A Cultural History of Western Fashion

BLOOMSBURY VISUAL ARTS
Bloomsbury Publishing Plc
50 Bedford Square, London, WC1B 3DP, UK
1385 Broadway, New York, NY 10018, USA
29 Earlsfort Terrace, Dublin 2, Ireland

BLOOMSBURY, BLOOMSBURY VISUAL ARTS and the Diana logo are trademarks of
Bloomsbury Publishing Plc

A Cultural History of Fashion in the 20th Century published by Berg Publishers 2007
A Cultural History of Fashion in the 20th and 21st Century published by Bloomsbury Academic 2013
Reprinted 2015 and 2016
© Bonnie English
All materials not appearing in *A Cultural History of Fashion in the 20th and 21st Centuries*
© Nazanin Hedayat Munroe, 2022

This edition published by Bloomsbury Visual Arts 2022

Bonnie English and Nazanin Hedayat Munroe have asserted their right under the Copyright,
Designs and Patents Act, 1988, to be identified as authors of this work.

For legal purposes the Acknowledgements on p. xiv constitute an extension of this copyright page.

Cover design by Liron Gilenberg
Cover image: Dress by Madeleine Vionnet, Paris, 1938. © Apic/Hulton Archive/Getty Images

A catalogue record for this book is available from the British Library.

A catalog record for this book is available from the Library of Congress.

ISBN: HB: 978-1-3501-5088-1
        PB: 978-1-3501-5089-8
        ePDF: 978-1-3501-5090-4
        eBook: 978-1-3501-5091-1

Typeset by RefineCatch Limited, Bungay, Suffolk
Printed and bound in India

To find out more about our authors and books visit www.bloomsbury.com
and sign up for our newsletters.

A Cultural History of Western Fashion

From Haute Couture to Virtual Couture

Bonnie English
Nazanin Hedayat Munroe

BLOOMSBURY VISUAL ARTS
LONDON · NEW YORK · OXFORD · NEW DELHI · SYDNEY

FIGURE 0.1 *Model for Gimbel's Department Store wearing Paul Poiret, March 1914. Photo by Bain News Service. George Grantham Bain Collection. (Library of Congress.)*

Third edition dedication, Nazanin Hedayat Munroe:

Dedicated to Alia, Reza, Sara and Layla, who will fashion their own futures

*And to Eshy joon, whose elegant style played a huge role
in my interest in fashion and textiles*

Second edition dedication, Bonnie English:

*Dedicated with love to
my beloved daughters, Sarah and Katie,
and to my parents, Edna and Bruce,
to whom I owe everything.*

CONTENTS

Conclusion 255

ILLUSTRATIONS

ACKNOWLEDGEMENTS

I would like to thank my editor at Bloomsbury, Georgia Kennedy, for her excellent suggestions and support during the process of revising this edition. My sincere appreciation also goes to Dean David Smith, Business Department Chair Lucas Bernard, and the administration at NYC College of Technology – CUNY for supporting my research and publication goals. It would be impossible to discuss fashion without attentive students, and to this end I extend my appreciation to my students in the Business & Technology of Fashion program, whose questions and comments in class helped contextualize my approach to fashion for future industry professionals. Lastly, I must thank my husband, who was extremely patient while listening to the many drafts of this volume; and my father, who has supported me throughout my career.

Introduction

A Cultural History of Western Fashion: From Haute Couture to Virtual Couture discusses how fashion reflects the essence of society, responding to many aspects of culture including art, music, politics and popular media. Approaching fashion as both a barometer and a response to the cultural milieu during which new styles are developed, this volume takes into account various factors in order to present a history of fashion as a record of social and ideological movements. Beginning with the mid-nineteenth century founding of haute couture, the volume follows the development of fashion to the digital era of the twenty-first century, demonstrating how dress styles change in response to major shifts within society at large.

The recognition of fashion as a significant aspect of culture has been illustrated in recent years by the rise of the celebrity designer, the increased number of blockbuster fashion exhibitions held in key international museums, and the proliferation of academic fashion texts published which underline the interdisciplinary connections between the applied arts, design, fine art, film and the fashion industry. By providing a sociohistorical review of major trends that have emerged since the late nineteenth century, *A Cultural History of Western Fashion* will consider the significant role that couture and ready-to-wear designers have played in the interpretation of the fashions of their day.

The more we learn about the history of fashion, the more we realize the nature of its complexity. We broadcast our views about world events, environmental concerns or social issues through dress. In some cases fashion represents conformity, and in others it is a rejection of social norms. Fashion can incite revolution, or represent revolutionary thought. Although fashion is rarely seen as an artistic practice, it is consistently in dialogue with the art world, sharing the ability of art to transform the mundane into a profound truth. As trends enter and exit through the revolving door of time, each one brings a new message of social contemplation. Ancient silhouettes and textile patterns are borrowed and transformed to metamorphosize identity, turning tradition on its head. By challenging social conventions, fashion – like art – evolved in new directions not hindered by tradition, rules or moral standards.

In both commercial and cultural terms, the seemingly whimsical nature of fashion is offset by its weight as a trillion-dollar industry that has contributed to new business practices, as well as changing the way people communicate through dress. The contextual relationships that exist among designer fashions, popular culture, big business, high-tech production, e-commerce and the impact of digital media will be discussed and analysed throughout the volume.

A central argument of the book is based on the premise that, while haute couture reigned supreme at the turn of the twentieth century based on the concept of exclusivity and luxury materials, its relationship with mass-produced clothing changed significantly as developments in manufacturing and the rise of designer brands diminished the hierarchy of fashion.

Fundamental to a designer's success was the ability to critically analyse communal and cultural trends and to know intuitively when to respond to social change. For example, Chanel's working-class background allowed her to respond pragmatically to the shortage of fine textiles by replacing them with pedestrian fabrics in the period following the First World War. More importantly, the material symbolically represented a revolutionary – and at the same time bourgeois – response to the previous use of expensive haute couture fabrics. Understanding the reasons *why* changes have taken place and being able to contextualize these changes within a sociohistorical setting is paramount for the student, the emerging designer, the historian and the avid follower of fashion history. Considering fashion from a cultural studies perspective helps to frame it within a broader context, to engage with multicultural and multidisciplinary issues, and to forecast future developments. This invokes an obvious question: if one does not know the past, how can one possibly contemplate the future?

Since the 1960s, many fashion designers have emerged from art schools as well as fashion institutions, and conceptualization in the design, as well as the art, process has become an essential part of the work. In simple terms, both fashion and art have become ideas rather than objects or products. In fact, the question of whether fashion is art is no longer relevant. Since the 1980s, fashion displays have become akin to art installations, and fashion shows became a type of performance art. Contemporary fashion garments can be viewed in exhibition spaces and have been purchased by galleries and museums for their permanent collections. International fashion exhibitions have become a huge draw for museums as the public is able to identify with both the functional and aesthetic appeal of the work. And as more fashion is viewed and consumed in the digital world, the merging of function and fantasy has come to represent the future – or at least one major direction – for the industry's growth.

The book is arranged both thematically and chronologically, although some chapters inevitably overlap the same period of time. Chapter 1 'The Commercialization of Fashion' outlines the inherent paradox of the founding of haute couture as exclusive apparel for the privileged, which is paralleled by the rise of the department store as a social equalizer for the upper and middle classes. 'The Artistry of Fashion' examined in Chapter 2 contemplates early twentieth-century relationships between fine and applied art forms in the wake of mechanized production, and attempts to merge art practice with dress. In Chapter 3, the move towards 'The Democratization of Fashion' is discussed, as haute couture changed its model and machine-made clothing was increasingly widely distributed following the First World War. In Chapter 4, 'The Americanization of Fashion' studies the development of the US fashion industry from a manufacturing hub to a major design leader, focused on Seventh Avenue as the home of ready-to-wear. Chapter 5 investigates changes in haute couture following the Second World War, and alternative fashion that permeated the social landscape in the 1960s, in turn influencing high fashion – thus resulting in 'The Popularization of Fashion'. While mainstream fashion evolved into a more widespread and accessible phenomenon, countercultural movements sought individualized ways to dress.

Chapter 6 studies 'The Postmodernization of Fashion' illustrating how anti-fashion became a vehicle to express dissent, ideology, meaning and memory as it became more closely allied with individualism and the search for greater intellectual depth. Chapter 7 further discusses 'The Deviance of Fashion' through alternate presentations within the system, ranging from satire to contemplation of the human condition. Both chapters address the ways in which visual tropes from non-Western cultures became a form of sartorial pastiche which heralded the development of street style. As fashion has become an increasingly globalized industry, world events have also affected the way that clothing is created, marketed and distributed. Chapter 8 returns to the

American industry which produces 'The Lifestyle of Fashion' in which designers become the brand, and clothing becomes the representation of uptown and downtown cultures. Chapter 9 considers 'The Corporatization of Fashion' which has mirrored political unrest and instability, economic downturn and the effect of industrial globalization, explaining how these world events have substantially impacted upon individual designers, corporations, retailers and associated fashion businesses. As environmental issues and social justice concerns inform consumer spending and prompt social corporate responsibility, the industry is slowly moving towards 'The Sustainability of Fashion', the focus of Chapter 10. The final chapter of the book looks at ways that technology has introduced new concepts for physical and virtual fashion: 'The Digitization of Fashion'. Replacing the department store model, the mainstream world of fashion is now dictated by the propagation of styles, ideas, and e-commerce through the internet, and fashion has become to some extent an image-based experience. Social media has become a powerful force displacing the old model of fashion advertising through a public-driven market, in which consumers create trends as much as follow them through favourite influencers.

One of the glaring omissions from the first and second editions of this text was the inclusion of designers and consumers outside the mainstream fashion system, an important issue that needs to be addressed by the industry at large. As a new generation of fashion historians develop a more diverse world view, a fuller picture of society's relationship with dress is emerging. Although a thorough review of worldwide contributions to twentieth century fashion to the present day is beyond the scope of this book, the context has been broadened to include designers from diverse backgrounds working outside the establishment, and to note the non-Western textiles and garment forms utilized in both haute couture and ready-to-wear.

A Cultural History of Western Fashion will provide cultural and historical insight into some of the many developments which have changed the world of fashion over the past century and a half. Although this volume doesn't cover all periods, designers and every fashion trend of the twentieth and twenty-first centuries, it outlines the major factors that turned the tide away from exclusivity and regulation in fashion towards a more streetwise, casual and individual way of dressing, and contemplates the evolution of fashion in the context of cultural change.

1

The Commercialization of Fashion

Introduction

This chapter will look at shifts within clothing production and purchasing that occurred in the mid-nineteenth century. These shifts were instigated by many factors, from technology and economics to music and art, laying the groundwork for the contemporary fashion industry. As textile technology sped up the process of cloth-making, overall costs were lowered, making wardrobes available to the middle- and lower-middle classes. This sudden availability of new clothing increased rather than met the demand, becoming the arena in which artists and designers found a fresh audience willing to indulge their creations both elaborate and mundane for the sake of appearance.

As the middle class continued to grow, the upper classes distinguished themselves by association with a new professional: the couturier, who created ensembles to be custom fitted for an exclusive clientele. Middle-class patrons found a way to participate in this display of wealth by buying imitations of these creations, either made by their dressmakers and tailors, or manufactured in factories and sold in department stores. As soon as the upper classes set a trend that the middle classes followed, the wealthy elite adopted a new style to differentiate themselves, starting the cycle anew.

Dress and society in Europe before the twentieth century

Dress has always functioned as a marker of social status and wealth. Prior to the nineteenth century, changes in fashion were gradual, and social class was represented by high quality textiles, rather than garment styles. The development of 'fashion' as we know it now – a specific style of dress prone to frequent changes – is in many ways the result of a marked increase in manufacturing and distribution during the nineteenth century. Textile and garment-making are slow, labour-intensive processes, which made clothing a precious commodity. Only the very wealthy could afford whole wardrobes; the working class, who were often responsible for textile and garment production, generally had a few sets of everyday clothes and one set of 'Sunday best'. Clothing was often repaired and reused, and handed down from one generation to the next. Much of what differentiated everyday and special occasion garments was the fabric: historically, the more colour and pattern in one's clothing, the more expensive it was to produce. Much of this expense was material as well as technical, requiring expensive dyestuffs and skilled labour to produce woven patterns in materials such as silk, or colourful prints on fine cotton, which until the eighteenth century were primarily exported from India to Europe.[1]

Technological advances during the previous century in fibre spinning – from the Spinning Jenny to the Water Frame, and finally to the Spinning Mule perfected by Samuel Crompton in 1779 – meant that cotton and wool yarns were readily available for weaving textiles. The invention of the fly shuttle in 1733 by John Kay sped up the weaving process, decreasing the number of workers needed per loom. The Jacquard loom, invented in 1801 by Joseph Marie Jacquard, functioned on an automated system of punched cards that made the creation of pictorial woven textiles faster and easier to produce than the centuries-old draw loom. Finally, the mechanical sewing machine, patented originally by Elias Howe in 1846 and reengineered by Isaac Merritt Singer in 1851, hastened the rate at which all these textiles could be fashioned into garments. As this technology increased the rate at which apparel fabric could be produced, and the expansion of railroads across Europe and North America made the transportation of goods faster and more reliable, fashion became an important commodity, particularly for those who could afford expensive clothing as a marker of social standing.

As clothing production increased in speed, so did changes in fashion. New styles were historically determined by royalty and aristocracy, with the middle classes of society emulating their dress. From the mid-seventeenth century onwards, elaborate dress styles for the elite emulated French court dress, which then became popular among royalty and aristocrats across Europe through travel and diplomacy. These styles were further popularized through descriptions

FIGURE 1.1 *Lewis Wickes Hine. Fourteen-year-old spinner in a Brazos Valley Cotton Mill. West, Texas, November 1913. Child labour in the textile industry was common, though much debated by social reformers, in the nineteenth and early twentieth centuries. (National Child Labor Committee collection, Library of Congress.)*

in travelogues, letters and illustrations in fashion plates. Once new styles became popular, expensive fabrics and trims were distributed through textile merchants anxious to increase sales to the lower gentry and upper middle class, whose dressmakers and tailors copied the styles. By the 1840s, the desired silhouette for women had become a fitted bodice accentuating an impossibly tiny waist with a floor-length spherical skirt. This silhouette employed a tightly fastened corset and up to six separate layers of stiffened fabric called crinoline to create the desired fullness of the skirt. The bodice and overskirt required several metres of expensive luxury fabric, making each gown a rather expensive investment. Upper-class husbands and fathers were driven into debt outfitting young wives and daughters, who tried to avoid wearing the same dress too often for fear of appearing middle class (even if they were).[2]

The use of both corsets and petticoats created health problems for women, from back pain to breathing problems, a point with which nineteenth-century feminists and physicians took issue (Mitchell, ed. 2018).[3] In the 1850s, the development and widespread use of steel as a new material lent itself to the invention of the cage crinoline. An armature of steel hoops linked by cloth tapes creating a semi-spherical frame, the cage created the desired silhouette of a full skirt by suspending the outer layer of fabric, eliminating the need for multiple petticoats. This style was adopted by both Empress Eugénie of France and Queen Victoria of Britain, and soon became the mark of a fashionable woman. The cage had a telescoping effect, so women could sit while wearing it.

Although this was a relief from the weight of the underskirts previously worn, the exaggerated shape of the cage was fodder for great criticism in its time. Punch magazine, a satirical publication based in London, dubbed the period of 1857 to 1867 'Crinolinemania' and published cartoons with humorous depictions of the style. More significantly, the sociological implications of placing a woman in such a restrictive ensemble reduced them to objects of decoration, meant solely to be admired by men (Pomeroy [1882] in Mitchell, ed. 2018: 82–3). Male and female critics alike took issue with the fashion. In 1863, journalist Harriet Martineau wrote an intentionally shocking column entitled 'A Wilful kind of Murder' listing multiple instances of women wearing crinoline cages who had been burned alive when they got too close to the fire grate or a lit candle (reprinted in Mitchell, ed. 2018: 103–9). Martineau's article cited coroners' inquests throughout West Middlesex, including London, where the oversized gowns were custom-made for wealthy patrons. The enduring popularity of these full-skirted creations, still known as the 'ball gown' silhouette named after its ideal setting, perpetuated the lower-class work of the needlewoman, a skilled worker spending up to fifteen hours a day in a poorly lit room sewing garments for the upper classes. The demand for clothing was particularly high during the Season, a period lasting approximately six months from January to June, when Parliament was in session and wealthy estate owners came to London.

By the mid- to late 1860s, the cage was abandoned for a new contraption: the bustle, an armature or padding that protruded backwards at a right angle from the waistline of the woman, creating a prop on which to drape a large pouf of fabric. Although the width of this style was more manageable than the spherical cage, women now had a rather large protrusion in the back supporting the fabric, placing considerable weight on the waist and lower back. Also worn with a corset, the hourglass-shaped bustle silhouette would remain the dominant fashion until the turn of the twentieth century.

Menswear in Europe also underwent a dramatic change, from colourful and ostentatious court dress to a more subdued style during the nineteenth century. Based on the court attire of Louis XIV (r. 1643–1713) and fashioned from mainly French, Spanish or Italian patterned silk textiles, seventeenth- and eighteenth-century dress for aristocratic men consisted of a knee-length coat, fitted waistcoat and matching breeches in colours such as rose pink, emerald green

FIGURE 1.2 *John Tenniel.* 'The Haunted Lady.' *Cartoon from Punch Magazine, 1863. Dressmaker enthusing over the wonderful gown that has been made for an aristocratic client. In the mirror, we see a vision of the exhausted, wasted needlewoman, whose underpaid labours have created the exquisite gown. (Photo by: Universal History Archive/Universal Images Group via Getty Images.)*

or rust orange. Accessories included coiffed white powdered wigs, a silk scarf tied into a floppy bow at the neck, lace cuffs, silk stockings and satin shoes. Tiny triangular hats or feathers were fixed to the wig for the finishing touch, an overall look that became popular among aristocracy throughout Europe. Despite the French origins of this style, during the French Revolution (1789–99) the style for silk satin suits with knee-length breeches was rejected by the masses for its association with the ruling class. Working men and their sympathizers from the upper classes preferred striped plain weave cotton or wool fashioned into ankle-length *pantalons*. These social revolutionaries were referred to as *sans-culottes* (French, without knee-breeches), signifying the Proletariat class' break with aristocratic ideals and their fight for social justice (Takeda et al., 2015: 24). These changes in menswear would prevail from the early nineteenth century onwards.

From the latter half of the eighteenth century, fashionable Englishmen who travelled through Europe on Grand Tour returned wearing these elaborate ensembles, earning them the derisive nickname 'macaroni' (after the cuisine they would have eaten while in Italy). The appearance of these young men included a spyglass and feathered ornament in a curled, oversized wig; mocked in contemporary theatre works such as David Garrick's play *The Male-Coquette* (1757), the 'macaroni' was noted as having exclusive and elitist attitudes toward fashion (Takeda et al., 2015: 15–16).

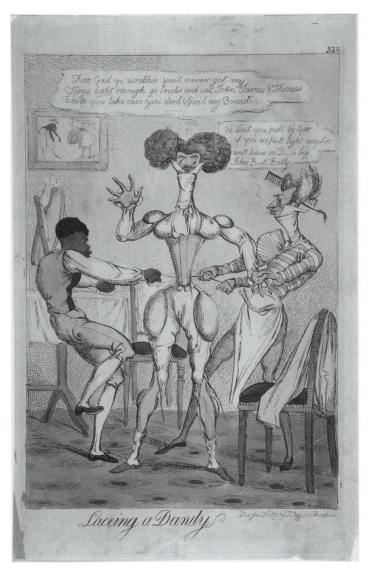

FIGURE 1.3 'Laceing [sic] a Dandy.' *Published by Thomas Tagg, 26 January 1819. This illustration by an anonymous British artist shows a Dandy being laced up by his French hairdresser (right) and an assistant. The central figure identified as the 'dandy' derides the men for not lacing his corset tightly enough, while the hairdresser protests the bulge of his Lord's 'John Bull Belly'. The dandy desires to have the idealized male physique: a narrow waist offset by broad shoulders and thighs, which are achieved by padding, complementing the hourglass look for men. (Collection: The Metropolitan Museum of Art, NY [69.524.35]. Rogers Fund and The Elisha Whittelsey Collection, The Elisha Whittelsey Fund, 1969.)*

From the early decades of the nineteenth century, a revised vision for menswear developed. Credited to an influential social climber named George 'Beau' Brummell (1778–1840), court circles gave preference to a new style: a fitted three-piece ensemble made of dark woollen cloth. The desired appearance for men thereafter shifted from ostentation to subtlety, with an emphasis on tailoring and fit exacted by experts on Savile Row, where London tailors had grouped their establishments (Takeda et al., 2015: 173). As in France, these elements changed throughout the century, with breeches rejected in favour of full-length trousers or pantaloons. The tail coat, a double or single-breasted jacket cut short in the front with a long solid or split panel hanging to the knees in the back, remained an essential element of formal dress. Day dress by the second half of the century for men included a morning suit, or trousers paired with a frock coat, a skirted jacket to the mid-thigh that had evolved from British hunting attire into an element of formal day wear. Even this more austere style of dress could become very costly, as each suit was custom-made from worsted wool and other high-end materials. Despite the changes in cloth and cut from the more conspicuous styles of the eighteenth century, English men still paid conspicuously close attention to their appearance (Takeda et al., 2015: 173). Some even went so far as to wear boned corsets at the waist, emulating their female counterparts (Takeda et al., 2015: 168). These more extreme practices earned these men the reputation of being dandies, who were mocked in print publications and criticized by intellectuals for being profligate and vain.

For the working classes, clothing had little to do with 'dress' or signalling one's position in life, but purely served a functional purpose. Everyday clothing for the working class shifted with the rise of factory jobs in textile and other mills. Factory workers were expected to provide their own clothing, and banned immediately from wearing cage crinolines or other voluminous styles in which the cloth was likely to get stuck in the grinding machinery. Men and boys soon adopted trousers over breeches for practical and health reasons. For those in service at a large manor house, the uniform was provided for them, but considered property of the estate: dresses, caps and aprons for housemaids, livery for footmen, and formalwear for high level employees such as the butler. In most cases, garment styles indicated the extent of physical labour involved in the job; tight-fitting clothes were not practical for excessive movement, and therefore represented a man of leisure, a gentleman. However, despite the absence of a cage crinoline, female servants were still required to wear a corset which was considered a proper and necessary undergarment.

Agricultural workers, including slaves in the United States and the British Colonies, were often expected to make their own clothing, from spinning fibre to weaving coarse unbleached fabric known as osnaburg, to sewing their garments. By the nineteenth century, ready-made clothing could also be obtained for slaves, but it was primarily made of the same coarse cloth, indicating their status. Runaway slaves were often identified by their garments, so in order to escape, they had to obtain the more expensive clothing worn by free men or women. In some instances, hand-me-down clothing from employers, or clothing purchased with cash or by barter, provided enslaved people a means of obtaining better quality garments (Shaw, 2012). This remained the case until the abolition of slavery in the British colonies (1833) and the United States (1865).

The ability to change life circumstances by donning the right outfit was one that held both positive and negative connotations among all social classes. Fashionable Americans followed the fashions of Europe with a one- to two-year delay, but these elaborate ensembles were considered ostentatious in the Puritanical US; there were moral implications to the display of means. Kate Haulman (2014) analyses the political effects of fashion in eighteenth-century America, revealing the complexity of fashion's power as an indicator of religious morality for groups such as the Quakers, who stressed plain attire as a sign of virtue, and derided heavily trimmed silk ensembles as a symbol of vanity and frivolity. Despite these early social pressures to downplay one's appearance, fine clothing continued to differentiate the social classes. Due to the absence of an established aristocracy in America, there was some fluidity within the social hierarchy, and the right clothing could provide entry into a new lifestyle.

Social implications of dress

Thorstein Veblen, the late nineteenth-century American economist and sociologist, underlines this notion of the 'pecuniary canons of taste' as the dominant economic factor impacting the evolution of dress in the late 1880s. In *The Theory of the Leisure Class*, originally published in 1899, Veblen analyses the privileged few, referencing the division of labour as the underlying foundation for the development of the leisure class. Coining the terms 'conspicuous consumption' and 'conspicuous leisure' among others, Veblen hypothesizes a hierarchy of the ways in which consumerism has become a tool for demonstrating social stratification. Veblen, along with German philosopher Von Jhering, developed theories about the 'trickle-down' effect: the emulation of higher social classes by lower classes in the social strata as a means to elevate the appearance or impression of social status. With regard to Victorian fashion, he asserts that the hindrances of female dress represented a woman's economic dependence on a man, as well as being a reflection of male pecuniary strength (Veblen, [1899]1965). Veblen's argument suggests that individual or family status was the motivating factor for the emulation of dress within Victorian society.

The theories of the trickle-down effect and conspicuous consumption were developed in different directions as the twentieth century redefined this practice. Quentin Bell, who relies heavily on Veblen's work to provide a framework for his own study, argues that this theory is limited because it is time- (or period-) specific – in this case, to a nineteenth-century sociological determinant. Bell's classic text *On Human Finery* (first published in 1947) refers to this as 'class solidarity,' and concludes that 'the usual desire of the great majority of those who follow fashion is not so much to achieve personal distinction, as to emerge discreetly into a "distinguished class"' ([1947] 1992: 181). He maintains that the most important overall determinant in the history of dress is the condition of the class struggle. Bell argues that fashion was a European product which was never to be viewed as a 'universal' condition of dress ([1947] 1992: 115). However, he adds: 'Within any stratified society, you are almost certain to have a classification of dress', maintaining that this 'challenges the lower strata to compete with the higher strata'. Bell further explains:

> Emulation occurs where status can be challenged, where social groups become strong enough to challenge the traditional pattern of society, in fact, in those places where a strong middle class emerges to compete with the aristocracy and, at a later stage, a strong proletariat emerges to compete with the middle class.

> [1947] 1992: 115

In Bell's terms, if the middle class has the financial and the political power – which seems to have been the case in the late nineteenth century – the distribution of wealth allowed for more than one social class to afford 'the luxury of sumptuous dress' ([1947] 1992: 113). In other words, a society that is changing will produce fashions that are also changing due to the striving of the middle classes to emulate their social superiors; and this, in turn, stimulates greater production of consumer goods.

Complementing and refining Bell's theory, other cultural studies researchers have underlined the notion that while lower social class groups attempt to emulate the tastes of higher groups, this causes the latter to respond by adopting new tastes that will re-establish and maintain the original social superiority. This was particularly evident in the nineteenth century, when the simulated attempts of the bourgeois class to imitate *le bon monde* of an elitist society found middle-class women packing dusters or newspapers under the backs of their skirts to replicate the modish bustle backs of high fashion. However, recent research by Vivienne Richmond presents a more nuanced analysis of class emulation in her publication *Clothing the Poor in Nineteenth Century England* (2013), which includes primary accounts and records. Richmond argues that, while the middle classes struggled to emulate their social superiors, the lower classes were in fact emulating their peers. Identifying a broad base for the 'poor' that includes those born into poverty as well as those who found themselves impoverished at some point in life, Richmond discusses the practice of pawning clothing as a way to regain lost funds. This in turn allowed thrifters to purchase garments intended for a higher-class consumer at a discounted rate. Once there was no longer a code arising from social distinctions, fashion soon ceased to be a prerogative; rather, it became a question of means. In summary, these trends signalled the relatively fluid social and cultural structure and economic consumption that would prevail in contemporary Western societies.

The rise of haute couture

Prior to the Modern era, the established canons of taste in the arts – including fashion – were once considered to be the exclusive priority of aristocrats. While cultural debate questioned the extent to which other groups, notably the *haute bourgeoisie* and the *demi-monde*, played a part in establishing these canons, the gap between the classes was apparent. Pierre Bourdieu (1930–2002), French sociologist and intellectual, refers to taste as one of the most vital stakes in the struggles fought in the field of the dominant class and the field of cultural production in his essay 'The Aristocracy of Culture'. Bourdieu explains that: 'The upper class propriety treats taste as one of the surest signs of true nobility and cannot conceive of referring taste to anything other than itself' (1984: 11). By linking cultural practice to social origin, Bourdieu emphasizes the discrete nature of the cultural exchange between the upper-class intellectuals and the bourgeoisie, in which their 'self-interested representations of culture' provoke 'mutual lucidity and reflexive blindness' (1984: 12).

Elitism in fashion has always been linked closely with status and social class, with success, and with what was perceived to be impeccable taste made publicly visible through dress. For centuries, royal courts used fashion as a means of publicizing their superiority, strength and influence across Europe. Looking again to the French monarchy, Louis XIV demanded that his courtiers pay scrupulous attention to their grooming, and insisted on the conspicuous display of finery at all palace events. He maintained a mental inventory of the garments worn by the female members of his entourage to ensure that his reputation was not tarnished if one was seen wearing the same garment too frequently. He believed that this form of dress code upheld the wealth and opulence of his court.

In the second half of the nineteenth century, a new dictatorial hierarchy arose with the 'fashion designer as artist/genius' as distinct from the humble dressmaker or *couture à façon*, and a new form of elitism in fashion replaced the old. This time, however, it was one determined by pecuniary rather than class dominance. Fashion historian Christopher Breward (2003) argues that this elite sector of the fashion market relied on an exclusivity necessary to sustain high prices through a deliberate glorification of the role and identity of the couturier. Citing a combination of factors, Breward identifies hand-sewing, bureaucratic control and creative vision as the underpinnings of the success for couture houses (2003: 50). Haute couture demanded labour-intensive specialized sewing techniques, sustained by high prices.[4]

Arguably, haute couture in fashion was also determined by this heightened taste for luxury; more importantly in economic terms, haute couture became an interface between the luxury silk manufacturers of Lyons and the world of the aristocracy. Fine fabric, sumptuously embellished with a layer of lace, delicate beading and rich hand embroidery, enticed women of high society. Certainly, couture relied on expert craftsmanship in sewing and great attention to detail and fit. It was these custom-made creations that would be the most coveted objects in society from the mid-nineteenth century onward.

Charles Frederick Worth

This advent of changing cultural values is reflected in the clientele of Paris' first haute couture designer, Englishman Charles Frederick Worth. Despite his recognition by fashion historians as the 'founding father' of haute couture, Worth played both sides of the dichotomy he created. On the one hand, he designed for members of royalty and fitted aristocrats; on the other, for grand divas of the stage.

Worth began his career in Paris with the celebrated textile manufacturer Maison Gagelin, where he began designing dresses for his French wife, Marie Vernet, made from the firm's textiles. The popularity of her gowns led to several custom orders, including two orders for the wife of the Austrian Ambassador; these were spotted and admired by Empress Eugénie, the beautiful wife of Napoleon III, who invited Worth to court (Tortora and Marcketti, 2015: 356). Contradicting the usual role of dressmaker – as an employee who took directions for style from her patroness – Worth brought a fully-made gown to the empress, and she favoured him with her patronage thereafter (Givhan, 2015: 11). The support of the empress enabled him to open his own business in Paris on the Rue de la Paix in 1858 with his business partner, Otto Bobergh. Worth quickly gathered a clientele of aristocratic women at the French court. He created hundreds of garments for the influential Eugénie, who determined fashionable taste in the royal court at a time when the demand for luxury goods reached levels unsurpassed since the French Revolution of 1789. In 1869, the empress officially appointed the House of Worth as the court dressmaker, and Worth's label bore the royal crest. The success of his fashion empire was also measured by his employment of 1,200 workers by 1870. For the opening of the Suez Canal – an important historical event – the empress felt that she needed no fewer than 250 of Worth's dresses.

Worth's creations did not escape the attentions of the British crown. When he was invited to create a wedding dress in 1866 for the very fashionable Alexandria, Princess of Wales, he fortuitously took advantage of the opportunity to create a 'new' silhouette. Worth replaced the circular crinoline, and introduced a narrower skirt with a bustle back, a silhouette that dominated fashion for the next thirty years.

In addition to designing clothes for many members of European royalty, including the Princess de Metternich, Princess Maria of Austria and Empress Elizabeth of Austria (the fashionable wife of Franz Joseph I), Worth was also adept in marketing his work to a much broader clientele. Significantly, he was one of many of the early haute couture designers to recognize the financial opportunities inherent in the American market. He attracted the attention of wealthy patrons, including the American Rothschilds and Vanderbilts. When a wholesale trade was established between France and America and Australia, his gowns were shipped internationally in huge steamer trunks, as by then his name had become synonymous with Paris fashion. His clothes were purchased by department stores such as Sears Roebuck and Montgomery Ward in the

FIGURE 1.4 *House of Worth, ball gown, Paris, France c. 1872. This bustled evening gown was worn by Mrs. William De Forest Manice, the donor's grandmother, at both the French and English courts during the reigns of Napoleon III and Queen Victoria. (Collection: The Metropolitan Museum of Art, NY. [46.25.1a-d]. Gift of Mrs. Philip K. Rhinelander, 1946.)*

United States, as well as by other major outlets as far away as David Jones in Australia, which had a buyer in its head office in London. David Jones, like many other department stores, also set up in-house workshops to copy the trends of many of the Paris models.

To ensure a perfect fit, Worth could use up to seventeen pieces of material in a single bodice. To ensure expertise in construction, his seamstresses were organized in specialized workshops as skirt-makers, bust-makers, sleeve-makers or hem-stitchers. While the majority of Worth's garments, for example, were entirely hand-sewn, with the advent of the mechanized sewing machine, there was a growing trend towards using the machine to sew the main seams of the garments. Designers not only chose the fabric and determined the finishing techniques, but they also produced the models that were commercially distributed.

Herein lies the dichotomy: Worth was attempting to juggle an exclusive, one-of-a-kind garment market (which provided him with great status within an elitist upper-class society) with an international commercial fame (which led to greater financial returns). As early as the 1870s, Worth's name frequently appeared in ordinary fashion magazines, including American *Vogue*, created by Arthur Turnure in 1892. This had the result of spreading his fame far and wide to women beyond courtly circles.

As a clever business entrepreneur, he also expanded his repertoire of clients to include famous singers and actors of the day, recognizing that his garments would be seen by a much wider audience if they were worn by popular public figures. He supplied performance costumes and personal wardrobes to famous stage performers including Sarah Bernhardt, Lillie Langtry, Nellie Melba and Jenny Lind. In 1883, Langtry – an internationally well-known celebrity – purchased enough gowns to fill twenty-two trunks for her European performance tour. So, while Worth attempted to establish himself as a creative artist who produced exclusivity for a privileged class, at the same time he compromised haute couture ideals by also catering for a middle-class clientele with no defined social currency. This social paradox will be discussed further in Chapter 3.

The success of Worth's business model soon encouraged others to open their own couture houses. In order to open an haute couture establishment in Paris, one had to be approved by *Le Chambre Syndicale de la Couture, des Confectionneurs et des Tailleurs pour Dame* (Trade Association for Couture, clothing manufacturers and tailors for women), formed in 1868. In 1910 the organization's name was changed to *Le Chambre Syndicale de la Couture Parisienne*, and in 1945 to *Chambre Syndicale de la Haute Couture*, following the legal registration of the term 'haute couture'. Specifications were set forth to determine what constitutes a couture house; these include custom-made creations, a minimum staff of twenty, and a minimum collection of thirty-five ensembles including day and evening wear presented to the press in Paris twice per year. By 1946, there were over one hundred couture houses in Paris, a number that is much reduced today. The organization is now known as *Federation de la Haute Couture et de la Mode*.[5]

Early couturiers and couturières include the Callot Soeurs, Jeanne Paquin, Jacques Doucet, Jeanne Lanvin and many other smaller establishments whose legacy has yet to be thoroughly studied. These couture houses were effectively Worth's competitors, and supplied the ever-growing demand for luxury dress towards the end of the century. Despite the large numbers of seamstresses, tailors, lace-makers and embroiderers employed, it was the purchase of expensive silks from textile manufacturers that required most of the capital. Following Worth's example, many couture houses had a clientele comprised of both royalty and aristocratic Europeans as well as moneyed American clients. Wealthy Americans were looked down upon as *nouveau riche*, but their wealth – mostly obtained through manufacturing during the Industrial Revolution – was required by couturiers to keep their high-end business model from running a deficit. Like

Worth, many couturiers also created stage costumes, which increased the visibility of their creations to a broader spectrum of society.

The influx of popular culture into mainstream society signalled a shift in the previously held elitist notion of what constituted status in society. While haute couture designers were dressing not only heads of state and socialites but also stage celebrities, artists too were using depictions of popular performers to draw the attention of the middle class to their work. In the famous Moulin Rouge cabaret in Paris, one of the star performers of song and dance, Jane Avril, was often depicted in Henri de Toulouse-Lautrec's work. While Toulouse-Lautrec was primarily a fine artist, he was drawn to the commercial processes of lithography, as it allowed him a greater

FIGURE 1.5 *Jules Cheret,* Jardin de Paris *poster, c. 1890. The Cherettes not only set the fashionable mode, but also alluded to the moral licentiousness of working-class women in Paris. (Photo by © Historical Picture Archive/CORBIS/Corbis via Getty Images.)*

spontaneity of line and more expressive characterization of his figures in his graphic design work. It could also be reproduced many times over. With the rise of the graphic design industry in the 1880s and 1890s, images of popular culture – themes, events and products – were used deliberately in poster designs to attract the new middle-class audience and to integrate art and life. Ultimately, the emergence of the poster as an art form by 1900 led to a cultural shift in the visual arts. The art dealers who sold the work to the public and established a commercial market became the new artistic patrons, replacing the educated members of the academy who had previously determined the canons of taste.

Jules Cheret, named the French father of the modern poster, used the actor and dancer Charlotte Wiehe to create a prototype of the young, vibrant and emancipated middle-class woman of the latter nineteenth century. Cheret's elongated female figures became famous in a series of designs he created for Job cigarette papers, and used throughout his advertising illustration career. These young women became known as his 'cherettes'. These posters became important sociological tools because, by being adopted as the 'new art' of the middle classes, they reflected the changing attitudes and mores of that particular society.

By the turn of the twentieth century, the women's suffragette movement was gaining momentum, and young women were trying to emulate the looks and attitudes of the emancipated women from working-class backgrounds depicted in these posters. The role and direction of art and fashion reflected this changing culture, where an evolving interaction between fashion, art and popular culture emerged.

The rise of consumerism

With the rise of the middle-class consumer, economic factors implicit in the improved production systems, mass manufacture, incentive advertising and marketing techniques – including visual display and merchandising, and wider distribution markets – were influential in the evolving democratization of fashion, which sought to make stylish clothing universally available to the masses. Undoubtedly, the social and economic expansion of the middle class led to increased social mobility, which activated a shift in aesthetic considerations away from an elitist culture towards a popular culture. Prior to this period, early mass-produced goods, especially ready-made clothing, were viewed with suspicion and purchased out of necessity rather than choice due to financial constraints.

Discussing the ways in which technological development and new marketing strategies facilitated the new social mobility, early studies by fashion historians such as Elizabeth Ewing (1986) and Michael Miller (1981) observe how improved production systems, wider distribution markets and incentive advertising schemes would systematically cater to a large national market. Beverly Lemire (1991) also points out that the availability of cheap, yet fashionable, ready-made attire initiated by the bourgeoisie was responsible for the bridging of this social gap. She indicates that, even in the eighteenth century, there was a great demand for 'popular' fashions amongst the working classes. This was facilitated by a dramatic increase in the production of cotton clothing 'which swept from London's court to Manchester's courtyard, with the help of newspapers and magazines' (1991: 324). As Ewing suggests, this marked the beginning of a new cycle of fashion-making and fashion-selling that would become the means of bringing fashion to millions of women (1986: 122). In France, the first good-quality ready-made clothing appeared in 1824 with the opening of La Jardinière Maison in Paris. Within twenty years, 225 establishments were operating in France with the further democratization of fashion becoming possible in the 1850s when mechanical sewing machines were introduced, along with die-cutting appliances and the emergence of the women's dress pattern industry. The Singer sewing machine undoubtedly provided the greatest impetus in the growth of ready-to-wear clothing, as it dramatically reduced the construction time required to make garments, thereby reducing production costs and lowering the price of apparel.[6]

The availability of ready-made clothing for both men and women coincided with the development of the department stores, and these factors were instrumental in the emergence of a culture of consumption that eroded social class barriers. Large department stores such as the Bon Marché were stocking shawls, cloaks and tippets, as well as garment linings and millinery items, and this trend escalated with the introduction of a ready-to-wear department in the 1860s. According to Miller (1981) in his historical retrospective of mass-merchandising at the Bon Marché, ready-made menswear, including shirts and ties, was expanding rapidly by the 1870s, and extensive advertising in the 1880s of 'dresses completely made' suggested that ready-to-wear was beginning to encroach even on the fashion trade (1981: 50).[7] Despite this evidence, it is difficult to ascertain the extent to which ready-to-wear was usurping private dressmaking businesses. Lipovetsky (1994) argues that the first manufactured dresses made utilizing standard measures did not appear until after 1870 and that manufacturing techniques produced primarily the loose-fitting elements of dress, including lingerie, mantillas and coats; for the rest, 'women continued to turn to their dress-makers, and went on doing so for a long time' (1994: 83). Lou Taylor corroborates this observation in her study of woollen cloth in Britain, noting that the firm of S. Hyam & Co., men's outfitters and tailors of Manchester and London, advertised riding habits that were 'matchless in price and make' to custom-made garments; and also that outdoor garments that were not form-fitted were easily made up by the burgeoning ready-to-wear companies for the fashion-conscious middle-class female consumers (1999: 31). Certainly a study of the popular fashion journals of the 1870s such as *The Queen*, *La Mode Illustrée*, *The Young Ladies' Journal* and *La Mode Pratique* reveals numerous advertisements for ready-made garments by individual fashion companies and major department stores. By the turn of the twentieth century there was a great abundance and diversity of mass-produced merchandise available, but the stigma that they were poorly made fashion goods took a long time to dispel.[8] In advertising at this time, greater emphasis was being placed on marketing techniques than on the products themselves. This focus on advertising over product quality, coupled with the namelessness of most designers, contributed to the lack of acceptance of mass-produced goods in the nineteenth century (Hollander, 1988: 358).

While one might assume that this factor would dissuade upper-class purchasers, it is debatable whether or not it would have concerned middle-class consumers. The process of the democratization of fashion during the nineteenth century was arguably most pronounced in the United States because of the nature of its fluid social structure (Crane, 2000) . As a relatively new nation, American society did not have the lang-standing aristocracy that was painstakingly documented and maintained in Europe, and therefore presenting the image of wealth through clothing was potentially enough to buy one's way into the social elite. This created a high level of competition accompanied by an obsession with fashion, and the desire of Industrialist wealth to compensate for their modest past (Banner, 1984: 18, 54). The display of fashion was not only an indication of wealth, but a display of taste, which in turn demonstrated the elite virtues of the upper classes. Fashion accessories such as gloves, canes and watches became obvious signifiers of middle-class male 'upward aspirants'. Watches with gold chains were much sought after by working-class men, and were occasionally provided as props by photographers to add 'momentary prestige' to appearance of the sitter (Heinze, 1990: 89).

The social equalizer of the department store

As consumer culture grew with the advances in garment production technology, department stores led the way to the modern development of mass-merchandising. The Bon Marché, an early example of a modern department store, was developed in Paris by Aristede Bouçicault from a dry goods store bearing the same name first established in 1838. Becoming a partner in 1852, Bouçicault implemented a new business plan: fixed prices, a refund and exchange programme, advertising and a broader range of merchandise. This initiative is outlined in Georges d'Avenel's 1898 essay 'The Bon Marché' ([1898] (1989), which deals with the influential Parisian department store. D'Avenel credits the entrepreneurial skills of Monsieur Bouçicault with making this establishment the *apothéosis* of all modern department stores. D'Avenel points out that the success of the Bon Marché resulted from a number of factors. First, Bouçicault sold cheaper, often mass-produced, goods with a guarantee of quality – normally only given for more expensive merchandise. He relied on the premise that it was far better 'to sell in great quantity than to take much in profit'. Second, he introduced a revolutionary step in merchandising: the institution of fixed prices, which did away with 'bargaining' or determination of the price on the conspicuous appearance of the buyer. Third, clients were able to inspect the goods without an obligation to buy and, if they were dissatisfied with their purchase, a *'rendu'* would be arranged (d'Avenel, 1989: 59). Fourth, according to Artley (1976), prior to the 1850s Parisian retailers 'regarded their shops as private places or extensions of their homes', and therefore a new consideration of the psychology of the customer had to be introduced by Bouçicault in the manifestation of an establishment extolling 'modern methods of retailing' (Artley, 1976: 6).

Miller's comprehensive study of the Bon Marché (1981) also examines the success of the store based on Bouçicault's approach to reconciling his employees with his master plan for a paternalistic work environment, while courteously servicing the bourgeois customer, exploring this symbiotic relationship in the age of mass consumerism. Finally, the vastly increased expenditure on advertising, used to promote 'special sales' of goods, precipitated higher financial returns. This point is detailed by Émile Zola's novel *Au Bonheur des Dames* (The Ladies' Delight) (1883), a fictional account presumably based on the business ventures of the Bon Marché. The commercial success of the Bon Marché was duplicated internationally with the advent or refurbishment of major department stores in many cities in Europe, Britain and America. In Germany, the great Wertheim department store was built on Berlin's Leipziger-strasse by Alfred Messel between 1896 and 1899, and Samaritaine was built in Paris by Franz Jourdain and Henri Sauvage in 1905. In Australia, David Jones opened its doors as a department store in Sydney in 1877 with great fanfare, and became a public company in 1906.

In England, Harrods was established at its Knightsbridge London location in 1849 by Charles Henry Harrod, and refurbished by his son Charles Digby Harrod into a grand structure following a fire in 1883. With the motto *Omnia Omnibus Ubique* (Latin, 'all things for all people everywhere'), Harrods sought a universal appeal and offered a wide variety of products from medicine to clothing, attracting consumers from all class backgrounds. The goal of providing goods for anyone who could afford them permeated early department store philosophy. In the United States, the first department store was Lord & Taylor (established in 1826 by Samuel Lord and George Washington Taylor), followed by Macy's (founded 1858 by Rowland Hussy Macy) and Bloomingdale's (founded 1872 by Joseph and Lyman Bloomingdale) in New York City.

Marshall Field's in Chicago had been in operation for three decades by the turn of the century. Owned by the wealthiest man in Chicago at the time, the flagship store located on State and

FIGURE 1.6 *Lord & Taylor's store, 20th Street & Broadway, c. 1870. The flagship Lord & Taylor store was considered the prototypical American department store. These commercial establishments were grand structures with each floor dedicated to a broad range of consumer products. This stereograph is from the 'American Views' series. The double image would be viewed with a stereoscope, giving a 3-D effect. (Library of Congress.)*

Washington Streets was designed and built by Henry Hobson Richardson, one of America's great pioneering architects. Deemed an architectural landmark, this 1892 building was six storeys high and, despite its conservative exterior, was celebrated as one of the earliest 'distinctly American' modern buildings. In 1978, it was designated a National Historic Landmark. A magnificent large Tiffany ceiling made of glass mosaic pieces – the first to be made entirely of *favrile* iridescent glass – adorned the store and added to its sumptuous display. Field himself is considered to be one of the leading figures in the development of the department store. Marshall Field's was the first American department store to establish a European buying office, which was located in Manchester, England. It was also the first American store to open a restaurant and to offer a bridal registry. Both American and European department stores fashioned their stores on the premise that, with all facilities such as rest rooms, restaurants, theatrettes or exhibition spaces provided, the customer could spend an entire day enjoying the ambience of the store, therefore encouraging repeat visits and increased sales. This retail success was led by Harry Gordon Selfridge. Based on his experience with Marshall Field's, Selfridge set out to create his own version of the department store. Arriving in London in 1906, the self-made Selfridge hired Daniel Burnham and R. Frank Atkinson to build his grand department store on Oxford Street, which opened in 1909. Revolutionary in having its display windows lit up at night, Selfridges also encouraged customers to linger by instigating some of the more successful features of Marshall Field's, furnishing their store with public restrooms, a restaurant, lounging areas for husbands, and entertainment for children while women shopped.

In America, Macy's opened its flagship store in Herald Square on Broadway in 1902, advertised widely as the largest department store in the world. Broadway was New York's leading street, and its first cable car lines were completed in 1893 with underground conduits to avoid having poles and overhead wires. Electric trams, or trolley cars, carried hundreds of potential customers past Macy's doors every day, and its large display windows enhanced its products' appeal to buyers.

Perhaps the most important aspect of this development of consumerism, concurrent at the time Veblen was writing (1899), is echoed in the following observation from James Allen's early text *The Romance of Commerce and Culture*:

> The rise of modern marketing also forced a shift in economic theory away from production to consumption – away from the idea that the value of products resides in the cost of production and towards the idea that the value derives from subjective consumer demand or desire in relation to supply.
>
> 1983: 6

Allen's summary is central to the argument that there were three main marketing strategies developed to promote consumption: first, methods of presentation and display of goods; second, the use of the 'seduction theory' as a sophisticated psychological marketing approach; and third, the escalation of mass media advertising. These mass-marketing techniques stimulated 'conspicuous consumption', increased product production and generated the emergence of the autonomous consumer object. This was the case not only in England, France and America but also in Italy; the emergence of fashion as a consumer object is explored by Carlo Marco Belfanti and Elisabetta Merlo's research on the Italian department store Alle Città d'Italia in Milan (Merlo and Belfanti, 2019). Particularly in Europe, these pronounced profit-oriented sales techniques of the first two decades of the century highlighted a growing sophistication of entrepreneurial skills. Fashion advertising became symptomatic of the commodification and commercialization of modern society, literally and symbolically.

Intellectuals and artists became critical of the growing materialism implicit in business enterprise at the time. These new commercial merchandising techniques did not escape the attention of the avant-garde artists Pablo Picasso and Georges Braque, who seized upon the opportunity to appropriate small sections of commercial logos into their collaged work. The *papier collé* entitled *Au Bon Marché* of 1913 is an exception in so far as Picasso appropriates a large lingerie advertisement without alteration or fragmentation from Samaritaine, a major Paris department store, and juxtaposes it with another large lingerie advertisement from its commercial rival, the Bon Marché department store. This referential and commercial juxtaposition is heightened by the aesthetic juxtaposition of the different typefaces used by these stores. The blunter and more traditional sans serif lettering of the word 'Samaritaine' contrasts visually and associatively with the more decorative and stylish curvilinear trademark of the Bon Marché.

In the collage, discordant forms visually create the illusion of a seated female figure, and Picasso has strategically placed the words '*trou ici*' (hole here) near the figure to indicate sexual suggestion. After all, he is suggesting, what more is lingerie than an enticement to the boudoir? Picasso is almost certainly mocking the underlying motivations and stereotyping implicit in fashion advertising. While this kind of direct social or cultural comment is atypical of Picasso's work, it undoubtedly anticipates the ways in which some French and German Dadaist artists used advertising materials in their collages to link fashion imagery and social commentary. The psychological ploys of mass-marketing that motivated the human psyche became an inherent part of the fashion advertisements of the day, and in turn were facetiously implied in the work of the avant-garde artists of the early twentieth century.

Ultimately, the display of merchandise in glass vitrines, attentive employees who worked on commission, and the opulent environment of department stores all contributed to the appearance of exclusivity sought after by middle-class consumers, and played upon by merchants. Elizabeth Wilson identifies the clients of department stores as primarily middle class in *Adorned in Dreams,* a study of fashion and modernity first published in 1985. She points out, however, that 'this ambience of service rather than commerce gave an illusion of aristocratic life, and in this way old forms of class and personal relationships persisted in the midst of the new' (Wilson, 1985: 149). The illusion that the venue itself afforded an elevated status, one which previously only the upper classes could have enjoyed, held great appeal for the bourgeois customers. As both upper- and middle-class clients frequented the stores, it would seem that – at least superficially – it led to a greater levelling of the social classes. This factor relates more to department stores in England than to those in the United States or Australia, where social class distinctions were not as pronounced.

More importantly, because bourgeois culture was on display, it allowed for greater divergence of thought regarding what constituted popular culture and how social processes structured lifestyles and determined 'taste' in consumer goods. Bourdieu's *Distinction* (1984) suggests that taste in cultural goods functions as a marker of class. The shop assistant's position, for example, allowed young women a status above that of factory workers, and provided them with the means to be well dressed. Shop Girls were provided with a dress uniform, usually in all black, and were paid a small salary in addition to being provided with dormitory-style housing and meals. It thus became far easier for a woman to 'dress above her station in life', and social mobility was possible provided one could emulate and sustain the illusion. This was equally true of customers who indulged in expensive garments on credit.

According to Zola, this was symptomatic of the bourgeois culture which extolled consumptive virtues to the extent that it exploited and even victimized people – women, in particular. In his novel *Au Bonheur des Dames,* he describes 'how definitions of the feminine came to be linked with such psychological disturbances as the new department store madness – kleptomania. As the modern world became more affluent and prone to overproduction, excess and indulgence, the practices of everyday life, such as shopping, were identified as sources of instability, even of insanity' (cited in Finkelstein, 1996: 97–8). However, Saisselin, in his book *The Bourgeois and the Bibelot* (1984: 36–9), disagrees with this proposition. Explaining a woman's relationship with the department store, he argues that whether it is in New York, Chicago or Paris, the results are the same. The advantage to the female customer is 'undeniably in her aesthetic education', and he underlines that, through the staging of theatrical effects, 'the aesthetic experience was generalized and democratized'. Elsewhere, Saisselin compares 'the striking similarities of the structures, spaces and methods of exhibiting objects in museums and department stores' despite the 'social, aesthetic and theoretical differences between the objet d'art and the consumer object' (Saisselin, 1984: 42).

The impact and influence of this increased consumerism and visual display of fashion upon early twentieth-century artists such as Pablo Picasso, whose work broke away from the expectations of the fine art establishment, and Marcel Duchamp, whose work would later influence postmodernism (Chapter 6), is significant. The subsequent emergence of the modernist and postmodernist concepts of 'art as object' and 'art as product' become manifest in Duchamp's ready-mades and the 'café' assemblages created by Picasso before the outbreak of the First World War in 1914. The relationship between early twentieth-century consumerism, art and fashion will be further explored in Chapter 2.

Summary

Modes of dressing prior to the twentieth century reflected social class, and were the primary means of establishing one's place in society. The working class dressed in functional and inexpensive garments, while the middle classes aspired to match the appearance of the upper classes, who in turn emulated the sovereign and members of the court. This is reflected in women's fashions such as the cage crinoline and corset, both of which were costly and required assistance for dressing, implying wealth and prestige. The move to the bustled silhouette shifted the form of the ideal female to one that still placed emphasis on unrealistic body proportions created by hazardously restrictive underpinnings, and also required a tremendous quantity of luxury fabric. Nevertheless, these styles were in high demand due to the establishment of haute couture in Paris by Charles Frederick Worth and his contemporaries, who furnished European royalty as well as wealthy American clients with elaborate ensembles. Despite the expense and exclusivity of owning a Worth gown, the entrepreneur's business interests extended to collaboration with theatre actors and less expensive models created for department stores, which were now emerging as the great social equalizer. Catering to the bourgeois as well as the middle class, these establishments developed a business model that relied upon advertising, mass-merchandising, and an emphasis on customer service in lavish environments to give their customers the sense of importance they craved. The development of technology such as the sewing machine made the labour-intensive process of assembling garments faster, and in spite of having to overcome the reputation of shoddy workmanship, this paved the way for the ready-to-wear industry that would dominate fashion for decades to come. Major changes in the production, distribution and marketing of clothing from the mid-nineteenth century led to more commercially available goods being made available to a broader spectrum of society.

Notes

1 Printed fabrics for apparel for high-end patrons in Europe were primarily prints (chintz or calico) which came from India and were popular in France and England. In the early eighteenth century, when these expensive imports were banned, French and English fabric printers developed printing methods including woodcut and copper plate printing.

2 In earlier centuries, sumptuary laws governed the type of dress style and fabric that was permissible. Dressing in luxury fabrics, for those outside royalty and the aristocracy, was considered 'dressing above one's station' and was a punishable offense, as it constituted fraud. Sumptuary laws in the Western world date to the Roman period and continued into the seventeenth century.

3 For nineteenth century British critiques of dress for women by both male and female authors, see Mitchell, R. (ed.) (2018) *Fashioning the Victorians,* London and New York: Bloomsbury Publishing.

4 Research by Beverley Lemire (1991) suggests that the ready-made clothing industry and consumerism were well under way in the eighteenth century in Britain. In particular, she discusses ready-made gowns that could be purchased for eight shillings by working-class women in 1777 (1991: 313), cheap, ready-made leather breeches sold at the Rag Fair in the late 1780s (1991: 315), fifteen types of plain cotton hose available by the 1770s (1991: 316), and ready-made cotton shirts for working men which appeared regularly in drapers' ledgers from 1791 (1991: 316). However, it must be noted that the eighteenth century ready-made industry catered only to the working classes, as the garments were considered inappropriate for middle-class consumers.

5 This information follows that available on the web site of the Federation de la Haute Couture et de la Mode https://fhcm.paris/en/the-federation/history/ (accessed 18 September 2019). For a scholarly analysis regarding developments in the role of the Chambre Syndicale, see Kurdjian, S. (2019) 'The Cultural Value of Parisian Couture' in Steele, V. (ed.) *Paris, Capital of Fashion,* 141–63, London and New York: Bloomsbury Publishing.

6 Stanley Chapman and his colleagues (Chapman et al., 1993) argue that the British ready-made clothing industry was essentially complete by 1860, a date at which the sewing machine was only beginning to come into widespread use – indicating that the sewing machine added to, rather than instigated, the trend for ready-made clothing. He maintains that the 'rapid development of ready-made [garments] in the 1840s and 1850s stimulated a demand for machinery rather than vice versa' (Chenoune, 1993: 22–3)He points out that the sewing machine was fifty times faster than the quickest seamstress, but because some parts of the garment were not accessible to the machine, there was a considerable resistance to its use.

7 Evening gowns, wedding gowns and other dresses continued to be available to individual demand, cut to fit the client.

8 Letter from A. Bouçicault to his secretary M. Karchon, 16 September 1876, which calls for greater publicity concerning the store's ready-to-wear dresses.

2

The Artistry of Fashion

Introduction

The early twentieth century witnessed the rise of several artist-led workshops in Europe and later in America, in which the aesthetics and philosophy of mass manufacturing of objects, including apparel and textiles, were challenged. The common goal of the workshops discussed in this chapter were to equate the status of the so-called fine and applied arts by creating a unified aesthetic across all media. In fashion, the burgeoning ready-to-wear industry was counterbalanced by the popularity of theatrical and elegant garments in the world of haute couture. Paul Poiret, Mariano Fortuny, Madeleine Vionnet, Sonia Delaunay and Elsa Schiaparelli all approached fashion design from an artist's perspective. As fine and applied arts were considered essential components of creating an idealized environment, the question of 'democratization' was further pondered by both designers and artists. This chapter will reinforce the threads that tie fashion and art practice together.

Artist-led workshops

The twentieth century led to the rise of a new concept in the bifurcated practice of 'art' and 'craft': the artist-led workshop, which eliminated the hierarchy of the fine and applied arts that had been prevalent since the Renaissance. Established in major cities in Europe and the US, these organizations generally consisted of practicing artists, architects and designers who pooled their talents to create a unified aesthetic. The result was a collection of both consumer goods and architectural spaces that embodied an ideal environment, in which viewers could attain a higher level of appreciation for beauty – connecting them to a higher level of thought, action and experience.

Gesamtkunstwerk of the Weiner Werkstätte

In 1903, architect Josef Hoffmann and painter Koloman Moser partnered with the wealthy industrialist Fritz Waerndorfer to create the Weiner Werkstätte (Vienna Workshop) in Austria. Inspired by John Ruskin, William Morris, and the Arts & Crafts movement active in the last quarter of the nineteenth century in the UK, the Werkstätte aimed to reunite beauty with functionality in handmade objects. The rise of factories had created a disdain for mass manufacturing among the Haute Bourgeoisie, who had the means to purchase finer objects. The Werkstätte began with two of Hoffmann's architectural commissions in 1904–5, the Sanitorium

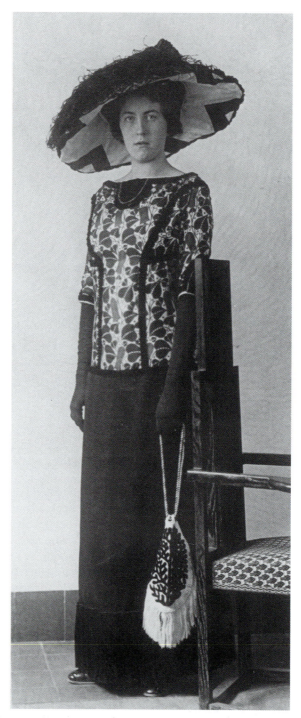

FIGURE 2.1 *Model wearing a blouse made with 'Apollo' fabric designed by Josef Hoffmann at the Wiener Werkstätte, 1911. Werkstätte garments had a minimum of pleating or trim, and simple lines that allowed the textile repeat pattern to dominate the look. (Photo by Imagno/Getty Images.)*

Purkersdorf near Vienna and the Palais Stoclet in Brussels, which included interior decoration and furnishings. Initially the textiles for these endeavours were outsourced, but these early commissions led to the establishment of textile and fashion design departments within the Werkstätte. The development of these separate areas of specialty within the Werkstätte, both employing a similar and complementary aesthetic, is based on the concept of *Gesamtkunstwerk*: creation of a 'total work of art' in architecture and design.

In addition to establishing their own School of Arts and Crafts, the Werkstätte employed both full time and independent artists, such as Viennese Secession painter Gustav Klimt, to create designs for textiles and other applied arts. The resulting aesthetic incorporated abstract geometric or floral designs with bold colours, juxtaposed against a dark outline or background. Fashion and textile departments were created as separate entities from *c.* 1910, led by Edouard Josef Wimmer-Wisgrill, employing over eighty artists during the next twenty-two years. Drawing inspiration from the Mediterranean and the Islamic world, textile designs such as 'Apollo' and 'Pompeii', 'Mekka', 'Konstantinopel' and 'Ispahan' [Mecca, Constantinople and Isfahan] make reference to travels and fascination with the East by the upper classes of Europe. Pattern swatches were arranged into books for customers, and could be used for both furnishings and apparel. Interiors and their inhabitants reflected the aesthetic of the Werkstätte ethos: clean, simple lines and colour combinations in jewel tones, quite different from elaborate Victorian styles in muted hues. The garments produced with these fabrics were high-waisted, linear ensembles that laid pattern upon pattern with minimal trim – the opposite of the corseted, bustled silhouette

FIGURE 2.2 *Fabric pattern 'Mekka' by the Wiener Werkstätte, Vienna, 1911–13. Textile patterns are named to reflect the Eastern inspiration for these brightly coloured designs. (Photo by Imagno/Getty Images.)*

propagated by the House of Worth (see Chapter 1). Fashions created with Werkstätte textiles were advertised on painted postcards by Moser and other painters, and textiles were featured in the International Art Exhibition in Rome (1911), among others, to critical acclaim.

Waerndorfer – whose own home was furnished with Werkstätte creations – declared bankruptcy in 1913, resulting in a reorganization of the workshop. This restructuring led to greater expansion of the textiles and fashion departments, which by 1916 had their own showrooms separate from the main Werkstätte premises, indicating the financial success of these areas. Klimt's paintings of women in Werkstätte garments included wealthy patroness Federika Bier-Monti (1916), as well as his muse and mistress, Emilie Flöge, popularizing the look of these loose colourful garments. Emilie and her sisters were proprietors of Schwestern Flöge, a high-end couture house in Vienna, who often used Werkstätte textiles for their dresses.

Werkstätte objects were well-crafted and made of high-quality materials, catering to the socio-economic elite. Like any couture house in Paris, the Werkstätte relied upon the patronage of wealthy patrons and celebrity clients whose homes were featured in journals. Wimmer-Wisgrill displayed his own apartment decorated with matching Werkstätte textiles in *Das Interieur*; the same issue included a drawing of his sofa, resembling the stage set for the Vienna production of Wagner's *Der Rosenkavalier* (1911). Despite its popularity throughout the First World War, funding for these handmade objects was tenuous, and eventually the workshops could not compete with cheaper, plentiful goods produced during the Interwar years. Although the Werkstätte closed its doors in 1932, the impact of its ethos – artists and designers working together to create artistic objects for everyday use – would inspire several other artist-led workshops.

Bloomsbury and the Omega workshop

In 1913, as the Werkstätte experienced the height of popularity throughout Europe, a group of artists in London formed the Omega workshop at 31 Fitzroy Square. Created and funded by art critic Roger Fry, this collection of painters and designers were active avant-garde artists exploring colour and abstraction. The founding members of Omega were known as the Bloomsbury group: artists, writers and intellectuals who first met in 1905 to discuss their mutual disdain of all things Victorian. The group's main members were sisters Vanessa Bell and Virginia Woolf (née Stephens), respectively a painter and a writer; art critics Roger Fry and Clive Bell, Vanessa's husband; and write Lytton Strachey. Later the group would be joined by Duncan Grant, a painter who would live most of his life with Vanessa Bell at their country house, Charleston in Sussex, following her estrangement from her spouse. The cohesive group were among the first artists in Britain to practice abstract painting, inspired by a pivotal exhibition of the work of Picasso, Gauguin, Van Gogh and other post-impressionists. They named their workshop 'Omega' after the last letter in the ancient Greek alphabet, indicating that their works were the final statement in good design.

Contrary to the Victorian practice of amassing objects as a form conspicuous consumption, the Omega artists believed that handmade decorative objects could elevate the spirit. One of their most public displays of the goods produced was at the Ideal Home exhibition of 1913, where the group displayed curtains and furniture upholstered with Omega designs by Bell, Grant and others. Hand-painted screens, rugs and murals were included in the early productions of the workshop. However, these handmade objects were expensive and required a wealthy clientele.

Similar to the early years of the Werkstätte, Omega founded its ethos on the premise that art and design should be complementary practices that produced a unified visual environment. Textiles and fashion in both workshops began as tangential experiments that proved to be more fruitful than expected. Vanessa Bell began using Omega printed linens and other textiles in dress

FIGURE 2.3 *Furniture and textiles from at the Omega workshops by artists connected with the Bloomsbury group in 1913. (Photo by Topical Press Agency/Getty Images.)*

design around 1915 – a good business move, as fashion proved to be more financially tenable than other goods during the war. Their patrons included the group's intellectual friends as well as the social elite in London, from E.M. Forster and George Bernard Shaw, to Lady Ottoline Morrel, a wealthy patron. Despite financial subsidies from Roger Fry, the workshop was closed in 1919 due to expensive production costs, a lack of patronage, and internal staff issues, but the impact of the Bloomsbury group and Omega is still acknowledged today.

Building Better Design: The Bauhaus

As the Omega workshops were closing, the Staatliches Bauhaus was established by architect Walter Gropius in Weimar, Germany (1919–23). Later relocating to Dessau (1923–31) and Berlin (1931–3), the Bauhaus was a state-sponsored art school and design think tank. Bauhaus faculty were prominent avant-garde artists who strove to improve quality of life through well-designed objects and buildings. Mirroring the concepts put forth by the Werkstätte, the Bauhaus established various areas of specialty to create a unified guild that expressed respect for the practice of all artistic forms, from architecture and cabinet-making to textiles and painting. Resident faculty were known as 'masters' and worked with student apprentices on prototypes and commissions, establishing a 'foundation' program that included drawing, painting, two-and three-dimensional design and colour theory – the model still used by art schools today.

Bauhaus philosophy encouraged designs of functional objects suitable for mass production, an effort to democratize access to high-quality design. Prominent Bauhaus masters included painters Wassily Kandinsky, Josef Albers and Paul Klee; industrial designer Marcel Breuer; theatre and costume designer Oscar Schlemmer; typography designer Maholy-Nagy; and weavers Gunta Stölzl and Anni Albers, each of whom led the weaving workshop in turn. The goal of the weaving studio was to create fabrics that were suitable for use in Bauhaus environments, employing the rectilinear motifs and colour experiments that also defined painting in this period. Stölzl encouraged the use of unusual materials, such as cellophane, metal and fibreglass, collaborating across departments. Bauhaus textiles were both handmade art objects, as well as designs that could be manufactured en masse, suitable for furnishings and fashion.

The weaving workshop was primarily composed of women at the Bauhaus. This was due to Gropius' belief that women were not suitable for manual labour or spatial planning required in fields such as architecture or sculpture, and assigned them to the weaving workshop instead (Loho, 2019). Reflecting on the contributions of women artists and designers, Anscombe (1984) argues that it was the familiarity of abstract designs on textiles that led to the acceptance of the avant-garde 'abstract' art seen in the museums. She observes the significant fact that: 'The character of the early Bauhaus textiles . . . mark[s] a departure from the textile patterns produced before the war in its abandonment of conventional patterning and naturalistic ornament, as in Russia (Constructivism), Paris and Vienna (Weiner Werkstätte), it was primarily through textile design that the current ideas of abstract art were brought to a wider public' (1984: 136).

In the years leading up to the Second World War, the Bauhaus experienced increasing pressure from the conservative German right-wing government to curtail their activities and remove faculty who did not conform to their political ideals. The school closed in 1933, and many of the masters fled Germany and ultimately Europe; Josef and Anni Albers went on to teach at the Black Mountain College in North Carolina, and later Josef taught at Yale University. Anni went on to become a prominent fibre artist specializing in tapestry and pattern weaving, writing the seminal treatise *On Weaving* in 1965. She was the first woman to have a solo exhibition at the Museum of Modern Art in New York (1949). The impact of Bauhaus principles and aesthetics still resonates in textile and fashion today, from inspiring high-end designers Mary Kantrantzou and Rosetta Getty, to an Anni Albers-inspired collection at the fast fashion giant, Uniqlo. Contemporary exhibitions celebrating the 100-year anniversary of the Bauhaus in 2019 include 'The Bauhaus and Harvard' at Harvard Art Museums and 'Anni Albers' at the Tate Modern.

Design in America: Cranbrook Academy of Art

In America, the early twentieth century brought a similar interest in artistic unity, primarily inspired by the avant-garde movements in Europe. The interplay of architecture and design is exemplified in the collection of buildings and grounds at the Cranbrook Educational Community in Bloomfield Hills, MI. The 319-acre farmstead was purchased by newspaper magnate George Booth and his wife, Ellen Scripps Booth, in 1904. After commissioning Albert Kahn to build the family manor home, the Booths set about creating primary and secondary educational institutions and an Academy of Art, with a unified aesthetic across architecture and interiors based on the principles of *Gesamtkunstwerk*. As the harbinger of mid-century modern design, the Cranbrook aesthetic featured telescoping geometric patterns that repeat throughout each building on doorways, gateways, leaded glass windows, furniture, wainscoting and textiles. The grounds are dotted with elaborate gardens enhanced by the bronze figural sculptures of Swedish sculptor Carl Milles.

The visionaries for this aesthetic were Finnish husband and wife, architect Eliel Saarinen and textile designer Loja Saarinen. In addition to his commissions for the Cranbrook educational community, Eliel went on to design several Detroit-area landmarks; Loja designed the interior furnishing textiles for Cranbrook Schools, as well as having her own independent business, Studio Loja Saarinen. The Academy of Art was founded in 1928 as an artist colony, and codified in 1932 as an educational institution. Both Eliel and Loja Saarinen were heads of their respective departments of Architecture and Urban Design (1932–50) and Weaving and Textile Design (1929–42) at the Academy of Art. Eliel Saarinen was also the first president of the Academy (1932–46). Although there was no 'fashion' department as such, the Saarinens' daughter Pipsan led a fashion class at the Academy, and Loja was known for making her own clothes (Mayman, 2019). Activities at the Art Academy included fancy dress-up balls such as the 'Crandemonium' ball (1934), not unlike those at the Bauhaus, in which extravagant and sometimes outlandish costumes were constructed. The textiles produced at Cranbrook were emulated far and wide, used for both interior furnishings and dress fabrics. The weaving and textile design department produced a number of influential students, including Frances Knoll (co-founder, Knoll, 1938), Jack Lenor Larsen (founder, Larsen Textiles, 1951), and fibre artists Anne Wilson, Nick Cave and Sonya Clark, among many others.

Haute couture at the turn of the twentieth century

In Paris, the turn of the twentieth century brought significant changes in dress. Social gatherings in the upper classes called for a parade of haute couture garments that created a virtual theatre in which to display new ideas, an idea made literal by the couturier Paul Poiret.

Paul Poiret: The King of Fashion

The son of a French textile distributor, Poiret was raised with a love of fashion and exotic fabrics. He learned the basics of couture and costume design while apprenticing with Jacques Doucet (1898–1901), where he designed the famous 'Aiglon' costume for actress Sarah Bernhardt, and a hand-painted black cape for the lead actress Rejane in the theatre production of *Zaza*. Following this early exposure to theatrical costume, Poiret was employed at the House of Worth (1901–2), where he created an Eastern-influenced cloak entitled 'Confucius'. Taking inspiration from the loose cut of Eastern garments, Poiret was fired for presenting a black kimono-style cloak to a Russian princess who found it deplorable. Despite this setback, Poiret founded his own couture house in 1903, where he proceeded to follow his Orientalist-inspired visions to great success.

Poiret modelled his designs on his wife and muse, Denise, a slender young woman who had grown up in the French countryside without the frills and fit of the bustled, corseted silhouette. Poiret's primary style was one that eliminated these underpinnings by working with the high-waisted, linear silhouette also taking root in Vienna at this time. In November 1911 while touring his latest collection, Poiret visited the Werkstätte in Vienna, and purchased several of their colourful abstract textiles for use as coat linings and dress fabrics.

Poiret's most significant contribution to fashion in the early part of the century was to bring his love of patterns and garments from Far Eastern and Islamic lands into the Parisian vocabulary. Although textiles from Asia had been used to create European clothing for centuries, Poiret incorporated (and perhaps appropriated) garment cuts and features that had been used in these cultures, introducing wide-legged harem trousers, pantaloons and hemlines weighted down by tassels. He created a sensation in 1911 with his costume ball, 'The 1002nd Night Party,' [making reference to the 1001 Arabian Nights story, a medieval tale taking place in Abbasid Baghdad]. Poiret's directions to his 300 guests were to dress in costume or to purchase

FIGURE 2.4 *French comedian Cora Laparcerie (1875–1951) as Myriem in a costume by Paul Poiret for the play 'Le Minaret' by Jacques Richepin. Photo from French paper* Le Theatre. *Paris, May 1913. Poiret's costume design for the play 'The Minaret' was based on the prototype of the 'lampshade' tunic design worn by his wife Denise, at the 1002nd Night Party held on 24 June 1911. (Photo by Apic/Getty Images.)*

one on site: he offered turbans, harem pants, and his own hybrid creations known as 'lampshade tunics', ensembles featuring iridescent fabrics forming an 'A' shape through a wired hem just above the knees. This was modelled by Denise Poiret, who played the part of the 'Sultan's favourite' and was locked in a golden cage, released by Poiret into the crowd as part of the theatrics of the event. The lampshade tunic was so popular that it found its way to both theatre and couture in the following seasons. On his first journey to America in 1913, he found that he was being called 'The King of Fashion' and that the lampshade silhouette was being copied far and wide.

In 1912, several large department stores staged more spectacular theatrical presentations of Paris couture fashion disguised under the exotic 'Garden of Allah' theme. Similarly, Paul Poiret

FIGURE 2.5 Sorbet *evening dress by Paul Poiret, 1913 (front view). Silk satin, chiffon, glass beads. The lampshade silhouette was admired equally as couture creation and costume for theatre. Poiret's Orientalist designs shocked and amused his Parisian clientele, and were widely copied throughout the fashion world. (Photo by Chicago History Museum/Getty Images.)*

staged a production of 'Le Minaret' during his 1913 American tour (Troy, 2003). He created an ideal of sophisticated luxury, and his presence at the events resulted in the outstanding commercial success of his collection. A year later, Poiret used the Théâtre de la Renaissance in Paris to stage a play called 'Aphrodite', where an opulent spectacle of couture fashions distinguished the actors in the five-part drama. The success of these ventures suggests that theatricality was used as a clever tool in bridging the gap between culture and commerce (Troy, 2003).

Poiret did not develop his ideas in a vacuum. A precedence for Eastern dress and textiles was established for modern audiences in 1910 when Serge Diaghilev's Russian Ballet (Ballet Russes) performed *Schéhérazade* in Paris to huge crowds. While it was held as a cultural event, the fashion designers saw how movement, drama and visual spectacle could enhance the clothing that was worn. Not only was it the first time that the famous dancer Nijinsky had appeared outside of Russia, but it was also the first time that a European audience had seen the experimental costumes and stage settings of Léon Bakst. The dramatic experience of this single production, with its bejewelled garments in brilliantly juxtaposed hues, had a historically unparalleled impact upon its viewers. Poiret's exotic collections were further popularized, but more importantly the ballet's impact reverberated through every branch of the arts. The Russian Ballet 'became a catalyst of culture' and, furthermore, 'the critics found it hard to determine what to praise first – the choreography of Fokine, the dancing of Nijinsky, the dazzling costumes and sets by Bakst which exploded into Parisian fashion and interior design, or the unfamiliar music of Rimsky-Korsakov' (Lloyd, 1991: 35).

The goddess silhouettes of Vionnet and Fortuny

As Poiret focused on the East for inspiration, other couturiers were looking to the Mediterranean. Nineteenth century archaeological excavations had brought the sculptures and artefacts of Hellenistic Greece and ancient Rome to Europe in the form of reports, prints and engravings, and the draped bodies of goddesses became a subject of both fantasy and fashion.

In France, the couturière Madeleine Vionnet opened her atelier in 1912 after apprenticing as a dressmaker with the Callot Soeurs, whom she would later credit with teaching her high-end couture skills, followed by work at the atelier of Jacques Doucet. The loose silhouettes that were to dominate the 1910s were an appropriate segue into the soft, clinging silhouette that was to define Vionnet's work. Like Poiret, Vionnet was inspired by the art forms prevalent in Europe at the time, including exhibitions at the Louvre and other venues displaying friezes excavated from ancient Greek sites, such as the Parthenon. She was not alone in her admiration of Grecian dress: Isadora Duncan, the mother of modern dance who started her career in the late nineteenth century dancing in the drawing rooms of the social elite, dressed in belted shifts meant to emulate the caryatids of the Parthenon. This overlapping of fine and performing art with fashion helped to stimulate public acceptance of these non-Western styles.

Vionnet achieved her Grecian goddess look by cutting whole garments on the bias, the first known couturière to attempt this. In order to emphasize the natural curves of the body, her creations lacked structure and required wrapping or belting the gowns, resembling the peplos and chiton of ancient Greece. These goddess silhouettes became all the rage among the Paris elite, and by the start of the First World War she had a loyal clientele. Working in Rome from 1914–18, Vionnet returned to Paris and re-established her couture house in 1919, remaining en vogue for the next twenty years. Vionnet's style would become ever more influential through the

FIGURE 2.6 *A model wears a floor-length Madeleine Vionnet dress cut on the bias, with wrapped bodice draped over one shoulder, September 1935. (Photo by Roger Viollet via Getty Images/Roger Viollet Collection/Getty Images.)*

costume designers of Hollywood, whose starlets – Jean Harlow, Marlene Dietrich and others – were often dressed in bias-cut gowns created by costume designers for seductive promo shoots. In 1924, Vionnet entered into a distribution agreements with Fifth Avenue retailer Hickson, who showed an exclusive collection of gowns; the following year, Vionnet opened her own salon in New York City, followed by a location in Biarritz. Her New York store offered a prêt-à-porter line of her wrapped and belted dresses, which were adjustable and had only to be fitted for height.

Throughout the 1930s, Vionnet continued to update her classic style through her manipulation of new materials. In her final seasons of 1938 and 1939, many of her evening dresses were made

FIGURE 2.7 *Model Sonia in a summer evening dress by Madeleine Vionnet in Paris, 1938. The halter neckline, belted waist and delicate layers of tulle are hallmarks of Vionnet's style in the late 1930s. (Photo by Apic/Getty Images.)*

with tulle and gold lamé, fabric woven or knitted with thin strips of synthetic fibres coated with metallic film, in imitation of luxury metal-thread textiles. She gave her gowns fullness by adding synthetic horsehair on the outer hem of the garments, creating volume without adding weight, and complemented by a form-fitting bodice. Greatly admired by other couturiers in her time, Vionnet epitomized the serious dressmaker whose style long outlived the fads introduced by other designers. Political changes in France during the Second World War forced Vionnet and many other couturiers to close the doors of their fashion houses, but the label was resurrected by Guy and Arnaud de Lummen in the mid-1990s. Since 2009, it has been owned by Goga Ashkenazi and rebranded as a sustainable company.

The elegant ensembles of Mariano Fortuny also reflected an admiration for Hellenism, as well as the history of luxury silk production in Europe. Fortuny, a Spaniard, came from a family of artists. Following the early demise of his father, Fortuny spent his youth in Paris and later moved to Venice with his mother. Showing great promise as a painter, Fortuny nevertheless shifted to theatre and set design. Inspired by Wagner's historic characters, he created his first costume piece: the Knossos scarf, a rectangular shawl reminiscent of the Greek himation.

Inspired by the ancient Greek bronze sculpture 'The Charioteer of Delphi' (found in 1896), Fortuny set out to recreate the draped garment of the figure. In partnership with his wife Henriette Negrin, whom he met in 1897, Fortuny created the first Delphos Dress (c. 1907). He achieved this by inventing a specialized pleating technique, the exact process of which is still a mystery, the only surviving evidence a patent for heated ceramic rollers that may have been used to set the pleats. Fortuny dresses were columnar, made of silk overdyed in several layers with natural colourants, and belted loosely at the mid-section. These goddess-like dresses were often layered with voided velvet or compound-woven silk textiles with a small matching drawstring pouch, reminiscent of Italian Renaissance garments and metal-thread silks from Islamic lands. The whole ensemble conjured images of luxury, royalty and mythic deities.

Maintaining a couture house in Paris, Fortuny kept his main operations in Venice, where he established the Palazzo Fortuny (now a museum dedicated to his legacy). Fortuny's commercial success was expanded in partnership with Elsie McNeill Lee, an American interior designer who had become enamoured of Fortuny's fabrics. Becoming the exclusive distributor of the couturier's fabrics and fashions in 1928, Lee popularized the Fortuny look among the New York elite based in her Madison Avenue showroom. By Fortuny's death in 1949, Lee had married an Italian count and took over operations in the Venice factory, as well as maintaining the New York showroom until her death in 1988. Delphos dresses remained a staple of the House of Fortuny until about 1960, inspiring couture in Fortuny's time and beyond, including: Paul Poiret, Madame Grès, Christian Dior, Roy Halston Frowick and others.

Art and fashion

As a symbiotic relationship emerged between the fine arts and the applied arts, this led to a more conceptually enhanced aesthetic direction in fashion. Fine artists such as Sonia Delaunay in Paris successfully applied the dynamics of this modern visual language to a utilitarian art form: clothing. By applying aesthetic concerns to both fashion and textile design, Delaunay pioneered the practical application of abstraction to everyday objects, and thus consolidated the link between the art and design movements of the post-war era. In particular, Delaunay was able to apply her colour theories (originally meant for her canvases) directly to textile designs which, in turn, were used in the production of simply constructed garments.

FIGURE 2.8 Vogue *1935: Mrs William Wetmore modelling pleated gown by Mariano Fortuny, standing in front of printed fabric. Fortuny's skill with fine pleats and natural dyes created ephemeral garments that emulated Grecian prototypes. (Photo by Lusha Nelson/Condé Nast via Getty Images.)*

Sonia Delaunay: Simultaneous contrast of colours

For Sonia Delaunay, painting was a form of poetry in which colours were words, and the pattern of the colours created rhythms in the composition. Her early life as a painter was closely allied with that of her husband, abstract painter Robert Delaunay, and with their experiments in colour orchestration and the founding of the art movement called Orphism in 1913. When she first moved to Paris from Russia in 1905, there was a great deal of interaction among Russian and Western European artists, and she met most of the avant-garde artists including Picasso, Braque and Derain (Heller, 1987: 122–3). A systematic development from painting to applied art and craft, fashion and textile design emerges throughout Delaunay's career. Her brilliance as a colourist is generally acknowledged, and this talent inspired her to experiment extensively in media other than pigments.

Delaunay viewed fashion design as an alternate mode of artistic expression, and her interest in fashion as a commercial enterprise is overshadowed by her conceptual interests in bringing material to life. When questioned about her fashion design in an interview for *The New York Times* (4 December 1977), Sonia remarked: 'I wasn't interested in fashion, but in applying colour and light to fabrics.' Her colour theories of 'simultaneous contrasts' were inspired by Michel Eugène's theories of colour, in turn based on Gustav Chevreul's book *On the Law of the Simultaneous Contrast of Colours*, published in Paris in 1839. Her first Simultaneous Dress of 1913 was a patchwork of different textures and colours, combining her abstract colour paintings with the aesthetic of Picasso and Braque's experimental Cubist collages. Immediately, with the interplay of colours and abstract form, the leap from fine art to fashion was complete. Delaunay famously commented to Tristan Tzara, Dadaist poet and occasional collaborator, that: 'If painting has become part of our lives, it is because women have been wearing it!' (cited in Anscombe, 1984: 120). Her friendship with Tzara and her ideological ties with the Dadaist painters and poets were demonstrated in her series of robes-poèmes (dress poems) of 1922. The robes-poèmes consist of a series of abstract dress designs in which geometric blocks of colour are interspersed with lines of Tzara's Dada poetry. As the body moves, the interrelationship of colour and text becomes very fluid and creates a variety of different simultaneous juxtapositions. One robe-poème called 'The Eternally Feminine' caressingly played with the wearer's body, with the 'l' appearing at the bend of an arm, and the 'e' at the fingers (Madsen, 1989: 180). Ideologically, her comprehension of the ephemeral nature of fashion as opposed to the enduring values of institutionalized art would have appealed to the Dadaists.

Delaunay's collaborative work with Tzara extended to designing costumes for his notorious play entitled 'Le Coeur à Gaz' in 1923, which featured Satie's music, Van Doesburg's sets and Man Ray's films. While the immortality achieved by this Dadaist production was due to the outrageous nature of the play, the resultant publicity brought Delaunay's costumes to the public eye. The solid cardboard costumes, which conceptually bridged the gap between dress and sculpture, did not allow for much movement (Richter, 1965: 190), and their 'direct audacity' was described by the Dadaist René Crevel in 1920 as being 'immediately impressive' (Cohen, 1978: 187). 'Sonia's costumes', as they were described by Madsen (1989), 'were renderings of stiff, formal bourgeois evening attire on cardboard encasements that parodied the clothes and characters' (1989: 189). Avant-garde spectacles like Dada performances and poetry readings[1] helped to break down earlier notions about clothing as a cover for the body, replacing them with an image of the body as a fluid screen, capable of reflecting back a present constantly undergoing redefinition and transformation (Chadwick, 1990: 257). In a similar vein, early 1920s Bauhaus theatre also featured elaborate sculptural costumes and set design for Oskar Schlemmer's Bauhaus Dances and Triadic Ballet, in which the dancers resembled mechanical puppets.

Delaunay's theatrical costumes have been compared with Picasso's costume designs for *Parade* of 1917, featuring elements of his Cubist collages as large cardboard cut-outs adorning the dancers.[2] Interestingly, this analogy has been overshadowed by Damase's remark that 'Delaunay's costumes were still more original' and 'few works can be said to have such a far-reaching impact' (1972: 131) – a comment which perhaps refers to Delaunay's important contribution to modern fashion design. According to Buckberrough (1980: 64), 'the following year, cardboard costumes exhibiting the same frontal, abstract conception as those from the play (and perhaps based on its designs), were paraded before high society'. These geometric futuristic creations became the forerunners of Delaunay's textile and fashion designs of the 1920s, and in 1923 the Lyons textile manufacturer Bianchini-Ferier commissioned her to design fifty patterns for fabrics. This event launched her commercial designing career.

FIGURE 2.9 *Two women wearing swimsuits designed by Sonia Delaunay. Right, in light blue silk embroidered in red, white and green. (Photo by Luigi Diaz/Getty Images.)*

Delaunay's financial success resulted from the production of the initial textile designs for the Lyons textile firm. In Paris in the same year, she marketed her work in a fashion booth at the Bal Bullier. In 1924 she established a clothing boutique, the Atelier Simultané, on the Boulevard Malesherbes for printing simultaneous textiles and producing a wide range of clothing and accessories. While she primarily hand-painted 'simultaneous' fabrics and tapestries for a growing private clientele, her influence as a designer had a considerable impact on international fashion trends. Her overseas market – particularly in America – was steadily improving. Delaunay documents that 'scarves, ballet costumes, bathing suits, and embroidered coats, employing the principles of collage, were sold throughout the world' (Cohen, 1978: 211). The fusion of art and commercial enterprise in decorative design was heralded at the 1925 'Exposition des Arts Décoratifs et Industriels Modèrnes' in Paris, where Delaunay's fashions, textiles and paintings were displayed in the Boutique Simultanée, a business enterprise collaboratively run with the furrier Jacques Heim. This international exhibition reflected modern industrialized post-war culture and art. Buckberrough (1980) points out that, after this important event, 'the "modern style" typified by Sonia Delaunay's creations took precedence in the French decorative arts' (1980: 67).

Not only is Delaunay's accreditation of bringing modern art into modern life mirrored in the doctrines of other modernist movements in the 1920s – including the Bauhaus – but the creation of this universal visual language through the confluence of form and function dominated the machine aesthetic which arose out of the technological 'renaissance' of the 1920s. While some complained that Delaunay's fashion and textile designs were elitist in nature, as they were prohibitively costly and therefore aimed at the wealthy, she counteracted this claim by attempting to interface with industry by the mass production of her patented *tissu-patron*. Adapting them to commercial reproduction, these fabric patterns pre-packaged the dress pattern with the textile fabric, thereby protecting the unity of the design while being marketed at a minimal cost to the consumer. While this enterprise should have been successful, in practice it was not, as the standardization of the design did not allow for individual figure variations, and consequently most women found that they needed individual alterations for a proper fit. She promoted this modernist idea in her public lecture given at the Sorbonne University in Paris in 1927, entitled 'The Influence of Painting on Fashion Design', where she emphasized the 'constructive' aspects of dress – which she stated were 'clearly influenced by painting', maintaining that 'the cut of the dress is conceived by its creator simultaneously with its decoration' (Cohen, 1978: 206). She reinforced this belief later in her autobiographical text of 1967, when she argued that the true beauty of an object is not an effect of taste, but is ultimately tied to its function. She also emphasized that the mechanical and the dynamic were the essential elements of the practical dimensions of that time.

Undoubtedly, Delaunay's major contribution to the decline of elitism is evidenced by the application of her artistic theories to design in the applied arts rather than by the practice of mass-producing her goods. Her most significant contribution centres on her prophesies for fashion production in the future. In her essay, 'Les Artistes et L'Avenir de la Mode' (first published in 1931; see Cohen, 1978: 208), she forecasts that the future democratization of fashion will 'raise the general standards of the industry' and suggests that the primary aims of industry should be twofold. First, she predicts that laboratories of research dealing with the practical design of clothing will develop in a way that closely parallels the necessities of life. Second, she suggests that industries will lower the costs of production by mass production of goods and will concentrate on the expansion of sales. Delaunay's endorsement of ready-to-wear fashion in the late 1920s is recorded in her autobiography, *Nous Irons Jusqu'au Soleil* (Delaunay 1978):

Before the inescapable reign of ready-made clothes, we were enjoying the last days of the 'modèle unique' before the first liberated women would be imitated by thousands of others. The ready-to-wear clothes would reclaim the conquests of the 1920s and the poem-dresses would fill the streets.

1978: 93

Delaunay's contribution to the redefinition of textile and fashion design within the context of the fine arts cannot be underestimated. Until recently, Sonia Delaunay has not been fully accredited for the very important role that she played in extending and expanding the traditional aesthetic boundaries of art and design. Retrospective exhibitions of her work in Europe include 'Les couleurs de l'abstraction' at Musée d'Art Moderne in Paris (2014–15), and 'The EY Exhibition Sonia Delaunay' at the Tate Modern (2015).

Elsa Schiaparelli: Surrealism in fashion

As opposed to creating fashion in the traditional sense, Elsa Schiaparelli created a more explicit form of statements inspired by art. Schiaparelli found her inspiration in the use of paradoxical imagery, which often shared Freudian associations apparent in the work of the Surrealists[3]. The boundless development of novelty in her design and her unorthodox use of materials were instrumental in her ability to undermine the serious nature of traditional haute couture – a factor that often caused conflict with her peers. Schiaparelli did not have couturier training and was part of the artistic contingent made up of painters, writers, poets and film-makers in 1920s and 1930s Paris. Like Dada's anti-art, which challenged the canons of the salon and the art academy, Schiaparelli questioned the notions and structures of institutions such as Parisian haute couture with a type of anti-fashion.

As with Delaunay, Elsa Schiaparelli's fashion career evolved from a fine art base. When she turned to fashion design, her work always retained a direct link with artistic methodologies. It was her association with the Dadaists and Surrealists which provided a wealth of symbolic meaning to each of her works. Throughout her designing career, she redefined and reconstituted the interrelationship between fashion and art. Despite her nonconformist attitudes and practices, she rose to an eminent position of power and influence in the world of haute couture. Like many of the Dadaists, her work 'took the form of an insurrection against all that was pompous, conventional, or even boring in the arts' (Chipp, 1973: 367). She eroded traditional and elitist practices through the use of unconventional materials, included explicit sexual imagery in the decorative detail of her garments, and used memorabilia from popular culture in her work.

A prime example of Schiaparelli's fascination with unusual materials and motifs led her to commission the Lyons textile firm, Calcombet, to produce silks and cottons with a pattern printed from newspaper clippings about her. The text juxtaposed fragments of articles written by fashion editors and journalists – including both favourable and unfavourable descriptions written about her work! Some authors speculate that this visual displacement was either inspired by Picasso's daring collages of 1911 or by the newspaper hats that she had seen Scandinavian fisherwomen wear (Palmer White, 1986: 38). O'Neill (2005: 181) argues that 'the designer was herself keen to maintain that the overarching inspiration had been a Cubist painting by Picasso that had used newspaper as a collaged material'. In fact, he speculates that: 'It may well be that she got the idea from the Dada artist, Kurt Schwitters himself, as she was well versed in modern art and was acquainted with many of the practitioners.' Scandalous as this was in the 1930s, this form of self-critique foreshadowed later post- modernist practice.

Schiaparelli's ability to combine the commonplace and the sensational into a single item is evident in her clear plastic necklace decorated with coloured insects that appeared to crawl over the wearer's neck. Not only is this a visually bizarre piece, but it stimulates a tactile sensory response. It seems that an art nouveau necklace featuring hybrid creatures, created by the famous French turn-of-the-century jeweller Lalique, inspired this piece. The unorthodox subject matter and the combination of precious and non-precious materials synthesized in the piece were properties that characterized both art nouveau and Surrealist work.

The Surrealist phenomenon is manifest in the world of dreams, derived from the imagination as a duality of rational/irrational, or the actual as opposed to the depicted. This juxtaposition of opposing realities heightens the paradoxical nature of the work. In this way, Schiaparelli's work employs the conventional framework of formally tailored garments as a foil for meticulous Surreal embroideries, which were 'inspired by a range of historical and traditional embroideries including magnificently embroidered ecclesiastical vestments' (Wilcox and Mendes, 1998: 104). For Wilcox and Mendes, Schiaparelli's work 'alternated between the bizarre and the lyrical' (1991: 50), deliberately using provocative combinations of ancient and modern techniques and materials in order to 'unite the best of the fine and decorative arts' (1991: 120). In this respect, Wilcox and Mendes underline the crucial link between Schiaparelli's fashion and both art nouveau and Surrealist art practices.

In 1934, Schiaparelli first employed the firm Lesage et Cie to produce hand-embroidered belts and later necklaces, yokes and trompe l'œil collars in a highly coloured and baroque style. At the time, it seemed inconceivable that she could single-handedly revive this flagging industry. Palmer White (1986) consistently observes that no other couturier has ever done more to promote embroidery than Elsa Schiaparelli. Summarizing Schiaparelli's career, Wilcox and Mendes (1998) add that: 'Slowly, in a reaction to the beading of the 1920s, she returned to the use of embroidery materials employed centuries before – paillettes from medieval times – and asked for designs recalling stained-glass windows and liturgical ornamentation of the sixteenth century' (1998: 64). While Schiaparelli's collection themes determined the embroidered designs, Palmer White adds that Poiret argues that 'she conceived the garments that would enhance the embroidery' (Palmer White, 1988: 63). It was precisely the fairly unremarkable cut of her garments that so effectively allowed the ornamentation to capture the attention and imagination of the viewer.

Working closely with Albert Lesage, Schiaparelli encouraged him to experiment with innovative materials and techniques: 'Albert used . . . Murano-blown glass for little flowers; glass stones and beach pebbles; he crushed gelatino beads to lend them the appearance of hammered coins; and employed metal to reflect its new uses (in the modern machine age)' (Palmer White, 1986: 62). These collaborations culminated in such extravagant projects as the elaborately embroidered suit of 1937, where Schiaparelli cleverly incorporated the use of ruby mirrors as part of the bodice design. These were strategically placed across the bustline, creating not only a baroque sumptuosity, but imparting a theatrical touch – mirroring the reflection of the viewer. These mirrors, perhaps used in jest as a means to divert voyeurism, were considered incompatible with high fashion.

Schiaparelli created, by innovative synthesis, a certain eclectic and non-exclusive 'exclusiveness'. She blatantly used artistic techniques meant to 'trick the eye', and appropriated symbols from one visual context for use in another. The assimilation of optical deviations within an elitist framework of fine fabric and craftsmanship created a visual anomaly. The impact of her work was heightened by the interrelationship of the Surrealist psycho-sexual imagery with the traditional framework of embroidery, Lesage and beaded techniques. Schiaparelli, having emerged from a fine art background, embraced the artistic circles of artists, poets and writers and became a great friend to many of the Dadaist artists, including the notorious Salvador Dalí. So much of her work underscored the symbiotic relationship that has always existed between fashion and art.

Significantly, the earliest influences upon Schiaparelli's work were two major exhibitions in 1925: the 'Exposition des Arts Décoratifs et Industriels Modèrnes', Paris and the first Surrealist exhibition held in Paris. The former display of applied arts made Schiaparelli aware of the new materials that heralded the new machine age, and she subsequently adopted technological innovations and exploited the use of industrial materials such as plastics, latex, cellophane, rayon crêpe, coiled spring and wire into her work.

The Surrealist exhibition of 1925, in particular, inspired Schiaparelli to produce her earliest design sensation, the *trompe l'œil* (Fr. *trick of the eye*) woollen Cravat sweater, two years later. The hand-knitted top, created to Schiaparelli's direction by an Armenian couple in Paris specializing in knits, appeared to be decorated with a bow at the neckline. While the illusion of the three-dimensional butterfly bow was sustained at a distance, it diminished as the viewer approached the wearer, forcing the viewer to participate in the joke when the visual paradox was discovered. This visual deception expounds the Surrealist idea that reality is often an illusion.

While Schiaparelli's use of paradoxical Surrealist imagery emerged in the 1920s, it gathered strength in the 1930s and reached its zenith in 1937 and 1938. In collaboration with Salvador Dalí, she produced the Desk Suit of 1936, which incorporated a vertical series of true and false pockets that were embroidered in strong raised relief (bourré) to look like drawers, with buttons for knobs. In this visual and conceptual paradox, the woman and her job become inextricably interwoven. As becomes evident, Schiaparelli's garments – like Dalí's three-dimensional pieces – should be interpreted within a social context. Through their appropriation of paradoxical imagery, her designs conjure symbolic associations that often relate to irrational feelings, sensory stimulations, totems and myths, and which seem to change depending on their environmental or social context. The symbolic associations inherent in her designs are also explicit in her choice of materials. For example, a tactile fabric that she called 'treebark' resembled its name and encompassed the body as bark enshrouds a tree trunk. Literally, the garment became a second skin, and at the same time created a visual dichotomy. In 1943, the use of cellophane, velours and glass fabrics called rhodophane dominated Schiaparelli's collection. *Vogue* described rhodophane as 'a brittle and fragile fabric with the transparency of glass, but it doesn't shatter like a window-pane'; glass belts 'which resembled Pyrex but were paper thin' adorned these unequivocal, sensational new garments (Palmer White, 1986: 31). In this 'New Art', Schiaparelli created another conceptual paradox: a glass covering for the female body not unlike the glass display cases and windows in the department stores.

When Schiaparelli appropriated and recontextualized fabrics, their tactile surfaces enhanced both sexual and sensual provocation. This is evident in her dresses made in billiard table felt, and the rubber-lined hostess blouse that converts to an apron for kitchen work. This use of materials normally associated with the world of bars and brothels also juxtaposes the concept of elitist fashion in a non-elitist form. The erotic nature of The Tears Dress (1937–8) is implied, for example, in Schiaparelli's collaboration with Salvador Dalí to produce a textile that appeared to be covered in rips or tears. This illusion creates a visual fantasy that invites a tactile response to the actual fabric, something that needs to be handled as well as viewed.

In this way, Schiaparelli's work illustrates the convergence of elements of humour and provocation, in both Surrealist fashion and art. According to Palmer White, Schiaparelli ignored the propriety associated with hats and instead 'gave them a playful and sometimes even satanic dash of humour' (1986: 100). Commenting on this tendency, Cecil Beaton (1954) refers to the 'invention of her own particular form of ugliness' which 'salubriously shocked a great many people' (1954: 184). The substantial role of humour in Schiaparelli's work is particularly evident in the Dalí-inspired Mutton Chop Hat, which went perfectly with a suit embroidered with cutlet motifs, the bathing suit with wriggling fish printed on the stomach, handbags that looked like telephones or birdcages, and long black gloves with clear windows for fingernails. Like certain art exhibitions, her collections were thematically presented; her Circus collection of 1938, for example, incorporated buttons depicting acrobats and, in one instance displayed (like a billboard) the words 'Beware of the Fresh Paint' on the back of a dress.

Other haute couture designers preferred overt political commentary to sardonic wit. After the election of the Socialist Front Populaire in 1936, when 'strikes were declared throughout France', Schiaparelli 'brought out her Phrygian Bonnet, a symbol of freedom from enslavement, which the strikers had adopted' (Palmer White, 1986: 101). Historically, the Phrygian bonnet had been worn to identify freed slaves in Roman times, and was later adopted by the revolutionaries during the French Revolution of 1789. Schiaparelli was not alone; after the Nazi occupation of Paris in 1940, couturière Madame Grès themed her collection on the Revolutionary tricolore ribbons that proletariat sympathizers wore, indicating her nationalism.

Like many Dadaist works, Schiaparelli's productions were always the result of collaborative effort. She liaised with expert knitters, furriers, dyers, jewellers, embroiderers and artists such as Dalí, Cocteau, Vertès, Van Dongen, Giacometti and Christian Bérard, questioning the concepts of uniqueness in both haute couture design and fine art. More generally, Schiaparelli mirrors the sentiments of the Dadaists when she refers to dress designing as a particularly transient art. This echoed Jean Cocteau's view that: 'Fashion dies very young, so we must forgive it everything' (quoted by Steele, 1988: 251). Similarly, Laver wrote that: 'A fashionable dress is attractive (only) in the context of contemporary taste' (1967: 117). Schiaparelli (1954) declared her practice to be 'a most difficult and unsatisfying art, because as soon as a dress is born it has already become a thing of the past. Once you have created it, the dress no longer belongs to you. A dress cannot just hang like a painting on the wall, or like a book remain intact and live a long sheltered life' (1984 [1954]: 26). *Vogue* editor Michael Boodro (1990) mused that the heyday of Surrealism perhaps represented the most intimate connection between art and fashion, when 'rationality was decidedly not the point'. Boodro argues that: 'Surrealist fashion was created in a spirit of fun, to amuse, to shock and – like so much else invented by the Surrealists – to question the basis on which judgements about art are made' (1990: 125–6).

Perhaps the visual paradox of Surrealist iconoclasm, initially conceived in film, was more effectively communicated through fashion and the applied arts than by two-dimensional media such as painting or photography. Fashion relates more directly to the conditions of life and to the nature of society, and this underlines its dominant appearance in the work of the Dadaists. Whereas Max Ernst used fashion imagery to elucidate, visually, the psycho-sexual associations of Freudian psychology, Schiaparelli created a more direct and dramatic paradox in her Shoe Hat of 1938 – a work which refers to the 'repressed unconscious', where the 'device of displacement is at play within the language of clothes' (Evans and Thornton, 1991: 61). At the

FIGURE 2.10 *The Duchess of Windsor (Mrs Wallis Simpson) sitting on the grassy edge of a pond on the grounds of Châteaux de Candé, in Schiaparelli's lobster dress. Simpson was photographed by Cecil Beaton in the custom creation for a* Vogue *article intended to restore her international reputation, but Schiaparelli was not afraid to poke fun at the woman who lured the king away from his throne. (Photo by Cecil Beaton/Condé Nast via Getty Images.)*

same time, it uses a sexual symbol, normally used to encase a foot, upon the head. Two other examples might include the Medusa-like head placed on the shoulder of a cocktail dress (whose writhing tendrils of hair suggest sexual provocation) and the 1937 Dalí-inspired Lobster and Parsley garment of white organdie (in which the image is strategically printed over the pubic area).[4] This gown was designed for Mrs Wallis Simpson, the American divorcee who famously inspired King Edward VIII to abdicate the throne of England in 1936, invoking scandal for both Simpson and the crown.

If the visual juxtaposition of such images elicits erotic symbolic significance, the images also serve to heighten the element of shock and sensationalism within the context of haute couture. The increasing notoriety of Schiaparelli's work not only challenged those established hierarchies through which meaning is ascribed to fashion, but questioned the traditions of one of the most elitist institutions of Parisian culture in the first half of the twentieth century. As Schiaparelli wrote in her 1954 autobiography: 'A dress has no life of its own unless it is worn, and as soon as this happens, another personality takes over from you and animates it, or tries to, glorifies it or destroys it, or makes it into a song of beauty.'[5]

FIGURE 2.11 Vogue *1952: Black bouclé Shetland stole with oversized insect pin, both by Schiaparelli. The designer liked to invoke a squeamish response in her viewers by juxtaposing beauty with the grotesque. (Photo by Robert Randall/Condé Nast via Getty Images.)*

Summary

The impact of the philosophy and aesthetic of the art world undoubtedly influenced fashion in the early twentieth century. The reorganization of the hierarchy of fine and applied arts at workshops such as the Werkstätte and the Bauhaus encouraged the interaction of painters and sculptors with textile and fashion designers, elevating the status of fashion and textile design to art. Designers such as Poiret took his influences from theatre and traditional Eastern garments, while Vionnet and Fortuny emulated the ruins of goddesses from Hellenistic Greece. Delaunay brought her own art to life by applying colour theory and interdisciplinary Dada practices within the arts to the world of couture, recognizing the forthcoming dominance of the ready-to-wear industry as a way to democratize fashion. Schiaparelli's collaboration with Surrealist artists simultaneously mocked and celebrated the world of haute couture by maintaining the elegance of handmade garments and employing symbolism and wit.

Notes

1 Hugo Ball, reciting the sound poem, *Karawane*, at the Cabaret Voltaire on 23 June 1916, wore blue cardboard tubes on his legs, a huge cardboard collar, and a blue and white striped witch doctor's hat (Goldberg, 1979: 40).

2 'Parade' was a ballet created for the Ballet Russes, with music composed by Erik Satie, and one-act play by Jean Cocteau (1916–17). Pablo Picasso created the sets and costume, and it was first performed at the Theatre du Chatelet in Paris on 18 May 1917. Briefly summarized, the performance is inspired by a sideshow on a Paris street, borrowing heavily from dance halls and vaudeville. The main characters are a Chinese conjurer, two acrobats and a young American girl. Reproduced by the Joffrey Ballet in 1976, the whole performance unfolds as a dream or dreamlike state. The programme note, written by French writer Guillaume Apollinaire, describes the play as 'a kind of surrealism', a term coined by his 1903 original script and later becoming the official name for Surrealism as an artistic genre (1920).

3 Surrealism was founded in 1924 by Andre Breton and his followers, introduced by a short brochure entitled the *Surrealist Manifesto*. The group had formed after breaking with the Dadaists, led by Tristan Tzara – reportedly following the 1923 performance of *Le Cœur à gaz*, the play featuring Delaunay's costumes.

4 Dalí's motivations were often criticized by other members of the Surrealist movement. When his art and his behaviour became overly sensationalist and publicity-seeking, they expelled him from the group.

5 This excerpt was made available online through the Victoria & Albert Museum, London. Available online at: https://www.vam.ac.uk/articles/shocking-life-by-elsa-schiaparelli (accessed 19 April 2021).

3

The Democratization of Fashion

Introduction

This chapter investigates the methods used to achieve a greater 'democratization' of fashion: the concept that well-designed clothing can be made available throughout the social hierarchy. The rise of fashion advertising created new notions of consumerism and beauty, and the proliferation of print media created ample opportunity for imitation, as did the development of a new occupation: in-house designers working for department stores and manufacturers. As fabrication methods improved, mass-produced clothing became more difficult to distinguish from haute couture, particularly with the increasing occurrence of piracy in the fashion industry. Couturiers, therefore, had to decide whether to embrace or battle against the copyists who were stealing their designs. Coco Chanel's rise to success in Paris mirrors social movements demanding equality among the classes following the First World War by juxtaposing working-class clothing with elite concepts of luxury. In Soviet Russia, designers strove for garments that functioned as equalizers, echoing the tenets of Communist theory.

Changes in commerce and social structure

The rise of the fashion industry in the late nineteenth and early twentieth centuries foreshadowed a development towards greater 'democratization' of fashion. Major changes in society, particularly in terms of social class structures and the status of women, were to greatly impact the direction that fashion would take during the 1920s. Hollander (1983: 85) notes that: 'Prior to 1918 ... a gentleman did not dine with his tailor, or a lady with her couturier.' The dictates of European hierarchical class structures determined that 'society had never before opened its door to couturiers, however talented they may have been, and those creative women had been relegated to the status of *faiseuses* or "dressmakers"' (Charles-Roux, 1981: 182). However, Hollander (1983: 85) argues that, after the First World War, 'old social hierarchies were rearranged' and both artists and designers 'rose abruptly on the social scale'.

In the decades leading up to the First World War, bourgeois fashion was merely a poor imitation of that worn by the privileged classes. As production methods became more sophisticated, the visual difference between haute couture and mass-produced fashions became less manifest. Wilson (1985: 79) argues that 'wholesale couture' or 'middle-class fashions' also developed. Several firms developed 'distinctive house styles and good design', which became 'as important as good quality'. The character and nature of commercial design was changing internationally. According to Ewing (1986: 135), in Britain for example, the firm of Jaeger claimed that 'you can no longer tell a shop girl from a duchess'. This company originally manufactured and sold garments wholesale in London in the 1890s, and in the 1920s employed professional designers to produce 'elegant, fashionable clothes at moderate prices' for the mass-market.

Increased democratization of fashion came to fruition in the 1920s, when three preconditions were met: a competitive pricing system, advanced manufacturing technologies which produced goods that were well made and designed, and an effective distribution network. It is widely acknowledged that the increase in the number of 'multiple stores' or chain stores in the 1920s was rivalling the number of department stores, which seemed to have reached their numerical peak. Moreover, the consumer focus of these chain stores was aimed at the increasingly large and prosperous working classes. This new means of fashion distribution targeted all sectors of society in much the same way as the department stores had done in the nineteenth century.

The chain stores offered open displays of merchandise, variable sizing, self-selection and fixed prices. A new niche marketing approach appealed directly to working women, whose numbers had increased dramatically and who were enjoying their new financial independence. Significantly, this reflected an important development in social history. As Caroline Seebohn (1982) notes, another major factor in 'democratizing the fashion industry' was that 'designers like Chanel were creating simpler, more practical clothes for women who were active, held jobs, and sought comfort instead of artifice' (1982: 184).

The art of fashion advertising

Marketing strategists insist that the continuity of visual seduction in the fashion industry is based on the desirability of innovation and change. History has indicated that the laws of mass production and consumption decree that, in order to keep the wheels of the economic capitalist system turning, consumption has to be continuous and on an ever-increasing scale.

Throughout the late nineteenth and early twentieth centuries, 'orchestrated needs' or desires in the fashion industry were created systematically. Clothing styles not only changed from year to year, but changes in social structures – including connotations of 'status' – and developments in technology led to innovations in clothing design. Miller's *The Bon Marché* (1981) recounts that, by the 1890s, the store was selling cycling apparel for both men and women; ten years later, coats for automobile drivers were on sale (1981: 185). In 1904 in London, Burberry devoted a 254-page catalogue almost entirely to ready-made sportswear. As the merchandisers discovered, consumers purchased goods primarily based on the style rather than any obvious functional benefit, communicating a lifestyle of wealth and leisure in line with the objectives of conspicuous consumption. It was primarily this concept of 'conspicuous consumption' that established the visual dominance of fashion design and advertising imagery in the pre-war years.

Fashion and textile goods predominated in store merchandising from the early 1800s onwards. The growth of ready-to-wear fashion paralleled the growth of the *grands magasins* in Paris, which originally were 'drapery and fancy goods stores' (Miller, 1981: 34). By 1906, forty-one out of fifty-two major divisions of Bon Marché involved either fashion or dry goods. This visual dominance of fashion imagery was complemented by the wide distribution of department store and fashion distributors' catalogues, which advertised the new styles, special sales and mail-order services, and by the use of full-page advertisements in the daily press. Distribution figures were enormous. In 1910, Bon Marché sent out 1 million catalogues for one 'white sale' to the provinces alone (Miller, 1981: 61–2). While this sort of advertising was extensive and geographically widespread, more sophisticated techniques developed prior to the First World War marked a 'revolution in marketing'.

As early as autumn 1874, the grand London department store Debenham & Freebody produced a special mail-order catalogue directed at American visitors in London, advertising its stock of authentic Parisian mantles, costumes and millinery (Taylor, 1999: 35). In America, catalogue selling was led by Sears Roebuck & Co., a firm that declared: 'We sell everything'. Between 1893 and 1894, the catalogue increased in size from 196 pages to 322 pages. By 1895, it was 502 pages long, and bridged the gap between rural and urban consumers. In country areas, clothing had previously been purchased for its practicality, but the catalogue offered greater choice of 'garments with style'. Like the department stores, it provided one-stop shopping and the fulfilment of wishes and desires.

Selling consumption was a matter of seduction and showmanship. Discussing the difference between the nineteenth-century mimetic catalogues, which stressed value for money and consumer choice, and the later editions, which persuasively used psychological associations inherent in the purchase of goods, Alan Tomlinson (1990: 9) observes that: 'The commodity has acquired an aura beyond just its function. The commodity now acts "on" the consumer, endows him/her with perceived qualities which can be displayed in widening public contexts.' In turn, Miller (1981) suggests that 'mass-marketing demanded a wizardry that could stir unrealized appetites, provoke overpowering urges and create new states of mind' (1981: 165–7). For Miller, 'the bourgeois culture was coming more to mean a consumer culture . . . the two were becoming interchangeable' (1981: 165). The 'image' of the product was paramount as it was closely tied with the status of ownership, whether the goods involved were fashion items or household appliances such as vacuum cleaners, electric refrigerators or automobiles. This form of conspicuous consumption, once restricted to the upper classes, now enticed middle-class individuals in the consumption of commodities.

According to de Grazia's *The American Challenge to the European Arts of Advertising* (1991), another important factor that was to greatly influence the direction of advertising in Europe in the 1920s was the influx of American business and advertising agencies such as J. Walter Thompson, N. W. Ayer & Son and Erwin Wasey (1991: 36). These firms promoted a more rational persuasive technique, commonly cited as the American 'hard sell' approach. By incorporating a 'press insert' in the advertisement, information was combined 'with persuasive reasoning'. This 'salesmanship in print' was often 'backed up by ostensibly scientific data and testimonials from prominent social figures', and sold the beneficial properties rather than the functional aspects of the product. The 'intentional blurring of the "real" reading material and editorializing for consumer products' was achieved by using similar page formatting and typographical print for both news articles and advertising sections within the publication (de Grazia, 1991: 241). From another American perspective, Ewen (1976) argues that Veblen's theories relating to the conspicuous consumption habits of the leisure class of the nineteenth century were 'now propagated as the democratic ideal' within mass advertising in the 1910s and 1920s. As Ewen subsequently observes, 'in order to sell the commodity culture, it was necessary to confront people with a vision of that culture from which the class bases of dissatisfaction had been removed' (1976: 79). Unlike Americans, Europeans were always more reluctant to accept mass consumerism as a utopian ideal – perhaps as a historical result of their more structured social class system (Clair, 1991: 238).

Many mass media critics confirm Veblen's characterization of advertising as a strategy that trades on a range of human frailties. The advertising copywriters seem to direct their persuasions towards human weaknesses at all social levels. This is consistently evident in both the popular magazines such as the Parisian *Les Annales*, as well as the more elite publications such as *Vogue*. Personal insecurities based on the dictates of improving oneself fostered the consumption of a vast array of new cosmetic and perfume products. In the early 1920s, the Helena Rubenstein cosmetic empire was built on the foundations of this consumer culture. The glamorous image of women in the cosmetic, fashion and advertising world projected a desirability that could be purchased in a mass-production economy. The quest for an idealized youth dominated facial soap advertisements, which promised rejuvenated complexions and wrinkle-free skin as a result of using their preparations. While these products offered at least short-term juvenility, cosmetic surgery and the wearing of toupees guaranteed immortality. Not surprisingly, a veiled illusion was created, as the consumers to whom the advertisements were directed were rarely categorized with regard to specifics such as age, marital status, ethnicity or any other characteristic – thereby sustaining a universal appeal.

Advertising – especially in the era following the First World War – stimulated women's needs in particular. Not only had women continued their role in the household, but they were increasingly in paid employment as well. They became a new 'niche' market as potential financially independent consumers. Advertisers appealed to the 'narcissism' of a woman's self-concept by offering goods that promised higher status and a means of increasing self-esteem, as well as intimating sexual attractiveness and helping her to maintain her security within the family structure. For both men and women, the concept of fear, which consequently created emotional vulnerability, became the main motivating factor in advertising in the 1920s. The most pressing fears were the fear of losing one's job, the fear of failure in courtship or marriage, or the fear of what others might think or say. As class was no longer a barrier, women were enticed to dress as fashionably as their wealthier counterparts by purchasing mass-produced copies of designer garments, ensuring that they would not be considered socially inferior. In America, in particular, some advertisements not only emphasized that these ready-made garments were 'exact copies' – or at least inspired by Paris originals – but also gave them a certain exclusivity by giving them a 'name' label of their own. For example, Franklin Simon & Co. marketed the Bramley ensemble as an exclusive line of ready-to-wear fashion garments that could not be sold by any other distributor, including that the designs had been registered in the US patent office in their Spring 1925 catalog.

By the 1920s, women were coerced through consumer fantasy into thinking that they could express their own individuality and personality regardless of economic limitations, class restraints and conflict. In other words, the needs of the consumer economy effectively became a woman's needs as well. The use of 'social psychology for understanding and directing consumer behaviour' investigated 'human association and motivation', and this in turn created 'lifestyle advertising'. The association of a particular commodity with a whole way of life was a remarkably successful advertising technique. The purchase of the product promised happiness, security and pleasure, and its absence resulted in personal failure and despair. Ultimately, materialism and superficiality were nurtured by the growing advertising industry, the use of psychological associations was the key to advertisers' promotions.

These changes were accelerated by cheaper production of goods for a mass-market; more appealing and more 'lifelike' visual display modes, which tempted the middle-class consumer; more enticing merchandising methods, which attracted a wider consumer audience; and the growth of more accessible distribution centres, which offered numerous attractions for all members of the family. When this was coupled with increasingly sophisticated advertising and promotional material that catered to the weaknesses and frivolities of all classes of society, a decided shift was becoming more apparent – from what had been a relatively elitist marketing sector in society to a broader-based consumerist market.

Flooding the American market: Reproductions and fakes

By the end of the First World War, couturiers found that costs were rising, both for wages and materials of which there was still a shortage. For those couturiers who had closed their doors four years earlier, it was difficult to cover their initial business costs. In an attempt to bolster the industry, the French government pressured the banks to extend their overdrafts. Even the larger houses were suffering financially, and it became almost a necessity to extend their markets to larger – and therefore lower – income groups. No longer could the haute couture designers afford to work exclusively for individual clients and exclude everyone except the very wealthy. The dichotomy underlining the work of early haute couture fashion designers forecast the inevitable growth of the democratization of fashion in the twentieth century. On the one hand, couturiers were producing extremely expensive items for elite patronage, yet on the other they were distributing copies at reduced prices to a widespread middle-class market. As touched upon in Chapter 1 with regard to the business practices of Worth, Suzanna Shonfield (1982) describes how, by the late 1870s, 'C. F. Worth was beginning to run his "salon de couture" on an almost industrial scale, resulting in "blatant duplication of models"' (1982: 57–8). This was due to the expediency of the new sewing machines and the use of standardized patterns with interchangeable parts, leaving only the cutting, finishing and embroidery to be done by hand. By using these divided labour practices, with the only variation being the different fabrics that were used, an unstable discourse between originality and reproduction resulted. Nancy Troy, in *Couture Culture* (2003), provides valuable insight into the commercial practices of a number of leaders in the French fashion industry, including the designers Charles Frederick Worth, Paul Poiret, Jeanne Paquin, Madeleine Vionnet and Sonia Delaunay, and underlines the contradictions inherent in their work.

Most designers, especially Paquin, Worth and Poiret, recognized the important role that the American market played in achieving international and financial success. Jeanne Paquin, who first opened her salon in 1891 and was considered the first important woman in haute couture, often remarked that the American market 'is the most important in the world'. Similarly, in his book *Some Memories of Paris* (1895), Worth became famous for this quip:

> Some of the Americans are great spenders . . . I like to dress them, for, as I say occasionally, 'they have faith, figures and francs' – faith to believe in me, figures that I can put into shape, francs to pay my bills. Yes, I like to dress Americans.
>
> 1895: 193–4

Troy (2003: 24–5) points out that Worth sold models designed to be copied by others – especially American dry goods and department stores – in the 1860s, which subsequently necessitated the introduction of house labels to identify genuine Worth products, as many of the garments looked identical. This was akin to artists signing their work as a means to validate the originality and uniqueness of their creations. Despite this, by the late 1880s the Worth label itself was being fraudulently copied, and imitations were flooding the market. With the consumer goods market expanding so rapidly, protection by copyright laws became mandatory, with the brand name used to authenticate the product.

According to Troy (2003: 10), when Poiret decided in 1916–17, that it would be fortuitous to establish a US market, he designed a line of dresses which he named after his workshop, called *Hotel de Couture*. Their styling was particularly intended to appeal to American women, and by affixing a special label to these items of clothing, they were identified as 'authorized reproductions'. Having compromised the elite nature of his dress range, he had effectively created a new category of fashion. Yet, when he organized a tour to America with five of his models, he found that he was unable to protect his intellectual property as his 'reproduction' designs were being undermined by an extensive system of fashion piracy that he could not control. (See Chapter 4, in which the means and methods of piracy will be explored in more detail.)

Madeleine Vionnet – highly esteemed by her fellow designers for her technical and aesthetic prowess – was particularly outraged about copyists, and went so far as to include her fingerprint on her garment labels to identify and validate the original nature of the dresses. Despite this, Vionnet – like Poiret and Worth – continued to be exploited by the fashion counterfeiters who sold unauthorized copies of her designs in department stores across the United States. In another attempt to counteract this fraudulent practice, Vionnet ran a notice in the trade journal *Women's Wear* in August 1921, warning her customers that her work was copyrighted and could not be reproduced without a licence.[1]

As her label was uniquely identifiable, she tried to sue a number of French and American firms and department stores for selling illegal copies. The contradiction inherent in Vionnet's actions was not that she was against selling copies of her work to the American market, but rather that she tried to devise a scheme where she received royalties for the licence to copy, thereby controlling the products' production and circulation. While the complexity of her work, based on her trademark bias cut, was very difficult to copy, it was not impossible. When, in 1923, a lawyer named Louis Dangel became Vionnet's business manager, he founded a new anti-piracy group, the Association for the Defence of the Plastic and Applied Arts, which demanded that the French government enforce an international copyright to protect the creative intellectual property of the Paris fashion designers (Troy, 2003: 330–1). Not all designers agreed to join, as they were not *entirely* opposed to the American paradigm of mass-marketing. Coco Chanel was one of those designers.

Coco Chanel: Pauvreté de luxe

Gabrielle Chanel, better known as 'Coco', was one of the most influential female designers of this transitional period. A woman who rose out of a working-class background, she was the first haute couture designer to consider the functional aspects of dress, rationally deconstructing women's dress through cut, fabric and simplicity of design. Chanel is best known for popularizing the 'Little Black Dress' (1927), in which she appropriated a mourning colour to create a new definition for day-into-eveningwear. Playing upon the French word for boy, her ensembles pioneered the *garçon* style, in which women's curves were minimized with drop-waist dresses that ended at the knee, an objectionable length even as late as 1924. Her clientele included the *gratin* of Parisian society, as well as wealthy Americans, who represented licentiousness and independence. Both Coco Chanel and Elsa Schiaparelli are frequently credited with playing a major part in both the aesthetic and social revolutions that occurred in fashion in the 1920s and 1930s, but this can also be seen as a response to the revolutions already taking place.

Chanel's work deliberately disrupted and overturned social class indicators insofar as it discarded the dominant concept of conspicuous consumption as a means of achieving status. Her relentless promotion of working-class attire in the early years led to a social paradox, where 'dressing down' became the epitome of elitist fashion: *'pauvreté de luxe'*. The foundations of elitism in haute couture were weakened further when fashion edicts dealing with uniqueness, originality, stereotyping and sobriety in haute couture were questioned by mass-production techniques and the rise of prêt-à-porter. While the bastions of haute couture had been protected and defended for fifty years by the quality of materials and garment construction, as well as the techniques employed in their work, many haute couture designers no longer applied these criteria in their workrooms. Poiret, in his book *En Habillant L'Époque* (1931), comments on this lamentable decline of elitist practice and refers directly to designers such as Chanel and Schiaparelli, in its demise. 'It has profited them considerably,' argues Poiret, 'but at the same time they have forfeited the title of couturier and fashion creator' (Ewing, 1986: 99).

In October 1926, American *Vogue* proclaimed: 'The Chanel "Ford" – the frock that all of the world will wear – is of black crêpe de chine. The bodice blouses slightly at front and sides and has a tight bolero at the back'. It conformed to a universal standard that was characterized by simplicity, a streamlined silhouette and a distinct lack of unnecessary detail. In the 1920s, the industrial design emphasis was on function, and the total modularization of all of the component parts of the machine. Ford's famous retort, when referring to his Model T Ford, that 'it didn't matter what colour it was, as long as it was black' epitomizes the uniformity of the machine age aesthetic that dominated design in the 1920s. The key to this success was 'the impersonal simplicity of the dress' (Neret, 1986: 172) and the fact that Chanel had produced a 'standard which appealed to every taste' (Mackerell, 1992: 11).

In other ways, Chanel's innovations underlined the modernist adage of functionalism and the use of modularization and standardization as the basis of mass production. As Wilcox and Mendes (1998) observe, Chanel was renowned for her customary attention to detail and her dressmaking skills, which she perfected over many years. She insisted that pockets could hold cigarettes and that buttons and buttonholes were functional and not just decorative appendages. While Chanel's use of expensive trimming saw her work described as *'pauvreté de luxe'*, it was very much part of the machine aesthetic of the modernist period. In terms of embracing new technological materials, Chanel used innovatory resins and plastics in her 'fake' costume jewellery.[2] This new fashion style was based on the concept that jewellery no longer had to advertise one's status and wealth, but had instead become a symbol of popular aesthetic taste. Laver and Probert (1982) insists that Chanel was the designer who displaced the tradition of elegance that dominated the era prior to the First World War, and that she undoubtedly helped to change the way status was shown through dress.

Chanel achieved her stylistic *coup d'état* by two means: her choice of new materials; and the adaptation of men's clothing for womenswear. During the war, the knitted material called 'jersey', which had previously only been used for hosiery and underwear, had stockpiled in the textile dealer Rodier's warehouse. It was an improbable material for haute couture to consider, as 'it seemed totally unsuitable for tailoring, too poor and soft' (Charles-Roux, 1981: 105). Jersey was described as being a 'drab, beige colour and having a hard-to-handle weave', and was 'primarily worn by sportsmen and fishermen' (Mackerell, 1992: 22). Chanel bought the entire surplus in 1916 for a very competitive price, despite the fact that it defied 'the conventions of luxury', and consequently its adoption by haute couture 'called for purer lines and created a

FIGURE 3.1 *Vogue 1926: Illustration of Chanel's Little Black Dress, 'The Ford'. The dress is paired with a tall black cloche hat, pearl earrings and necklace, thin geometric bangle bracelets and black pumps. (Illustration by Condé Nast via Getty Images.)*

revolution in costume and appearance' (Leymarie, 1987: 57). Her metamorphosis of this poor man's material into couture fabric caused a fashion revolution – the first time in haute couture that a cheap 'second-class' material was used as an outer garment. When Chanel officially went into haute couture at 21 Rue Cambon, 'her lease forbade her from making dresses'; however, as 'jersey was not considered a fabric', she was not breaking the law (Galante, 1973: 36). It was subsequently adopted as an excellent medium for mass production, expanding the ready-to-wear trade.

Significantly, this humble fabric introduced an element of popular culture into traditional haute couture. Devoid of superficial trimmings, these early tricot garments designed by Chanel exuded an effortless style, which emphasized comfort and ease of wearing and epitomized the liberation of youth. There was no stiffness or defined shape. Her two-piece suits featured a slightly gathered skirt and a long jacket, with the material looking limp and quite unremarkable.

It was exactly this commonplace appearance that seemed so revolutionary at the time. Chanel used jersey on such a massive scale that she opened her own factory at Asnières, initially called Tricots Chanel and then later Tissus Chanel (Mackerell, 1992: 27). Other 'popular' or non-elitist materials were incorporated into Chanel's haute couture collections, such as tartan, quilting and the synthetic fabric rayon – called 'artificial' silk. The manufacture of artificial silk was perfected in the 1920s, and was eminently suitable for Chanel's 'little black dresses' because of its excellent draping qualities. Similarly, when the supply of expensive furs was interrupted, Chanel 'turned to the more modest furs, like beaver and rabbit, thus transforming the shortage into an opportunity for greater inventiveness and style' (Leymarie, 1987: 57). This broke 'the bounds of hierarchy and tradition', since 'even a woman of modest means could afford a fur stole, or a fur wrap of fox, worn casually across the shoulders' (Bailey, 1988: 130).

As an innovator in textile usage, Chanel also introduced British tweeds into the female fashion domain. She procured her fine tweeds from Linton Tweed Ltd of Carlisle, and in 1927 opened a boutique in London where she sold tweed cardigan suits 'which moved with the body and did not crease' (Mackerell, 1992: 28) as both summer and winter fashion. Fashion historians have documented that Chanel's strength lay in her affinity with the fabrics she used. Valerie Mendes (in Mendes and de la Haye, 1999: 12) argues that 'some couturiers are irrevocably associated with their favourite materials' and that 'certain fabrics can develop a symbolic relationship to the fashion trends of a particular period'. In this instance, 'textured tweeds were perfect for Chanel's classic suits'. Chanel's choice of informal and comfortable fabric suited the more active lifestyles of women, and provided suitable corporate dress as more women were working outside of the home.

Another significant contribution to the democratization of fashion was Chanel's direct appropriation and popularization of male attire, which recognized and reflected the changing status of women in this modernist era. As well as using male fabrics, she drew inspiration from divergent sources such as the straight jackets that Marines wore, men's woollen sweaters, cuffed shirts and cufflinks, Norwegian male work clothes, sailors' flared trousers and her nephew's English blazer. In 1920, she launched her masculine-style baggy yachting trousers, and in 1922 her wide-legged flared beach pyjamas (Mackerell, 1992: 33).[3] Writing from a feminist perspective, Evans and Thornton (1991: 57) argue that Chanel's contribution to women's fashion was an 'adaptation of the forms and details, but above all the meanings, of a certain type of masculine dress to that of women'. Specifically:

Her approach to style was analogous to that of classical male dandyism – that essentially masculine cult of distinction which was crucially mediated through dress. Dandyism offered the possibility of social mobility, something which was of the first importance to Chanel personally, and more generally to women in the changing social climate in the early years of the century.

1991: 57

Cecil Beaton (1954) similarly observes that:

Women began to look more and more like young men, reflecting either their new emancipation or their old perversity . . . and that as a dress designer . . . Chanel was virtually nihilistic, for behind her clothes was an implied but unexpressed philosophy: the clothes do not really matter at all, it is the way you look that counts.

1954: 162

For Hollander (1983), Palmer White (1986) and Evans and Thornton (1991), Chanel's adaptation of male attire was not primarily used to promote fundamental feminine psychology or feminist ideology; rather, it employed a lack of gender stereotyping as a seductive principle. In Hollander's terms: 'Chanel was never a feminist' and it was her view that a woman's 'practical success was never to preclude the sovereign aim of being seductive' (1983: 84).

An equally significant hypothesis is that the masculine model of power allowed greater social mobility within a male-dominated culture (Evans and Thornton, 1991: 57). If fashion is recognized as a cultural construction, then independence and equality in female dress should reflect the changing values of that society. The understated female bodies of the 1920s attempted

FIGURE 3.2 Vogue 1927: *Two women depicted wearing fashions by Chanel: at left, a heavy Scotch tweed coat with a homespun woollen dress that matches the lining; at right, a tweed suit with a striped lining and matching sweater. Chanel's reappropriation of tweed for couture was one of the many ways she challenged elitist notions in couture. (Illustration by Pierre Mourgue/Condé Nast via Getty Images.)*

FIGURE 3.3 Vogue *1928: Elizabeth Shevlin in Condé Nast's apartment, wearing knit straw cloche with black cockade decoration, designed by Agnes; crepe and jersey dress; and geometric-printed scarf by Chanel – items carried in her new boutique. (Photo by Charles Sheeler/Condé Nast via Getty Images.)*

to create a physical and social profile equitable to that of their male counterparts. Arguably, Chanel's appropriation of 'masculine power' and her 'adaptation of the meanings of masculine dress to that of women' (Evans and Thornton, 1991: 57) contrasts with Schiaparelli's apparent indifference to the seriousness and restrictions of masculine meaning in dress. For example, Chanel adapted the masculine uniform of red riding coats into evening redingotes and later into ladies' housecoats (Palmer White, 1986: 99). Yet did these clothes necessarily redress women's undermined position in society?

Interestingly, both Chanel and her great rival, Schiaparelli (see Chapter 2) created a stylized man's dinner jacket covered with black sequins. Chanel's garment was created in 1926 and Schiaparelli's in January 1931. While Chanel's version reflected her liking for 'gaudy rich ornaments on the surface of a simple structure' (Hollander, 1983: 83), Schiaparelli contributed to 'reducing the gap between the sexes' by creating 'hard chic' clothes which had 'a militant, masculine quality' (Palmer White, 1986: 97). Both garments reflected the relative financial independence and assertiveness of the post-war woman. Schiaparelli's model mimicked a more mannish mode, with widened and squared shoulders that seemingly 'concealed feminine vulnerability in an almost belligerent manner' (Palmer White, 1986: 97). This silhouette was to become the dominant look of the 1940s, and seemed to forecast the 1980s concept of 'power dressing' for women. Both designers question the representation of sexual identity in dress, and reflect the changing social mores of the 1920s. According to Palmer White (1988: 59): 'Schiaparelli, like Chanel, accentuated youthfulness and freedom of movement' and 'in the battle of the sexes, Schiaparelli's clothes reflected an entire social revolution: defensive by day and aggressively seductive by night'.

Chanel's success was based on her ability to perceive and meet the demands of a changing commercial market. It is interesting to compare how, in much the same way, fine artists such as Sonia Delaunay and the Russian Constructivists Varvara Stepanova and Liubov Popova – who will also be discussed in this chapter – linked fashion, as an applied art, more closely to fine art trends in the 1920s and 1930s (see the section on Sonia Delaunay's work in Chapter 2). This underlines the notion of the synthesis of the visual arts that evolved across all media in this modernist period.

Like the avant-garde artists, both Chanel and Schiaparelli became major figures in breaking down traditional fashion concepts and institutions. Both substituted non-status or atypical materials for luxurious fabrics; both adapted male working-class attire for female wear; and their philosophies regarding reproduction superseded the need for exclusiveness and uniqueness in their work. Schiaparelli's ability to convert something ordinary into a witty item of high fashion can be compared with Chanel's successful introduction of artisans' clothes into upper-class society. While Chanel's reputation in haute couture evolved from an initial adherence to the 'functionalist theory' of the machine age (discussed later in this chapter) and an astute assessment of the economics of supply and demand which emerged out of wartime restrictions, Schiaparelli's notoriety emerged from her anti-fashion and her close alliance with the fine art world.

Thus far, this chapter has outlined the ways in which Chanel and her contemporaries contributed to the decline of elitism in haute couture by breaking down traditional concepts and ways of merchandising fashion. Chanel deviated from the elitist nature of haute couture both by creating a 'working-class look' through her choice of non-luxuriant fabric – her inspiration being drawn primarily from working-class male attire – and by embracing a philosophy of copying and mass production, which denied exclusiveness and uniqueness. In this respect, certain parallels can be drawn between Chanel's iconoclastic alternatives and the Cubists' attempts to fuse art and life. Braque and Picasso, for example, used unorthodox materials in their collaged work, incorporated the world of popular culture into their compositions, and used reproduced imagery which reflected the commercial and social stereotyping of the bourgeois world. Diaghilev's production of 'Parade' (1917), created in conjunction with Jean Cocteau and Pablo Picasso, incorporated music and choreography influenced by the dance halls in Paris, traditionally considered entertainment for the working class. Just as visual paradoxes informed the work of the Cubists, social paradoxes informed the design work of Coco Chanel. With her 'poor boy' fashions and imitation jewellery, she aimed to create an image of middle-class informality rather than emphasizing the affectations of the upper classes, yet her garments were consistently priced in a bracket far above the economic means of the average working girl. As Ruth Lynam (1972) points out: 'The simplest suit or dress from the House of Chanel cost as much as gold and silver embroideries of other designers' (1972: 119). Despite the apparent lack of what Veblen (1899) refers to as 'conspicuous consumption' in her garments, hems were always hand-rolled and weighted chains were inserted into the backs of the jackets. When she dressed her clients in garments of austere simplicity, she would then heap strands of costume jewellery around their necks, on their wrists, hands and ears. Even if the pieces of jewellery were made of rubies or emeralds, Chanel once commented that they would do, 'so long as they look like junk!' (Lynam, 1972: 118). Was it perhaps this incongruous juxtaposition of poverty and expense that created her fashion success? And did she really 'democratize' fashion if her original creations were too expensive for consumers below the upper class?

Jean Patou: Style meets scandal

While Chanel's popular style was ubiquitous in both Europe and America, her most formidable rival in the 1920s and early 1930s was Jean Patou, the debonair gentleman of Parisian haute couture. Originating from a successful family, Patou's father owned a tannery and his uncle was a furrier. Patou began working with his uncle in 1907 and branched out into his own clothing business as early as 1912. He trained as a tailor and dressmaker before establishing his couture house, Patou et Cie, in 1914. His foray into fashion was disrupted by the First World War, but after serving in the French army he resumed his career in 1919. Opening his establishment at 7 Rue Saint-Florentin, Patou lured the Parisienne *gratin* to his collection of elegant, richly embroidered or beaded eveningwear. Having been deployed to the Eastern front during his time in the military, Patou admired the folk costume of the Mediterranean and Eastern Europe. Exposed to the colourful needlework of these regions, similar elements would adorn his dress and coat designs in the 1920s, juxtaposing modernity with tradition.

In addition to his skills in tailoring and dressmaking, Patou's success was a result of his charismatic personality and business savvy. He specialized in elegant, minimalist clothing for day and eveningwear with clean lines and understated embellishment. Patou also offered the active women of the 1920s sportswear, including the famous tennis player Suzanne Lenglen, who was dressed by Patou both on and off the court. Lenglen debuted a shockingly knee-length tennis skirt with a sleeveless shirt and headband in 1921, replacing the traditional hat and dresses worn on the court. In 1925, Patou opened *Le Coin des Sports* (The Sports Corner) on the ground floor of his couture house, expanding his business to swimwear, golf, riding habits and ski apparel. He added an embroidered monogram to most of his sportswear, publicizing his collection while also creating a status symbol for his clients. Much of his daywear reflected the popularity of his pleated tennis dresses, and were variations of this style. This look was achieved with separates made of knitted cardigans and shells in silk or wool, paired with a kick-pleated skirt.

FIGURE 3.4 Vogue *1928: A model wearing a two-piece bathing suit by Jean Patou, with a belted striped sweater top and wool jersey shorts. Sportswear for the upper classes comprised a separate section of Patou's couture house. (Photo by George Hoyningen-Huene/Condé Nast via Getty Images.)*

Although his clientele included the European aristocracy, Patou also dressed stage and film celebrities, such as the Dolly sisters and Josephine Baker, scandalously associating his style with the chorus girls and flappers that emulated these stars. Patou's clientele also included a large number of wealthy Americans. He catered to the US market by holding a competition for six models whom he referenced as 'collaborators', a publicity event well documented by the press, further promoting his label. As the first couture house to show his clothes on American models, Patou's collections shocked the elite of Paris by co-opting flapper style with high-end garment construction. This was in line with Patou's reputation as man about town: he was a consummate bachelor and womanizer, a showman who turned up at casinos and clubs to mingle with the European and American upper classes. As an entrepreneur, Patou registered hundreds of products, from natural fibres to notions and trims, as well as other items. To complement his

FIGURE 3.5 *Jean Patou choosing his models in the United States for his French atelier. Patou was the first couturier to show his dresses on young American models, selected on a trip to New York with carefully planned press coverage of the event. (Photo by Keystone-France/Gamma-Keystone via Getty Images.)*

cocktail dresses, Patou branched out into perfumes, sold in a 'bar' box – the most famous of which is 'Joy'. Drawing on this popularity, he opened his 'perfume bar' for clients to have a drink between fittings in 1921. The American-style bar was a growing trend in Paris for ex-pats, especially after the Prohibition (1920–33) forced establishments selling liquor in America to go underground as 'Speak Easy's. The presence of Americans and Europeans, men and women, all drinking together in a couture house broke several social norms, adding to the allure of House of Patou.

Despite the overwhelming popularity of 1920s fashion in the style of Chanel or Patou, not everyone in Paris was taken with the garçon style and knee-length pleated skirts. In particular, the Café society – intellectuals and artists who spent time in cafés discussing philosophy, art, and mingling with the 'beautiful people' – despised and criticized this style of dress. Perhaps in response to this, and to differentiate himself from Chanel and other designers copying his work in the late 1920s, Patou returned a natural waistline and lengthened hem to his dresses. By 1930, favour for the soft bias cut dresses of Patou and Vionnet had superseded Chanel's drop-waist rectangular dresses, heralding a return to romanticism and femininity in apparel.

FIGURE 3.6 Vogue *1933: Two models wear evening gowns by Jean Patou in the living room of Mr Charles de Beistegui's Paris penthouse. Patou's return to a lengthened silhouette pleased the café society of Paris, and set a new trend for the romantic garments that would dominate the 1930s. (Photo by George Hoyningen-Huene/Condé Nast via Getty Images.)*

These longer silhouettes were especially popular for the cocktail hour between 6.00 and 8.00 pm. For his American clients, Patou created ensembles with removeable accessories that could transition from day to eveningwear, such as capes or wraps with a sleeveless gown. Patou's expertise was colour, and by 1931 he began creating his own palette and textile designs for each major collection showing. Patou's collection showings were held in the evenings, and heralded as the biggest events in Paris during the mid-1920s, challenging Chanel's popularity. However, his success was cut short by his sudden death in 1936, and many of his stylistic advances were overshadowed by Chanel's continuation as a major force within fashion up to and beyond the Second World War.

Fashion and functionalist theory

The new and innovative stylistic trends popularized by Chanel and Patou can be contextualized within the development of modernism. The modernist period in the visual arts, which spanned the Interwar years of the 1920s and 1930s, evolved from the technological developments and inventions of the First World War, and had an unprecedented impact upon all of the visual arts, including fashion and jewellery design. New man-made materials such as cellulose acetate and viscose rayon, originally developed respectively by Celanese and Du Pont as parachute fabrics to replace silk, broadened fabric choices for designers. Materials such as lucite and other synthetic plastics in the 1930s led to the invention of plastic zippers and buttons, as well as more artistic uses, such as Schiaparelli's experimental accessories (see Chapter 2). The automated knitting machine, which began producing on an industrial level in factories during the mid-nineteenth century, was capable of creating finely knitted yard goods en masse. These technological advances were fundamental to creating the relaxed styles that defined modern fashion.

The modernist age was the machine age, where functionalism and practicality prevailed. According to the 'functionalist theory' popular during the 1920s, the structure of the form was determined by its function and the use of superfluous decoration was considered incompatible with machine production. 'Form follows function', a term coined by architect Louis Sullivan and expanded in practice by his pupil Frank Lloyd Wright, became the modernist slogan. Wright's buildings are characterized by simplicity and elegance of design based on the concept that the building's function should determine its layout, as well as obtain cohesion with its environment.

This modern visual language of abstraction – characterized by simple, geometric and modularized forms reminiscent of machine technology – was 'implicit in the development of modernism' (Lynton, 1980: 19), and inherent in the design work of Russian women artists Varvara Stepanova and Luibov Popova. Their work epitomized the ideals of the machine age aesthetic through their attention to structure and material, the underlying mathematical structure of their designs, and their use of bold, dynamic colour. Along with Sonia Delaunay, these artists expanded and extended the traditional aesthetic boundaries of art and design through their fashion and textile design and fulfilled the aims of the modernist movement.

Stepanova and Popova: Russian constructivism

Unlike many designers focused on fashion as a business, the work of Stepanova and Popova was directed by utopian socialist ideals. The two women were not haute couture designers, but ideologically committed artists whose contribution to modernist principles in relation to dress, aesthetics and functionality countered commercial fashion. Encapsulated in their work was the Russian Constructivists' philosophic ideal that clothing as an art form should impact directly on the masses. Prior to the 1917 Russian Revolution, communists saw fashion as a bourgeois phenomenon, having no social utility other than that of elitism (Stern, 2004), and the two designers led the field in cultivating a different approach to fashion. Somewhat ironically, Stepanova's aesthetic approach to fashion design more closely paralleled that of Chanel, whose basic concern with the union of structure and form was shared by the Constructivists.

Popova and Stepanova both came from a dressmaking background and placed great emphasis on technical skills. It seems that in both capitalist and socialist societies, this utilitarian-oriented design work led, in varying degrees, to increased industrial production and the greater merging of artistic and commercial activities. Both Stepanova and Popova had moved towards utilitarian clothing and textile design by 1921, as they were strongly motivated to serve the people and committed to the practical application of Constructivist ideals.[4] Unfortunately, the influence of Russian fashion and textile design was not as extensive, nor did it have the same degree of influence, as Delaunay's work. Yet their work shared the same dynamic interplay of diagonals, the simulation of crisp, clean lines, and the clarity of brilliant hues, and was more in keeping with the tenets of the machine age aesthetics.

Perhaps the remarkable visual similarity between the work of artists such as Delaunay and that of the Russian Constructivists can be explained in part by historical, economic and circumstantial factors. Delaunay, while a French citizen, was born in the Ukraine (Russia), and Russian folk art is quite evident in her early work (see Chapter 2). According to Anscombe (1984) and Chadwick (1990), the post-war years reflected a time of diverse artistic activity, which advocated the identification of avant-garde art with modernist design as a means of bolstering the French economy. In Paris, after the war, there was a social milieu of artists, designers, couturiers, writers and photographers in which an 'extraordinarily rich interplay of ideas existed', and which led to 'numerous collaborations in cabarets, illustrated books, ballets and schemes for interior design' (Anscombe, 1984: 114–15). Women designers actively involved in the applied arts benefited from this cultural environment and, turning to textile design, they supported the French textile industry's efforts 'to recover quickly from the slump caused by the war' (Chadwick, 1990: 257). Additionally, as Chadwick observes: 'The years during which Delaunay was most involved in textile and clothing design in Paris correspond to the period when Russian artists sought to find socially useful applications for their aesthetic theories' (1990: 257).

In Russia, a similar economic deprivation existed where 'crippling shortages of raw materials after the Revolution and civil war of 1918–21' prevented the actualization of many plans and theories of the avant-garde artists and architects (Chadwick, 1990: 257). According to Chadwick, the only exception was Moscow's large textile industry, which was able to mass-produce the Constructivists' abstracted fabric designs, where 'kinetic forms symbolized emancipation and mobility' (1990: 257). While this work was ideologically sound, in accordance with the Russian Constructivists' ideals, the Russian historians Sarabianov and Adaskina (1990) argue that the production itself presented its own conditions as the technology of the textile print factory was geared towards printing small repeats (1990: 302). Lodder (1983) confirms that, at the beginning of the 1920s, industrial production was at a third of pre-war levels as 'materials and technological standards were limited' (1983: 145). It seems that Tatlin, Stepanova and Popova were the only Constructivist artists who attempted to put their projects relating to fashion into operation. The establishment of a standardized pattern was facilitated by Stepanova's self-imposed limitations. She used only a compass and ruler to design her work, which usually consisted of two-coloured patterns based on the circle, triangle and rectangle. This form of reductionist, formalistic art

МАВРУША

FIGURE 3.7 *Constructivist costume design by Varvara Stepanova, for the play 'The Death of Tarelkin' by A. Sukhovo-Kobylin, 1922. Stepanova's designs for the play included both costumes and sets, but were underappreciated by Meierkhol'd, the director. (Photo by: Universal History Archive/Universal Images Group via Getty Images.)*

reflected the universal rhythms found not only in the organics of nature, but also in the systematic workings of well-oiled machines. Symbolically, several interpretations have been postulated. Laurentiev (1988) suggests that 'the geometric construction can be interpreted as the mechanization of the artist's labour', that it 'reflects the world of industry in graphic form', or perhaps functions 'as an expression of the principles of technological form' (1988: 83). These mechanistic analogies clearly imply that Russian Constructivist textile work was inextricably immersed in, and directed by, the industrial process.

Popova's textile designs also emphasized an ultimate simplicity printed on ordinary cotton, yet the use of geometrical forms originating from her abstract painting did not appeal to the masses, who continued to prefer cloth printed with floral techniques (Stern 2004: 55). Lodder (1983) stresses that only the women's textile designs, rather than dress designs, progressed successfully beyond the conceptual stage (1983: 145–6), and she also points out that one of their greatest contributions was 'this new formulation, by a radical reassessment of the design process, which co-related the design process for cloth and clothing' (1983: 146). Significantly, it was this necessity for a total design process that inspired Delaunay to conceive her *tissu-patron*, her early experiments in paper patterns that accompanied her signature fabrics, allowing consumers to size, modify and make their own clothing.

FIGURE 3.8 *Design for a dress, 1924, by Liubov Popova. The stark lines of the garment's silhouette and geometric pattern represent functionality, and therefore modernity, in clothing. (Photo by Fine Art Images/ Heritage Images/Getty Images.)*

The Russian avant-garde's attempt to revolutionize clothing by designing anti-fashion garments only impacted upon a minority of individuals who used their dress to express their total commitment to Communist ideology. By the 1930s, it had become apparent that clothing would not become an instrument of socialization, nor would it be used as a social condenser – workman's overalls would not replace traditional male garments, and individual dress would not be superseded by collective dress that offered utility, protection and anonymity.

Dressing thousands: The birth of prêt-à-porter

Mass production in its true sense did not evolve fully in the world of high fashion until after the Second World War, but it became clear during the Interwar period that this was the direction in which fashion was headed. Chanel was one of the first haute couture designers to open a small ready-to-wear section in her *maison* in 1929. Duplicates of the same garment were offered for sale in a range of sizes, with the price including one alteration. Other designers followed suit, and by the mid-1930s the majority of haute couture salons in Paris offered similar ready-to-wear lines. Chanel's philosophy of fashion design was determined by her belief that 'a fashion is not just for one person, nor even for a group; if a fashion is not popular with great numbers of people, it is not a fashion' (Beaton, 1954: 163). She observes that 'a copy could only be a copy', but also recognizes that 'imitation was a visible sign of success' (Carter, 1980: 59). In his biography, *Chanel Solitaire*, Baillen (1973: 72) quotes a tempestuous Chanel as saying: 'I don't create fashion for three or four tarts.' As late as 1953, Chanel reiterated these feelings: 'I am no longer interested in dressing a few hundred women, private clients; I shall dress thousands of women' (*Vogue*, February 1953). This statement forecasts the future destiny of haute couture.

Chanel's sense of timing and her ability to seize the moment were crucial to her success. Chanel was 'a pioneer of the new casualness' (Hollander, 1984: 83), with comfort and practicality becoming her trademark. Chanel recognized that the rigid concept of social stratification had changed in the 1920s, as the economic instability of life at this time did not make it unusual to see Russian grandees in Paris working as taxi-drivers and grand duchesses employed as models. Marly (1980) comments: 'There were some proud names who had become poor' (1980: 147). The lifestyles of the rich and fashionable were changing dramatically. Many well-to-do women could be seen riding on trams, trains and buses, and this necessitated clothing that offered greater freedom of movement. A less rigorous social stratification, and the move away from sartorial formality in dress, encouraged Chanel to extend the formal boundaries further by introducing working-class garments into the world of haute couture. Horst observed that 'In those days, fashion wasn't for elegant women only. It was a part of life. Women who didn't have much money had little sewing ladies around the corner who copied the designers ; . . . It was Chanel who made it all simpler' (cited in di Grappa, 1980: 72)

While Laver (1995: 235) has alluded to Chanel as 'an important part of the whole artistic movement', it is interesting that she never considered herself to be an artist. This was in contrast to Poiret, who was insistent on promoting the illusion that he was a creative artist who was not concerned with commercialism. Even the performance of the Russian Ballet's *Schéhérazade* (1910), which exerted unprecedented influence upon the arts in general in Paris (and underlined the direction of Poiret's designs), did not impact directly upon Chanel's work. 'We're in trade, not art,' Chanel said, 'and the soul of trade is good faith' (Baillen, 1973: 75). She defined dressmaking rather as a technique or a craft – a trade by which one could earn a living. Arguably, a considerable amount of attention has been paid in biographies to her social contacts with many artists, writers and intellectuals, but there is little evidence that art ever specifically inspired her work.

This is not to preclude her participation in the world of art and performance, however: Chanel designed costumes for 'Le Train Bleu' (The Blue Train, 1921), in which Diaghilev's Ballet Russes performed a contemporary performance set at a bathing resort at the French Riviera. With scenery by Jean Cocteau and a front curtain designed by Pablo Picasso, the athletic movements of the ballet worked perfectly with Chanel's knitted sportswear. The 'synthesis' or common thread that tied the visual arts together in the 1920s was based on the 'machine age aesthetic', as it was called, which was fashioned not only by the fundamental shapes of machine imagery but by the flat planes and simple geometric shapes evident in non-Western art. Unknowingly, Picasso initiated the Cubist movement when he created a landmark painting in 1907 entitled *Les Demoiselles d'Avignon*. He introduced a new spatial language, where three-dimensional, cube-like forms were arranged in a two-dimensional space; this art movement developed well into the 1920s and impacted on the majority of decorative artists. While Richard Martin, in his book *Cubism and Fashion* (1988), cites examples of Chanel's work, he argues that it was more plausible 'that it was not the art of Cubism, per se, but the culture of Cubism that influenced fashion, just as the culture of Cubism might be said to align it with new ideas in theatre, literature and, eventually, the movies' (1998: 16). A year earlier, Leymarie (1987) made a similar statement when she argued that Chanel's 'consecration of humble fabrics and furs paralleled the poetics of Cubism' – just as, in 1912, Braque 'had invented the breakthrough of the *papiers collés* [collages]' into the fine arts, thereby rejecting the traditional mode of painting (1987: 57). Mackerell (1992), who is considered a major authority on Chanel's interest in art, describes how Chanel hired the Russian Futurist artist Iliazd, who had designed textiles with Sonia Delaunay in 1922 and who, in retrospect, may have strengthened her ties with Cubism. As Mackerell suggests, this involvement seems to establish some link between Chanel's fashion and the fine arts: 'Chanel's combination of pure lines and plain colours often drew comparisons with the contemporary art movement, Cubism, with particular reference to the Analytical phase which ennobled humble materials and muted colours' (1992: 23). Reflecting on the interplay that did exist between fashion designers and fine artists in the 1920s, the modernist photographer Horst P. Horst perhaps best summed it up when he stated that, at that time, 'Everybody worked together, talking fashion and art' (cited in di Grappa, 1980: 71). However, direct references did not dominate the aesthetic of Chanel's work as they did the collections of Schiaparelli.

The Scottish Arts Council's *Fashion 1900–1939* catalogue concluded:

> In fact, despite her great friendship with artists such as Picasso and Cocteau, Chanel seems consciously anti-art; even her salon was modish rather than modern; she, alone among the young couturiers, never appears in *Bon Ton* which, in its 1920 prospectus, sets out to be 'the mirror in which all the arts are reflected'. Equally indicative is her derisive comment on her archrival Elsa Schiaparelli as 'that Italian artist who makes clothes'.

Summary

Haute couture as an elitist, artistic practice shifted after the First World War, when couture designers expanded to prêt-à-porter, and copyrighted their designs for use by manufacturers. Chanel, Patou, Vionnet and their contemporaries in Paris began to redefine the role of the couturier by developing a relationship to prêt-à-porter through licensing and authorized copies. Arguably, the most successful couture houses responded to market demands, a capitalistic feat that helped to propel fashion to the fifth largest industry in France in the 1920s.

Both Chanel and Patou had American clients and experienced imitation by American manufacturers as a sign of success. The prevalence of mass-produced clothing reflected the pecuniary strength of the middle class, and the active role of women in society requiring practical, comfortable clothing. Advances in technology allowed for better manufactured materials and garments at prices the average consumer could afford, resulting in the growth of the fashion industry. However, moderate prices and increased demand came at the cost of human labour, an issue that will be discussed in Chapter Four.

Notes

1 Vionnet was one of the first haute couture designers to copyright her designs by photographing the garments from the front, back and side. These photographs were then lodged with the Chambre Syndicale in Paris.

2 Costume jewellery was made from plastic products introduced in the 1920s as a result of war technology. It was the first time that imitation jewellery was worn with couture clothing.

3 Various Eastern garment forms were introduced into Western fashion as loungewear. The word 'pyjama'(American spelling: pajama) is from the Urdu *pae-jama*, referring to loose trousers covering the legs; usually part of an ensemble consisting of a long tunic, worn by both men and women. The British became familiar with these garments during the Colonial era in India (1858–1947). The kimono was introduced as a beach coat, yet more importantly was seen as a simple modular design, being made up of eight pieces, which became a canvas for asymmetrical decoration. Asian art has consistently impacted upon Western artistic sensibilities since the nineteenth century, and particularly upon the decorative arts – including fashion. The Philadelphia World's Fair in 1876 provided an opportunity for American artists and craftspeople to view Eastern decorative art for the first time.

4 Stepanova was the wife of artist Alexander Rodchenko, one of the founders of the Russian Constructivist movement. As a founding member of the Russian Constructivist Group (1921), he and his colleagues, including Stepanova and Popova, approached art-making as disciplines that were skill-based, and that art should serve a social function.

4

The Americanization of Fashion

Introduction

This chapter looks at the social phenomena and technological advances that laid the foundations for the ready-to-wear clothing industry in the United States. Known as prêt-à-porter in France, ready-to-wear became synonymous with American fashion. Retail strategies, changes in design style and manufacturing methods will also be discussed relative to the development of American ready-to-wear. New York's garment district, with its prolific apparel manufacturing, could not have been developed without the inexpensive labour force comprised mostly of immigrants, women and children. Labour was a major source of contention from the nineteenth century, prompting social reform and new legislation.

As mass-produced clothing became readily available to the lower classes, an American couture sector developed among a diverse group of wealthy consumers. In addition to bespoke and luxury clothing that could be purchased at high-end department stores, Hollywood also became a driving force in fashion during the 'Golden Age' of the 1930s to 1950s. Meanwhile, street styles in minority communities gained prominence as a political statement, propagated by stage and film celebrities.

Slop shops, sweatshops and factory work

In America, the earliest ready-made clothing (historically called 'off-the-peg') came from so-called 'slop shops' that aimed to provide inexpensive garments for sailors, labourers and slaves during the late eighteenth century.[1] These slop shops, prevalent on both sides of the Atlantic in port cities from at least the eighteenth century, sold Pea jackets [Pea coats], waist coats, shirts, and trousers known as 'slops', as well as frame-knitted items like stockings (Putman, 2010: 42–4). Defined by large, visible stitches and inexpensive cotton or linen fabrics, the consumer of these garments earned the reputation of being a 'sloppy' dresser. Nevertheless, advertisements and illustrations depict polychromatic ensembles with striped and patterned fabrics and a variety of garment types, indicating that patrons had options in with regard to their selections. Surviving garments provide clues as to how this clothing was made in the era before standard sizing: garments were loose and adjustable, fastening with drawstrings and ties, indicating a one-size-fits-most approach. Contemporary illustrations mock not only the ill-fitting garments, but also the retailers derisively known as 'slops-sellers' and the men that wore slops during this era of bespoke clothing. Ultimately, since the consumer base for these off-the-peg garments was working class, ready-made clothing would be associated with the lower social strata well into the early twentieth century. In order for the industry to gain solid footing, three major issues needed to be resolved: clothing needed to be more stylish, indicating improvements in fit and function; mass production had to be affordable, to keep prices low; and public perception of ready-made clothing had to improve. These developments slowly transformed public perception throughout the nineteenth and early twentieth centuries.

As fashions for upper-class men became less form-fitting throughout the nineteenth century, tailoring establishments found that they could create a collection of ready-made clothing to sell during the slow season (Putman 2010: 32). In pursuit of a greater profit margin, tailors would cut the pattern pieces and allocate sewing to widowed or orphaned women, who were willing to work for far less than men with the same skill set. The 'sewing woman' worked long hours at home or in dark workrooms for little pay, inciting sympathy from upper-class women and social reformers. In 1845, Horace Greely – founder and editor of the New York *Daily Tribune*, and leader of labour reform – wrote of the conditions of nineteenth-century labourers in New England, including occupations in the garment industry, as a form of wage slavery (Greely, 1845).[2]

The ready-to-wear industry in the US grew exponentially in the latter half of the nineteenth century, as sewing machines became more affordable. The patent pool formed by Howe, Singer, and other inventors of sewing machine parts in the 1850s dropped the price of the sewing machine from $25 to $5 (Palmer, 2015), and companies such as Singer offered payment plans.[3] This allowed entrepreneurs to set up clothing production shops with a moderate capital investment, taking orders from manufacturers while sub-contracting piece work. This type of arrangement meant that clothing was cut into pattern shapes at the factory and then assembled and finished in other locations, and sub-contractors were paid for each finished piece upon delivery – a practice known as 'piece work'. Often, this system pushes employees to work more quickly in order to complete the garment, but quality suffers. Often, sub-contractors would spend long hours to complete their order by unreasonable deadlines only for payment to be reduced or denied, as the contractors complained about quality.

In addition to delivering low quality goods, these contractors – the 'sweaters' – developed a reputation for greed, underpaying workers to create garments in crowded conditions in order to keep costs low. The sweaters, in turn, were competing for work from manufacturers, who hired the lowest bidder in order to keep up with the continually lowered cost of clothing. Many sweaters went out of business after a year or two, unable to keep up with demand and price cutting by manufacturers, who had to keep up with the price cutting of retailers. Much of this cycle was perpetuated by large department stores (see Chapter 1) buying garments wholesale. Although the proliferation of ready-made, affordable clothing delighted most middle-class consumers, these goods came at a steep price for the labour force.

Labourers in the garment industry were primarily immigrants, who came to the US en masse to escape religious persecution or seek financial gain. From the 1850s, the first wave of immigrants began arriving in New York and Boston from Ireland, followed by Swedes and Germans after 1865; by the 1890s, Italians, Polish and Jews from Russia and Eastern Europe arrived. These immigrant groups – who settled in great numbers in New York City, but also in Boston and Chicago – became the labour force for the ready-to-wear clothing industry.

In the 1860s, the majority of mass-produced garments were uniforms for Civil War soldiers; by the 1880s, men could buy fully manufactured suits, and loose clothing styles that allowed for differences in body shapes. Womenswear items were also available off-the-peg, but these were generally cloaks and other styles that didn't require precision sewing or fit. A task system was established by the Eastern Europeans, with specialists working on one aspect of garment construction: cutting, basting, sewing, pressing and finishing were the main jobs and were often executed in the same area of town where immigrants lived. Once completed, the garments were delivered to middlemen who interfaced with manufacturers, who in turn sold these goods to department stores.

In New York, labourers lived and worked in Manhattan's densely populated Lower East Side, where poorly ventilated tenement houses were built without proper sewage drains and diseases were prevalent. This was an equally serious problem in the overcrowded slums of Victorian London, documented in Charles Kingsley's social critique *Cheap Clothes and Nasty* (1850), and his subsequent publication the same year, *Alton Locke, Tailor and Poet*.[4] Kingsley identified and named the practice of tailors sub-contracting sewing work to others as the 'sweating system' based on the amount of labour involved in making Victorian garments. As with the American practices, workers were paid for finished pieces rather than hourly work, resulting in a very low standard of living for these skilled labourers.

By 1891, terms including 'sweatshop' (originally sweat-shop) based on Kingsley's description of the 'sweating system', were cited by factory inspectors in New York and included a social critique of the whole system (Bender, 2002: 15).[5] Sweatshops could be located in small rented rooms or low-income housing such as tenements, where families would eat, sleep, cook and work in cramped, squalid conditions. Children were often participants in the arduous process (see figures 4.1 and 4.2). Jacob Riis, a journalist and Danish immigrant, illuminated the problems of New York tenement slums through photographs and in his book *How the Other Half Lives* (1890). Riis describes in detail the live/work conditions in the tenements where ready-made clothing was being assembled:

> It has happened more than once that a child recovering from small pox, and in the most contagious stage of the disease, has been found crawling among heaps of half-finished clothing that the next day would be offered for sale on the counter of a Broadway store; or that a typhus fever patient has been discovered in a room whence perhaps a hundred coats had been sent home that week, each one with the wearer's death warrant, unseen and unsuspected, basted in the lining.
>
> Riis, 1890: 109

Riis' reports confirm the health hazards of the clothing being produced in these disease-infested sweatshops, for which inspectors had been on the lookout. Despite garments being 'aired out' after finishing, the public – now apprised of the facts – was concerned that ready-made clothing produced in tenement sweatshops was carrying these diseases from one location to another. In 1892, New York factory laws prohibited domestic sweatshops by banning sewing machines in the tenements without a permit. Unions were formed between consumers and trade workers protesting sweatshop conditions and wages, demanding better working conditions as a public health concern. The National Consumers' League (formed 1899) distributed lists of responsible manufacturers and retailers, indicating 'sanitary' clothing with a coloured hang tag. 'Needle trade' unions were also established, including The International Ladies' Garment Workers' Union (ILGWU) in 1900, and its counterpart for menswear and textiles, the Amalgamated Clothing and Textile Workers of America (ACTWA) in 1914.

Although many tenement sweatshops had been replaced by factory work by the turn of the century, factory jobs did not offer a significant improvement in working conditions. Factories were still sweatshops, and workers were often locked in for ten or more hours per day in crowded, poorly ventilated conditions, many of which led to health issues. Worker strikes resulted, such as 'The Uprising of 20,000' (November 1909 to February 1910), when workers

FIGURE 4.1 *Lewis Wickes Hine.* Jennie Rizzandi, 9 year old girl, helping mother and father finish garments in a dilapidated tenement, 5 Extra Pl., NYC. *New York, NY, January 1913. Hine's notes read: '11:30 A.M. They all work until 9 P.M. when busy, and make about $2 to $2.50 a week. Father works on street, when he has work. Jennie was a truant, "I staid [sic] home 'cause a lady was comin".' (National Child Labor Committee collection, Library of Congress, Prints and Photographs Division.)*

across the country protested in solidarity with a walkout at the Greenwich Village-based Triangle Shirtwaist Factory in New York. Working-class women were supported by the so-called 'mink brigade', a group of wealthy women who stood in line with picketers, attracting widespread press of the strike.

Despite the 'Protocol of Peace' agreement for better working hours and pay reached by labour leaders and employers in February 1910, disaster soon overshadowed the progress. On 25 March 1911, just over a year after the strike, a tragic fire at the Triangle Shirtwaist Factory resulted in the death of 146 young, mostly female immigrant workers, who could not escape the flames due to crumbling fire escapes and locked doors; in lieu of incineration, many jumped to their deaths from the ninth floor. Although factory owners Isaac Harris and Max Blanck were prosecuted, they were never charged, and the whole case was seemingly swept under the rug.[6] The catastrophe became a symbol of the kind of worker abuse that was largely ignored in garment sweatshops; nevertheless, these practices continued until Franklin Delano Roosevelt's New Deal was enacted in the 1930s. Legislation such as the Fair Labor Standards Act (1938) established a minimum wage of twenty-five cents an hour and a 44-hour work week, decreasing the profits of contracting and shifting the industry toward the government standard of ideal factory working conditions.

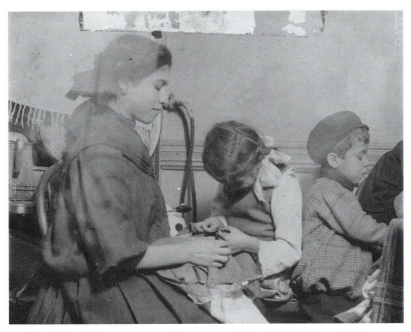

FIGURE 4.2 *Lewis Wickes Hine.* Garment Workers on East Side 4:30 P.M. Vincenzie, 14 years old. Jovannina, 9 years old. *New York, NY. January 1910. Although laws dictated that children under the ages of thirteen could not legally work, younger children often participated in garment-making in tenement sweatshops. (National Child Labor Committee collection, Library of Congress, Photographic Prints Division.)*

FIGURE 4.3 Two women strikers on picket line during the "Uprising of the 20,000", garment workers strike, *New York, NY. February 1910. (George Grantham Bain Collection, Library of Congress.)*

FIGURE 4.4 *Al Ravenna. Photograph for the New York World-Telegram & Sun. Men pulling racks of clothing on busy sidewalk in the Garment District. New York City, 1955. (New York World-Telegram and the Sun Newspaper Photograph Collection, Library of Congress.)*

By the 1930s, the new factories were clustered in Manhattan from 25th to 42nd Streets, between Sixth and Ninth Avenues. This area became known as the Garment District, with the southern portion known as the Fur District. Manufacturers and designers were mainly located between 28th and 38th streets along Seventh Avenue, dubbed 'Fashion Avenue', where one could see racks of garments being rolled down the street from the factories to the design offices (in America, 'off-the-peg' became known as 'off-the-rack').

Despite the social and political issues surrounding the garment industry, consumer demand drove the growth of ready-to-wear. The fluid social structure of American society became more receptive to off-the-rack fashion for its people, which crossed all social class boundaries and no longer carried the stigma of its previous history.

Fit and function

One of the initial challenges of creating manufactured clothing was a lack of standard sizes. Historically, Western European clothing was long and loose, fitted to the body with belts or metal fasteners. As clothes were cut and sewn to accentuate certain parts of the body during the Renaissance (*c.* 1500 and later), the need for a series of pattern pieces was necessary to create the proper style and fit each individual's proportions. In addition, luxury cloth was expensive, and the aim was to waste as little as possible. According to Joy Spanadrel Emery (2014), the oldest books on pattern making date to sixteenth century Spain, with French pattern books published in the following century specifically demonstrating how to lay pattern pieces across the width and length of the fabric (Emery, 2014: 5–6).[7] It is no surprise that these books appear just as fashion becomes an ever-changing phenomenon, providing tailors and dressmakers with templates and guides for creating the newest styles. By the early nineteenth century, tailors were using one of two systems to create fitted garments: the proportional scale, in which the body is assigned a series of proportional measurements; or the direct system, based on specific measurements (Emery, 2014: 8). These were created for individual customers as templates; most tailor shops didn't have incremental tape measures until after 1820, instead measuring each customer with a strip of paper and marking the relevant points for reference (Putman 2010: 67). However, these systems refer to bespoke traditions, and did not lend themselves easily to ready-made clothing until the growth of the paper pattern industry.

By the 1850s, paper patterns were available for purchase in England for tailors. A number of books on pattern drafting for womenswear were available for dressmakers by the late nineteenth century, such as Charles Hecklinger's *The Dress and Cloak Cutter* (1877) and T. H. Holding's *Ladies Cutting Made Easy* (1885). Trade journals also became popular in England and America, many of which contained block patterns based on the proportional system of drafting (Emery, 2014, 15). The major theme of all these publications was to figure out how to create a system of sizing for patterns that could be easily adapted to a variety of body types. Although it is difficult to trace the demographic purchasing publications and patterns, one can see how conveniently paper patterns, along with the sewing machine, made the production of ready-made clothing. The growth of the paper pattern industry also created the ability for individual women to set up sewing machines at home, to quickly sew clothing for herself and her children, as well as run a home business sewing for other people. The earliest company distributing paper patterns in the US was Demorest, which provided coloured paper patterns 'with or without trim' from the 1850s. By the mid-1860s, Demorest had opened a chain of display stores and a magazine, which

FIGURE 4.5 *American dress chart, front of lady's dress Danville, Indiana, c. 1868. Paper patterns allowed middle-class women to emulate the dress styles of the elite for a fraction of the cost. (Popular and applied graphic art print filing series, Library of Congress.)*

included patterns as an insert. Surviving patterns from this period indicate a dearth of instructions describing garment construction; as the industry grew, pattern instructions became more standard. Dressmakers could buy the pieces for an ensemble at reduced rates, for use and for sale, putting promotional cards in their windows to advertise the latest styles by the 1880s.

In 1863, former tailor Ebenezer Butterick began selling patterns for boys' and men's clothing, expanding to dresses by 1866 and patenting his patterns – a practice not pursued by the Demorest company. Butterick is also credited with developing a proportional sizing system: sizing for children was correlated with the age of the child, and numbered as such (size 3–6 was for a three-to-six-year-old, etc.). Butterick developed ten different sizes for women's shirts based on the bust size (28 to 46 inches), as well as creating proportional measurements for the torso: for example, Butterick explains in his company periodical, *The Metropolitan*, that a 32-inch bust determined a 24-inch waist (Emery, 2014, 54). Following the success of Butterick's business model, *Harper's Bazaar* began to include paper patterns in their publication as early as 1867, followed by Scottish tailor James McCall, who immigrated to New York in 1869 (Emery, 2014, 42). By 1871, Demorest also offered patterns in a range of sizes based on Butterick's proportional approach (Emery, 2014, 40), establishing the system that would be in use for the ready-to-wear industry in the following century. The bulk of paper patterns were intended for the home seamstresses, but dressmakers also bought and used paper patterns (or modified them), as a more expedient way to create templates for rapidly changing women's fashions. Technology to mass produce paper patterns was also developed in the 'cut-and-punch' method, in which a fabric model was traced onto a stack of tissue paper, cut by hand with a sharp knife, and punched with round holes to indicate the pattern part using a metal machine (Emery, 2014, 51–2).

Although French and English pattern companies were established in the last quarter of the nineteenth century, the industry was strongest in the United States, primarily due to improvements in the US Postal service and expanded railroad lines connecting the vast continent from east to west, making cloth and patterns more readily available. The US companies established Canadian and European offices, and the fascination with French fashions continued to be a dominant force well into the first decade of the twentieth century, especially as couturiers licensed their house labels for patterns that were distributed through periodicals such as American *Vogue*. Butterick, McCall's and Vogue are still the dominant pattern-makers for home sewers today, and much of the popular DIY movement today finds its roots in the practice of producing clothing for oneself. Ultimately, as the fit of clothing improved, these changes helped to close the gap between ready-made and custom-made clothing.

In context of the democratization of fashion, the affordability of the sewing machine, development of mass-produced paper patterns, and the development of sizing systems were as much a driving force as the ready-to-wear line of Chanel, whose originals were way out of the price range of the average consumer. Between these two poles of couture and home sewing lay the fertile ground for a ready-to-wear industry available to the middle class, comprised of quality mass-produced clothing.

Piracy in fashion

Paris couture continued to steer fashion in the 1920s. Middle-class consumers could buy dresses, coats and sportswear 'in the Chanel style' from department stores such as Franklin Simon & Co., who designed their own line in New York and produced high quality ready-to-wear garments. Although Franklin Simon & Co. patented some of their designs to demonstrate authenticity, other manufacturers were less concerned with originality. Manufactured clothing for women was essentially comprised of copies of Paris designs, brought to the US through a sort of fashion espionage, the mechanics of which are described in detail by American couturière Elizabeth Hawes in *Fashion is Spinach*, her tell-all memoir and manifesto against the ready-to-wear industry.[8] Hawes describes her experience as an illustrator (i.e. copyist) while working in Paris from 1925 to 1928, and her observations at a Jean Patou fashion show:

> I was to sketch the Fords. A Ford is a dress which everyone buys. Patou decided in advance what models were to be Fords. His showmanship was perfect and unique among the couturiers. He [Patou] put Fords on six at a time, all alike in line and different in color. This, Mesdames, is No. 46. Here are six of them. You will each order this dress. You will all go home and make six thousand more. My job was to get the Fords down cold. There were at least thirty to a Patou collection and Weinstock [her employer] wouldn't buy more than eight ... From my sheltered position, I took elaborate notes and sometimes sketched.
>
> HAWES, 1938: 59

Until the end of the 1920s, it was the habit of American buyers to purchase several dozen copies of each selected model in Paris and retail them to a wealthy clientele, and then to make a thousand copies to sell at lower prices. The principal Parisian fashion houses in 1925 were listed as Chanel, Patou, Lanvin, Vionnet, Lelong, Molyneux and Piguet, and the fashion export market was a valuable contribution to the national economy. Many salons had expanded their premises and hired as many as 500 people to cope with the demand. After the stock market crash of 1929, prohibitive customs duties began to make the luxury trade almost impossible, with duty of up to 90 per cent imposed on the cost of the model. However, models imported on a temporary basis for the purpose of copying were allowed into America duty free. These toiles (patterns cut out in linen) were sold for 100,000 francs each, with full directions for making them up. Ironically, this practice of licensing designs, which theoretically controlled their reproduction and circulation, would ultimately lead to the destruction of the exclusivity of haute couture. Economic factors in the form of tariff restraints were also a major factor in restructuring the international fashion market, and accelerated the development of the ready-to-wear industry internationally. These restraints, imposed during both the First World War and the Depression, compounded this industrial shift.

Fashion piracy was costing the couturiers thousands of francs each year, and further hastened the introduction of ready-to-wear garments. The illegal copying of haute couture designs could not be prevented by the French authorities because it occurred in foreign countries. Infringement of copyright was the subject of the Hague Agreement of July 1928, which was promulgated 'as an international instrument of protection. It covered all designs and models registered with the *Organisation Mondiale de la Propriété Intellectuelle* in Geneva' (Palmer White, 1986: 167). Ironically, Palmer White has concluded that, despite these protective measures, in the 1920s and 1930s, 'few members of the national fashion organizations could be bothered to proceed to any such registration' (1986: 167). Significantly, in 1929, three of the key fashion houses – Lelong, Patou and Chanel – introduced their first prêt-à-porter lines. This event officially heralded the demise of haute couture and the rise of designer ready-to-wear clothing. Although the rampant piracy of French fashion was a persistent problem for the couturiers in Paris, this was an inevitable step for the development of the American design industry, one supported by a consistent (if discontented) indigenous labour force.

While it would seem that Chanel undoubtedly made a major contribution to fashion's redirection – along with a number of other influential designers of the time, notably Jean Patou – international monetary factors determined that the world of haute couture could no longer afford to ignore the fashion demands and economic strength of the bourgeoisie. For example, long before Chanel's name was first mentioned in an American *Vogue* magazine article in April 1923 titled 'Chanel Opens Her Doors to a Waiting World', this elitist magazine had been printing regular feature articles for several years with titles such as 'Where Modes and Moderate Incomes Meet', 'Dressing on a Limited Income' and 'Ways to Alter Your Old Fashions'. In American *Vogue* in the years following the war, it became quite common to see advertisements for copies of 'Paris originals' and lists of distributors of lower-priced ready-to-wear garments. Already by that time, the editors of fashion magazines were appealing to a potentially vast new market.

American couture

The editor of American *Vogue*, Edna Woolman Chase, had always attempted to avoid the possibility of American fashion isolation by placing American fashion within the context of Parisian culture, and by encouraging the French to present their clothes within a theatrical format at various American fashion fêtes. She soon realized that a different marketing strategy had to be adopted to take advantage of the changing market. Chase persuaded the new director, Condé Nast (who purchased *Vogue* in 1909), that the women of American high society could be coerced into buying models from the top New York houses if the event benefited a French charity. *Vogue*'s first show attracted the cream of New York society. The display of 125 models included the work of Henri Bendel, Mollie O'Hara, Bergdorf Goodman, Gunther, Tappe, Maison Jacqueline and Kurtzman, as well as many other elite houses. This event sparked controversy in Paris, as many – including Poiret – saw it as an attempt to 'throw off the yoke of Paris' by 'instituting American styles' (Poiret, 1915). Even Worth's successors, sons Jean-Philippe and Gaston-Lucien, alluded in an interview with *The New York Times* (20 December 1912) to his concern that American designers might develop a viable fashion industry of their own which would compete with the Europeans. This marked the beginning of the rise of the American super fashion consumer, whose desired image was meticulously assembled by the editors of America's fashion magazines for middle-class women, such as *Harper's Bazaar* and *Vogue*.

Upper-class consumers could purchase Paris originals from Bergdorf Goodman or Henri Bendel. While the exclusive Bergdorf Goodman store had sold Parisian dresses to wealthy New York socialites from 1925, when Wall Street crashed in 1929, this market disappeared. Not one American commercial buyer attended the Paris collection showings in the first season after the stock market plunge. The US government slapped a 90 per cent tax on all imported clothing in order to encourage local manufacturers to provide alternative models.

The first couturières opened establishments in New York during the 1920s: Jessie Franklin Turner, Valentina and Elizabeth Hawes rivalled the French market with elegant, bespoke styles. Turner specialized in exotic tea gowns, intended to be worn when receiving guests at home; her upper-class clientele also attended sporting functions and vacationed at the beach, requiring ensembles for these events (Reeder, ed. Diehl 2018). Valentina created draped gowns and silhouettes, modelling them herself in high society and in print advertisements. Hawes had been trained in the couture tradition in Paris, and had been employed as an illustrator, designer and stylist from 1925 to 1928. Establishing her label in New York in 1928, she created couture dresses while advocating for women's comfort over tradition. She also briefly entered the ready-to-wear market during this period, but writes disparagingly of the problems with the manufacturing industry caused by poor fit and materials in *Fashion is Spinach*. Hawes herself had sold copies of Paris fashion to New York designers, whom she considered copyists and thieves, and was convinced that manufacturers would not want their designers to create original work (Hawes 1938: 126).[9] Further explaining the inner workings of the ready-to-wear system, Hawes refers to the business entrepreneurs – often Jewish immigrants who had experience in garment manufacturing – who had invested their money into this new industry by establishing their own businesses. Their factories started to produce hundreds of copies of the French best-sellers by sending designers to Paris and sneaking them into couture showings disguised as rich Americans or luxury department store buyers. After sketching the models (or buying sketches from an illustrator like Hawes) they would rush back to New York and make copies of the Paris style: knock-offs of the couture originals. This system persisted well into the twentieth century; it was only in the 1930s that new ideals for American style were formed through a combination of an organized manufacturing industry, promotions in retail, and fashion images propagated by print media.

Couturières such as Hawes, Turner and Valentina were not the only style-makers in America at this time. African American designers such as Zelda Wynn Valdes and Ann Cole Lowe worked across racial groups, creating couture gowns for wealthy patrons of diverse backgrounds. Valdes established a successful dressmaking business outside New York City in the 1930s, and maintained a steady clientele of prominent African Americans. Opening a location on upper Broadway in 1948, Valdes created the wedding gown and bridesmaid dresses for Nat King Cole's wedding to Maria Hawkins Ellington the same year. She specialized in creating fitted, embellished gowns for celebrities such as Jazz singers Ella Fitzgerald and Joyce Bryant (Diehl 2018). Valdes' designs were high quality, with high prices: a gown could cost between $800 and $1,000. Valdes also publicized her gowns through benefit fashion shows throughout the 1950s and 1960s, creating show-stopping designs. Conscientious of the limitations placed on women of colour by the mainstream fashion industry, she was one of the founders of the National Association of Fashion and Accessory Designers (NAFAD) in 1949, promoting the work of young black designers and organizing annual conventions around the country. She formed a relationship with Hugh Hefner of *Playboy* when she created several bunny costumes for the club in 1962, going on to stage several fashion shows there; from 1970, she began designing for the Dance Theater of Harlem, a relationship that went on for nearly thirty years until her death in 2001.

Ann Cole Lowe trained in dressmaking alongside her mother in her home state of Alabama, whose commission designing ball gowns for the governor's wife was completed by sixteen-year-old Lowe after her mother's death in 1914. On commission to create dresses for a society wedding, she moved to Tampa briefly before going to New York City to study design in 1917. Lowe's reputation as a highly skilled couturière spread among the wealthy and famous, where the Rockefellers and Du Ponts were among her clients (Davis and Grabowski 2018); in 1946, Lowe designed a blue floral gown worn by Olivia de Havilland to the Oscars ceremony. However, while many white American designers had won the battle for having their names on the labels, Lowe remained unacknowledged for another twenty years. In 1950, Lowe opened her first boutique in Harlem, later moving to Fifth Avenue. Lowe primarily had a steady clientele of wealthy white women, and designed the illustrious wedding gown of Jackie Bouvier Kennedy in 1953, along with the bridesmaid dresses. Lowe's signature gowns were embellished with elegant silk appliqued floral motifs; Kennedy's gown was adorned with large floral medallions executed in the trapunto technique. Although Lowe's work was on par with other couturiers, unlike Valdes, she charged notoriously little. The Kennedy bridal party dresses were ruined in a flood at the atelier one week before the wedding and had to be remade at a loss of $2,250. Lowe couldn't break even with her expenses, and was forced into bankruptcy – although an anonymous donor reportedly paid her back taxes, possibly Jackie Kennedy (Davis and Grabowski 2018). Following these misfortunes, Lowe went into employment for Saks Fifth Avenue as head designer at the Adam Room, as well as designing dresses for Neiman Marcus, Henri Bendel and Hattie Carnegie.

The 'American Look' in ready-to-wear

By the late 1920s, the American fashion industry began to produce high quality ready-to-wear that combined the casual lifestyle of Americans with the class and repute of European designer goods. New York City became indicative not only of the place of manufacture of ready-to-wear clothing, but of the lifestyle of the upper middle class, who wore sportswear to indicate leisure. Broadly defined, American sportswear included clothing for town and country, collegiate wear, and resort wear (Arnold, 2009). Advertisements meant to evoke memories or idealized images of an athletic, leisurely lifestyle appeared in journals such as *Vogue* and *Harper's Bazaar*. Sportswear also incorporated workwear for women: models photographed in the busy streets of New York represent the sleek silhouette of a modern woman rushing to her job, emphasized by the sharp lines of steel skyscrapers in the background. These images represent not only the American lifestyle, but New York as the location in which modern society finds its identity.

The role of retail in the establishment of American style was developed through a promotional program spearheaded by Dorothy Shaver, 'First Lady of Retailing' (Braun, 2009), who worked her way up from salesgirl to president of Lord & Taylor's department store (1924–49). Shaver's early contributions were to create the Bureau of Stylists (1925), followed by an exclusive line of products for Lord & Taylor. Stylists in the New York location tended to customer needs for out-of-towners who came in specially to shop at the store, choosing wardrobes for customers upon request and fitting them in their hotel rooms (Braun, 2009: 80). The Stylists later became Lord and Taylor's Personal Shopping Department, creating the prototype for modern-day personalized services. In 1928, Shaver organized an exhibition of French furniture and painting at the Department Store's Fifth Avenue location: *Exposition de L'Art Decoratif et la Peinture Francaise* (Exhibition of French Decorative Arts and Painting). Combining the drama of a gallery opening and Hollywood premiere, Shaver's clever merchandising attracted over 300,000 viewers during the month-long display, and won her accolades as a publicity genius (Braun, 2009: 82). The event resulted in a wave of Modernist design throughout the US, and increased stock value for Lord & Taylor.

This positive public response led Shaver to create the Contempra Group of International Arts, in pursuit of all-American designers (1928). The first designers were recruited in 1929 to create American-themed fabrics; in 1932, Shaver inaugurated the 'American Look' [aka American Designer] campaign featuring the work of three designers in an exclusive luncheon and fashion show on 17 April: Elizabeth Hawes, Annette Simpson and Edith Reuss, later recognized as the 'First Rank' of American Designers. (Braun, 2009: 98) The next round of designers include Hawes and Muriel King, followed by a third round with Clare Potter, Alice Smith and Ruth Payne. Shaver's campaign was furthered through the public relations efforts of Eleanor Lambert, who took on these young designers as clients and promoted their work. Initially, the American Look campaign did not give credit to designers by name, instead referencing manufacturers (Hawes, 1938: 181) Although press coverage was excellent, it would take eight years for the newspapers to finally start naming designers, signalling a turning point in the industry emphasizing design over manufacturing.

Shaver increased her show of support for American designers in 1937 by creating the Lord & Taylor Awards, which offered a $1,000 prize to the outstanding designs in several categories, including fashion. One of the first recipients of the award, Clare Potter, focused on colourful clothes with clean lines and minimalistic silhouettes for women with busy lives. Focusing on the American lifestyle and the need to combine comfort with smart dressing, Potter contributed to the early development of American sportswear.

Claire McCardell, an early Shaver protégé and in-house designer for Townley Frocks, developed her clothing on the basis of an adjustable silhouette, using belts or ties to allow the wearer to fit the garment to her body proportions. Adopting Vionnet's bias cut, McCardell's first successful design was dubbed the 'Monastic', a tented dress with a long string belt that could be tied around the body to create a ruched torso and full skirt. Her clothes combined elegance with childish playfulness, ranging from draped bathing suits (Fig. 4.6) and rompers, to pinafores and halter-neck sundresses. In September 1940, Lord & Taylor created their Designer's Shop to showcase American designers, including McCardell. In 1942 Diana Vreeland, fashion editor of *Harper's Bazaar*, challenged designers to create a utilitarian garment that an average middle-class housewife could afford; McCardell won the challenge with her Popover dress, a wraparound

FIGURE 4.6 Vogue *1945: A model wears a grey V-midriff swim suit with polka-dot ascot by Claire McCardell. McCardell's draped bathing suit appeared in many iterations throughout her collections. (Photo by Serge Balkin/Condé Nast via Getty Images.)*

FIGURE 4.7 Vogue 1949: *A model wears a small jacket and pleated skirt with cummerbund by Claire McCardell. (Photo by Horst P. Horst/Condé Nast via Getty Images.)*

dress made of calico cotton that came with an oven mitt, and sold for $6.95.[10] Vreeland's challenge was in response to new restrictions on cloth usage following America's entry in the Second World War. Regulation L-85 (March 1942) limited the amount fabric that could be used, the use of natural materials including silk, wool and leather, and metal used in zippers and other notions, challenging designers to find new approaches to garment construction and materials.

Ultimately, the closing of many of the French design houses after the German Nazi occupation of Paris in 1940 led to the success of an indigenous American fashion design industry. Vera Maxwell revolutionized sportswear with her approach to utilitarian garments. Creating the jumpsuit worn by women for factory work during the Second World War, Maxwell's design was popularized by posters of Rosie the Riveter. For leisure wear, Maxwell responded to the limitations imposed by fabric restrictions imposed by L-85 by designing coordinates in plain fabrics – garments that could be worn in different combinations to give the illusion that one's wardrobe was larger than it actually was. Other sportswear designers such as Bonnie Cashin would continue the practice of creating ensembles with interchangeable pieces, now known as separates. Although all sportswear was created on the principles of comfort, adjustable fit and streamlined silhouettes, each designer – including Tina Leser, Emily Wilkins and others – created a signature detail, such as Cashin's leather trim, Maxwell's softly tailored suits, Leser's artistic printed and painted dresses, or Potter's pajama pants. Beach wear and play wear had a large market, and designer Carolyn Schnurer combined casual clothing with garment details from around the world, inspired by her travels. One of the first lines for teens was developed by Emily Wilkens, who created youthful styles with adjustable waistbands and hemlines. These simple concepts, later coupled with the development of machine-made knits and elastomeric fibres, solidified ready-to-wear principles that still define American design.

In the summer of 1940, five retailers led by Fashion Group International orchestrated a series of promotions and fashion shows promoting American design, timing the events carefully so the press could attend all of them. The retailers also allowed pre-publicity photo shoots – usually forbidden due to the high probability of knock-offs – to appear in *The New York Times*. In *The American Look*, Rebecca Arnold notes (2009:16–17): 'Although sportswear began as a reflection of elite, leisured lifestyles, in the interwar period it increasingly came to represent the dynamism and flux of modernity and the city.'[11] Photographed in The Hamptons or similar locations where

FIGURE 4.8 *Mrs R. Fulton Cutting Modeling Summer Outfit, 1949. Even the very wealthy dressed in American ready-to-wear for leisure and comfort. (Photo by Genevieve Naylor/Corbis via Getty Images.)*

FIGURE 4.9 *Bonnie Cashin 'Eskimo Pants' of Navy blue and white polka-dotted silk , worn by Barbara Lawrence, blonde beauty featured in the 20th Century film 'You Were Meant For Me'. (Bettman/Getty Images.)*

the New York wealthy vacationed to escape the city heat and crowds in the summer, American Look models redefined the beauty ideal to one of sleek athleticism.

New synthetic fabrics being produced by textile mills in Europe and America were used by manufacturers to reduce the cost of garments, thereby giving greater impetus to the ready-to-wear market. Rayon, which had been developed in France and marketed as 'artificial silk' as early as 1888 by Compte Hilaire de Chardonnet, found its place in the American ready-to-wear market during the Interwar years. Nylon, used primarily for stockings but also for clothing requiring stretch, was developed by Wallace Carruthers of Du Pont laboratories in 1937, and contributed greatly to the reduced cost of clothing. These lab-made materials became particularly useful for garment production during the Second World War in response to the restrictions defined by L-85.

Despite rationing, the 'Dean of Fashion' Norman Norell created elegant ready-to-wear that combined couture details with American style. Beginning his career in the late 1920s, Norell joined business partner Anthony Traina in 1940 as head designer of Traina-Norell. Like

FIGURE 4.10 *The sleeveless jacket designed by Norman Norell, 1945. Norell worked as a fashion designer with Hattie Carnegie. As the head of design and co-founder of Traina-Norell, the 'Dean of Fashion' defined American luxury ready-to-wear. (Photo by Genevieve Naylor/Corbis via Getty Images.)*

McCardell, Norell's contributions are numerous, and include the chemise dress and hand-embellished sequined evening sheath. Signature details include sailor collars on cotton organdy dresses, and large 'pussycat' bows dressing up cocktail dresses. Marketed for upper middle-class women, his off-the-rack line ranged from casual separates to evening wear, equally admired and sought after by American high society and deemed equal to the designs of Paris. Norell's work was the focus of a major exhibition at the Museum at FIT, 'Norman Norell: The Dean of American Fashion' (2018), which examined the breadth of his designs and its lasting impact on luxury ready-to-wear.

Changes in menswear: Shirts, jeans, and suits

The evolution of menswear follows a similar path as that of womenswear, with the ready-to-wear industry in America gaining a foothold in the first half of the twentieth century. Groundbreaking technology included the development of denim workwear by Levi Strauss in the nineteenth century, and the self-folding collar patented by John M. Van Heusen (1919), making button-down shirts more comfortable for growing numbers of office workers. These major developments laid the groundwork for men's business attire for decades to come.

What we now identify as a dress shirt was first worn as a type of undergarment covered by a waistcoat and overcoat, as discussed in Chapter 1. The button-down shirt was to become one of the largest mass-production markets in the fashion industry. It dated back to 1881 when Moses Phillips and his wife Endel began sewing shirts by hand and selling them from pushcarts to local coal miners in Pottsville, Pennsylvania. The shirt business expanded into New York City after Phillips' son bought the rights to a soft collar design by John M. Van Heusen, a Dutch immigrant who patented a self-folding collar in 1919. Forming the Phillips–Van Heusen Company, they marketed the first collar-attached shirt in 1929, and the Van Heusen shirt became a staple item in every man's wardrobe. This development was concurrent with the sleek, bias-cut necktie patented by Jesse Langsdorf (1926), creating a more comfortable alternative to stiff bowties or ascots with layers of fabric at the folded over at the neck. Improvements in the fit of ready-to-wear clothing, such as having neck size and arm length determined in standard sizes, made way for styles such as the drape suit of the 1930s, a loose ensemble with wide shoulders and a broader cut in the chest and back that gave the effect of a narrow waistline and athletic physique. Inspired by the debonaire Prince of Wales (also King Edward VIII of England, and later the Duke of Windsor), this was his signature style: loosely fitted bespoke suits in grey flannel developed by his tailor, Frederick Scholte, in the 1920s. A contrast to the heavy dark frock coats and tail coats of the early twentieth century, this style came to be known as the 'English Drape' suit. A version of this cut with slight differences in construction became popular in the US by the late 1930s, known as the 'American Drape' suit.

As American men became more fashion-conscious, and ready-to-wear elements of middle-class clothing became affordable, garment styles were marketed to them directly. As early as 1931, Arnold Gingrich published an influential magazine called *Apparel Arts*, which was the first male fashion magazine aimed at tradespeople, manufacturers, wholesalers and retailers in order to promote better design, presentation and marketing strategies for mass-produced fashion products. He also published *Esquire* magazine in 1933, which was used to show the fashion-conscious public that stylish clothes did not necessarily have to be produced by the tailors of London's Savile Row. Chenoune, in his *A History of Men's Fashion* (1993: 188), notes that by 1937, subscriptions for the monthly magazine had reached 728,000. It promoted ways to match shirts, suits and ties according to fabric, patterns and colours, and devoted long articles to the wool industry, manufacturing standards and store improvements; this, in turn, gave a major boost to the American ready-to-wear market.

Another staple in every wardrobe is jeans, but the popularity of denim as a fashion fabric overshadows its humble beginnings. Levi Strauss, a twenty-four-year-old Bavarian immigrant, left New York for California during the gold rush era to sell rough canvas overalls to miners. The trousers were hardwearing, with pockets that would not tear when filled with gold nuggets. When Levi Strauss introduced his first basic pair of 'waist-high overalls' in 1853, he had no competitors. He replaced the tough canvas (which the miners complained was causing chafing) with a cotton twilled cloth from France called serge de Nîmes. This name was shortened to 'de Nîmes', from which the term 'denim' was created. It appeared in *Webster's Dictionary* for the first time in 1864. Later, in 1873, Strauss added the distinctive double-stitched pockets and, in partnership with Nevada tailor Jacob Davis, patented the process of putting metal rivets in the seams for strength. Branding was completed with the large, leather two-horse label that was added in 1886 and the red tag attached to the back left pocket in 1936 to identify the Levi's 501 brand at a distance. The marketing image conveys the value of the Levi Strauss brand: they are 'the real deal' – authentic, original, dependable. Levi's would expand its marketing throughout the twentieth century to broaden its demographic: in 1934, they introduced 'Lady Levi's' when they realized women on the ranch and the farm were borrowing their husbands' jeans. During the Second World War, the American government declared that Levi's were an essential commodity and sales were restricted to defence workers. Following the Second World War, Levi's began an aggressive marketing campaign to young boys and teenagers, hailing the casual pants as appropriate for school and play.

By the 1950s, jeans had been further popularized by the insurgence of western films, which promoted the adventurous and romantic image of actors such as Gene Autry and Roy Rogers. Also, jeans were immortalized as a symbol of youthful revolt in movies such as *The Wild One* (1953) featuring Marlon Brando, and *East of Eden* (1954) and *Rebel Without a Cause* (1955) featuring James Dean. Young men started wearing a black or brown leather jackets with blue jeans and mimicking the insolent casual body positions and poses of these legends of the silver screen, slouched against walls with their hands in their pockets. Jeans were adopted by typical middle-class teenagers, the offspring of white-collar businessmen. Levi's successfully capitalized on the notion that it had emerged from a working-class base, and this appealed to a generation of anti-establishment baby boomers, leading to its symbolic identity as the uniform of revolution.

Fashion in film: Costume designer as couturier

One of the greatest homogenizing influences on global fashion has been the spread of American popular culture. Both Eastern and Western cultures became seduced by the widespread distribution of American Hollywood films. Cinema often acted as a catalyst to determine the direction in which fashion was headed, displayed in the dress of the characters and further promoted in short newsreels of fashion shows by American and Parisian couturiers (Finamore, 2009). The cinema proved to be an inexpensive and exciting form of entertainment for mass consumption, and was an effective escape from reality during the Depression and the war years.

During these stringent times, support actors were often hired for their smart hats or coats rather than their talent, as the production houses were limited to a shoestring budget. During the silent film days of the 1910s and 1920s, exaggerated appearances and gestures were necessary to provide greater dramatic appeal for the audience, so effective costumes for the heroes and heroines of the silver screen were paramount. Dress played a key role in the development of plot and characterization.

The seductive 'vamp' of the 1910s and 1920s, which included Theda Bara, Pola Negri and Gloria Swanson, had dark hair and heavily kohl-rimmed eyes. The vamp was a femme fatale who enticed men to ruin through games of love and passion, often dressed in revealing costumes for films such as *Cleopatra* (Theda Bara in 1917) or *Zaza* (Gloria Swanson in 1923) inspired by Orientalist haute couture and designed by Norman Norell. In addition to glamorizing the imagined past in historic dramas, dress played a key role in the development of plot and characterization, an aspect of fashion in film that would resonate throughout the Golden Age of Hollywood. Throughout the 1920s, the 'vamp' look would decline in popularity, in favour of the flapper look (Finamore, 2009). The musicals of the 1930s provided visual spectacles that allowed Hollywood to 'transform itself into a "dream factory", where film images created suspense, humour and a distraction allowing people a temporary flight from their bleak, everyday reality' (Gronemeyer, 1999: 78). Film designers in Hollywood produced clothes that rivalled those of the French couturiers in quality, expense and glamour, and which had an enormous influence on the public (Crane, 2000: 139).

A new genre of American dressmakers or stylists emerged, whose names became synonymous with Metro-Goldwyn-Mayer (MGM), Warner Bros. and Universal Studios. They included Gilbert Adrian, Travis Banton, Howard Greer, Walter Plunkett and Edith Head. Some of these designers also did some work for the wholesale trade in America. Adrian, in particular, began his career in the Garment District of New York and then progressed to Hollywood, where he worked for MGM and created the immortal 1930s silver screen look. In 1932, Adrian's most successful design was a white organdy dress with ruffled shoulders, designed originally for Joan Crawford in the film *Letty Lynton* (1932). Macy's Cinema Fashions boutique sold 500,000 copies of the dress in 400 stores across the US, starting a new fashion trend (Poulson, 2009). Adrian left Hollywood in 1941 to start his own ready-to-wear line, after designing the memorable costumes for *Marie Antoinette* (1938), *The Wizard of Oz* (1939) and many other films. Walter Plunkett was immortalized for the costume collection he designed for the classic epic *Gone with the Wind* in 1939, in which Scarlett O'Hara (Vivien Leigh) used the green velvet material and tieback tassels of old Victorian curtains to make a seductive gown to woo the wealthy Rhett Butler (Clark Gable). William Truvilla cemented Marilyn Monroe's status as a sex symbol with his designs as well, from the strapless hot pink gown for *Gentlemen Prefer Blondes* (1953) to the iconic halter-neck dress for *The Seven-Year Itch* (1955) which allowed the breeze from a New York subway to scandalously flare the dress up over her head, exposing her undergarments.

However, the lengthy career of Edith Head still lingers as legend in the world of Hollywood costuming. In addition to costuming Gloria Swanson for *Sunset Boulevard* (1950), she also costumed Audrey Hepburn in *Roman Holiday* (1953). Head worked with director Alfred Hitchcock on several of his thrillers, creating whole wardrobes for actress Grace Kelly in *Rear Window* (1954) and *To Catch a Thief* (1955). Her masterwork lay in the dual wardrobes created for Kim Novak's character in Hitchcock's *Vertigo* (1958), in which Novak plays two identical but different women, defined by their diametrically opposite fashion sense. Head won a record eight Academy Awards for costume design between 1949 and 1967.

The need for Hollywood to have its own roster of costume designers was, in some ways, an outgrowth of earlier partnerships with design houses that did not work out. While key European fashion couturiers were hired to design clothes for major productions, such as Poiret's historic interpretations of Renaissance garments for *Queen Elizabeth* (1912) and Lucile's costumes for the mini-series *The Perils of Pauline* (1914), many of these partnerships did not come to fruition. Erté never completed the costumes for the film *Paris* (1926); Elsa Schiaparelli's garments for Mae West's 1937 film *Every Day's a Holiday* were made in Paris, but when they arrived in the Hollywood studios, it was discovered that they were far too small to fit her. When Chanel designed her functional but drab sportswear for Jean Renoir's *La Règle du Jeu* (1939), the audiences left the theatre disappointed, as they had anticipated that they would see costumes that were more spectacular. Movie stars also became associated with particular styles of dress, which were advertised in *Vogue* and *Seventeen* magazines. In addition to reflecting popular styles of the day, fashions created for films also held sway over the ready-to-wear industry. Hollywood was a formidable advocate of fashion, extending its influence over a broad spectrum of society.

Menswear also shifted in response to Hollywood plot and costume. The gangster movie genre was established with *The Roaring Twenties* (1939) from Warner Bros., starring Humphrey Bogart and James Cagney. Just as the early American immigrants discarded their previous identities by discarding their traditional clothing, movie producers – many of whom were children of immigrants – used this same technique of changing costumes to reflect the changed circumstances or characterizations of the anti-heroes in their films. In certain ways, these movies applauded the power and influence that the mafia leaders wielded – it was an era when the young tough guy from the slums of New York could be raised to the level of a demi-god in the eyes of his peers. His clothes indicated his tough appeal.

Fashion as sociopolitical statement: Zoot suits

The 'zoot suit' of the 1930s and early 1940s was a broad-shouldered, wide-legged suit tapered at the waist and pegged at the ankles, believed to have originated in New York's Harlem neighbourhood. In effect, these were oversized, exaggerated versions of the American drape suit. Worn by performers and patrons at swing clubs and dance halls, Jazz greats such as Cab Calloway sported zoot suits on stage while touring, as well as in films such as *Stormy Weather* (1943), popularizing the style in major cities such as New York, Chicago and Los Angeles. The baggy cut of the suit, accessorized with a dangling watch chain and wide-brimmed porkpie hat, accommodated movement for dancers while jitterbugging and performing other athletic moves associated with swing dancing; but the zoot suit came to represent much more. The popularity of Jazz and Swing music among African American, Latino and other minority communities provided an identifier for these groups – a way to express their association with the music and dance tradition that was heavily criticized by conservative white Americans. Amplified by reports of wild dancing, heavy drinking and the use of cannabis in these establishments, soon the zoot suit became known as a symbol of delinquency among the mainstream.

Made of flamboyant colours and striped or patterned cloth, zoot suits are also associated with Dandyism: a way to display pride in ones appearance while attracting attention to an eye-catching ensemble. This was especially important for minorities in the US, who were treated as second-class citizens and struggled with poverty and inadequate education. The zoot suit bore a visual message stating to American society that these groups should not be ignored. This basic desire for recognition became political, however, after L-85 restricted the use of fabric: these oversized suits suddenly became rebellious and anti-American. Tailors who made them – there was no way to buy one from a department store, and no designer exclusively associated with the design – worked underground to avoid prosecution. The struggle between social groups came to a head during the 'zoot suit riots' in Los Angeles (3–8 June 1943), when a large group of servicemen, off-duty policemen and civilians attacked a group of Mexican-American zoot-suiters known as 'pachucos' in the streets. Tearing the suits off their bodies, the violence escalated for three days before servicemen were banned from leaving their barracks, and the zoot suit was outlawed in Los Angeles. After the Second World War, zoot suits disappeared from popular culture, although they have been more recently recognized as a significant fashion statement in exhibitions such as *Reigning Men: Fashion in Menswear 1715-2015* at the Los Angeles County Museum of Art.

Summary

American fashion emerged in the first half of the twentieth century through a series of important foundational advances in the industry. Ready-to-wear garment manufacturing in New York and other metropolitan areas relied heavily on an overworked, underpaid work force comprised mainly of immigrants. Advances in technology for heavy duty industrial cutting and stitching, the development of a uniform system for sizing clothes, and the paper pattern industry all contributed to what would become ready-to-wear fashion. Early in the twentieth century, garments were primarily copies of French couture, and piracy was an ongoing problem in the industry at large. A small but significant couture sector developed in New York City, which included designers catering to the Social Register in both white and African-American communities. The major turning point for American fashion came with the isolation and rationing resulting from the Second World War, shifting credit from manufacturers to individual designers. Shifts in menswear also happened in the first few decades of the twentieth century, creating more comfortable clothing for professionals and denim for working-class men, creating the visual identifier of white and blue collar workers. The focus on sportswear as the representation of American lifestyle was a significant break from the traditions of Paris. Advances in lab-made fibres, garment construction and marketing all contributed to these developments. As zoot suits ruled the dance floors and stages in Jazz clubs, Hollywood films rose to prominence as both a representation of ready-to-wear and couture fashions, as well as the instigator of new styles.

Notes

1   There seems to have been a shift to buying ready-made garments for slaves in the last decade of the eighteenth century. George Washington writes in 1782 of his plantation producing enough wool and linen to have the majority of his cloth woven at Mt Vernon; however, in 1793 he writes of slaves receiving ready-made clothing. It is not clear if these were purchased from slop shops. See George Washington's Mt. Vernon, Digital Encyclopedia, 'Slave Clothing': https://mountvernon.org/library/digitalhistory/digital-encyclopedia/article/slave-clothing (accessed 23 January 2020).

2   Horace Greeely (1811–72) was a journalist and social activist who fought for labourers' rights in New York. He founded the *Tribune* in 1841, and used the paper's columns to editorialize. Social reformers in the mid-nineteenth century such as the Associationists were against both 'chattel slavery' and 'wage slavery' and sought fair wages for labourers, particularly in the garment industry.

3 Prior to the formation of the patent pool for the sewing machine, multiple companies were each taking small profits from the machinery they had developed, driving up the price of the machine.

4 Kingsley's *Alton Locke, Tailor and Poet: An Autobiography* (1850) is a novel about an aspiring working-class boy who accepts an opportunity to become a tailor's apprentice, but ultimately ends up at a sweatshop. Along with Kingsley's *Cheap Clothes and Nasty*, a social critique published the same year, these works illuminated the dark underworld of the sweated tailor's trade for Victorian readers.

5 For a historic analysis of sweatshops and labor reform, see Daniel Bender, 'Sweated Labor: The Politics of Representation and Reform', in *International Labor and Working-Class History* (No. 61, Spring, 2002), pp. 13–23.

6 Ironically, the lawyer who secured the not-guilty verdict for the proprietors of the factory was a former garment worker and immigrant, Max D. Steuer. A detailed narrative of the Triangle Shirtwaist Fire is Von Drehle, D. (2003), *Triangle: The Fire That Changed America* (New York: Atlantic Monthly Press). The Kheel Center at Cornell University has records available at: http://www.ilr.cornell.edu/ trianglefire/

7 For a detailed list of early European publications on tailoring, see Joy Spanadrel Emery (2014), *History of the Paper Pattern Industry*, 5–6.

8 Hawes describes her experience as an illustrator (i.e. copyist) while working in Paris from 1925 to 1928, including her work as a stylist and designer at the small couture house of Nicole Groult, Paul Poiret's sister. See Elizabeth Hawes (1938), *Fashion is Spinach* (New York: Random House).

9 See *Fashion is Spinach*, section titled 'Hawes in America: "Buy American: All American Women Can have Beautiful Clothes"' for her critique of ready-to-wear manufacturing practices. Hawes writes: 'I had gazed upon the bosses of American mass production in Paris. I considered them a bunch of thieves. I had sold sketches to their designers to such an extent that they were merely copyists in my estimation. I could not be under the illusion that any manufacturer would want original designs.' (126)

10 McCardell later recounted that the Popover dress was based on a Victory Garden cover-up dress she had designed. See White, C. (1998) 'Celebrating Claire McCardell' in *The New York Times*, Section B, page 15 (17 November).

11 Rebecca Arnold notes that the architecture of New York City, particularly skyscrapers such as the Empire State Building and the art deco design of the Chrysler Building, was maximized as a part of fashion photography stylizing the 'American Look'.

5

The Popularization of Fashion

Introduction

Following the Second World War, changes in the business of fashion were as important as fashion itself. Just as wartime restrictions and limited interaction with Europe encouraged a more independent aesthetic in American fashion inspiring growth in the industry, haute couture began to give way to a new kind of high fashion: luxury ready-to-wear. Couturiers, recognizing the dominance of ready-to-wear over Parisian couture as the economic driving force of the industry, continued to be taste-makers among the elite, while also taking cues from youth culture. While some couturiers continued in the bespoke tradition, new paths to financial success came through licensing deals with department stores, further blurring the lines between haute couture and ready-to-wear. These important developments established the contemporary fashion industry, in effect modernizing the old system that survived from the mid-nineteenth century. The generation growing up during the 1950s – the 'baby boomers' – would propagate the cultural explosion manifested in the arts including music, film and fashion. Dress would symbolize modern ideology to the extent that a fashion scene independent of the established system would be created. This dissemination of ideas that would permeate both couture and ready-to-wear brought together the two approaches to dress, ultimately establishing popular culture as the new voice of fashion.

Haute couture following the second world war

Several established couture houses, including Chanel and Vionnet, closed their doors in 1939–40 following the Nazi occupation of Paris. It would be more than a decade before Chanel made her comeback, and Vionnet's label did not reappear until the twenty-first century. Parisian couture may have disappeared entirely had it not been for the pioneering efforts of Lucien Lelong, who insisted on keeping the centre of the industry in France, despite the difficulties presented by the Nazi occupation.[1] Some couturiers had remained as mainstays of Parisian fashion, such as Fortuny and Schiaparelli, although demand for their styles would decline following the war.

However, the period following the Second World War offered an opportunity for couturiers in Paris to regroup formally as an industry, opening up opportunities for new designers and new business models. Fashion in the 1950s was defined by the retrospective style of Christian Dior, whose protégé Yves Saint Laurent defined and revolutionized popular trends in the 1960s, acknowledging the effect of streetwear as a major influence on high fashion. Among the couturiers whose work continued to attract a steady elite clientele while continuing stylistic developments, Cristóbal Balenciaga was a clear leader in the industry.

Christóbal Balenciaga

Like Vionnet, Balenciaga was renowned for his exquisite cut, tailoring and finishing techniques – the epitome of haute couture. He was unrivalled as an innovator, creating new silhouettes that drew inspiration from historic precedents. Beginning his career in his homeland of Spain in 1917, he opened fashion houses in Barcelona and Madrid. Balenciaga would draw upon his cultural heritage throughout his career in subtle ways, from the use of 'Spanish black' to the flamenco-inspired ruffles and tiers in evening gowns. Approaching his creations as sculptural works, Balenciaga drew inspiration from the art world in a different way than his contemporaries. When he opened his couture house in Paris in 1937, Schiaparelli's surrealistic collections were being fêted by every fashion journalist around the world (see Chapter 2). The influence of painters such as Salvador Dalí and René Magritte, who were known for their juxtaposition of 'opposite realities' to create a new visual paradox – with clocks melting over the table edges (Dalí, *The Persistence of Memory*, 1931) and steam trains emerging from fireplaces (Magritte, *Time Transfixed*, 1938) – were evident in her work. However, Surrealism impacted upon Balenciaga's work in a different way.

Balenciaga's work is more attuned to other Surrealist artists – including Max Ernst, Hans Arp and Joan Miró – who used biomorphic abstract shapes to create an 'otherness' not seen before in the fine arts. The silhouettes of these organic shapes lent themselves to sculpture as well as painting, and for Balenciaga these forms realized new forms on the body. Miró and Ernst painted personal themes by using amoebic signs and symbols seemingly painted in a spontaneous way, while Arp sculpted curvilinear shapes that related to the organic forms of nature and suggested growing body parts. Reformulating these forms to complement the body, Balenciaga's curved silhouette became the dominant style in the 1940s and 1950s. He is most famous for his evening gowns, in which the fabric was either manipulated into a distinct shape, or elaborately embellished to create a sumptuously textured surface. Balenciaga used stiff materials such as gazar silk that would hold their shape, but relied on expert cut to create simple, elegant forms, such as the 'Tulip' dress (1965) or the 'Envelope' dress (1967). His greatest talent was his ability to mould garments into sculptural creations, such as his black silk taffeta Balloon (or Pumpkin) dress of 1950, photographed by Irving Penn for *Vogue*. His evening concepts were often reinvented for daywear as well (Fig. 5.2). Renowned as a very prolific designer who was credited with creating every major silhouette of the 1950s and 1960s, his influence on a generation of designers was unparalleled. His sculptural work was often copied by Dior, Balmain, Givenchy, Fath and Griffe in the 1950s, and his work consistently appeared on the cover of *Vogue* magazine.

While the dominant colour for eveningwear in the 1950s was black, as it effectively highlighted the silhouettes of the garments in interior spaces, popular daytime colours such as turquoise, yellow ochre, mauve and reddish brown became the decade's signature hues, drawn directly from Balenciaga's own palette. Significantly, these have inspired many Spanish artists (including Miró), as they reflect the natural landscape of their homeland – the earth, the sea and the sun-drenched stucco houses. Considering that these colours became the dominant hues of the 1950s, it is an indication of the immense influence that Balenciaga wielded over fashion. Due to the great respect afforded him by his fellow designers, he has often been dubbed the 'couturier's

FIGURE 5.1 Picture Post: *1951 An evening dress designed by Cristóbal Balenciaga with crisp white cotton pique cut away at the front to show a full skirt of soft black silk flounces. Balenciaga's Spanish heritage informs this tiered evening gown, reminiscent of flamenco dresses. (Photo by Bill Brandt/Getty Images.)*

FIGURE 5.2 Vogue *1953: A model wears a sleeveless white dotted cotton balloon jacket by Balenciaga over a black wool dress. Balenciaga's organic forms transformed fabric into wearable sculpture. (Photo by Henry Clarke/Condé Nast via Getty Images.)*

couturier'. However, by the late 1960s the influence of haute couture was already usurped by younger styles worn on the street. Recognizing the impact that youth and street culture would have, a theme explored throughout this chapter, Balenciaga decided in 1968 that it was time to close his doors. *Harper's Bazaar* Australia wrote in September 1984 that, as the greatest perfectionist among his generation of couturiers, he felt that the life which supported high fashion was finished. His lasting contribution to couture was celebrated at an exhibition at London's V & A Museum, 'Balenciaga: Shaping Fashion' (2017–18).

Christian Dior

Dior is best remembered as the couturier who brought femininity back to the catwalk following the shoulder pads and V-shaped silhouettes of Schiaparelli, and the boyish garments of Chanel. He had worked for LeLong during the war, gaining technical expertise and providing him the opportunity to work on historical dress for the film *Le Lit à Colonnes* (1942), during which mid-nineteenth-century dressmaking and garment styles captured his attention. Opening his own couture house in December of 1946, Dior designed the 'Corolle' collection (Fr. *petal*; indicating Dior's vision of women as flowers), unveiling it in February 1947. Among the voluminous silhouettes, the 'Bar' suit captured the attention of *Harper's Bazaar* editor Carmel

Snow. Proclaiming it to be the 'New Look' (May 1947), this silk ensemble consisting of a narrow jacket with padded hips over a full pleated skirt, emphasizing a tiny waist, became the dominant silhouette for women over the next several years. Although the overall shape created by the garments is reminiscent of nineteenth-century precedents, Dior achieved his look through corsetry applied to the garments, rather than the woman; layering of stiffened petticoats or cage crinolines were replaced by expert pleating techniques. Evening dresses were often strapless or revealed décolletage in a coquettish way, embellished or accentuated by floral silks and embroidery. Hats and gloves often figured as part of the overall silhouette.

FIGURE 5.3 *The Dior 'Bar' suit from the 1947 Paris collections was comprised of a pale tussore hip-padded jacket, nipped in at the waist, and pleated jersey skirt at calf-length, paired with a wide-brimmed hat. His daytime dresses were midi-length, allowing for narrow ankles to peek through from the voluminous fringe of fabric. (Serge Balkin/Condé Nast via Getty Images.)*

FIGURE 5.4 *Vogue 1947:-Models wearing pleated satin dresses with leather belts by Dior. The 'New Look' promoted a return to full skirts and an hourglass silhouette. (Photo by Erwin Blumenfeld/Condé Nast via Getty Images.)*

According to Dior's biographical accounts (1956), the profligate use of luxury textiles was a deliberate statement of the post-war demand for a return to personal luxury (Martin and Koda, 1996). Fabric rationing during the war years in Europe and America led to significant changes in garment design, as noted in Chapter 4. 'Utility' clothing of the early 1940s, such as Maxwell's jumpsuit design and McCardell's Popover Dress, were mirrored by similar styles in England. Wartime propaganda dictating the reuse and conservation of fabric had led to a nostalgia for luxurious garments. By embracing historical luxury textiles and silhouettes, Dior had re-established Paris as the epicentre of couture, and became the fashion leader of the following decade. It should be noted that this was not met with universal praise, as there was criticism from the public towards indulgence during a time when many European countries were rebuilding their resources following the war; nevertheless, responding to critical acclaim, the 'New Look' prevailed.

In addition to his success in couture, Dior's business was supported by a management team that skillfully executed plans for licensed products such as fragrance Miss Dior (1947) and a ready-to-wear collection launched in New York (1948); by the mid-1950s, there were branches in major cities across the globe (Font, 2009). Despite the 'New Look' setting trends across fashionable society in the Western world, Dior's style had been evolving from the full-skirted silhouette to the 'H' silhouette: streamlined day suits for womenswear in grey flannel, and belted dresses in neutral colours.

FIGURE 5.5 *February 1957: Model wearing 'Bobby', a smart tailored suit with matching hat from the Spring Collection at Christian Dior Paris. Dior's style shifted from full to fitted throughout the 1950s, especially for daywear. (Photo by Keystone/Getty Images.)*

The fortuitous hiring of a young assistant in 1955 – Yves Saint Laurent – provided the House of Dior with a veritable heir when its founder passed away suddenly in 1957, shocking the couture world. Saint Laurent successfully brought the Dior vision to fruition with the 'A' line silhouette featured in his *Trapèze* collection in early 1958, featuring shorter hemlines and considerably less tailoring, establishing new trends that would dictate style in the 1960s.

Yves Saint Laurent

Yves Saint Laurent opened his couture house in 1961, blending ideas from many sources which tapped the artistic, social and political feelings of his time. Following three years as the head designer at Dior, Saint Laurent founded his establishment with his partner, Pierre Berge, both of whom were fine arts enthusiasts and collectors. His love of both fashion and fine art would inform not only Saint Laurent's work, but unite these two fields in ways reminiscent of early twentieth-century couture.

In both fashion and art, the revival of the 1920s experimentation with colours, lines and optics (taught at the Bauhaus School of Design, and reflected in art deco styling) was fundamental to the development of hard-edged graphic lines juxtaposed with large, flat areas of colour during the 1960s. In the decorative arts – especially furniture and household design – bold, bright primary hues were used to highlight the properties of plastics and resins, new technological materials that had emerged from experimentation during the Second World War. Designers generally mirrored the work of the hard-edged painters such as the American artists Ellsworth Kelly, Kenneth Noland and Frank Stella, who were producing huge canvases saturated with flat, juxtaposed areas of colour formatted in minimal compositions. Bridget Riley's op art canvases of undulating lines, and Victor Vasarely's studies of geometric shapes, interpreted the extensive colour studies that were undertaken by Johannes Itten and Wassily Kandinsky at the Bauhaus. Vasarely investigated spatial properties in conjunction with his 'colour forms' – in which shapes, related to colour, form units of a more complicated grouping. The juxtaposition of complementary colour schemes creates a kinetic visual movement, when after-images are created by the eye itself.

These art and design movements seemed to impact directly on the work of Yves Saint Laurent. His Mondrian Dress of 1965 was designed to commemorate the work of the Dutch de Stijl artist Piet Mondrian (d. 1944, New York), whose non-objective painting helped to revive neo-Bauhaus optical colour studies in the 1960s. The creation of this famous garment (Fig. 5.6) paralleled a number of retrospective exhibitions of Mondrian's paintings in the Sidney Janis Galleries (1962 and 1963) and the Allan Frumkin and Marlborough-Gerson Gallery (1964) in New York, followed by an exhibition at Galerie Beijeler in Basel, Switzerland in 1965. In 1966, three major exhibitions of Mondrian's work were held in The Hague, Toronto and Philadelphia. After the opening night showing of Saint Laurent's collection, thousands of copies of the Mondrian Dress were reproduced by Seventh Avenue manufacturers.

It should be noted that Mondrian himself was a spiritualist who despised consumerism and cared little for fashion (Grovier, 2017). Unlike the Lobster dress and other collaborations between Schiaparelli and Surrealist artists, Saint Laurent's interpretation of art as fashion does not represent a meeting of the minds, but rather the reconfiguration of a famous painting as art for the body. Saint Laurent considered his work homage to the famous painter; but given the fact that Mondrian had died twenty years earlier, it's impossible to know how he would have felt about his spiritual art being transformed into fashion.

Saint Laurent appropriated pop art into his 1966 fashions, inspired by his friend Andy Warhol's work, and for the next thirty years he paid homage to many of the great twentieth-century artists, including Matisse and Picasso. In the 1980s, he employed the famous company of French embroiderers and embellishers, Lesage et Cie (founded in 1922) to copy, in sequins, Van Gogh's *Irises* painting, as it had just been sold for the highest auction price ever paid for a work of art. Being entirely embroidered by hand, it was said to be made from 250,000 sequins in twenty-two different colours, 200,000 individually threaded pearls and 250 metres (273 yards) of ribbon (Frankel, 2001: 206). Within the fashion industry, the irony implicit in this metaphoric work – the highest price paid for a garment as well – was appreciated by the audience and received top media coverage.

The fashion press loved the eclectic nature of each successive Yves Saint Laurent collection. The only constant element in his pastiche collections was change – characteristically, in keeping with postmodernist trends. Even in his early work, he challenged the seriousness of couture by introducing 'fun' clothes mimicking the beatnik look, followed by the sailor look and the 'gypsy' look historically rooted in Bohemian styles. His African collection was unveiled in 1967–8: garments made of beaded rows revealing the flesh below, and Safari jackets reflecting Afrika Korps uniforms combined with the casual dress style of Western men in Africa (Musée Yves Saint Laurent Paris n.d., 'First Safari Jacket'). Saint Laurent seemingly drew inspiration from

FIGURE 5.6 *Dresses on display at the opening night of the 'Yves Saint Laurent: Style is Eternal' exhibition at Bowes Museum on 9 July 2015 in Barnard Castle, United Kingdom. The 1965 Mondrian Dress is centre, with two designs from the 1965–6 Pop Art collection behind. (Photo by Ian Forsyth/Getty Images.)*

FIGURE 5.7 *Yves Saint Laurent, French designer with two fashion models, Betty Catroux (left) and Loulou de la Falaise, outside his 'Rive Gauche' shop, 1969. Saint Laurent's fascination with the growing popularity of Bohemian and Hippie trends is juxtaposed here with his Safari look. (Photo by John Minihan/Getty Images.)*

every world culture and every facet of street culture; does this cross-cultural nature of his work represent inspiration, or appropriation? The plurality of sources made for a fascinating range in his collection, blurring lines between high and low culture, couture and ready-to-wear, art and fashion. However, as popular as these styles were in their time and beyond (fashion trends referenced 'colonial chic' well into the 2010s), the origins of some of these design sources – the Afrika Korps were Nazi soldiers in Africa during the Second World War – are considered controversial by today's standards (MacDonell, 2019).

Other sources of inspiration came from theatre and performance. Just as the music, sets and costumes of *Schéhérazade* by the Ballet Russes inspired artists and designers alike to recreate an exotic and colourful array of theatrical costumes in the early years of the century, so did its influence impact upon Saint Laurent. This was evident throughout his 1960s collections, which were characterized by bright colours and rich brocades. As Yves Saint Laurent continued his involvement with theatrical costuming throughout his career, he developed an ongoing series of ensembles for the French performer Zizi Jeanmaire from 1963, designing feathered and sequined ensembles for the stage sensation. He designed garments for his friend and actress Catherine

Deneuve for the Surrealist director Luis Buñuel's 1966 film, *Belle de Jour*, and also designed Isabelle Adjani's clothes in Luc Besson's film *Subway* in 1988.

Historical films also inspired a return to historical dress in fashion. The classic film *Dr Zhivago* (1965), for example, set in post-Revolution Russia, motivated designers to create collars and cuffs trimmed with fur on their winter coats. Inspired by these visually rich historic styles, Yves Saint Laurent produced a Catherine the Great collection in the late 1970s, which featured sumptuous, richly coloured brocaded garments trimmed in black fur. His Russian collection of autumn/winter 1976–7 was considered to be one of his most magnificent in years, and was captured on the front page of both the *New York Times* and the *International Herald Tribune*. During this decade, classic cinema initiated a host of fashion revival styles, as movies of the 1920s, 1930s and 1940s were shown to audiences who enthusiastically engaged with the nostalgia of classic screen productions.

Saint Laurent was one of the first haute couture designers to openly acknowledge his interest in popular culture. Interestingly, when asked in an interview for *Dazed and Confused* (March 2000) what his greatest influence was, he replied, 'The fashion of the street.' He watched what the young were wearing, where they were going and what they were doing. According to Steele (1998), he was the most successful designer, in the long term, to combine couture with street style – and in some cases, to set the trends on the street. In sympathy with the student riots in Paris in 1968, he designed a Native American protest uniform complete with headband and fringe. The headband later became identifiable with those persons participating in demonstrations against the Vietnam War. This kind of cultural appropriation is considered highly insensitive today, but in its time it supplied a generation of anti-establishment youth with a kind of dress code that represented their ideology.

Just as he had introduced turtle-necked sweaters with black leather jackets in 1960, he continued to heed the dictates of the street. In spring/summer 1978, he showed the Broadway Suit – a man's suit with short, full trousers worn with a straw hat. 'I wanted to bring some humour into fashion: adapt the street humour, its freedoms, the arrogance of punk. But of course with dignity, luxury and style' (Saint Laurent, 1978, quoted in *Yves Saint Laurent Retrospective*, 1986).[2] In retrospect, Saint Laurent will be remembered as most famous for introducing the 'midi' trench coats that were worn over trousers, his tuxedo suits for women and the peasant dresses that he designed from 1973.

The combination of feminine features, such as frills, with a tailored masculine style created an ambiguity which many felt reflected the dual role of women in our society. This is particularly obvious in his T-shirt dresses and his *Le Smoking* (black tie) garments, both designed in 1966. With a transparent blouse and trousers tailored from a man's tuxedo, *Le Smoking* was to be worn at sophisticated evening parties and reappeared many times during the course of the next decade. Saint Laurent sensed that women in trouser suits, for both daytime and evening wear, would become a major fashion statement over the next four decades. In *Paris Match* (4 December 1981), he commented: 'If I had to choose one design among all I have created, it would be Le Smoking. Every year since 1966, it has been part of my collection. In a sense it is the Yves Saint Laurent trademark.' In the same year, he opened a number of Rive Gauche boutiques, which sold his designer ready-to-wear line. The *maison* of Yves Saint Laurent was consolidating its financial standing in the industry.

In significant terms, Saint Laurent made a decided contribution to the changing role of women in the 1960s. A feature article in the *New York Times* (13 January 2002), entitled 'When Trousers were a Statement', pointed out that 'people had forgotten what a big deal it was' when women started to 'wear the trousers in the family, along with men'. While the first famous

FIGURE 5.8 *A model wearing a pinstriped trouser suit by Yves Saint Laurent, 1967. The pantsuit for women challenged feminine mores of the 1960s. The tuxedo-based suit for evening wear known as 'Le Smoking' became his signature piece. (Photo by Reg Lancaster/Daily Express/Hulton Archive/Getty Images.)*

woman to be photographed wearing trousers was Sarah Bernhardt in 1899, and they featured in Poiret's *Les Choses de Paul Poiret* illustrated by Georges Lepape in 1911, it was not until the 1920s that they were introduced into fashion – primarily for sportswear purposes. They became a functional necessity during wartime, when women took on men's jobs in the factories, fields and ammunition depots, but it wasn't until the 1960s that evening trouser suits were designed for women to wear for formal occasions. While women in trousers were outlawed in many upmarket venues in the mid-1960s, by the 1970s most establishments had come to regard trousers as suitable attire for women. Saint Laurent, following in Chanel's steps forty years later, appropriated men's fashion in order to break down established gender codes in his creation of elegant women's trouser suits.

André Courrèges

Establishing his label in Paris in 1961, André Courrèges produced a sophisticated, structured style using geometric A-line shapes. Having been trained as an engineer, Courrèges moved to fashion as an apprentice to the couturier Balenciaga, where he became a master of cut and tailoring techniques. Approaching garment design as architecture for the body, Courrèges shaped his garments into stylized, futuristic forms. He combined his inventive forms with unexpected fabrics, such as gabardine, to create sleek women's trousers that could be worn for an active yet stylish lifestyle during the daytime, or in the evening – a radical proposal for the time. He developed a signature style through cut, channel seaming and banded hemlines, which created subtle abstract patterns on the surface of his clothing. However, Courrèges is best remembered for his experimental 'space age' designs, staged with his models moving like robots in rigid, choreographed movements. The 'space race' dominated the media, both in news broadcasts and in popular television science shows. The top ten movies of the 1960s included *Dr Strangelove* (1964), *Goldfinger* (1964) and *2001: A Space Odyssey* (1968), with television featuring the original series of *Star Trek* and *The Man from U.N.C.L.E.* Drawing upon popular interest in and imagined future, Courrèges identified these technological developments as 'a metaphor for youth' (Steele 1998: 278). The look was decidedly avant-garde, and his mid-calf, flat-heeled boots became an iconographic symbol of the 1960s. Courrèges' most famous designs were seen in his Space Age collection for spring 1964, which strongly featured silver and white PVC with bonded seams. The collection included silver 'moongirl' trousers, white catsuits and monochrome-striped miniskirts and dresses.

His famous client, Jacqueline Kennedy, immortalized the Courrèges look, wearing his above-the-knee, triangular-shaped pastel coats with matching pillbox hats and flat-heeled shoes. As he fervently believed in the democratization of haute couture for the modern young working girl, Courrèges produced a large ready-to-wear collection that was widely exported. His ambition to

FIGURE 5.9 *Models in New York City, 1965, wearing André Courrèges' Suspender Outfits with Barrel Skirts and Leather Cowl-Neck Blouses. Courrèges presented a sleek look that represented his ideas of the future of the space age. (Photo by: Universal History Archive/Universal Images Group via Getty Images.)*

establish workshops that produced clothing at 'boutique prices' for direct marketing was unsuccessful, but his look remained a classic icon of the 1960s.

Pierre Cardin

Professionally, Pierre Cardin followed a similar course as Courrèges, including working for Schiaparelli (1945–7) and the House of Dior as head of *tailleure* (Fr. men's tailoring) (1947–50) before opening his own salon in 1950. Cardin quickly realized the need to expand his market; by working with department store companies in the late 1950s, he developed very strategic business skills. He was the first couturier to sign a 'licensing' contract in which his ready-to-wear designs carried his name, but were manufactured and marketed by another company or group of companies. As the licensing contracts expanded into a diverse range of products, his label became a great international success. His early signature fashion work was minimalist, with strong graphic lines in contrasting colours that created geometric, streamlined shapes. He incorporated decorative features as an inherent part of the surface design, making jewellery redundant. Like Courrèges, he had a fascination for technology and a passion for architectural shapes.

In 1961, Cardin opened his first men's boutique, and soon became a world leader in menswear. He redefined men's suiting by minimizing excessive fabric and details, creating a 'cylinder' silhouette that followed the natural contours of the body. He popularized the popular high-buttoned and collarless 'Nehru' jacket (its namesake was Jawaharlal Nehru, the first Prime Minister of India). Worn by celebrities such as The Beatles in the mid-1960s, as well as young and middle-aged consumers, the Nehru style was agender, and relatively easy to replicate through home sewing patterns. He specialized in men's suits, which often had matching hoods, and popularized the double-breasted evening suit for men.

Cardin began working on small couture collections for women in 1953, presenting his first full womenswear collection in 1957. Following Vionnet, Cardin investigated the possibilities of both cowl drapery and the use of the bias, and often chose wool crêpe or jersey to create a soft and supple nonchalant look. He broke gender norms in 1958 by creating a unisex line of bodysuits, and opened his first ready-to-wear line in 1959, getting him briefly expelled from the *Chambre Syndicale de la Haute Couture* (he was soon reinstated). In 1964, he introduced the futuristic Moon Range to his womenswear collection, with female models wearing tabards over catsuits, with high leather boots and space helmets. He was an expert with materials, and he became a perfectionist with pleating, mastering every possible variation – sunray, pencil and cartridge. In 1966, his moulded dresses imitated sculptural shapes and his work, like that of Courrèges, took on an austere, minimalist appearance, which epitomized the scientific space race. Cardin, like Courrèges, is most strongly associated with his futuristic designs for the 'Cosmocorps' (1967) collections, which included the 'Space Age Suits' made of silver lame for both men and women. He invented his own synthetic fabric ('Cardine'), and experimented with other materials including vinyl as both appliqué embellishments and garment fabric. Cardin, renowned for his individualized collars, which were often gigantic and double layered, combined with geometric detail, was exceptionally experimental and innovative.

Cardin worked through his experimental ideas in couture designs, and once popularized, brought them to the masses in his ready-to-wear lines. Showcased in the 2019 retrospective exhibition 'Pierre Cardin: Future Fashion' at the Brooklyn Museum, Cardin's range of products included couture and ready-to-wear collections, accessories, furniture and industrial design.

FIGURE 5.10 *Space age outfits in silver vinyl by Pierre Cardin, on display at Fashion Week in Paris, 26 January 1968. (Photo by Keystone/Hulton Archive/Getty Images.)*

Clothing and popular culture

From the 1960s onwards, fashion changes accelerated at a more rapid pace than ever before. This is reflected in the proliferation and diversity of styles promulgated until the end of the century. In *Design After 1945* Peter Dormer indicates that by the end of the 1950s, a decided change had taken place in terms of design philosophy. European designers challenged the notion that good taste (or good design) was embodied by one particular aesthetic, instead promoting the idea that design challenges present multiple solutions (1993: 200). This unprecedented visual pluralism reflected an age of experimentation, diversified thinking and dramatic technological change with the advent of the computer age, an ever-expanding communications system and a growing popular culture.

As the litmus test of social consciousness, clothing became a metaphor that clearly indicated the anti-war and anti-Establishment feelings of the hippies in San Francisco and the sexual revolution of women in the Western world. Clothing was used as a counter-cultural device to publicly announce an alternative outlook on society. Crane (2000) provides extensive data gathered from surveys and interviews that relate to the role of fashion in the social construction of identity. Finkelstein argues that 'clothes are regarded as the visible manifestation of entire systems of value' (1996: 16). In the mid-1960s, marketing surveys in Britain indicated that more than 50 per cent of fashion and fashion products were being sold to young people in the age group 15–18 years.[3] Designers and marketers immediately shifted their consumer focus to accommodate this swing. Not only did it become necessary to increase the ready-to-wear market so that it was affordable to younger clients, but the rapidity of change was such that it deterred wealthy clients from buying couture, as it would only be fashionable for a short period of time.

The introduction of television in the 1950s and the growing popularity of the movies increased the impact of popular culture upon the masses. With the proliferation of fashion and women's magazines and social page coverage in the newspapers, journalists constructed the glamorous, fairy-tale lives of these celebrities. The impact of American popular culture upon youth, fashion and the visual arts was universal. Teenagers had the greatest disposable income in history. There was a new kind of prosperity, especially among the working classes, and young people wanted to express their own attitudes and tastes rather than those of their parents. Crane (2000: 172) argues that popular culture redefines social phenomena, and that the construction of personal identity is based on leisure clothes that are synchronized with TV, film and popular music. Fashion styles change each time musical styles change, and these trends are religiously followed by a huge audience of adolescents and young adults. Youth culture determines its own codes of fashion, and these codes are carefully monitored and reinforced by the popular cultural industries.

With Hollywood films reinforcing the substantial link between celebrity and sexuality, the charismatic Cary Grant and Clarke Gable, so often filmed in their lounging attire, built their silver-screen images on suave sophistication, refinement and glamour, while Marlon Brando and James Dean created theirs on the look of rebellious youth, whose black leather and jeans epitomized masculine sex appeal, street culture and revolution. The business suit, when worn by the refined, thrill-seeking playboy Sean Connery, reinforced the notion that its wearer was a gentleman, a modern James Bond.

Sci-Fi fantasy films, such as *Barbarella* (1968), provided designers with a large audience to try out new ideas. Paco Rabanne, the Basque-born couturier who designed Fonda's retro-futuristic costumes for the film, used revolutionary new methods, including electronic welding to seal seams of plastic garments in his Barbarella collection. The theme of engineered couture is evident in Rabanne's method of constructing chain mail garments by linking discs and squares using metal rings. His inventive architectural dresses were seen in other films as well, such as *Casino Royale* and *Two for the Road* (both in 1967) and by celebrities such as pop singer Francoise Hardy and models Twiggy and Brigitte Bardot. The proliferation of pop culture icons provided a bridge between high fashion and ready-to-wear through the shared ground of visual media, and gave consumers an identity toward which to aspire by emulating dress styles.

The Swinging '60s in London

As celebrity status for movie stars, television stars, pop singing idols, rock groups and fashion models increased dramatically during the 1960s, Carnaby Street in London became the fashion epicentre for the young. The prevailing fashionable look at the end of the 1950s was 'Mod' – the style worn by the 'Modernists' in London who wanted a look and lifestyle that challenged traditional norms, but didn't emulate the greasy leather look of 'Rocker' bikers, 'Teddy' boys sporting Edwardian suits and pompadours, or long-haired beatniks in cafes. These young Mods gathered in coffeehouses and dance clubs, listened to Jazz music, and soon adopted a uniform of slim-fitted Italian suits, giving a dandified appearance. Mod style was propagated overseas by bands such as The Beatles, who first came to America in February 1964. Although first adopted by men, women's Mod styles began to mimic the clean lines with their short hair, Ballet flats, bobbed hair and heavy eye makeup. This look was brought to mainstream fashion by a young Mod designer who added bright colours and a shortened hemline, revolutionizing fashion for young consumers who embraced the ethos of the lifestyle.

Mary Quant

With no formal training in dressmaking or couture, Mary Quant established Chelsea's first fashion boutique, Bazaar, in 1955 with her husband, Alexander Plunkett-Greene, and Archie McNair. Quant epitomized a new breed of designer trained at art school, unafraid to defy mainstream ideas and enthusiastically promote new ideals. The boutique capitalized on the buying power of the new, young clientele by specializing in a mode of dress that encompassed specific fashion accessories – bags, hats, jewellery, stockings and even cosmetics. Even more significantly, she defied the fashion system – which manufactured two new styles per year – by following current fads and changing her styling every six weeks. Interestingly, the Bazaar boutique pioneered a revival of old-time shopping patterns, when small, family-owned businesses catered for personalized service – a practice that diminished when department stores were conceived. The rise of the boutique in London paralleled the growth of retail chain stores (which were, by then, firmly entrenched in the United States) and of Marks and Spencer,[4] which had become 'a byword for democratic fashion in the 1950s' (Glynn, 1978: 214). Gaining popularity, the store expanded in 1975 by opening a branch in Paris.

When Quant introduced the shortest skirt in history – the 'mini' – it systematically excluded older and larger women from being entirely fashionable. Youthfulness became the new feminine ideal in the 1960s, and the central market became the working girl rather than the socialite of the pre-war years. It was a revolutionary, yet logical, step to take. Significantly, it signalled a turning point in fashion: the principal focus was no longer on the well-heeled, middle-aged fashion buyer; instead, the market catered exclusively for the young, who had a more limited budget. Quant used popular London tourist sites as a backdrop for her fashion photographs, and had her energetic, youthful models hop, skip and dance down the catwalks. Ready-to-wear had taken the reins from haute couture. Quant became the first 'designer' rather than 'couturier' to determine the new direction in fashion.

Quant used western movies as an inspiration for her first collection, which was presented in London in 1961, and then parodied childlike garments such as knickerbockers, pinafores, playsuits accompanied by knee-high socks, berets and pigtails. The 'off-the-peg' clothes – which initially she made herself – displayed shapes that were simple and two-dimensional. She created a visual paradox by using evening fabric for daytime wear and vice versa, combining bright, unexpected colour combinations and conflicting patterns. Her clothes were designed to appeal to those in their teens to mid-twenties, and were made from easy-care, crease-resistant, washable synthetic fabrics[5] suitable for an active lifestyle. Quant's rise in the fashion industry signified that clothes were no longer a sign of a woman's social position and income group. Hilary Radner quite rightly suggests that 'snobbery had gone out of fashion' (2001: 185). As home sewing grew in popularity with the new technologically advanced sewing machines, Quant produced designs for Butterick Patterns in 1964 to enable her styling to reach a larger market in a way that was affordable to all. Her philosophy towards dress has often been compared to that of Chanel: they both produced a holistic look with totally coordinated accessories.

According to Radner (2001: 186–8), 'The Look' was a term coined by Quant, made up of 'image, attitude and association' that underlined physical activity, dieting and the development of a confident self-image. Arguably, the concentration on 'self' materialized out of the reflectiveness of the baby boomer generation, and the notion of the expendability of taste, which broke fashion's rules. Fashion photographers responded to this emphasis on movement and the increased interest in sportswear quite literally, by constructing the effect of spontaneity in their fashion photography. According to *Vogue*, Martin Munkasci,[6] working for Fashion Editor Carmel Snow, created in fashion photography 'a new aesthetic of urban life ... stylistically, the genre exploits the techniques of immediacy (and disposability) that characterize the mass media in general' (Radner, 2001: 187–8). A new kind of fashion photography and modelling developed as well, pioneered by American Peggy Moffitt, whose asymmetric bob (courtesy of Vidal Sassoon) and gestural poses introduced the ideal woman as young, expressive and athletic. Models clung to helicopters, were dropped into haystacks and encased in plastic bubbles floating down the River Seine in Paris. Page layouts in fashion magazines were composed of images tilted on their sides to emphasize the diagonal line – which, in graphic design terms, created visual movement. The notorious photographer David Bailey helped to establish Jean Shrimpton as one of the leading fashion models, along with the boyish-figured Twiggy, in the 'Swinging '60s'.

FIGURE 5.11 *English fashion designer Mary Quant (front, centre), at her show of fashion footwear, 'Quant Afoot'. Quant's Mod look redefined youthful fashion in the 1960s. (Photo by George Freston/Fox Photos/Hulton Archive/Getty Images.)*

Alternative fashion

Fashion was no longer just about the label on your clothes, but the experience of finding clothing to express one's ideology and lifestyle. After Quant's Bazaar had demonstrated the need for young consumers to have a place to congregate as well as shop, boutiques opened up in fashionable hot spots in London on King's Road, Kensington, and Carnaby Street, offering a total shopping experience that included loud music, casual service, nominal privacy in changing rooms, and inexpensive, rapidly changing styles. This may sound identical to today's fast fashion boutiques, but in the 1960s this presented a radical shift from the typical experience in large, formal department stores filled with static trends and mass-produced goods.

The quintessential London fashion boutique was embodied by Biba. Founded in 1964 by Barbara Hulanicki, a fashion illustrator who started her own label with a mail-order catalogue business the previous year, Biba became a trendsetting label with its eclectic clothes. Starting as a casual boutique that turned into a superstore during the label's ten-year heyday (1964–74), Biba was a hotspot for celebrities as well as a moderately-priced store for the average young consumer. The Biba style is often described as romantic, including unusual earthy colours, floral prints, and styling the individual in a sleek 'skinny' silhouette with fitted sleeves and long hemlines. The overall look moved away from the Mod styles of the 1950s and early 1960s which had been the basis of Carnaby Street mainstream fashion. Unlike Quant's Bazaar, which included designs by other designers, all products in Hulanicki's store were exclusive to the Biba label, and short runs of designs meant fresh styles were available every few weeks.

Hulanicki and her husband Stephen Fitz-Simon, who managed much of the business side of the label, spent long days in the store, well attuned to what customers were seeking. A young mother herself, Hulanicki developed a childrenswear line in 1967 reflecting elements of Victorian children's clothing. Customers travelled from outside London to spend a day shopping at Biba, which not only represented the latest trends, but embodied youth culture of 1960s London; to shop or work at Biba was something of a status symbol, which only increased as celebrities embraced the store's eclectic style. Expanding her business into cosmetics, handbags and other products, Biba came to represent a lifestyle brand rather than a fashion label; celebrities such as Twiggy and Bianca Jagger were fond of hanging out at the art deco location, drawing throngs of admirers and fans. Changing locations from Abingdon Street to Kensington Church Street and finally High Street (1964–9), Hulanicki reached the peak of the brand's popularity with Big Biba, a seven-storey department store (1973–5). Following poor management and compounded by problems with shoplifting and a recession, Big Biba closed in 1975 and Hulanicki lost control of the Biba Limited to Dorothy Perkins, who had become a partner in 1969.

Hulanicki's boutique came of age alongside several others in London during the 1960s, including Hung on You, Top Gear and I Was Lord Kitchener's Valet. Kitchener's was founded in London's Portobello market in 1964, selling redesigned Victorian military clothing, which was in style at the time as British youth sought to redefine connections to authoritarian concepts of the country's colonial past. Redcoats designed at the shop were photographed on celebrities including Jimi Hendrix, Eric Clapton and John Lennon. The Beatles, whose military-inspired costumes on the album cover of Sgt. Pepper's Lonely Hearts Club Band were designed by M. Berman Ltd. and photographed by Sir Peter Blake, are essentially Victorian military suits fashioned in brilliantly coloured silk satin – a kind of rebellion in and of itself.

But the psychedelic zeitgeist was embodied by Granny Takes a Trip, founded in 1966 by Nigel Waymouth, Sheila Cohen and John Pearse, a Savile Row-trained tailor who ultimately became the main designer for the label. Inspired by Waymouth's collection of vintage clothes,

FIGURE 5.12 *Polka-dot minidress by Biba, May 1972, shown in the Manchester Daily Express, UK. The original caption reads: 'The way most men would like to spot a woman. This dotty mini-skirt, in red and white crêpe, has a matching jacket. Join the two bits with a polka-dot belt and they make a mini-dress. (Photo by SSPL/Getty Images.)*

the store started out selling refashioned vintage clothing, soon evolving into new clothes made with historic designs. Pearse shopped at Pontings and Liberty of London to buy cloth produced in the East, or inspired by Asian textiles, such as Indian bedcoverings that he fashioned into dresses, or William Morris florals used to make tailored jackets. Much of the affinity for these Eastern-inspired textiles went in hand with the hippie penchant for travel throughout Asia. These were often juxtaposed with Victorian and Edwardian military paraphernalia and design details. Despite its location in a then-unfashionable part of London – 488 King Street at the 'World's End' – Granny Takes a Trip was launched to success by a feature in a *Time* magazine article ('London the Swinging City', 1966). The boutique was famous for its ever-changing façade: a window that was smashed in by looters was covered in plywood that was alternately painted with murals including Native American chiefs Low Dog and Kicking Bear, followed by a Pop Art portrait of Jean Harlow; and then attached to the front half of Pearse's 1948 Dodge. But the real success lay in its clientele: the biggest names in rock music bought clothes at Granny's, including The Rolling Stones and The Beatles, who wore Granny's on the album covers of Between the Buttons and Revolver, respectively, in 1966. Inspired by the boutique's atmosphere and clothes, The Beatles opened their short-lived Apple boutique in December 1967, emulating the feel and style of Granny Takes a Trip. However, at the height of its popularity, Pearse left for Italy in 1968 to work in theatre, and in 1969 Waymouth and Cohen sold the shop to Freddie Hornik, who took the store in a new direction.

The 1960s witnessed the intersection of fashion, music and popular culture including drug use; the 'trip' was often a reference to experiencing the hallucinogen lysergic acid diethylamide (LSD). The bright colours and blurred edges induced by the visual and sensory experience of the drug inspired both art and fashion to shift in a new direction (Pinnock, 2018). In search of spiritual enlightenment, hippies travelled to the Middle East and India to join ashrams and orders, bringing home clothing from their travels, representing their new mind-set in opposition to the establishment. Music icon Cat Stevens (now Yusef Islam) converted to Islam, while Eric Clapton and The Beatles travelled to India to study transcendental meditation with Maharishi Mahesh Yogi (later exposed as a fraud). The interest in Eastern spiritualism, which was seen as the antithesis of the consumerism that had consumed the Western world, came to be represented by dress and textiles from these regions, indicating the wearer's unconventional ideology and international travel experience. As press coverage of hippie gatherings showed the colourful attire of this subculture, designers and manufacturers began incorporating elements of their style into mainstream offerings; by 1968, a 'Hippie-Gypsy look' was developed by American designer Ken Scott. Accordingly, there is some overlap between what was considered 'Hippie' style and what is now known as 'Bohemian'. Although the roots of what it means to be a 'Bohemian' date to the nineteenth century (see Chapter 6), both styles incorporated non-Western fabric and garment styles such as beaded and embroidered kaftans and collarless shirts. Anti-war sentiment in America was tied to Hippy beliefs to 'make love, not war', also indicating major shifts in sexual morality; and the phrase 'Turn on, Tune in, Drop out' coined by Harvard professor-turned-hippie-LSD-kingpin Timothy Leary (1966), encouraging young protestors to reject traditional education and lifestyles. Colour and curvilinear designs feature prominently in styles popular among this demographic, and came to represent anti-establishment views. In short, alternative fashion came to represent alternative lifestyles.

As Yves Saint Laurent had consistently noted, clothes were a form of protest. Handmade peace motifs, the marijuana leaf, love beads and headbands became symbolic expressions of a counterculture that resisted the influence of mainstream American society. The hippie culture adopted multicultural styling, including Afro hairstyles, facial and body painting and adornment – all of which had been adopted as a sign of 'Black Pride' during the Civil Rights Movement of the 1960s. Tribal customs such as ceremonial love-ins reinforced members' constructed identity as belonging to a rebellious and non-conforming social group. The hippie movement began in San Francisco's Haight-Ashbury area and spread quickly across the country. This subculture group refused to work, own property or material objects (other than a guitar), nor were they prepared to embrace the Great American Dream. 'Dropping out' became a romanticized, alternative lifestyle for the young, whose denim and patched dungarees became appropriated as a symbol of working-class, socialistic ideologies. Second-hand and vintage clothes were worn with hippie pride. The hippie movement had an unprecedented influence on global fashion, and very rapidly became a worldwide phenomenon. Haute couture designers, jumping on the bandwagon, sold the look – though not the dogma – to the highest bidder.

Zandra Rhodes

Rhodes, a British designer, was one of the first to capitalize on this new street style. Rhodes' colourful guise echoed her creations as a textile artist. She emerged from a textile art background, first studying at the Medway College of Art and then receiving a scholarship to continue her studies at the Royal College of Art in London. Like Quant and Hulanicki, she set up her own boutique, making up her own garments in the Fulham Road Clothes Shop. She capitalized on the labour-intensive 'ethnic' look, with hand-dyed chiffon and silk fabric in brilliant rainbow colours with hand-beaded or embroidered features. Rather than cut up textiles to create a highly tailored garments, she created large-scale prints, such as the 'Knitted Circle' series, as the template for long, loose garments based on the caftans of Asia and Africa. These 'ethnic' dresses suited progressive upper middle-class women who wanted to demonstrate their high-mindedness or their individualized personas. She dressed celebrities such as Cher and Freddie Mercury; in the 1980s, Lady Diana was a devoted patron.

FIGURE 5.13 Vogue 1970: *Model and actress, Natalie Wood wearing a hand-printed, chrome-yellow felt fabric with swirling scarlet pattern dress designed by Zandra Rhodes, of London. (Photo by Gianni Penati/Condé Nast via Getty Images.)*

Rhodes, a perfectionist down to the last detail, researched the themes of her collections thoroughly before she started to design specific textiles for each range. Her diverse influences, like those of Saint Laurent, came from history, nature, her travels, street styles and other designers' work. Her ranges have included the Chinese collection, the Ayers Rock collection, the Shell collection, the Zebra collection and the Conceptual Chic collection. In the 1970s, she became famous for her punk fashions, which she appropriated from the street (see Chapter 6 for a discussion of punk and Rhodes' involvement in propagating the style). She designed a range of wedding dresses made up of ripped white fabric, creating holes and frayed edges that were pinned together with 18-carat gold safety pins from Cartier – the ultimate juxtaposition of high fashion and anti-fashion (see Chapter 6). Still designing in 2020, Rhodes' work has been featured in several retrospective exhibitions at the Mingei International Museum in San Diego, CA (2011) and the Fashion and Textile Museum of London (2019–20).

Laura Ashley

Popular culture not only influenced designers such as Saint Laurent; when television sets became available to large sectors of the community in the 1960s, television programmes, as well as cinema, began to impact upon the stylistic direction of fashion. Series such as *Little House on the Prairie* (1974), set in the days of late nineteenth-century American settlers, kindled a historical revival of Victorian working-class dress. Classic books describing nineteenth-century life became popular, and reprints of old favourites such as *Little Women*, *Pride and Prejudice* and *Tess of the D'Urbervilles* flooded bookshops. Perhaps inspired by a reaction to an age of accelerating change which proliferated advancements in technology, this nostalgia for the past and a revival of idealized romanticism had a substantial impact upon both the literary and visual arts, including fashion. The British designer Laura Ashley revisited the look of the long pioneer dresses of the late 1800s. Ashley's business began in 1957 when she was making 'country overalls' for women, which evolved into long, country-style dresses. By the mid-1960s, they had become a fashion fad amongst the young. By using textiles covered in small floral designs, reminiscent of Victorian wallpaper designs from the Arts and Crafts movement, the dresses recreated a romantic simulacrum of the image of a simple, uncomplicated lifestyle. These loose-fitting garments, which allowed for total freedom of body movement (no underpinnings required), were quickly adopted by students and artists alike, and proved to be an ideal form of alternative dress. This 'granny' dress preceded the 'peasant' dress, and soon flowing, hand-painted and embroidered ethnic-look garments were entering high fashion in the couture houses of Yves Saint Laurent, Bill Gibb and Zandra Rhodes.

According to Laver (1995), the early 1970s paved the way for the stylistic pluralism of the 1990s:

Individuality and self-expression were paramount. Clothing was often customized with embroidered, appliquéd and patchworked designs. Tie-dyed T-shirts became popular. Colours were muted and textiles predominantly made from natural fibres. In Britain, at the top end of the market, Bill Gibb became famous for his stunning appliquéd and embroidered designs and Zandra Rhodes for her exquisite, ethereal, hand-screened silk and chiffon garments. In Italy, the Missonis did much to elevate the status of knitwear in fashion, incorporating subtle patterns and blends of colour.

1995: 266–67

Valerie Steele's *Paris Fashion* (1998) insightfully comments that the 'obsession with British and American popular culture' – seen across Europe and Asia in the proliferation of Saint Laurent's pea jackets and pop art dresses, and Cardin's use of industrial zippers – was actually generated from ideas that came out of Seventh Avenue rather than Paris.

Summary

Paris was reestablished as the epicentre of haute couture by Christian Dior following the Second World War. By the 1950s, couturiers such as Cardin and Saint Laurent expand into ready-to-wear offerings, also paving the way for the use of licensing. Courrèges and Cardin experimented with futuristic designs inspired by outer space, while in London Mary Quant developed stylish Mod ensembles for young consumers. As sentiment grew towards effecting social justice and changes to the established system, young people began to use clothing as a representation of their beliefs. The rise of the fashion boutique, featuring alternative dress and vintage clothing, is in sync with a growing movement among youth who want to live and dress differently from their parents. The 1960s were the first moment in modern fashion history during which popular youth culture influenced high fashion. Ironically, trends that were designed for maximum self-expression and originality would soon become mainstream, with Eastern-inspired designs and tie-dyed garments dominating the couture and luxury ready-to-wear runway by the end of the decade.

Notes

1 As President of the *Chambre Syndicale de la Haute Couture Parisiènne* (1937–47), Lelong played a critical role in preventing the Nazi relocation of Paris to Berlin as the centre of couture during the Second World War.

2 The Musée De La Mode, Paris staged the retrospective exhibition in summer 1986 and in Moscow in December 1986. It opened in the Hermitage Museum in Leningrad in February 1987.

3 Statistics indicate that this impacts to a considerable degree upon the young, as some studies – e.g. Pujol (1992) in Gare (2000: 180)—show that, of the percentage of French men who make a concerted effort to dress fashionably (including anti-fashion, approximately 45 per cent of the sample group), the majority are classified as young (under thirty years of age) or relatively young.

4 According to Glynn (1978), Marks and Spencer remained the classic of the genre, 'keeping up with its customers so adeptly that [they] could be anything from a duchess to a cleaner'. During the Interwar period, Marks and Spencer 'had a price limit (as did Woolworth's), which restricted its fashion sales: five shillings' (1978:11).

5 The fashion press in the US was largely supported by chemical companies which promoted these new fabrics, such as Bri-nylon, Ban-lon and stretch fabrics such as Crimplene and Lurex (Bliekhorn, 2002: 68).

6 There is some controversy regarding this claim. According to *Vogue*, the Munkasci photo of Lucille Brokaw was the first action photo made for fashion (see *Vogue*, 1 April 1947: 141 and 1 November 1954: 86; Radner, 2001: 188). According to *Harper's Bazaar*, the first fashion photograph taken on the move and on the street was taken by Jean Moral in 1932, but the most famous was Munkacsi's shot; both were taken for *Harper's Bazaar*.

6

The Postmodernization of Fashion

Introduction

This chapter will consider additional changes in the fashion system, with a focus on anti-fashion as an extreme postmodernist response. Postmodernism as a concept emerged in the 1960s as a mark of the end of the modernist approach to art and design. In fashion terms, it could be translated as anti-haute couture or anti-fashion. This could include the use of deconstructivist sewing, pattern-making or cutting techniques, which created a less than perfect finish. From one approach, it could reference fashion that produces a form of ugliness, breaking the codes of classical beauty. Alternately, it could be a self-mocking, self-reflexive comment on individual taste, or upon the fashion industry itself, or the attitudes and mores of a particular society or group within that society.

Postmodernism in fashion and art

The term 'postmodernism' was applied to art and design movements that emerged from the 1960s to the present day. Fundamentally, postmodernism can be characterized by a number of things, seen individually or in combination with each other. First, it is essentially anti-modernist – 'modernism' being a term referring to idealism and the concept of 'good taste' in design, which dominated the visual arts in the Interwar period.

Second, postmodernist art and fashion often appropriate imagery from earlier historical or cultural eras, or use material from other contexts. Revival fashion, or 'retro' fashion, revisits fashion styles from earlier decades or centuries, and can reveal cross-cultural or counter-cultural ideas. Combinations of a variety of ideas, styles, images, textiles, colours or patterns can create a form of *bricolage*, a range of pluralistic forms or a pastiche. Fashions might recontextualize imagery from artistic, popular cultural, industrial, scientific or mixed-media sources.

Third, art and fashion can be used as social or political markers, as they both have the capacity to advertise an individual's representation of self as well as critiquing society in general. This can be realized through the use of deconstructivist techniques, symbolic imagery, or the juxtaposition of different materials or images in the work to create a visual paradox; or simply the use of text to communicate the message. Postmodernist design often uses humour to create notions of irony, satire or parody, enhancing the power of the projected message.

Finally, postmodernist art and design embrace new technological materials and methods. Conceptual art can be recorded in digital form using electronic equipment; performance art can be recorded; and installations can be created when a number of objects interact with each other within a defined space. Materials other than fabric, such as paint, rhodoid plastic, PVC, resin, vinyl, see-through synthetics, reflective metals or industrial materials, can be used to dress the body (see Chapter 5). The fashion industry has been reliant on the technological development of new fabrics, textures and colours, as well as computer-aided design, to transform and reexamine materials and processes.

The aim of postmodernist design is to be provocative – in other words, to ask more questions than it answers. In our society, what constitutes 'good taste'? In *Vogue* in 1971, a feature article asked 'Is Bad Taste a Bad Thing?' (it featured a Yves Saint Laurent collection that mixed and matched diverse patterns in combination with each other). Has all fashion become anti-fashion? Why are postmodernist fashion designers defying conventions and forcing the viewer to reassess what constitutes acceptable design in today's technocratic society? Since the latter half of the twentieth century, fashion design has questioned gender constructs, sexuality and moral values, addressed humanistic and environmental concerns, and asked – either implicitly or explicitly – what value history plays in contemporary dress. Has fashion become a theatrical parade, a masquerade for individuals to mask or reveal their true identities? Just as artists have questioned 'What is art?', designers similarly ask 'What is fashion?'

The rejection of fashion

Anti-fashion has often been defined as a form of nihilism, in much the same way as a revolutionary break with tradition in the fine arts has been labelled 'anti-art'. When this deviation becomes accepted as mainstream, the notion of the avant-garde disappears. A study of historical fashion quickly reveals that, in revolution, the mode of dress becomes a badge of political affiliation, for example in 1780s and 1790s France during the French Revolution, when a sector of society – primarily comprising the young – known as *Les Incroyables* and *Les Merveilleuses* displayed extremes of dress as a means of expressing their rejection of the 1790s Reign of Terror period. Visual symbols were displayed by revolutionaries, such as the *tricolore* ribbon and *pantalons* worn by French revolutionaries, to represent their rejection of the aristocracy (see Chapter 1).[1]

A return to this exaggeration and distortion in dress emerged in the late 1970s and 1980s, when British punk recreated the most nihilistic fashion worn since the French Revolution. Effrontery in dress, obscenity in language and offensiveness in behaviour characterized the urban punk warrior. Punk fashion used visual violence rather than political violence to prompt a response from middle-class society. Elements of contrast and contradiction proliferated in the costumes of the street punks, whose tribal and ritualistic body accessorizing – body piercings, tattoos and mohawk hairstyles – suggested metaphoric links to earlier societies considered 'primitive' by the modern Western world. Punk music formed the backbone of this counter-cultural movement, which used dress to display its defiance of the establishments, the institutions and the canons of mainstream society.

Clearly, it seemed that there was one dominant aesthetic emerging in fashion – a look of poverty, which dominated street style clothing. Yet it was more than poverty; it was aggression, a demand for attention. In Britain, the young railed against the dominant ideology and punks replaced their more passive hippie counterparts. The economy in the early part of the 1980s was in recession, issues of global poverty dominated, and the disparities between rich and poor – even in the wealthiest nations – continued to rise sharply. England, by 1975, had reached its highest level of unemployment since the Second World War, with the young being the hardest hit

FIGURE 6.1 *Punks in London in the 1970s. Punk styling included mohawks, tattoos, body piercings and T-shirts with punk bands or slogans. (Photo by Erica Echenberg/Redferns.)*

– especially those who were the least educated and who lived in the lowest socio-economic areas of London. Britain's economy took a turn for the worse when Harold Wilson's Labour Party came to power and immediately imposed IMF (International Monetary Fund) restrictions on citizens, which many believed cut public expenditure and increased the cost of living. Angry working-class Britons felt that they had been betrayed by their own party. It was a time when youth reacted heatedly against the hypocrisies of the Establishment. This socio-political disorientation contributed to a social backlash in their music, their fashion and their lifestyle.

The Sex Pistols, the leading punk band in Britain, criticized the autocratic nature of the country with savagery and bitter humour through the lyrics of their *God Save the Queen* single: 'There's no future in England's dreaming.' John Lydon (also known as Johnny Rotten), lead singer of the Sex Pistols, complained: 'If you weren't born into money, then you might as well kiss your life goodbye; you weren't going to amount to anything ... you were told at school, you were told at the job centre, that you didn't stand a chance; you should just accept your fate and get on with it' (the Sex Pistols' documentary, *The Filth and the Fury*, 1996). When London's streets filled with rubbish due to the continuing strikes of the mid-1970s, Lydon decided that it would be fitting to wear torn trousers and garbage bags cut up to make T-shirts as an outrageous method of presentation – a new aesthetic. On a more conservative note, Barnard (2002) argues that: 'The punks produced their own music and clothing in opposition to the music and fashion system that had become monolithic, unadventurous and predictable' (2002: 136). A number of young artists alternated between art performances and punk performances, and one group called COUM Transmissions held a scandalous exhibition in London's Institute of Contemporary Art in 1976 called *Prostitution*, which documented Cosey Fanni Tutti's activities as a model for a pornographic magazine and resulted in the group being banned, unofficially, from holding any more public exhibitions in England. The following year, the Sex Pistols' records were also black-listed by radio stations (Goldberg, 2001: 182).

Art and fashion school students helped to define the new look, which became immensely design-conscious. Shiny gold industrial fabrics and plastic-coated cottons were used, along with metal fastenings including zippers, studs, spikes and safety pins. Zippers and webbing used for pockets were placed everywhere on the garment – the more bizarre the position, the better. For some, it was a revival of the 1950s look, with straight-leg drainpipe Teddy Boy trousers worn by men and voluminous angora sweaters worn by women. For others, the look was unisex – functional but sinister. Punks became increasingly hostile in their dress, adding tribal mutilations, body piercing and swastika tattoos, and accessories that symbolized their obsession with bondage and other sadomasochistic interests. They wore lavatory chains around their necks, used tampons as decorative accessories and featured pornographic imagery on their T-shirts. Their clothing was dirty, usually tattered and ripped, defiled with obscenities, and held together with pins and string. For the punks, fashion became ugliness – an external form of visual intrusion. They sourced their eclectic clothing and accessories from charity shops and found objects, produced home-made items, and even shopped at sex shops and army surplus stores. This insolent, anti-authoritarian presence appealed to disaffected youth around the world, and quickly became a global phenomenon. Interestingly, with time, this defiance ate through the very fibre of the entire fashionable world.

At first, punk fashion seemed quite distasteful to the *beau monde*. No one really wanted to be reminded of the pain of poverty, or the undignified way that it morally attacked individuals and families. The punk aesthetic was steeped in shock value, and it revered what was considered distasteful. As an anti-fashion statement, it was designed to disturb and disrupt the complacency of wider society. Statistics have indicated quite clearly that this fashion was a product of social economics. Historians thought it would be short-lived – merely a fad – but it has mutated over and over again, tied to global recessions that have continued into the twenty-first century. In the early 1990s, it was called neo-punk; in the mid-1990s, it evolved into a generic 'grunge' street style (see Chapter 8).

Vivienne Westwood: Anarchy as inspiration

Vivienne Westwood has had a long and influential career in fashion, despite her beginnings in anti-fashion. Rejecting her early training as a primary school art teacher and suburban married life, Westwood began her career in fashion with Malcolm McLaren in 1974, opening the SEX boutique in London. Primarily involved with alternative music, McClaren had managed proto-punk band the New York Dolls before becoming manager of the Sex Pistols.[2] Johnny Rotten (John Lydon) wore Westwood's clothes, and the Sex Pistols helped to put punk rock into the popular media with their loud anti-music and their obscene behaviour. Adapting punk aesthetic into her designs, Westwood's aggressive and visually provocative form of dress shocked the fashion audience in the 1970s. Not only did Westwood initially imitate the punks' eclectic DIY look, appropriating imagery from a diversity of sources, but she was able to sustain her anti-establishment reputation throughout her career.

Rebranding the SEX store in 1976, Westwood and McLaren reopened as Seditionaries: Clothes for Heroes and became an important resource for punk style and clothing. Focusing on the power of imagery, Westwood's work included torn and faded T-shirts printed with images meant to shock the viewer, such as the Jubilee portrait of Queen Elizabeth II printed on torn muslin, with a safety pin through her mouth (fig. 6.2) (also in the collection at the Victoria and Albert Museum, T.93-2002) or pornographic images. The SEX store sold to both punks and prostitutes, incorporating elements from bondage practices into garment design, such as straps, stilettos with spikes and latex dresses. Following key appearances by the Sex Pistols in 1975

FIGURE 6.2 *Designer Vivienne Westwood with Malcolm McLaren outside Bow Street Magistrate Court, after being remanded on bail for fighting. McLaren managed the punk rock group Sex Pistols, whose satirical song 'God Save the Queen' was banned in England; Westwood wears a T-shirt depicting Queen Elizabeth II's Jubilee portrait with a safety pin through her mouth – imagery akin to treason in earlier eras. (Photo by Daily Mirror / Bill Kennedy/ Mirrorpix/Mirrorpix via Getty Images.)*

wearing her punk garb, Westwood's hand-printed, distressed garments gained popularity, becoming relatively expensive for the sector on which it was based.

Westwood and McLaren renamed their shop World's End in 1981, staging their first catwalk show at Olympia for the Pirate collection and transforming the look from Westwood's previous punk aesthetic. Still maintaining its connection with the outlier, the Pirate collection was unisex and eclectic, including oversized ruffled shirts, striped Buccaneer trousers and wide sashes with non-Western prints and historic garment cuts. The ensemble was accessorized by pointed Pirate hats and buckled boots, which inspired the trend for pixie boots throughout the early 1980s. This visual 'plundering' of historical garments would inform Westwood's work going forward, which continued to evolve based on her research (Westwood, n.d. 'The Story so Far').

As punk was absorbed into the mainstream, Westwood moved away from her original style but continued to present subversive collections, creating new associations with dress for her viewers. Her early collections include Savages and Buffalo (Nostalgia of Mud) (1982) and Punkature (1983), in which Westwood explored outerwear as underwear, and the juxtaposition of bowler hats with layered tops and full skirts.

The 1984 Witches collection was inspired by New York artist Keith Haring's visual symbols, including garments knitted or printed with Haring's hieroglyphs. After Witches, Westwood's collaboration with McLaren came to an end, and her work continued to explore unexpected avenues. Paintings from the European Romantic period (seventeenth and eighteenth century) and historic English tailoring became the basis for several collections into the 1990s, including a play on the corset and bustle which now represented controversy, rather than conformity and confinement.

FIGURE 6.3 *World's End Fashion show for the Pirate collection, Autumn/Winter 1981/2, the first catwalk show of Vivienne Westwood and Malcolm McLaren, at Olympia, London, 1981. (Photo by David Corio/Redferns.)*

As writer Ted Polhemus ([1978] 2011) affirms in his seminal book *Fashion and Anti-Fashion*, the function of anti-fashion is to maintain constancy with style outside the organized system of fashion change. Just as the 1960s experienced the shift of hippie/bohemian dress from streetwear to high fashion, no longer signalling a break with the establishment, the subsequent appropriation of punk elements into the fashion system immediately recontextualized the style, creating yet another layer of meaning in the evolving definition of anti-fashion.

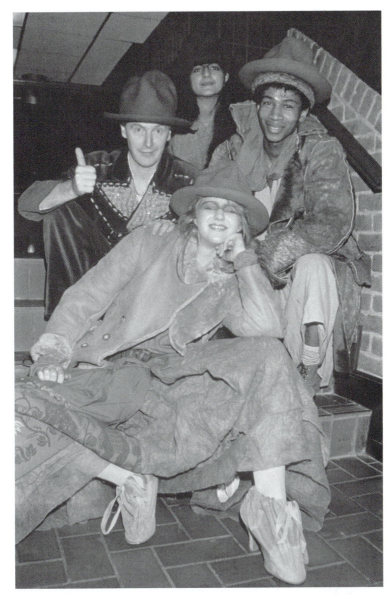

FIGURE 6.4 *Malcolm McLaren (left) and models wearing outfits from designer Vivienne Westwood's 'Buffalo' collection, London, February 1983. (Photo by Dave Hogan/Hulton Archive/Getty Images.)*

Zandra Rhodes adopted punk styling in the 1970s and 1980s as part of her repertoire, despite her early bohemian leanings. Rhodes's highly priced slashed and torn garments symbolized an economic irrationality – a social paradigm where a new ethic was embraced and the deconstruction of the fabric reflected, quite literally, the deconstruction of past values. There was an intrinsic irony in the adoption of this aesthetic into designer wear – an industry that fetched high prices as it seemingly mocked this underprivileged sector of society. Rhodes's collections, in particular, caused controversy. Polhemus (1996: 94) disparagingly comments that: 'The European fashion centres are churning out chic imitation punk garb and Zandra Rhodes – "High Priestess of Punk" – fattens her bulging bank balance by selling the punk image to Dallas, New York and Chicago.' He argues that the punk fashion was about anti-fashion and anti-commercialism – both of which Rhodes ignored. He insists that her garments defied the unexpected nature of true punk fashion, as everything she did was calculated and created with

FIGURE 6.5 *Zandra Rhodes attends the Costume Institute Gala for the 'PUNK: Chaos to Couture' exhibition at the Metropolitan Museum of Art on 6 May 2013 in New York City. (Photo by Dimitrios Kambouris/Getty Images.)*

the intention of being aesthetically pleasing. While Rhodes's Conceptual Chic collection is decidedly glamorous, Steele (2000: 97) argues that Westwood was the direct inspiration for Rhodes's designs. Unremittingly critical as Polhemus was, Rhodes' appropriation of images, themes and symbols from a different cultural context was inherent to her practice – a practice that would only continue in the cycle of fashion at large.

As discussed throughout this volume, cultural appropriation is simultaneously critiqued and celebrated in the fashion world; but in the context of punk styling, where did the appropriation begin? Were the street punks appropriating the traditions of tribal societies with the body ink, mohawks or body piercings practiced in ancient cultures, which once held social and talismanic significance? Was it an affront to the homeless population to purposefully distress fabrics and safety pin them together again, then sell these 'looks' at exorbitant prices? When mainstream designers began incorporating punk elements into their repertoires, they further disconnected from the original messages of these visual phenomena – and in disconnecting, are perhaps opening up new channels for communication.

Like so many of the street style fashions that were slowly absorbed by the fashion houses, copied by industry and then sold back to middle-class consumers, both hippie and punk fashions proved to be highly successful business enterprises. For McDowell (2000), hippie fashion ironically created a new form of status, that of 'dressing down to please oneself rather than dressing up to please others' (2000: 467). Identification with a particular group in society is considered one of the prime motives for wearing a particular form of dress. Polhemus and Procter (1978) argue that adornment allows us to assert ourselves as individuals, but it also allows us to identify ourselves as part of a social collective. Similarly, Batterberry and Batterberry (1982) contend that, for the hippies, self-expression in dress became an article of faith in their code of rebellion. In socio-political terms, their dress mirrored what they believed. When fashion designers embraced this look, the social value or currency inherent in their clothing and its social and political protest was diminished. By the end of the 1970s, and well into the 1980s, at least superficially, most fashion had become a form of anti-fashion, following the directions of a proliferation of subcultural modes of dress.

Fashion and music

The loss of punk's shock value created a void that would be superseded by the next 'New Wave' in fashion and music, and later identified by this moniker. The confluence of synthpop music and post-punk styling developed organically from a small group of club-goers in London in the late 1970s. Frequenting Billy's in Soho and an old cabaret, the Blitz – taken over by Welsh pop star Steve Strange and Rusty Egan in 1978 – this group of artists and musicians created original fashion ensembles weekly, gathering to admire one another's outrageous attire. The media referenced the group as the 'Blitz kids' (*Daily Mirror*, 1980) but settled on the term 'New Romantic' in response to the affinity for garments with elements from the early Romantic period of the eighteenth and nineteenth centuries. Strategically, the Blitz was located in Covent Garden between the Central and St Martin's art schools, and the venue's Tuesday night dress offered budding designers including John Galliano and David Holah of BodyMap a test bed for their experimental styles. Modelling their ensembles on a makeshift catwalk and self-referencing as 'Peacock Punks' or 'The New Dandies', admission to the club was reportedly based on the originality of the ensemble (BBC Documentary *The New Romantics* 2001). Often utilizing vintage garments as a base, this heterogenous group took a DIY approach to clothing, blurring gender lines through cross-dressing and heavy use of make-up. This same group was acquainted with Westwood through McLaren's involvement with music, and World's End pieces from the 'Pirate' collection were donned by musical groups: Bow Wow Wow's Annabella Lwin, Adam Ant, Duran Duran's John Taylor and Culture Club's Boy George are all photographed or filmed wearing Westwood's post-punk ensembles. The syncretism in the music echoed the look: Adam Ant added an extra drummer to his band to create a 'tribal rhythm' and to emphasize the warrior paint across his eyes, offset by the eighteenth-century-style military jacket and ruffled cuffs. Coiffure played heavily into the look: heads were half-shaved, teased with bouffant poufs, or falling across one eye hiding half the face; or alternately grown long and dyed rainbow colours, arranged in Caribbean-inspired dreadlocks. The visual pluralism of this period during the early 1980s echoed the postmodern ethos.

In musical performance, the theatrical element was amplified by the 'Glam' movement, one that embraced sequins and cross-gender dressing as part of the live performance. Originating in London, Glam musicians include David Bowie, Gary Glitter, Freddie Mercury of Queen and a number of post-punk bands that experimented with iridescent fabrics and styles. This overlapped with much of the androgynous look that included long hair, tight leather clothes, and heavy make-up seen on the members of Kiss or Alice Cooper, and other 'glam metal' bands. Led Zeppelin and Black Sabbath, whose sound was dominated by electric guitar heavily influenced by Jimi Hendrix in the 1960s, set the precedent later identifying this genre as 'heavy metal' or 'hard rock'. Their fans – mostly white suburban kids in Europe and America – identified with them by growing their hair long and wearing T-shirts printed with the band's logo or image, with jeans or leather pants.

In New York City, a new form of musical performance was created through the use of multiple turntables, amplifiers, and spoken word: the origins of rap. Beginning as spontaneous rhyming to a consistent rhythm, rap – its origins from the slang for speaking, or 'rapping' – developed into a genre that fell outside of musical norms. Rap was codified on the streets of New York City in predominantly Black and Latino neighbourhoods, addressing socio-political issues such as poverty and racial inequality; many of the same circumstances that plagued London during the punk era were mirrored in 1970s New York. Hip-hop – which was rap set to music – gained popularity once it was recorded by independent labels such as Def Jam Recordings, founded by Rick Rubin and Russell Simmons in 1983, signing groups such as LL Cool J, Run DMC and the Beastie Boys. The founding of cable TV and the first music-only channel, MTV (1981), brought the visuals of this era to a suburban international audience, playing heavily into the identity of hip-hop. Performing artists wore track suits and Adidas sneakers, while brightly coloured Graffiti art on subway trains and abandoned buildings were the backdrop for album covers and rock videos. Young artists in New York, such as Keith Haring and Jean-Michel Basquiat, brought the vibrancy of this artistic style into the formal art world; Haring, an admirer of Warhol's Pop Art, blurred lines between commercial and fine art when he founded his Pop Shop at 292 Lafayette Street in Soho in 1986, selling memorabilia and T-shirts with his iconic drawings.

The impact of MTV as a source for propagating 'underground' style through music videos to a broader audience cannot be overstated. By the early 1980s, the sheer lace blouses of Madonna, military-style jackets of Duran Duran, and colourful agender garb of Culture Club was emulated by fans across the globe. Steve Strange and a few other Blitz kids appeared in Davie Bowie's Ashes to Ashes video (1980), which pushed the boundaries of both video production and popularized the New Romantic look overall. This, again, plays into the question of how an anti-fashion style can maintain its symbolic function when it is absorbed into the mainstream.

Anti-fashion as feminism

Historically, deviations from expected styles of dress were viewed quite differently for women than for men. Early dandies such as England's Beau Brummel gained cultural capital by rebelling against the polychromatic fashions of the day, using their appearance to raise their status in society and inventing a new social order (see Chapter 1). Brummel's impeccably tasteful dress and personal demeanour were highly regarded, even amongst the aristocracy, and proved to be more influential than class identification. However, when women attempted to wear unconventional dress at the same time in history, it was seen as a cultural affront to the bourgeoisie. When the actress Sarah Bernhardt was photographed wearing trousers, she explained that she wore them only in her sculpture studio, for practical reasons. She appreciated that if women wore trousers or loose-fitting smocks, without corsets, it would be regarded as a counter-cultural assault on modesty, decency and femininity. According to Barwick (1984: 121), these clothes were 'outrageously different, contemptuous of convention, escapist, theatrical, for the Edwardians the whole Bohemian effect was outrageous'.

Finkelstein (1996) reiterates: 'Throughout the history of women's social and economic struggles, dress signals an individual's politics or morality' and that the wearing of trousers and bloomers 'has been regarded as a blatant signal of female sexual abandon and rebelliousness' (1996: 70). Beginning in the 1850s, women's rights advocates and health reformers began to provide women with more practical and healthy dress. Trousers worn under skirts constituted the initial effort; this began with the introduction of 'bloomers', based on full-legged Turkish trousers[3] and named after one of its proponents, Amelia Bloomer (Tortora and Marcketti, 2015: 362). This was followed by underwear reform and the adoption of aesthetic dress. Usually worn without corsets in the home, these empire-waisted garments were often constructed of draped layers of soft, transparent silk fabrics. They sometimes shared design elements with classical Greek or medieval clothing. The earliest visual examples of this clothing can be seen in the photographs and drawings of the family members of the pre-Raphaelite painters. The adoption of aesthetic dress was supported in large part through the efforts of the Liberty Company beginning in 1884.

The turn-of-the-century suffragettes purported to use 'male' strategies to lobby for their cause. When they attempted to burn down empty factories as a form of sexual protest, these acts outraged conservative members of society, who indicated that 'not only were they violating their feminine roles', but that they were 'advocating a range of unorthodox, even criminal practices' (Finkelstein, 1996: 70). When several members of the feminist group in London, including Emily Pankhurst, were jailed, they subsequently staged hunger strikes as a form of protest. Again, these actions readily provoked hostile reactions from the general public. Not only was the name of the suffragette movement blackened, but it discouraged the average woman from adopting its dress reforms. It is ironic indeed to note that, by the 1920s – when women in most Western countries had gained the vote, the right to own property and the right to be educated – this style of casual dress had become fashionable.

Some of Westwood's most innovative work came from her early years, when she used underwear as outerwear – a postmodern trend that was seen later in the collections of Gianni Versace and Jean-Paul Gaultier, amongst others. This move also highlighted the role of fetishism in sexuality – an issue that was assuming greater importance in critical thinking about the cultural construction of sexuality. Considering that the feminists of the 1960s and 1970s were full of rage and strictly anti-sexist in their views, the rebellious nature of Westwood's blatant use of sexuality did not seem to fit well with their ideological focus. Arnold (2001: 47) argues that

Westwood pioneered a fashion for young women that was threatening and overtly hostile, thereby freeing them from the need to aspire to a particular fashionable ideal of beauty. Mulvagh (1992) claims that Westwood was the only designer who directly researched gang cults among the young, and designed to suit this taste, while other designers such as Rhodes, Mugler, Montana and Gaultier merely applied the style to their collections (Mulvagh, 1992: 344, 356).

Women artists in the 1970s and 1980s also adopted a much more blatant and provocative stance in their work. Judy Chicago became infamous for *The Dinner Party* (1974–1979), where a large, triangular table was set with symbolic ceramic plates in homage to women's history, the plates featured a floral-like sculpture that was supposed to represent the female vulva. According to the artist, *The Dinner Party* aimed to end the ongoing cycle of omission in which women were written out of the historical record. The scale of the installation – 14.5 m (48 ft) on each side – visually symbolizes the magnitude of female achievement traditionally reserved for men.

As pottery, textiles and craft skills were seen as women's work at this time, these seemed to be the most appropriate media for parodying sexist society. American Barbara Kruger used graphic design to create a series of provocative posters that challenged the perceived stereotyping that women had endured for years. *Untitled (I shop therefore I am)* of 1987 portrays the previously held belief that consumerism creates identity.

Cindy Sherman uses clothing and performance art to depict stereotypical roles that women play in society in her *Untitled Film Stills*. Her methodology is based on constructing individual personas to reconstitute the identity of self and to mimic mass media's configurations of femininity. The series is both humorous and devastating at the same time. In another series, she questions the notion of the ideal female body when she uses prosthetic body parts procured from a medical supply shop to create garish robotic figures that mimic human actions. Also, her photographs of large, old, sagging women comment on a new ideal of beauty, and she deliberately turns genital imagery into a form of pornography. Cindy Sherman's practice (in the early 1980s) witnessed fashion's entry into art's discourses (Townsend, 2002: 50). Dressing up in designer clothing (from the collections of Gaultier and Kawakubo, amongst others), she bridged the gap between art and business. Townsend argues that:

Fashion has for some time taken its cues from art, not Hollywood . . . [and yet at the same time] art's response had largely been to incorporate fashion into its own histories . . . [Sherman's] costumed performances within the photograph referenced the emergence of a new generation of designers such as Jean-Paul Gaultier, one of whose jumpsuits was worn by the artist in *Untitled # 131*, 1983. Sherman also directly interpolated her imagery into the discourse of imagination and consumption, that she analysed by producing it in collaboration with a New York retailer, Dianne B, who used a range of the images for advertising purposes. What was, at one level, a critical commentary, became, through the process of its creation, an extension of the subject of its critique.

2002: 52

Not surprisingly, her ambivalent photographs were among those included in the Spring/Summer 1993 issue of *Harper's Bazaar*.

Both Sherman and Westwood share a similar sense of irony and irreverence, and combine an interesting aesthetic and concept in their work. Westwood reportedly stated: 'The only reason I'm in fashion is to destroy the word "conformity". Nothing's interesting to me unless it's got that element.' Her breakthrough came in 1989, when John Fairfield, the publisher of *Women's Wear Daily*, named her as one of the top designers in the world, amongst Yves Saint Laurent,

Giorgio Armani, Emmanuel Ungaro, Karl Lagerfeld and Christian Lacroix (McDermott, 2000: 10). In 2004 the Victoria and Albert Museum chose Westwood's work for a travelling exhibition – an honour rarely accorded to a living designer. She received an OBE (Order of the British Empire) for services to fashion in 1992, and in 2006 she was made a Dame.

Japanese conceptual fashion: Miyake, Yamamoto and Kawakubo

Much of contemporary anti-fashion was spearheaded by a group of Japanese designers who melded traditional Japanese garment forms with a different form of street style, presenting garments based on cultural preservation and inquiry, rather than protest. Their Zen-based beliefs, based on a preference for simplicity and naturalness, led them to create works unaffected by the shifting tides of fashion. The subtlety in their work and their distinctive stylistic philosophy have been sustained for decades on the catwalks of Paris.

Since the 1970s, the Japanese fashion design of Issey Miyake, Yohji Yamamoto and Rei Kawakubo of Comme des Garçons has had an unequivocal impact on Western dress. Offering a new and unique expression of creativity, they have challenged the established notions of status, display and sexuality in contemporary fashion. Ignoring stylistic trends, these Japanese designers work within a postmodernist visual arts framework, appropriating aspects of their traditional culture and embracing new technological developments and methodologies in textile design. Yet, at the same time, they infuse their work with meaning and memory. The subtleties inherent in their textiles and forms promulgate a new aesthetic in Western dress. Miyake, perhaps the most revered designer in Japan today, has consistently propagated new ideas, new materials and new design directions, which accommodate the modern lifestyle of contemporary women. While the work of Yamamoto and Kawakubo was initially framed as another form of anti-aesthetic, their contribution to the evolution of twentieth-century fashion has been more profound. Their understated work underlines the notion that culture, conceptualization and experimentation can be integral to fashion, as they are to art. By the end of the century, they had helped to change the face of fashion irrevocably.

Postmodernist fashion relies on visual paradox – underclothing becomes outerwear, new is replaced by old, and propriety in dress is replaced by a total lack of respect for the display of status and value systems. Highly priced, slashed and torn garments symbolize an economic irrationality. A social paradigm is created and a new visual ethic is embraced. The literal deconstruction of fabric and finishing techniques seemingly reflects the deconstruction of past values.

Harold Koda, Fashion Historian of the Metropolitan Museum of Art, referred to this new concept of dress, as seen in the work of Yamamoto and Kawakubo, as the 'aesthetics of poverty' – a phrase that seemed to aptly describe the new dress code. This duality of an extravagance (designer fashion) masked in the garb of noble poverty creates a paradox particular to the Japanese culture. In the traditional tea ceremony, the highly refined and polished are fused with the rough and the natural. The aim is to create an effect of sublime beauty, expressing naturalness and ease. The Japanese preference for understatement is coupled by a love of old things that imply accretions of time. In their poetry, for example, they acknowledge that perishability is a necessary element of beauty and the words exemplify their grief over the fragility of both beauty and love. In their pottery, they choose simple and irregular forms, perhaps cracked, as they represent both humility and an appreciation of the traces of the individuality of the potter. These aesthetic sensibilities are integral to the work and philosophy of these contemporary Japanese fashion designers.

In Western terms, Koda compared the 1980s trend with the 1890s, a time that also 'saw decadence as an aesthetic ideal' (Martin and Koda, 1993: 97). In ideological terms, dress design has undoubtedly responded to social, political and economic instabilities throughout history. In the 1970s, 1980s and 1990s, global events such as high rates of unemployment, youth revolutions, anti-war sentiment, global poverty and environmental catastrophes impacted greatly upon the conscience of society, and became implicit in postmodernist visual arts practice. While cultural differences existed, both punk fashion and the work of Japanese designers Yohji Yamamoto and Rei Kawakubo reflected this practice. The Japanese fashions were characterized by torn, ripped and ragged fabric, and uneven and unstitched hemlines – a disarray that was quite subversively calculated. Subsequently, due to their unprecedented influence, a new form of anti-fashion emerged as the dominant aesthetic in the early 1980s.

For centuries, Western fashion has doggedly adhered to a structured and tailored fit, which extols the virtues of sexuality, glamour and status – the mainstay of European haute couture design. Returning to Veblen's conspicuous consumption as the key motivational role that the display of wealth in dress has played throughout history, this visual sumptuosity reflected individuals' standing in society, their status in a hierarchical order, and defined their position within a social class system. While Veblen questioned the need for this perceived pecuniary emulation, he argued that this material display of wealth reflected a 'status anxiety'. Arguably, this nineteenth-century notion of social class elitism gradually lost momentum as waves of middle-class consumerism blurred the distinctions between the classes throughout the course of the twentieth century. As history has shown, this growing 'democratization' of fashion eventually led to a contradiction of modernist ideals and practices.

What defined modernist haute couture fashion – the uniqueness of the design, fine finishing techniques, unblemished surfaces, exquisite tailoring and hand-sewing – gave way to the predominance of mass-produced prêt-à-porter clothing. Yet this new culture of dress presented by the two Japanese designers actually appeared to mock the exclusivity of the earlier modernist fashions. In fact, according to fashion historian McDowell (1987), the Japanese designers Kawakubo and Yamamoto 'made few concessions to traditional Western ideals of dress, chic or beauty' and their clothes were 'as much a statement of philosophy as they were of design' (McDowell, 1987: 178).

The overall construction of both Yamamoto and Kawakubo's work was based on the Japanese kimono, an uncut garment that is shaped to the body by the addition of the *obi*, a wide sash. Approaching dress as uncut cloth that is shaped to the body, rather than shaping the body to fit the clothes, was an idea that had not been explored in modern Euro-American fashion. These avant-garde designers produced clothes that appeared radical to Western eyes, and could almost be seen as a homage to their country's past and a challenge to the increased Western influence there (Carnegy, 1990: 20).

After training in both Japan and Paris in fashion, Yamamoto created Y's, his ready-to wear line evoking Japanese work uniforms. In 1976 he created a menswear line, holding his first Tokyo catwalk shows in 1977. Yamamoto's 1981 collection with Kawakubo included oversized, asymmetrical distressed garments paired with flat shoes worn by peasants in Japan, an intentional rejection of the polished appeal of contemporary fashion. The media reaction to their collection was derisive; headlines screamed 'Fashion's Pearl Harbor' with Kawakubo described as a 'rag picker' and the overall look declared 'Hiroshima Chic'. Their models, dressed in black deconstructivist clothes, looked cadaverous, with either shaved heads or seemingly dirty,

FIGURE 6.6 *Yohji Yamamoto. Spring/Summer 1986. Yamamoto's collection moved away from oversized black garments in this collection, adding shape by wrapping the torso, and using prints and colour. (Photo by Niall McInerney.)*

unkempt hair, with pasty white faces that were 'devoid of make-up, apart from a disturbing bruised blue on their lower lips' (Mendes and de la Haye, 1999: 234). Arguably, the fashion press saw this work as a political statement – and perhaps it was. While punk fashion in Britain could be discussed within the context of a generational protest – one that relied on provocation, visual obscenity and hard-core sexuality – deconstructivism in the garments of the Japanese designers could symbolize, in a more passive and discreet way, their reaction to Japan's historical position in the post-war years.

During and immediately after the Second World War, Japan suffered years of austerity, and this impoverishment was imprinted on the minds of many. For two decades, in the 1930s and 1940s, Japan had suffered a very stringent economic environment. Japan was one of the poorest countries in Asia, and these years are commonly referred to as *kuraitani* – the Valley of Darkness. Arthur Golden's *Memoirs of a Geisha* (1997) describes, in an anecdotal passage, the feeling of desperation in 1945:

> Anyone who lived in Japan during this time will tell you that it was the bleakest moment in a long night of darkness. Our country wasn't simply defeated, it was destroyed – and I don't mean by the bombs, as horrible as they were . . . During the period of a year or more, I never once heard the sound of laughter. I've often observed that men and women who were young children during those years have certain seriousness about them; there was little laughter in their childhoods.

1997: 349

Both Yamamoto and Kawakubo grew up in post-war Japan; the context of their early collections can be better understood if viewed in this context of despair and darkness. It should be noted that, despite the initial reluctance within the fashion system to accept Yamamoto's work as beautiful, the popularity of oversized, layered black garments as daywear during the 1980s – especially in New York – was adopted by mainstream fashion through the influence of the designer's conscientiously anti-fashion collections. Yamamoto has been described as a designer who is driven by an existentialist philosophy, and whose work elicits an intellectualism that ties form with meaning and memory. In his autobiography *Talking to Myself* (Yamamoto, 2002) he asserts: 'Dirty, stained, withered, broken things seem beautiful to me'. The Japanese term *hifu* refers to a form of anti-style, and is seen as an undeniable element of Yamamoto's dressmaking. According to Yamamoto, one can actually feel *hifu* clothing – its confusion, shabbiness and disarray – as if it were reflecting a meagreness of spirit or sadness in the people wearing the clothes. In other words, the disarray of the fabric mimics the emotional fragility of the wearer. This merging of the emotional, intellectual and aesthetic encouraged many viewers to see Yamamoto's collection showings as a form of performance art.

He describes his work as being 'contradictory' to the commercialism of Western fashion. He creates clothing that has a universal appeal, a timeless quality – clothes that are meant to last a lifetime. In the 1980s, he was greatly inspired by the 1930s photographs of August Sander, taken in the American Midwest during the Depression years. Images of farmworkers ploughing the dusty fields in their faded and tattered work clothes, and women and children huddled in shanty doorways, elicit an honourable dignity that he tried to emulate in his own collections. Yamamoto observes: 'I like old clothes . . . clothes are like old friends . . . What makes a coat truly beautiful is that you're so cold you can't live without it. It's like a friend or member of the family. And I'm terribly envious of that' (quoted in Chenoune, 1993: 305).

By placing Yamamoto's work within the framework of postmodernist visual arts practice in the 1980s and 1990s, it is difficult not to consider the work of conceptual artists such as Annette Messager, Christian Boltanski and a number of the postfeminist artists, who used clothing as a means to evoke an emotive response in their work and to link art with the everyday. Messager placed worn-out dresses under glass in wooden display boxes and hung them on the wall like paintings. Her *Histoire des Robes* (History of Dresses) series in 1990 is an affirmation of the feminine, and dramatically evokes a sense of melancholia and lost identity. Boltanski used actual lost property from railway stations to memorialize the unknown owners. These personal effects relate to the themes of loss, death and memories that have been buried. They are meant to remind us of the experience of remembering.

Authors often compare the work of Yamamoto and Kawakubo, as they were close friends for ten years. Kawakubo also finds beauty in the unfinished, the irregular, the monochromatic and the ambiguous. Placed within the context of Zen Buddhist philosophy, this translates as an appreciation of poverty, simplicity and imperfection (Leong, 2003). Kawakubo asserts that she does not have a set definition of beauty:

> I find beauty in the unfinished and the random . . . I want to see things differently to search for beauty. I want to find something nobody has ever found . . . it is meaningless to create something predictable.
>
> quoted in KAWAMURA, 2004

Kawakubo's conceptualization is inherent in her philosophy towards design, as she is always projecting forward to the future – pushing boundaries. 'It's not good to do what others do. If you keep doing the same things without taking risks, there will be no progress,' she said (*Undressed*, 2001). Kawakubo relies on spontaneity in her work: 'I could say that my work is about looking for accidents. Accidents are quite important for me. Something is new because it is an accident' (*Undressed*, 2001). While her work is uncompromising in its anti-fashion directions, like that of Yamamoto, it is still very personal and self-reflective. Despite the obvious push against the fashion system, Kawakubo commented in 1983 'I am not protesting against fashion. This is something else, another direction' (Metropolitan Museum exhibition guide for Art of the In-Between 2017: 3).

Redefining popular culture through heritage

Another strong link that ties both Yamamoto and Kawakubo to Miyake is their shared Japanese cultural heritage. This embracing of their indigenous culture could be read as a backlash against a previous celebration of 'outsider' popular culture. All three designers insist that the underlying influence of the kimono in their work is profound, agreeing that it is the space between the fabric and the body that is most important.[4] This negates the blatant sexuality of fitted Western clothes, and introduces the possibility of layered or voluminous clothing that becomes a sculptural form of its own. Yamamoto paid homage to traditional techniques, incorporating the ancient Japanese technique of *shibori* (indigo resist-dyeing) in his Spring/Summer 1995 collection.

Kawakubo comments on the 'gender-neutral' design of her kimono-inspired constructions: 'Fashion design is not about revealing or accentuating the shape of a woman's body, its purpose is to allow a person to be what they are' (*The Story of Fashion*, 1985). This is abundantly clear in her Spring/Summer 1997 collection Body Meets Dress, Dress Meets Body, where padded sections were added to the clothes to distort the back and hips of the body, thus critiquing the notion of the perfect female shape. Kawakubo stated: 'I want to rethink the body, so the body and the dress become one' (Metropolitan Museum exhibition guide for Art of the In-Between 2017: 8). This is very much in keeping with postmodernist practice, where self-critique and reflection challenge accepted norms of life and society. Does sexuality always have to be determined by body shape?

Kate Betts (2004) argues in *Time* magazine that Kawakubo invites an open interpretation of her work, but also suggests that this collection calls for some level of self-awareness. Kawakubo

FIGURE 6.7 *Rei Kawakubo for Comme des Garçons. Spring/Summer 1997. This collection, 'Body Meets Dress, Dress Meets Body', explores visual distortions. Often referenced as the 'lumps and bumps' collection, Kawakubo created asymmetrical forms through padding to challenge viewer expectations of feminine ideals. (Photo by Niall McInerney.)*

described her clothes as being for 'modern, working women. Women who do not need to assure their happiness by looking sexy to men, by emphasizing their figures, but who attract them with their minds' (Van Godtsenhoven et al., 2016: 229). This inherent feminist critique – obvious in both her words and her work – was echoed not only in many different forms in arts practice in the 1980s and 1990s,[5] but also in literature, media advertising, film and dramatic production.

Miyake's work comments on the recontextualization of the kimono to create a different aesthetic milieu. Miyake rejected the traditional forms of Paris collection clothing. Through the inventive use of fabric and successive layering, he developed a concept of fashion based on the 'essence' of clothing: the wrapping of the body in 'One Piece of Cloth' cloth, the underlying philosophy of his collections since 1971. He created anti-structural, organic clothing which takes on a sculptural quality that suggests a natural freedom, expressed through the simplicity of its cut, the abundance of new fabrics, the space between the garment and the body, and its general flexibility. Miyake stated: 'I learned about space between the body and the fabric from the traditional kimono . . . not the style, but the space' (Knafo, 1988: 108). Like Kawakubo, Miyake's designs also have parallels with architecture. His structures in bamboo recall Samurai armour, a rigid house for the body. These constructions exemplify ideas of the body moving within a space beneath an outer space (Holborn, 1988: 120).

Similarly, Yamamoto redefined male clothing forms when he introduced his Autumn/Winter 1985/6 'unstructured' men's collection with baggy, pleated trousers – a draped look that approximated Turkish harem trousers. Suit jackets lost their tapered waists, linings and padding were removed, and the way sleeves were mounted changed the male silhouette dramatically. Different textiles were used, such as soft, elastic fabrics made of viscose and crêpe yarns, and this new redefined form heralded the direction towards comfort and simplicity. Perhaps more importantly, Yamamoto saw this new aesthetic as a reflection of a new 'ideal of clothing'. He said: 'People don't "consume" these garments: they might spend their entire lives in them . . . that's what life is about. Real clothes, not fashion' (Chenoune, 1993: 305).

Another major factor that unites the postmodernist work of Yamamoto, Kawakubo and Miyake is their interest in experimentation in textile design. The Japanese fashion empire is built on the framework of its textile industry – just as, for centuries, the French industry has been. Kawakubo's use of textiles that conveyed meaning is inherent in her development of distressed fabrics: she worked with weaver Hiroshi Matsushita to reformulate the fabric on the loom to create various-sized holes that appeared as rips or tears. This experimentation was evident in Kawakubo's 'lace' or 'Swiss cheese' sweaters, knitted in stocking stitch with holes placed at random to create a slashed effect.

Some textile designers believed that, with growing industrialization and complex technologies, a more humanistic approach was needed in the creation of new textiles. In Japan, when one defines imperfections in fabrics, it is called 'fabric hand', as these aberrations are considered precious (Niwa, 2002: 238). This is used as an inherent criticism of the mechanical uniformity in textile production and experimentation with new methodologies in textile design. Matsushita refers to this technique as 'loom-distressed weaves'. In postmodernist terms, it is called 'deconstruction'.

Miyake is renowned for his research in textile technology. In his ongoing series of collections, Pleats Please, which first appeared in the Spring/Summer 1989 collection, the designer reinterpreted traditional pleating techniques by adding the pleats after the garment was sewn. The interplay of pattern and colour is heightened by the technique of heat-setting pleats in the synthetic fabric, referencing origami techniques and creating a kaleidoscopic effect with colours that move with the body. Pleating became one of Miyake's ongoing themes; *Interview* magazine

FIGURE 6.8 *Issey Miyake. Fall/Winter 1985. By utilizing shibori, a resist-dyeing technique used for centuries in Japan, Miyake references the rich textile traditions of his cultural heritage. (Photo by Niall McInerney.)*

quotes Miyake as saying: 'Pleats give birth to texture and shape all at the same time. I feel I have found a new way to give individuality to today's mass-produced clothing' (Saiki, 1992: 34). The series attests to Miyake's desire to produce adaptable clothing that is both functional and reflective of modern simplicity in an egalitarian society.

Textiles reference Miyake's cultural heritage in many different ways. He included *shashiko* – a Japanese technique for quilting cotton – for coats, and he also used a fabric called *tabi-ura*, formerly reserved for the bottoms of the fitted Japanese sock. Paper, originally used as a lining for winter coats worn by the ancient farmers, has been reintroduced in his collection showings. 'There are no boundaries for what clothes can be made from. Anything can be clothing,' he says. Miyake is inspired by the natural forms of shells, seaweed and stones. The oil-soaked paper used so commonly in the traditional Japanese umbrella is re-employed to form a translucent coat:

FIGURE 6.9 *Issey Miyake. Fall/Winter 1994. Miyake launched his 'Pleats Please' collection in 1993, created by heat-setting polyester to create a permanent pleat. (Photo by Niall McInerney.)*

The model glows through this golden paper skin, like an insect set in amber ... One of Miyake's most innovative images is found in the bark of a tree. The body can move inside a tube of fabric as if in a caterpillar skin. He asked: 'Did you know there's a tree in Africa where the bark comes off completely? It's round, just like a tube of jersey. I wanted to make something woven that was warped like African bark.'

PENN, 1988: 15

Architect Isozaki compares this to the hollow, seamless, sacred garments woven for the gods – which became the legendary prototype of human clothing. It becomes an archetypal dress, a universal, circular form (Holborn, 1988: 120). Perhaps this served as an inspiration for his APOC (a piece of cloth) collection in 1999, an ongoing series, where Miyake introduced a flat tube of white fabric that could be cut into a variety of garments – literally a capsule wardrobe.

Miyake's contribution to the invention of new synthetic fibres cannot be underestimated. In *Miyake Modern*, Simon (1999) remarks that one of the most remarkable aspects of his work is determined by 'an understanding of textile fibres, both natural and synthetic, and of fabrics, both hand-woven and traditionally dyed, as well as high-tech textiles that are not woven at all' (1999: 45). Mitchell, Curator of Fashion in the International Decorative Arts department of the Powerhouse Museum in Sydney, suggests that Miyake's work aims 'to rediscover the traditional beauty of a Japan which is disappearing; to emphasize the importance of industrially produced clothes by using synthetic materials' (quoted in English, 1999). It all offers fashion a focus as it walks backwards towards the twenty-first century, and offers suggestions for the future (Benaim, 1997: 7).

Conceptualization in postmodernist Japanese fashion

Both appropriation and recontextualization play a key role in the definition of postmodernist practice. Miyake's book *East Meets West* (1978) includes an essay by his close friend Arata Isozaki, the architect of the Museum of Contemporary Art in Los Angeles, which consolidates Miyake's link between his fashion design and architecture. The publication underlines the close association Miyake has always maintained with other art practitioners. For example, Leni Riefenstahl's photographs of the Nuba stimulated Miyake and fellow art director Eiko Ishioka. They both viewed the Nuba as magnificent specimens, wonderful human surfaces, as abstract as these African tribesmen's body designs. In 1989–90, Miyake used a stretch fabric to create a series of tattoo-like bodystocking garments that fitted the body closely. By embracing ethnic beauty, he treats the garments as a second skin. His collaborations with other visual arts practitioners have not only created a culturally diverse interface in Miyake's work, but have also infused it with a richness of symbolic reference and meaning.

All three Japanese designers rejected change for change's sake, and instead chose to work on the refinement and evolution of previous collections. This evolution of an idea was the basis of Japanese fashion. The conceptual process of serialization, revisited by many conceptual visual practitioners since the 1960s, is integral to the Japanese approach to design.

Miyake, Yamamoto and Kawakubo are often described as niche designers – designers who do not follow stylistic trends or directions. Unlike their European and American 'stylist' counterparts, they have not exclusively embraced the revivalist or popular cultural imaging that has inundated Paris catwalks for decades. The riotous and multifarious themes that we see in the repertoire collections of Alexander McQueen, Jean-Paul Gaultier and Vivienne Westwood find no place in the work of the Japanese designers. Nor is it likely that these designers will ever be nominated as possible head designers of other 'mega' fashion houses. Obviously, the uncompromising nature of the Eastern designers' work eliminates their suitability for such a role, despite the fact that the international press voted Kawakubo the leading designer in Paris in 1987.

The conceptual underpinning in their design work also explains why, in the early 1990s, their reputation as leaders in the international fashion arena was consolidated (English, 2004). It could be argued that Miyake, Kawakubo and Yamamoto all offered a meaningful alternative to the superficial, regressive and over-designed work of so many of the Western designers in the 1990s. Their work – more closely allied with postmodernist practice – did not fall neatly within the dictates of the established fashion industry, and as a result was not consumed by its self-imposed boundaries. Perhaps this is why it has appealed to noted art photographers such as Irving Penn, Nick Knight, Robert Mapplethorpe, David Sims and Inez Van Lamsweerde, whose photographs underline the notion that fashion can step beyond its immediate frame of reference. For example, the publication entitled *Issey Miyake: Photographs by Irving Penn* is a collaborative effort between the Japanese designer and the Western photographer, printed by Nissha in Kyoto (Penn, 1988). Three tons of Miyake's designs were shipped to New York, where Penn made his own choices. Penn, like Miyake, 'employs an art of reduction – his fashion photographs are emptied to allow the geometry of his clothes to be the sole uncluttered force. Penn's photographs are contextless, the subject without the surround' (Holborn, 1988: 118). In a similar way, Japanese landscape and woodblock print artists also concentrated their images by juxtaposing them with bare, unadorned elements. Penn presents Miyake's clothing as flattened, near-abstracted images in a white nothingness. The clothes disclose nothing of the bodies underneath, and sexuality often becomes ambiguous. Penn places Miyake's clothes within a neutral space to underline the notion that fashion can be seen as a reconsidered form.

Kawakubo worked collaboratively with American postmodernist artist Cindy Sherman in 1994 to promote her Comme des Garçons clothing (Glasscock, 2003). She sent Sherman garments from each of her collections to use as she wished. Sherman produced a series of unconventional photographs, which 'centred on disjointed mannequins and bizarre characters, forcing the clothing itself into the background'. Sherman presented Kawakubo's clothing in masquerade settings, but the confrontational, theatrical images are not about clothes, but rather a form of performance art. Sherman is renowned for her interpretations of mass media stereotypes of femininity. Her critique of 'fashionable' photography is in keeping with Kawakubo's approach to the business of fashion design, which is strongly inspired by the values of the contemporary art world.

Kawakubo also deconstructed accepted merchandising strategies by participating in the design of her shop interiors and exteriors. Her minimalist approach encompassed cracked concrete floors, warehouse tables for display of folded goods, and old refrigerator cupboards for storage. In 1999, she designed an architectural landmark building as Comme des Garçons' home base in Tokyo, with a curvy 30 m (98 ft) expanse of street-level glass screen printed with blue dots. From the outside, it creates a pixilated effect, with the customers appearing to be moving across a huge television screen like actors on a set. This type of self-reflectivity considers the notion that media advertising not only reinforces mass-market consumerism, but also becomes a reality in itself. Japan's willingness to embrace the avant-garde is evident in its fine art, architecture and fashion design. Japanese design had an unprecedented impact on Western design during the twentieth century. The designers Miyake, Yamamoto and Kawakubo produce work that is imbued with the history of the past, yet looks dynamically towards the future. They have become leaders in the international fashion industry. Their clothing has created a visual language that strengthens the converging line that exists between fashion and art. Miyake is amused when his work is so often referred to as an art form, stating that: 'Clothes are more important than art.'

Younger designers, who are apprenticed to these leading fashion masters, take many years to develop their trade under the tutelage of their employers. In Japan, it is called *enryo* – a supreme void of ego that demonstrates complete dedication to the group. For Westerners, it is a kind of learned humility. Naoki Takizawa, designing for Issey Miyake, combines a mixture of new and different materials to discover unexpected forms. Using a disciplined approach, he experiments with space age materials, some developed by NASA scientists, and combines them with natural fibres. Making clothing that conforms to Miyake's functional philosophy towards design has allowed Takizawa to continue the evolution of the company's Pleats Please collection. In 1993, he was the key designer of Issey Miyake menswear, and in 1999 he became head designer of the Issey Miyake label, leaving Miyake to concentrate on his APOC line. Like his mentor, Takizawa collaborates effectively with other renowned visual arts practitioners, and in his Autumn/Winter collection of 2004/5, entitled Journey to the Moon, he incorporated the popular cultural images of Japanese artist Aya Takano. In this collection, distinctively Japanese animé figures set in pale blue and pink futuristic landscapes embody eccentric street-style imagery.

Kawakubo's protégé, Junya Watanabe, has become one of Japan's leading fashion designers. His design work is aesthetically challenging and he, like Takizawa, has continued the traditional heritage of experimental textile development. His work relies on complex construction techniques, tactile surfaces and a sculptural interplay of light and shade. While he extends Kawakubo's conceptual approach to fashion, his work responds to existing stylistic trends more directly. He pays tribute to historical revival, and playfully paid 'witty and irreverent homage to Coco Chanel with ropes of pearls entwined in the necklines of dresses or stitched to the hems of ever more complex ruffled and draped creations' (Lowthorpe, 2000) in his Autumn/Winter collection of 2000. Political reference aggressively appeared in his 2006 Spring/Summer collection, where 'violent head coverings created out of ripped gaffer tape, tattered mohair, studs, pins and nails were the order of the day' (Frankel, 2006).

A new generation of Japanese designers – many of them graduates of Central St Martin's in London – have joined the ranks of existing design studios, or have ventured to create new businesses of their own. Tao Kurihara joined Comme des Garçons in 1997, and – working initially on the Tricot line – studied directly under Watanabe for eight years before she was allowed to create a modest collection in 2005, at the age of thirty-one. Her collection, inspired by lingerie, was described as a confection of wool and lace translated into coquettish corsets and shorts. She now works with her own team of six designers.

Summary

Anti-fashion exists as a relational concept opposed to the organized fashion system. Although this postmodern concept originated in the 1960s when streetwear dominated the popular aesthetic, alternative dress codes of the 1970s and 1980s presented a visual mode to dissociate from and reject the establishment. Drawing upon tribal and folk traditions, punks presented a unified identity that expressed apathy and anarchy through dress by intentionally shocking the viewer. The impact of dress in popular culture is amplified in the 1970s with the union of Westwood and various musical groups in London. In the early 1980s, New York hip-hop style is also fused with music and popularized through MTV.

Design from Japan would also challenge traditional fashion through the works of Miyake, Yamamoto and Kawakubo. Visually adjacent to punk in its use of distressed fabrics, conceptual Japanese garments acknowledge the superfluous nature of fashion itself, while also presenting itself within the larger system. The 'aesthetics of poverty' inform both punk and Japanese anti-fashion, and were soon emulated by luxury ready-to-wear and couture, shifting its symbolic meaning. Based on this cycle, styles that are considered anti-fashion in one year become fashionable the next season, and the look of anti-fashion must keep changing – ironically linking it to the very system it rejects.

Notes

1 In late eighteenth-century France, growing disenchantment with the corrupted Bourbon court forced the dematerialization of colour and fabric in their garments, with skirts shrinking and jewellery disappearing. Ribeiro (1988) describes a young man of one of the first families in France 'attending the Theatre in boots, his hair cropt [sic] and his whole dress slovenly' (1988: 70). Clearly, it had become unhealthy to advertise one's elitist position in society. Again, the crinolines, bustles and corsets disappeared and rich fabrics were replaced with muslin, cambric or calico. At the same time, history also acknowledges the irrationality of dress worn by the *Merveilleuses* and the *Incroyables* during the 1790s Reign of Terror. A volatile mixture of youth rebellion and political dissent lent itself to the wearing of unkempt, crumpled clothing: men had long, straggly hair and wore exaggerated cravats and extremely high-waisted pantaloons with undersized vests; women wore oversized bows and bonnets, shapeless garments and had wild, untamed hair.

2 Numerous authors, including Sabin (1999: 3), insist that punk originated in New York in 1973 because of the existence of early punk bands such as the Ramones, Television and the New York Dolls, and point out that New York punk had a distinctly different look, sound and attitude to that which emerged in London in 1976.

3 Ironically, when Paul Poiret introduced 'harem pants' fifty years later—the same 'Turkish trouser' garment style that bloomers were based upon—he was hailed as an artistic genius.

4 The great value attached to kimonos and textile design is evident in the involvement of some of Japan's most famous artists in the design of the garments, such as the nineteenth-century print-maker Utamaro. Kimonos are considered art objects, handed down from generation to generation, and they have defined and contributed to the Japanese tradition of beauty.

5 Feminist artists such as Barbara Kruger, Cindy Sherman, Moriko Mori and the Guerilla Girls, among others.

7

The Deviance of Fashion

Introduction

Any deviance from the established social class differentiation, in terms of dress, was viewed as a serious threat to an ordered society. Historically, the wealthy and famous relied upon haute couture to produce their fashionable look, and a system was set up in which the couturier working from the epicentre of Paris created new styles every season, changing what was in fashion. These styles were thereafter copied and 'trickled down' to middle- and lower-class consumers through department stores carrying mass-produced garments.

A major disruption happened in the system during the Second World War, providing opportunities for local systems in New York and other locations to emerge and develop styles that suited their population, such as the American Look (see Chapter 4). Following the war, Dior's success with his 'New Look' collection in 1947 re-established Paris as the epicentre of couture, but the very nature of the industry had been changed by the rise of luxury ready-to-wear and licensing deals made between couturiers and department stores.

However, another major shift happened during the 1960s: the social strata that had been dictating fashionable dress shifted from the elite to the lower classes and to what the younger generation was wearing in the street. This is often referenced as the 'trickle up' (or 'bottom up') phenomenon.

As the twentieth century moved closer to the end of the millennium, the influence of street style increased, creating a give-and-take with couture that threatened the established system. A deviant approach to fashion emerged on the fringes as a postmodern representation of a total rejection of society's rules. However, unlike the beginnings of punk and street style, this new countercultural approach added satire and social commentary to define and differentiate their approach from within the fashion system.

Franco Moschino

Italian designer Franco Moschino used a neo-pop approach to create anti-fashion statements. Using irony as a postmodernist tool to critically comment on fashion orthodoxy, his work was considered both avant-garde and fashionably provocative. Within a similar visual arts framework, Moschino used both text and design to humorously communicate parodic messages. For example, he blatantly designed a ticker tape rendition that wrapped the body but left the buttocks exposed. With text running across the back spelling out 'C–H–E–A–P' in large letters, he produced a zany but tasteless comment. On another level, he combined Duchamp's conceptualism with baroque extravagance. He capitalized on the 1980s obsession with designer labels by creating a unique signature style for his customers, whom he said 'had their own distinct personalities'. At the same time, he produced pastiches of the work of other designers – commenting, for example, on the banality of much commercial fashion of the Calvin Klein type by producing his own line of underpants, worn on top of trousers and bearing the waistband slogan 'To Be Shown in Public' (McDowell, 1997: 199). For *Uomo Vogue* fashion journalist Mariuccio Casadio (1997): 'Through art, performances and a passion for the provocative and unconventional, ever present in his designs, as well as through a unique conception of exhibiting space and an understanding of gesture and pose, Moschino still holds a prominent intellectual position in fashion' (1997: 19).

Unpredictability was a strong element of Moschino's work, and his fashion shows turned into performance art with an underlying ironic critique. T-shirts and other garments printed with 'Now is all there is', 'IN LOVE WE TRUST' and 'You can't judge a girl by her clothes' used verbal puns that were characteristic of his humour. Moschino 'highlights the cruelties and paradoxes of contemporary culture, the endlessly regenerated power of the ready-made and the din of forms and banality by which we are controlled and surrounded' (Casadio, 1997: 30).

In the late 1980s, Moschino embraced technology, using short videos to highlight a selection of the clothes in his collections. In a revisiting of the 1960s, he designed a dress constructed from plastic-coated cards that were linked together, in much the same way as Paco Rabanne did, but overlaid them with printed images and synthetic materials (such as fake hair) not normally used

FIGURE 7.1 *Franco Moschino, Spring/Summer 1993. Moschino explores the commercialization of the fashionista by printing her with a UPC code. (Photo by Niall McInerney.)*

FIGURE 7.2 *Franco Moschino, Spring/Summer 1994. Always questioning the relationship of art, fashion and consumerism, Moschino presents a model in a paper bag with his label, commenting on conspicuous consumption. (Photo by Niall McInerney.)*

in high fashion. He pumped up jackets and stoles by using inflatable PVC materials in his Couture! collection. He appropriated fun imagery from film, animation, media and pop culture, to which the young at heart responded. To a greater extent, his work is reminiscent of Schiaparelli when he uses a *trompe l'œil* effect to create visual paradox. His Organic Bikini (which was made by sowing and watering real grass), hats in the form of wedding cakes, and white handbags dripping with melted chocolate, all paid lip service to the visual irony of neo-Surrealism, which reinvented itself in the early 1980s. The Label Queen dress, created from shopping bags for a window display in his New York boutique on Madison Avenue, made a reflexive statement about excessive levels of consumerism in society – a consumerism generated by the fashion industry in particular during this era of conspicuous consumption. Upon Moschino's passing in 1994 at the height of his career, *Vogue* magazine created a tribute to his work featuring accolades from his peers, including Armani, Versace and Galliano.

Similar to Moschino's use of materials to create social commentary, Swiss artist Sylvie Fleury collects shopping bags featuring designer labels, which become part of her museological installations. In her work *Delicious* (1994), Fleury entices her audience to make associations with wealth, glamour, style and status. The contents remain untouched as they sit on the gallery floor. Labels such as Chanel, Armani, Tiffany & Co. suggest the purchase of luxury items such as clothing, perfume and jewellery. Jessica Berry (2005: 39–43) suggests that the artwork centres on the process of shopping and discarding, and constructs the notion that the act of acquiring, for fetishist collectors, is vital to their enjoyment of the object. Berry argues that, unlike the pop artists of the 1960s and 1970s whose work critiqued consumerism, Fleury presents the fetishized commodity collection as positive and desirable. Her work underlines the irony of the museum as 'department store' – an issue debated by art historians Emma Barker (1999) and Mary-Anne Staniszewski (1998), who agree that many museums have become indistinguishable from shopping malls in order to promote interaction between object and viewer – coming full circle to the relationship of commerce and art discussed in context of the nineteenth-century department stores, established concurrently with national museums (see Chapter 1).

Viktor & Rolf

Throughout the 1970s and 1980s, revivalist fashion was in full swing, with the recycling of styles from earlier decades becoming an endless cycle of monotony. It would seem that, by the 1990s, Western fashion had exhausted its endless appetite for change. In a constant search for novelty, some designers looked back to previous historical periods, while others found a need to react or contradict that which had gone immediately before. This lack of direction seemed to be broadcast in the growing superficiality of styles that led Suzy Menkes (2000), former Fashion Editor of the *International Herald Tribune* and online *Vogue International*, to call these trends 'the caricatures of fashion'. Since 1993, the work of the maverick Dutch artist-designer duo, Viktor & Rolf, has illustrated and satirized the bankruptcy of ideas prevalent in haute couture showings.

Viktor & Rolf's work highlights these stylistic absurdities and parodies the lack of originality by adopting Dadaist strategies including irreverence, affectation and sensationalism. In their 1998 collection, for example, their 'conceptual' couture fashions featured distorted figures and an exaggeration of forms as they piled one garment after another on the fashion model, until her slight form grew to enormous proportions. In both a literal and metaphorical sense, their pumped-up volumes created fashions that were larger than life. This provocative work inspires a number of postmodernist interpretations. As an art performance,[1] it breaks away from the linear progression of catwalk models to an accumulative progression of garments from the collection using only one model. It comments on the role of the body in contemporary fashion as a non-sexual and non-gendered object. Conceivably, it also comments on the theatrical pomposity of couture fashion, which creates garments that are more suitable for the stage than they are for life.

Viktor & Rolf introduced the visual pun into the shows for the Autumn/Winter collection of 2000, by parading an evening coat covered in little gold and silver bells; more bells were sewn inside the kimono sleeves of a wrap coat and, again, a tuxedo jacket was smothered with miniature bells scattered like sequins. Satirically, Suzy Menkes commented that couture was sometimes described as being 'fashion with bells on it' (2000) – this self-reflective critique of fashion was a product of postmodernist counter-couture (see Chapter 6). Often referred to as the 'kings' of the international avant-garde fashion scene, they have parodied European haute couture for its history of excessive sumptuosity, and the Japanese designers for their extremist use of black. Ironically, their Autumn/Winter collection of 2000/1, when they brought out their Stars and Stripes collection – their first ready-to-wear collection – was their greatest triumph. While seemingly mocking American nationalism and being dubbed 'the flag bearers', they saw American culture as being globally present so they chose various American fashion icons including sweatshirts, polo necks and jeans to 'kick off' their more commercial line, a mass-produced range of clothing.

Viktor & Rolf established their names as couturiers despite the fact that they sold almost nothing (Horyn, 2000a). Informed by a sense of humour, they ridiculed the pretentiousness of elitist fashion, breaking traditions and conventions by riddling their clothes with intentional errors and contradictions.

The conceptual approach of the designers means that they don't always make dresses: from a collection that consisted solely of placards painted with the words, 'V & R are on Strike' (when they were broke) to an art installation that only featured press clippings (about themselves), the designers take Warholian pleasure and fascination in knowing that printed exposure is the means by which they are understood and the means by which they continue.

O'NEILL, 2005: 182

In October 2003, a retrospective exhibition of their work was held at the Decorative Arts Museum in the Louvre to correspond to the 2003/4 Spring/Summer prêt-à-porter collection showings in Paris. Those who look for connections between conceptual art and fashion applaud the courage (or the folly) of their work. Their more recent work has drawn inspiration from the surreal, playing with concepts such as *tromp l' œil* in their 2010 collection of seemingly disconnected tulle gowns. The Spring/Summer 2016 Haute Couture collection 'Wearable Art' literally played with clothing as art: broken frames with blank canvas or printed with well-known paintings became

FIGURE 7.3 *A model walks the runway during the Viktor & Rolf Spring/Summer 2019 show as part of Paris Fashion Week on 23 January 2019 in Paris, France. The model's frilly baby doll style dress is contradicted by its message: 'I'm not shy, I just don't like you.' (Photo by Thierry Chesnot/Getty Images.)*

the edges of the garments, as if the work had been grabbed off the wall and smashed through the head of the model. The 2019 Spring/Summer collection played upon the idea of the 'fashion statement' by making a series of looks with large, simple statements in block letters such as 'Get Mean' and 'I'm not shy, I just don't like you' that resonate with social media's direct and unabashed commentary. The clothing serves as an exaggerated backdrop for these giant text messages, created in tulle as baby doll dresses or gowns to contrast the ultimate feminine references with rudeness.

Martin Margiela

Like Hausmann, Schwitters, Rauschenberg and the Arte Povera artists, Margiela chose debased and abject materials and deconstructivist methodologies to draw attention to a new type of anti-fashion. In a very objective, scientific manner, he analysed, dissected and recontextualized his garments. As if working with him in a laboratory, his assistant designers wore knee-length lab coats, an eccentric mode of dress that was copied by his devotees worldwide. Taking a postmodernist view of fashion design, he worked with a microbiologist in 1997 to grow mould and bacteria on the surface of a collection of garments, which was intended to eat away at the fibre of the textiles when placed outside in the weather for a period of time. A paradox is thereby created, where the clothing can be remembered as objects of beauty whilst they are gradually becoming objects of disdain. This theme was common in the 1960s conceptual art movement, when an artist might leave pieces of stale bread on the outside windowsill and photograph them at various stages of decomposition. Margiela's decomposing installation of work, entitled *9/4/1615* and exhibited in the sculptural court of the Museum Bojimans Van Beuningen in Rotterdam in 1997, forced Ingrid Loschek (2009) to speculate that Margiela was comparing this process of the natural cycle of creation and decay to the consumer cycle of buying and discarding. Some read the installation as a comment on the issue of consumerism for consumerist's sake; others suggested that his work spoke about the cycle of fashion by symbolically alluding to the deconstruction of couture. At this time, the relevancy of couture was being challenged, and the world was experiencing a period of rapid, destabilizing change.

A postmodernist reading would suggest that Margiela presents many different layers of meaning in his work and would advocate that individual viewers should respond with multiple interpretations. In the catwalk show of his 1999 Spring/Summer collection, Margiela plays with conceptual and real fashion by draping a model in a picture of a shirt, as it would be catalogued online. This Surrealist approach to fashion display – a nod to Magritte's 'Ceci n'est pas une pipe' – indicates his cynicism towards the very system in which he is operating.

Margiela's Size 74 collection, Spring/Summer 2000, features ridiculously oversized coats, shifts, lingerie and men's business shirts. These larger-than-life clothes dwarf the wearer and make the body appear to shrink in size. By challenging the visual proportions of high-fashion garments, the viewer is forced to 'see' the clothes differently. Irony, inherent in the sizing, is created by the paradoxical idea that sample designer clothes are usually too small to be worn by the average woman, as they range from American size 6 to 8 to fit a model's figure. Margiela's clothes in comparison are gigantic, causing the viewer to conceptually scale down the clothing, and in turn, this clever contradiction demands critical reassessment of the fashion system that makes implications about beauty ideals in the fashion industry.

Fashion theorist Caroline Evans describes his work as being 'much more experimental and "cutting edge" than that of many contemporary artists who use fashion motifs in their work'

FIGURE 7.4 *Martin Margiela. Spring/Summer 1999. Margiela plays with conceptual and real fashion by draping a model in a picture of a shirt. (Photo by Niall McInerney.)*

FIGURE 7.5 *Martin Margiela. Spring/Summer 2000. Margiela's creations evoke the breakdown of fabric and fashion itself through deconstructionist techniques. (Photo by Niall McInerney.)*

(Evans, 1998: 73). Margiela experimented with the paradoxical concept of the 'inside becoming the outside' or at least being reproduced to appear to be part of the exterior garment. One of Margiela's most sought-after pieces by museum curators was one in which he borrowed the covering of a tailor's dummy and recontextualized it into a waistcoat made of linen canvas, which he then re-draped over the original mannequin. This, of course, takes on a surrealist perspective – a contradictory vision. The designer also deconstructs and reconstructs ideas relating to fashion detritus. When second-hand or throwaway clothing is given a new lease on life, it contradicts the traditional elements of glamour, beauty and novelty. Undoubtedly, he appropriated this notion from the Japanese contemporary fashion designers whose work reflects the notion of *wabi-sabi*, or finding beauty out of ugliness.

Margiela also rejected the age-old concept of the 'artist-as-genius' and refused to become a celebrity designer, never appearing on the catwalk, shunning public appearances and social aggrandisement of any kind in order to retain his anonymity. Similarly, both Picasso and Braque negated the idea of the uniqueness of the artist's originality as well, by signing each other's work in the early 1910s, when they were developing their objective concepts of analytical cubism. Like the Dadaists, Margiela worked collaboratively with his team at the Maison Martin

Margiela and would not respond individually to queries or correspondences. He retired as the head designer of the label in 2010, following retrospective exhibitions of his work in Antwerp, Munich and London.

Alexander McQueen

McQueen's work deconstructed fashion using a different approach. Trained as a tailor on London's Savile Row (1984–7), McQueen was intensely interested in tailored construction, inspired by historic garments but always using his skills as a craftsman to subvert the viewer's expectations. Informed by his work for theatre production of *Les Misérables* during his apprenticeship with Gieves and Hawkes, and later by his work on the film 'King of the Wind' (1990) for Richard Harris' frock coat, his menswear balances the line between fine English craftsmanship while exaggerating details of historic dress. Following a brief stint in Milan working for Romeo Gigli, McQueen was accepted into Central St Martin's in the early 1990s.

FIGURE 7.6 *Alexander McQueen. Spring/Summer 1995. McQueen's collection was inspired by Alfred Hitchcock's 1963 thriller 'The Birds' featuring printed silhouettes of flocks in flight. (Photo by Niall McInerney.)*

FIGURE 7.7 *Alexander McQueen. Spring/ Summer 1995. The collection played with gender stereotyping, placing men in skirts and shirtless women in trouser suits. (Photo by Niall McInerney.)*

McQueen's graduate show shocked the audience with 'Jack the Ripper Stalks His Victims', referencing the notorious nineteenth-century rapist/murderer through deconstructed Victorian garments. The whole collection was bought by London stylist Isabella Blow, who later became the designer's friend and advocate. Always a fashion disruptor, McQueen's first collections for women were not well received; his Spring/Summer 1995 'Birds' collection referenced the 1963 thriller by Hitchcock, which drew upon the movie's themes of killer attack birds combined with roadkill. The garments were printed with bird silhouettes and textures that resembled tyre tracks and oil splotches.

His subsequent collection 'Highland Rape' the same year made him a target for feminists everywhere: McQueen contrasted his own family's Scottish tartan plaid with lace and leather to create slashed and torn garments, with models that bore blackish makeup resembling bruises on their faces and arms, as if they had been assaulted. Despite being flooded with criticism from the press and feminist groups, the designer insisted that the title was in reference to the rape of the Scottish Highlands by the English, who occupied their lands for centuries and ended the Highlander way of life. Retrospectively commenting on the collection in an interview for *The Independent Fashion Magazine*, McQueen remarked: 'The reason I am patriotic about Scotland because it's been dealt a really hard hand' (Autumn/Winter 1999). Following the controversial

FIGURE 7.8 *Sarah Jessica Parker and Alexander McQueen attend the Metropolitan Museum of Art Costume Institute Benefit Gala, 2006. Parker wears a dress from McQueen's 'Widows of Culloden' collection, while McQueen wears a kilt made from his family tartan. (Photo by Brian ZAK/Gamma-Rapho via Getty Images.)*

Highland Rape collection, McQueen reprised the theme in Widows of Culloden (Autumn/ Winter 2006/7), using his family tartan in a reinvention of traditional Scottish dress styles that included draped and belted tartans and kilts, as well as revivalist Victorian dress and slim fitted suits. For the opening of the Metropolitan Museum's gala benefit dinner that celebrated the opening of the 2006 exhibition 'Anglomania: Tradition and Transgression in British Fashion', McQueen arrived with Sarah Jessica Parker in coordinated ensembles made of McQueen tartan, stunning the fashion community.

McQueen's work left an indelible impression on all who witnessed the displays of performative fashion, creating new trends and recontextualizing garments through details. The low-rise look characterizing the 2000s were actually drawn from McQueen's 'bumster' style of the 1995–6

FIGURES 7.9 and 7.10 *Alexander McQueen. Spring/Summer 1999. Model Shalom Harlow is spray-painted by robots in a runway performance. (Photo by Niall McInerney.)*

collection, in which the designer celebrated the bottom of the spine as an erogenous zone (Bolton, 2011).

From 1996 to 2001, the designer went to Paris to become the head of Givenchy, after which he focused on his independent label with financial backing from Gucci Group (now Kering) until his passing in 2010. His outstanding collections from this period were featured in 'Savage Beauty', a retrospective exhibition at the Metropolitan Museum (2011). Highlights included garments from several collections, including 'Voss' (Spring/Summer 2001) which played with alternative concepts of beauty; his 2003 Spring/Summer collection with its recreation of a shipwreck and pirate-inspired garments; and his runway shows were unconventional, with shocking but philosophical themes, and a performative aspect that recontextualized the display of fashion. His Spring/Summer 1999 catwalk show featured model Shalom Harlow in a white dress on a rotating platform, being spray-painted by robots, while the 2006 'Widows of Culloden' featured a hologram of Kate Moss floating in space like an apparition in lace. His final collection for Spring/Summer 2010 was 'Plato's Atlantis' featuring the hoof-like footwear known as 'armadillo shoes' worn by Lady Gaga, and a morphing of animal forms which subvert the function of traditional garments. After the designer's passing, Sarah Burton – who designed Kate Middleton's 2011 wedding gown – took over the label as creative director.

Harajuku street fashion

The deviance of fashion was not a solely Western phenomenon. Designers of Japanese street style shared the DIY philosophy of their British punk counterparts, and adopted the use of plaid material, T-shirts advertising punk bands, ripped clothing and studded accessories. Unfazed by mainstream designer trends, they embraced the hyper-celebrity culture of Japan and recreated illusions of *manga* – a popular cartoon art form aimed at adults – and animé characters in their clothing. This subcultural form of dress was contextualized within a popular culture that was always transformative, dynamic and fundamentally linked to trends of disposability.

Japanese youth were introduced to European street fashion by Shoichi Aoki and Noriko Kojima, through the publication of a magazine called *Street* in 1985. Paradoxically, they promoted these overseas trends in Japan and, in turn, Aoki became famous for documenting the visual response of Tokyo's youth to these new trends. For his monthly *FRUiTS* magazine, launched in 1997,[2] Aoki photographed the self-designed street style dress paraded through the streets and parks of the trendy neighbourhoods of Shibuya and Harajuku, a district of Tokyo renowned for the street style fashions worn by the local teens.

A diversity of custom-made 'looks' burgeoned over a five-year period. These included girls – known as *wamono* – who wore a collage of traditional elements of Japanese ancient dress with kimono, sashes and *geta* sandals combined with second-hand and home-made items; the cult of 'cuteness' or *kawaii*, which encouraged a childlike appearance complete with plastic jewellery and toys worn as accessories, highlighted by an overabundance of the colour pink; the baby doll Lolita look, with frills and flounces; and the Gothic Lolita look, sometimes dominated by black Victorian mourning dress, which created an air of elegance and a nostalgia for an entirely fictional past. Blatant sexuality – manifested in fetishwear of red net stockings, black leather skirts and leopardskin-patterned fabrics, perhaps influenced by Westwood and Margiela – became another version of street fashion. Further appropriations of the western cowboy look (*ganguro*), the tanned and blonde California girl or Mountain Witch look (*yamamba*), and the

American hip-hop look for young men, added to this aesthetic pluralism. Not only did these borrowed looks take traditional meaning away from the original cultural referents, but also perhaps recycled them into a meaningless fashion pot-pourri. Such styles were dubbed 'dressing up', 'putting on a show', 'playing at costumes' – these words described an outsider's reaction to the new direction of fashion.

More critical commentators described this devotion to fashion as self-indulgent and dishonourable. Gothic Lolita, for some, signified a 'nostalgia fetish' or 'a form of drag'. The wearing of black vinyl kimonos or full punk bondage gear with whitened faces and blackened eyes conveyed a much more sexually aggressive appearance than their doll-like counterparts. Any public display of youthful intimacy or sexuality, whether in the community, on poster advertisements or in the media, was considered immoral before the late 1980s, and was not tolerated. The press referred to young women wearing 'Harajuku styles' as the 'Sirens of Tokyo'. Whether this individualized styling represents a candid critique of the role of women in Japanese society and culture is difficult to ascertain. Kinsella (1995) argues that 'this practice of performative dress-up provides a hyper-real form of what the Japanese call "cosplay" (or "costume play"), as well as a nexus between the old, the new and various connected ideas about identity in relation to culture, gender and youth' (1995: 247–8). If we agree that diversity in dress is complicit with street style, and therefore depicts identity as subject to constant change, then the Harajuku street style emphasizes the way different images of femininity show how tenuous commodity identity can be. Most commodity-oriented subcultures have become complicit in the niche marketing of their own identities (Kinsella, 1995: 226). Entire stores in the Harajuku area, for example, cater for a total Lolita transformation – the consumer's link to an alternative lifestyle.

In highly populated urban Japanese cities, where loss of individual identity becomes inevitable and highly dominant, traditional male structures exist within the society, street style dressing offers teenage girls and young women in their early twenties a form of escapism. The notion of attracting attention, yet hiding behind the safety of a group, suggests a personal insecurity that can both challenge and reinforce consumerism. As the notion of feminism is relatively unexplored in Japanese society, the diversity of street style dress allows for an investigation of different models of the feminine. Clothing can be a form of identity, an expression of creativity, a form of entertainment or performance, but at the same time it can act as a subtle mode of non-conformity – a passive critique that counters the Japanese ideology of order, control, uniformity and impersonality. According to Hebdige (1997), subcultures are both a play for attention and a refusal to be categorized:

> Subculture is, then, neither simply an affirmation nor a refusal, neither simply resistance against symbolic order nor straightforward conformity with the parent culture. It is both a declaration of independence, of Otherness, of alien intent, a refusal of anonymity, of subordinate status. It is an insubordination. At the same time, it is also a confirmation of the fact of powerlessness, a celebration of impotence.

1997: 404

The Japanese ability to synthesize the ideas and practices of other cultures is central to its success in the international design industry. Appropriation, pluralism and fragmentation are inherent in postmodernist practice, whether it is in the decorative, applied or fine arts. The visual anomalies or contradictions evident in Harajuku street style fashion are peculiar to the Japanese culture. More importantly, the style evolved from individual choice; it was not determined by designer trends or dictated by conglomerate ready-to-wear markets. The notion of difference, based on the adaptation of so many diverse local contexts combined in Harajuku street style fashion, suggests that this way of dressing was one of the very few which was resistant to the stereotypes of globalization.

In 1994, Jun Takahashi launched his Undercover label in Japan which attracted a cult following in the Harajuku district. According to *Gap (Japan) Press*, the well-known prêt-à-porter fashion magazine, commenting on the 2002/3 Autumn/Winter collection, Takahashi's appeal emanated from his independent vision, which employed a 'twisted' aesthetic. His new shop, opened in Tokyo in 1992, featured stuffed animals and one-offs that had been taken apart and remade, displayed in a glass showcase. The theme of his collection that year was Witch's Cell Division, where items were disassembled through fasteners and put together in different combinations, similar to robots with interchangeable parts. Black etchings, like tattoos, covered parts of the models' faces; moons, stars and witchery images decorated the garments – creating a unique and somewhat bizarre collection. In the same year, he launched his collection on the catwalks of Paris, under the sponsorship of Rei Kawakubo.

The Japanese label 20471120, created by Masahiro Nakagawa and Azechi Lica in 1992 reimagined streetwear for fashion-conscious Tokyo youth, juxtaposing it with elements of Western couture. The futuristic brand was originally named Bellissima and renamed in 1994 with the numeric label, representing 20 November of the year 2047 (a date realized in a dream), when Nakagawa believed the future would be represented by individuality, creativity and diversity (Leone, n.d.).[3] Nakagawa and Lica reimagined fashion by referencing popular culture such as animé, music and streetwear in Tokyo subculture. Nakagawa references his fashion influences as a broad range of twentieth-century designers, from Coco Chanel to Vivienne Westwood, Comme Des Garçons, Versace, Martin Margiela and others, with the common thread that they all referenced subcultures in their brand. The brand was embraced by Harajuku youth, while also applauded by Paris couture.

In 1999, Nakagawa took the brand in a new direction by repurposing previously owned clothing in his Recycle project. After interviewing the wearers about the memories associated with their garments, they were reassembled into new ensembles. In addition to his concerns about fast fashion and wasted materials, Nakagawa's project suggests that too many memories are being discarded with the clothing, commenting on excessive consumerism in Japanese society. Nakagawa created manga characters in a short graphic publication, Hyoma (named after its protagonist), to tell the story of how recycling (or as we call it now, upcycling) could change our way of life. The first Recycle project was followed by many other themed collections; Recycle project #3 identifies a specific look for each decade of the twentieth century, including a take on Dior's 1947 Bar Suit that mimics the hourglass shape but reimagines the jacket with camouflage fabric.[4] Hyoma appeared as the mascot on many of the brand's clothing, and these items are now popular with a new generation of fashion consumers who value the brand's legacy.

Fashion imagery and notions of gender construction

It is significant that the Belgian designers, Dries Van Noten and Ann Demeulemeester, emerged as the leaders in the latter half of the decade. Van Noten, named International Designer of the Year in 2008 by the Council of Fashion Designers of America (CFDA), followed the Japanese lead in terms of consistency in his design. His work demonstrated the Belgian fastidiousness for superlative construction and cut, incorporating classical elements into contemporary design, and he aimed to create clothing that could be combined in different ways by different individuals. This pragmatic approach has been essential to his success over the past decade. Demeulemeester, in particular, seemed to capture the essence of the 'urban warrior woman' in her collections, and as leading journalists explained, her designs manifested the new generation of self-determined women who were emerging. Demeulemeester's clothes reflected this belief with their brutal honesty, sophistication and practicality. With the global recession impacting upon the fashion industry quite dramatically, especially in 2008, her approach to design as a form of problem solving and not just for consumption's sake seemed quite realistic. The long-term 'stayers', including Lagerfeld for Chanel, Gaultier, Kawakubo for Comme des Garçons and Westwood, stood their ground to ensure that their collections had a strong commercial edge. By the close of the first decade of the new millennium, the distressed global economy had forced fashion designers not only to increase their diffusion lines but to initiate new collection ranges including menswear; to consider new methods of marketing and distribution; to reinforce their strong brand identities; to align themselves pragmatically with sports companies; to interface with biomedical research pursuing the domain of health and well-being; and to embrace emerging technologies.

Globally, other directions that emerged underlined the economic squeeze of the latter 2000s. LVMH and others who sell luxury goods have been forced to divest themselves of small and unprofitable companies originally purchased in the booming 1990s. In the 'age of rational dressing', they exchanged John Galliano for Alber Elbaz, who had previously been at Lanvin, and Hannah MacGibbon took Phoebe Philo's place at Chloe. Other 'takeover' houses like Prada bought and divested itself of Jil Sander (twice), and Helmut Lang, whose very lucrative and influential label had been renowned for his iconic flat-front pants and his low-rise denim jeans made from intricate washes coupled with T-shirts. When Prada did not invest enough in the

FIGURES 7.11 to 7.13 *Ann Demeulemeester, Fall/Winter 2000. Designs in Demeulemeester's collection kicked off the new millennium by heralding the coming of a new age for independent women, discarding old notions of gender stereotyping in fashion. (Photos by Niall McInerney.)*

brand, it faltered. With syndicates such as LVMH managing so many of the best-known brands, the constant change of head designers made it very difficult to keep track of who was where. Interestingly, the second largest luxury company in the world (behind LVMH), Compagnie Financière Richemont, which concentrates on watches and jewellery (Cartier) rather than clothing, was the company that was making the strongest financial returns. Similarly, by 2010, the magazine *Grazia*, known for its budget outlook, had taken over the premier position in the fashion reader distribution stakes. While *Vogue* put out its biggest American issue in September 2007, advertising had dropped dramatically by 2009, and, in response, the magazine began to run a more austere format.

Out of this economic quagmire, the first millennium ushered in the beginning of a new era, a period when women felt stronger and thought their voices might be heard in the sociopolitical corridors of power. Initially, there had been a trend towards a masculinized form of feminism in dress, bordering on androgyny. The favourite model of 2001, Eleonora Bosé, was the daughter of a legendary Spanish bullfighter, and her strong jaw line, closely cropped hair and tattoos made her the personification of the ultimate 'warrior' woman. She was photographed by Steven Meisel and Bruce Weber for Italian *Vogue* and appeared on the covers of numerous other magazine covers, including *Dazed and Confused, Nylon* and *Pop*. Tom Ford chose her to model the Gucci range, and *Women's Wear Daily*'s caption said, 'Think Marlon Brando' and described the models in both Milan and Paris that season as 'Tough Cookies'. Interestingly, this transgender image paralleled the rise of interest in queer theory publications. Feminist theory academic Suzanna Walters commented that 'an endless commodification of difference goes on in our culture, an endless search for a variation on a theme that will sell women slightly new images of themselves' (Trebay, 2001).

According to New York fashion journalist Gina Bellafante (2004), 'the rise of corporate superbrands narrowed the range of stylistic roles a woman could play'. She explained:

> Broadly speaking, she could cast herself in the role of the Gucci woman and look like the sort of sexually hungry powerhouse who always picks up the check. Or she could become a Prada woman – efficient, coolly nostalgic and erotically aloof. Or she could shop from the world of Marc Jacobs and his countless imitators and appear detached from everything but her own worked-over image of emotional absence.
>
> 2004

By 2006, the rest of the world caught up with Demeulemeester's concept of the new, self-assured, self-contained twenty-first-century woman. Her consistent nonchalant styling, striking the right balance between male and female elements, offered solutions to what women felt comfortable wearing. Sarah Mower (2006) described the image that Demeulemeester has believed in for twenty years as 'a strong urban female with an elegant-barbaric wardrobe'. Significantly, Menkes (2010) commented that 'this new decade's view of the strong woman is about nobility, rather than aggression', and she acknowledged that Demeulemeester might be the designer who had created the lexicon of the twenty-first-century modern woman.

Lipovetsky (1994) in *The Empire of Fashion* initially argued that individualism was the prime focus of fashion in the twentieth century. However, he added that, 'In the late 20th century, clothing no longer arouses the interest or passion it used to illicit' (1994: 120). Similarly, Andrew Hill argues that questions of individual identity within a postmodernist framework, have come to the forefront in a way not seen in earlier eras (2005: 67). He reinforced the idea that anti-fashion – which initially challenged the conventions of fashion – has, in turn, been accepted as mainstream, and this 'dressing down' was the outcome of the gradual shift towards 'casual' dress or 'lifestyle' dress (see Chapter 8). By the last decade of the twentieth century, it seemed that individualism in fashion no longer denoted difference. At that time, fashion was no longer a signifying power and instead reflected disenchantment with the world. A growing number of designers believed that fashion is a legitimate communication tool for sociopolitical advocacy, and its visual potency could be used to establish aesthetic direction in design and to reflect the cultural milieu of today's society.

Central St Martin's Caroline Evans also argued that a strong feeling of decadence and psychological trauma pervaded fashion collection showings in the 1990s and early 2000s. She explains that it was a period when experimental design and photography concentrated on the spectacle and not the essence of fashion. Just as the concept of deconstruction emerged in the 1980s with the socially challenged punks in London and the Zen anti-aesthetic work of the Japanese in Paris, at the turn of the century it was the Belgians, and, in particular, the work of Martin Margiela, who continued the social, sexual and aesthetic assault on the establishment. Margiela chose abject materials for his garments and destroyed any hint of the original functionality or exclusiveness. Bill Cunningham (2010) argues that deconstruction fashion is a cultural response to the social and political unrest of the times in Europe, and this zeitgeist constituted the emergence of countercultural fashion. The critics labelled it 'Le Destroy', and Alison Gill saw 'a mirror image in these decaying garments of social stress and degradation brought by the economic recession in the early 1990s' (1998: 30). Both Evans (1998) and Gill (1998) argue that the sordid urban locations chosen for Margiela's shows – empty car parks, warehouse corridors, an unused derelict Metro station and a disused hospital – added to the deconstruction of the notion of couture as glamorous. Other prominent Belgian designers, including Dries Van Noten and Walter van Beirendonck, followed this practice by holding collection showings in the snow around coal fires and in unheated tents. These cold settings were offset with natural elements and earth tones in the collections.

A polarity existed in the *fin de siècle* fashion trends, with Margiela and his experimental, dark and melancholic garments on the one hand and Galliano's vigorous and joyful creations that epitomized an age of luxury and excess on the other. Evans argues that both designers practiced a form of 'cultural poetics' that was 'caught up in an oscillation between novelty and decay, as cycles of consumption consign everything belonging to "yesterday" to the scrap heap' (2003: 37). Alexander McQueen seemed to be caught in the schism between these two worlds – glamorous collections expected by Givenchy and his own penchant towards outrageous, irreverent and spectacular narratives. His hard-edged collections, unashamedly sexual and subversive, revealed nipples; contained imitation body parts as adornment; and attracted controversy with collection titles such as the aforementioned Highland Rape (1995) and La Poupée (1997), in which a black model was restrained within a metal cage and was criticized by the press as representing bondage, slavery and the subordination of women. Many of these, and later, shows were inspired by the cult films of Stanley Kubrick, Pier Paolo Pasolini, Alfred Hitchcock and the dark photography of Joel-Peter Witkin.

After 11 September 2001, the world changed dramatically. A new type of *glamour noir* had emerged – one that relied on the paradox of reality and illusion contextualized by symbolic exaggeration and theatricality. Presentations became pretentious; they were a form of escapism, and fashion photography captured these images of excess, negativism and anxiety. Galliano's historical romanticism offered a form of staged escapism, while McQueen's creations, potent in their social and political meaning, spelled out the impending gloom-and-doom mind-set of the decade.

FIGURE 7.14 *Alexander McQueen. Fall/Winter 2001. The 'Voss' collection represented McQueen's oscillation between beauty and decay, drawing inspiration from nature through use of materials such as feathers, shells and a taxidermied hawk. (Photo by Niall McInerney.)*

Designer fashion responded to world events – terrorism, religious wars, ethnic conflicts and global recession. Fear, uncertainty and instability created a bunker mentality, and subdued colours and foreboding silhouettes began to dominate collection showings. Paris fashion in 2006 reflected the sombre mood of a world in turmoil. Lagerfeld's very long, dark layered clothes, ominous in black, set the mood for other collections.[5] Both Yohji Yamamoto and Marc Jacobs also featured a weighty look with sturdy fabrics and thick leg coverings concealing the body entirely. Fashion journalists referred to the 'Muslimization' of fashion – a religious influence where oversized clothes deny sexuality, and face coverings obliterate any sense of self

FIGURE 7.15 *Dries Van Noten ensemble. Van Noten references the decay of nature literally in this gown, with its dried leafy branches enclosed between layers of tulle. (Photo by Niall McInerney.)*

or individuality. Menkes wrote: 'What is hidden, secret and interior will become the new erotica' (2006). Simultaneous with this trend toward asexual clothing developed as a restructuring of gender concepts, the 2010s have seen a rise of 'Modest fashion' which caters to the population segment that was unwilling – for religious or philosophical reasons – to buy into the sexuality and beauty ideals of Western fashion. Although a growing number of Muslim designers have been developing fashion alternatives geared toward young women, corporate fast fashion store H & M and upscale labels including DKNY have been creating modest fashion collections since 2014. Hijab-wearing models, such as Mariah Idrissi and Halima Aden, have become powerful examples for young women who want to be stylish while dressing modestly. London hosted its own Modest Fashion week in 2017.

For a number of years, symbols of war and masculine aggression had appeared in designer collection showings. Some designers made extensive use of khaki or guerrilla warfare colours, while others relied on styling reminiscent of the 1950s motorcycle culture. A number of designers created survival coats – pocketed plastic coverings in which one's essential life possessions could be carried – while others included clothes that read like armour or uniforms (Prada's Miu Miu collection, 1 March 2006). Some designers, more directly, used text that appeared across the clothing, including Jun Takahashi for Undercover's display of antiwar T-shirts; Yamamoto's tops inscribed with the words 'Do Not Touch Me' seen in the October 2003 show; and Galliano's use of 'Dior not War' splashed on jackets and shirts. An atypical sense of sobriety dominated Watanabe's mostly black collection as early as October 2004.

It became common practice for designers to cover the heads of their models with scarves, veils and other wrappings, suggesting anonymity or victims caught up in espionage. For the Fall/Winter 2006/7 season, Takahashi's Undercover label showed models' heads completely covered, like the bags placed over prisoners' heads before execution. Vivienne Westwood also used a knitted cap that totally covered the model's face, and Viktor & Rolf's models wore pearl-and-rattan fencing masks with cocktail dresses, full-skirted suits and trenches that were a sly pastiche of 1950s French fashion. The colours varied from pebble to charcoal, with shades of grey dominating most collections. Trebay (2006) remarked that 'it's clear something ugly is going on', as the models appeared so sinister that they rivalled Robert Mapplethorpe's outrageous photographs of figures wearing bondage hoods and mummy suits. This mood of sweet melancholy apparent in fashion extended to fine art exhibitions as well. At the Neue Nationalgalarie in Berlin, the brilliantly curated exhibition 'Melancholy – Genius and Madness in Art' showed hundreds of works from the sixth century to the twentieth century that explored notions of sadness, melancholy, intellectual gravity and death (Von Hahn, 2006).

Like fashion, the visual arts adopted a postmodernist 'anti-aesthetic' and 'shock tactics' in their work. Instead of fashion's grunge, neo-punk or heroin chic revealing this anti-aesthetic, artists chose to use detritus materials such as garbage, rotting food and old car bodies in their work. Post-conceptual artist Damien Hirst exhibited his *The Physical Impossibility of Death in the Mind of Someone Living*, a shark in formaldehyde in a vitrine, at the Saatchi Gallery in London in 1992. In 1999, Tracey Emin was nominated for the British Turner Prize; at the exhibition she showed a work entitled *My Bed*, consisting of a dishevelled bed surrounded by detritus such as condoms, bloodstained underwear, bottles and her bedroom slippers. Both fashion and fine art received criticism for these tactics, though fashion was probably targeted more fiercely due to its perpetration of negative body ideals. Comparatively speaking, fashion had only recently defied conventional codes of propriety (emerging in the 1960s along with sexual permissiveness), whereas the fine arts had a long history of defiance and revolt.

The reinvention of menswear

One of the most positive and profitable developments to occur in fashion was the reinvention of menswear. Attention-grabbing collections and a sharper focus on male models have led to greater exposure of menswear on the international catwalks, in fashion photography and in magazine coverage.

In the 1980s, Gianni Versace presented the well-dressed male, styled in casual, colourful suits and silk shirts printed with historic Italian designs, as a new sex symbol. Versace's collections for women included use of leather and metal fabrics such as Oroton, a magnetic fabric developed by the designer. Ultimately, Versace's work played with 'masculine' and 'feminine' elements of colour, material and structure, subverting the expectations of the viewer. Jil Sander introduced her new menswear line in 1997, Galliano and McQueen in 2004, Demeulemeester in 2005, and the historic Savile Row brand Gieves was relaunched by British designer Joe Casely-Hayford in 2006. Net-a-Porter launched its dedicated designer website in January 2011 called Mr. Porter, offering more than sixty top menswear brands and providing style advice and trend forecasts for its male customers. Not only has there been a distinct increase in the number of designers presenting menswear collections at international showings, but a pervasive element of masculinity has dominated womenswear collections as well since the turn of the twenty-first century. While androgyny-dominated collections prevailed in the first few years, 'motorcycle chic' (aka 'biker chic') took the lead in many designer collections between 2004 and 2007, including Lagerfeld, Watanabe and Kawakubo and Gaultier's collection for Hermès, with studded and zippered black leather constructed jackets, caps and boots. While complementing the theme of the warrior woman, the trend towards nonpartisan, transgender dressing also reflected a growing recognition of both heterosexual and homosexual male standing in today's society. Undoubtedly, with a greater focus on the growing gay niche market, lucrative sales helped to sustain fashion's business status quo during the uncertain first decade of the new millennium. Alber Elbaz, director of Lanvin, used jewellery for the first time for his male models in the June 2010 collection showing, explaining, 'It's liberation for men' with necklaces of iron tusks, chains, black stones and wood, and designer Lucas Ossendrijver added, 'when women wear pants, men can wear jewellery' (*The Independent*, 28 June 2010).

During a decade characterized by economic downturn, it is not surprising that exceptional technical expertise on the catwalk was showcased, markedly reinforcing the value intrinsic to bespoke tailoring as opposed to mass-manufactured garments. This message was highlighted in a novel way when A. F. Vandevorst, in the March 2001 Paris show, showcased a man's trench coat made out of brown paper rather than fabric. While, historically, the suit has been the bastion of the English Dandy, and Savile Row the mecca for status and high-end business wear, designers have capitalized on present trends to highlight their extremely sharp tailoring skills, their fine craftsmanship, their devotion to structure and fit and their use of fine fabrics over embellishment and frippery. Men's tailored clothing has changed to reflect the interest in healthy and toned bodies. Paul Smith's very successful business enterprise has been built on an 'acute awareness of British bourgeois aspirations, combining a self-parodying humour' with reference to British history, 'when gentlemen played cricket, drank pink gin, ate curry lunches, and were reliably eccentric' (Breward, 2003: n.p.). While McQueen's work reflected a preoccupation with youth and youthfulness, Galliano resurrected his poetically romantic 'gypsy' persona, Van Noten consistently relied on exclusive fabrics to create a luxurious look and Jacobs promoted the retro classics through his reference to casual 'worn-out', second-hand clothes. Until he retired in 2005, Margiela's menswear captured the essence of imperfection, personality and eccentricity.

Long-standing menswear designers including Giorgio Armani, Helmut Lang, Jean-Paul Gaultier, Vivienne Westwood, Paul Smith and Veronique Nichanian at Hermès, are joined by a bevy of twenty-first-century newcomers. These include John Cavalera; the much-admired Christopher Bailey of Burberry; Stefano Pilati at Yves Saint Laurent, who has built his reputation on the elegant tailoring evident in all of his clothes; Nicolas Ghesquiere at Balenciaga, whom *New York Times* journalist Cathy Horyn (2004) described as 'the most important designer of

FIGURES 7.16 and 7.17 *Dries Van Noten, Spring/Summer 2000. Van Noten uses formal and informal elements of mens' suiting to juxtapose traditional tailoring with casual sportswear, reflecting elements of menswear in the 2000s. (Photo by Niall McInerney.)*

his generation'; and Hedi Slimane[6] at Dior, known for his cutting-edge, slim-line aesthetic styled for the rockers of the contemporary music scene. Legendary American labels, including Calvin Klein and Ralph Lauren, established the ultimate in men's casual lifestyle dressing (see Chapter 8).

Both John Varvatos and Rick Owens broke away from the conservative mould to introduce rock-inspired clothing, and in Owen's case, he offered the 'grunge meets glamour' look in Paris. Thom Browne teamed up with Brooks Brothers in 2006 to design his very successful high-end Black Fleece range and later, in 2008, was hired by Moncler to produce the Game Bleu 2009 menswear collection. Tim Banks of style.com described Browne as 'the master showman of fashion surrealism' when his astronaut-inspired models stripped off their jumpsuits to reveal two-button jackets, Bermuda shorts and knee socks underneath (Paris, 27 June 2010). Another newcomer, Alexander Wang, offered a slouchy, rolled-out-of-bed, edgy look that appealed to the young, and Californian surfwear label, Warriors of Radness (Rick Klotz), broke through the glass ceiling with his provocative T-shirts and board shorts.

In 2015, the Los Angeles County Museum of Art presented the exhibition 'Reigning Men: 1715–2015' exploring gender constructs of what constitutes masculine dress. While dandified men in the eighteenth century wore brightly coloured floral silk suits with matching breeches

FIGURE 7.18 *Thom Browne, Fall/Winter 2012/13. Models present creations by US fashion designer Thom Browne during his men's ready-to-wear collection on 22 January 2012 in Paris. Browne paired a pencil skirt, blazer and overcoat, presented on a model with a spiked face and head covering. (Photo by PIERRE VERDY/AFP via Getty Images.)*

and waistcoat, the shift toward dark, heavy three-piece suits reconstructed the look of the fashionable man (see Chapter 1). The twentieth century saw a move towards a more casual look, from sack suits and draped suits, to leisure suits or sport coats worn with jeans, to skate and surf wear popularized by California beach culture, while in the twenty-first century garments shifted in meaning by decontextualizing gender-specific styling.

FIGURE 7.19 *Thom Browne: Paris Fashion Week. Menswear Fall/Winter 2011/12. A model walks the runway at the Thom Browne show as part of Paris Menswear Fashion Week on 23 January 2011 in Paris, France. Elements of Victorian dress evoke anachronistic references. (Photo by Antonio de Moraes Barros Filho/WireImage.)*

Summary

Subversive designers such as Alexander McQueen worked with historical references and gothic themes to recontextualize fashion. As fashion became increasingly corporatized, the postmodernist movement in fashion grew to include designers such as Margiela and the Antwerp Six, as well as social critics such as Moschino and Viktor & Rolf. Since the last few decades of the twentieth century, fashion has been focused on subverting viewer expectations by delivering the unexpected, from gender-based styles to runway presentations. Agender dress and deconstructed clothing heralded a radical transition in the decades leading up to the 2000s, with the work of Dutch designers Demeulemeester, Margiela and Van Noten leading the inquiry in these areas of fashion. Designers Tom Ford and Thom Browne redefined menswear through their reinvention of classic forms.

Notes

1 Viktor & Rolf mimicked Gilbert and George's 'living sculptures' when they dressed in identical clothes and posed, like the earlier conceptual performance artists had in 1969, as a personification of art itself.

2 This culminated in the international publication of Aoki (2001).

3 Interview by Oliver Leone in Le Petit Archive (no date listed). Available online https://www.lepetitarchive.com/interviews-masahiro-nakagawa-one-of-20471120s-founders/ (accessed 21 April 2021).

4 For the Dior-inspired ensemble from Recycle 03 by 201471120, see object 2006/87/1 at the Museum of Applied Arts and Science: https://collection.maas.museum/object/360736

5 The website fashionwindows.com reports that Lagerfeld commented: 'If you read the daily papers, you are not in the mood for pink and green. We have to deal now with a whole world connected.'

6 Slimane left Dior in 2007 to concentrate on his photography but re-emerged in March 2012 as the creative director of YSL Womenswear.

8

The Lifestyle of Fashion

Introduction

American conservatism responded to the simplicity, versatility and comfort of ready-to-wear clothing. As a nation, Americans did not have the long-standing history of social class differentiation of their European counterparts. In many parts of the country – particularly the Midwest and the growing suburban areas of the large cities – they adopted a more casual, traditionalist lifestyle. In California, a relaxed 'beach style' evolved after the introduction of the Hawaiian shirt in 1946–7, together with Bermuda shorts, and the subsequent decline of business suits in favour of more ventilated and comfortable attire. New manufactured fibres such as nylon, polyester and spandex developed from the Interwar period onwards made it possible to utilize lightweight materials in garment manufacture. In Europe, both couture and ready-to-wear had taken on the traditional function of fashion by questioning its effects on consumers across the globe.

American sportswear designers

Following the early pioneering efforts of McCardell, Cashin, Maxwell and their contemporaries in New York (see Chapter 4), the period following the Second World War defined American luxury sportswear in the fashion industry. In the early 1950s, designer Bill Blass mingled with upper-crust society in New York, attaining a high position in New York society that aided him throughout his career. Observing the penchant for casual daytime dressing among the wealthy in New England, he manufactured comfortable garments made from quality materials. In the late 1950s, he began his career working for Maurice Rentner in the heart of the garment district on Seventh Avenue, and rose to the position of vice president, eventually taking over and changing the company name to Bill Blass Limited in 1970. Many of his sportswear designs included luxurious materials like cashmere or camel hair, and upscale details such as gold buttons. When women showed interest in the shirts and sweaters he designed for men, he opened his sportswear division for women, expanding his range to design workwear and eveningwear. His collections offered a mix-and-match sensibility that allowed consumers to work with bright colours and patterns. His true expertise lay in his business acumen: Blass set up licensing deals in products from perfume to luggage bearing his name, becoming one of the first American designers to become famous under an eponymous label.

Internationally acclaimed designer Geoffrey Beene utilized early training at the Chambre Syndicale and his apprenticeship at the couture house Molyneux (1948–51) to create designs that brought together Paris and New York. His expertise in cut led to creating architectural dresses with subtle interior structure, presenting a simple but elegant look. Beginning his career in New York at the dress house Harmay in 1952, his designs were recognized by *Harper's Bazaar* editor Carmel Snow, who featured one of his dresses in the magazine. Beene further developed his style during an eight-year stint at Teal Traina before establishing his own company in 1963 on Seventh Avenue. Some of his iconic designs include sequined football jersey dresses (1967) and evening dresses made from sweatshirt fabric (1968), both of which brought a more relaxed attitude towards upscale dressing. He designed garments based on the premise that a designer's role was to make people's lives easier, introducing ease and comfort into both women's and men's clothing. One of the first American designers to create a more affordable line, he launched the 'Beene Bag' label (1971); attempting to design a less structured look for men, Beene used soft fabrics such as jersey to produce more fluid designs, which he saw as a transitional garment between blue jeans and the tailored suit. Although these were not well received by the American fashion critics, in 1976 Beene became the first New York ready-to-wear designer to show a collection in Europe, where his look was well received.

Roy Halston Frowick, known by his label Halston, was born in the Midwest and renowned for his classic, simple styling. Halston followed the business model that would come to be standard for many high-end designers: he showed his custom-made collections in an uptown boutique on Madison Avenue, yet manufactured his ready-to-wear lines – sold in department and specialty stores across the country – on Seventh Avenue, the hub of the fashion manufacturing and wholesale trade. An early collection that he designed for Bergdorf Goodman was 'an attempt to bridge the gap between couture and ready-to-wear' (Morris, 1978: 92), but his *coup d'état* in ready-to-wear was the shirtdress that he designed in ultra-suede in the 1970s, which was to become a classic garment in every American woman's wardrobe. Halston also created designs in the classic bias cut established by Vionnet, creating halter neck or one-shouldered evening dresses with soft silhouettes inspired by Grecian precedents.

For those who wanted a less conventional approach to dress, designer Stephen Burrows offered colourful, body-hugging garments that emphasized eclecticism and exuberance. Beginning his solo career in the late 1960s at the height of hippie style, Burrows created colour-blocked jersey dresses that Diana Vreeland – by then, editor-in-chief of *Vogue* magazine – offered to feature in 'lettuce' [green]. Burrows, perhaps misunderstanding her suggestion, responded with a dress that featured asymmetrical tiers with rippled edges resembling leaves of lettuce, which quickly became his trademark. Throughout the 1970s, Burrows' body-conscious designs were seen throughout uptown and downtown nightlife in New York, resonating with street style. One of the few African American designers in sportswear, Burrows attracted a wide demographic and won his first Coty award in 1973. Both Halston and Burrows would define American disco style throughout the decade.

Arguably, American fashion emerged from the garment factories and from a tradition of ready-to-wear. This was in contrast to France, where ready-to-wear emerged directly out of couture. This divergence of approaches to fashion was displayed quite literally at a fashion show in France on 28 November 1973, dubbed by the American press as 'The Battle of Versailles'. Created as a fundraiser for the crumbling Palace of Versailles (near Paris) by publicist Eleanor Lambert and curator Gerald van der Kemp, the show featured five leading French designers against five leading American designers. The French line-up included Yves Saint Laurent, Pierre Cardin, Emanuel Ungaro, Christian Dior and Hubert de Givenchy; while the American group included Bill Blass, Stephen Burrows, Oscar de la Renta, Halston and Anne Klein (who brought her young assistant, Donna Karan). In contrast to the staged French showmanship and choreographed routines, the

Americans had their casual clothing modelled by a diverse group of models (including eleven African American women) who danced and skipped down the runway. The audience, consisting of celebrities and royalty including Princess Grace of Monaco, heiress Jacqueline de Ribes and artist Andy Warhol, were stunned and thrilled with the freshness of the American approach, which represented a coming of age for the ready-to-wear industry (Givhan, 2015).

Sportswear became synonymous with a casual, middle-class existence, and it coincided with the attitude that 'dressing down' in an elegant, comfortable manner was a subtle sign that one did not have to keep up appearances. In contradictory terms, it suggested wealth and good upbringing. Returning to Veblen's concepts in *The Theory of the Leisure Class*, the representation of 'conspicuous leisure' is evident as a mode of dress that gives the appearance that one leads an entirely useless or futile life, yet is undoubtedly a sign of status. In many circles of society at the time, conventional fashion was worn as a sign of social conformity, reflecting old-fashioned ideals and values.

This inherently conservative approach to design is apparent in the collections of many of the leading ready-to-wear designers, including Ralph Lauren, Calvin Klein and Donna Karan, whose international success began in the 1980s. Their work is often described as being 'classic', always appropriate and comfortably chic. American 'purist' fashion is characterized by clearly defined lines, splendid fabrics and perfect, yet formless, cuts. Fashion Editor Carrie Donovan makes a valuable comment when she argues that American designers create 'a style of dressing', as they are not interested in individual ideas but are particularly good at creating a concept.

Giorgio Armani is one of the few couture designers whose work has impacted upon American ready-to-wear. He was featured on the cover of *Time* magazine in 1982 for his revolutionary men's suits that broke away from the traditional mould. *Newsweek* (22 October 1978) described them as 'classically cut but not stodgy; innovative but never theatrical'. Armani's longer, unstructured jackets were comfortable, and suited the more casual approach to businesswear in the 1980s. As the architect of the soft shoulder, he removed the traditional padding; he also reintroduced a vintage double-breasted garment with long, deep lapels, similar in many ways to the zoot suits of the 1940s. His clothing questioned the traditional function of menswear, both artistically and culturally. He introduced the crumpled look of linen into menswear as well as womenswear, and his shapeless, oversized clothing bridged gender stereotypes. Like Chanel, he offered an alternative way of dressing – a new freedom that appealed to international men of all ages. Ironically, Armani was inspired by the film star Fred Astaire, whom he believed to be 'the supreme reference of elegance' in his 1930s suits. Crane (2000) believes that the American style of dress reached a pinnacle during this era, and 'had the greatest influence on 1980s and 1990s fashions' (2000: 174). Nevertheless, the Armani label raised the standard for American menswear design.

Ralph Lauren

Ralph Lauren, a leading American ready-to-wear designer, rose to fame through both designing and styling a high-end American look. Trained initially in classic menswear and specializing in ties, he designed for clients who 'did not want to stand out in a crowd', but who wanted their clothing – based on simplistic styling and the use of fine fabric – to reflect good taste and upbringing. The subtlety of this paradigm, based on 'lifestyle' or 'concept' dressing, underlined the success of many of the emerging designers in the 1970s and 1980s. Lauren launched his Polo menswear range in 1968, and three years later turned to tailored womenswear: shirts, blazers and suits that appealed to businesswomen even though they resembled sportswear. He is often quoted as saying: 'I stand for a look that is American', and alludes to the fact that he was inspired by the *Great Gatsby* look of the 1920s.[1] He is able to turn old classic looks into fresh, contemporary ones. Promoting this nostalgic image, his stores replicate a homey atmosphere, creating a feeling of well-being and relaxation.

Lauren's classic good looks, at prices that the upper middle-class American could afford, were the secret to his success. He combined quality materials, excellent workmanship and attention to detail with a carefully constructed image that applied not only to his products, but to his stores as well. The image he created was determined by clothing that gave the illusion of wealth; at the same time the wearer appeared to be nonchalant about his appearance. Much like the landed gentry, he might have been walking in the countryside, or sailing a yacht.

For the younger generation, this look mimicked those attending exclusive college preparatory schools – the term from which we get the moniker 'preppy' – whose look was defined by blazers and ties bearing school emblems, button-down shirts and khaki trousers for young men, or plaid skirts for young women. However, Lauren's exploration of American design did not end with the style of the upper crust. His western-inspired collections from *c.* 1980, known as Polo Country, explored materials and styles associated with the Southwest and the influences that still dominated there. Large silver belt buckles found in Native American metalwork was offset by denim ensembles, paired with chunky knitted sweaters featuring Navajo designs. Lauren's ads feature both sexes dressed in earth tones, wearing layered ensembles of shearling-lined leather or

FIGURE 8.1 Vogue *1976: Model Lisa Taylor wearing Ralph Lauren's plaid jacket and skirt suit with an olive turtleneck and brown boots. (Photo by Arthur Elgort/Condé Nast via Getty Images.)*

FIGURE 8.2 *Ralph Lauren, Spring/Summer 1989. Lauren's concept of Americana explored the styles of the Native American Southwest, heavily influenced by time spent at his Colorado ranch.*

suede jackets and tapered corduroy pants, with cowboy boots in embossed leather. The look was reflective of a renewed interest in the American West as part of the country's identity.

His women's line continued to garner inspiration from unexpected places, reflected in collections of full skirts and button-down shirts, with large belts at the waist. In 1993, Lauren launched his RRL line, which further referenced the raw denim of nineteenth-century gold rush miners, details from American military garb, and other vintage elements that would define Americana. Much of his style drew upon the essence of sportswear and casual chic style as worn by the upper classes, made available to a broader demographic.

Lauren's collections, though highly popular, were also critiqued for glamorizing wealth and the old-world order of social inequity that it represents. Contemporary artist Charles LeDray (Townsend, 2002: 118–21), sees Lauren's male clothing as mirroring a conservatism usually associated with an Oxford academic, an American preppy or one who claims aristocratic heritage. In order to critique the falseness that this type of clothing suggests, LeDray constructed a miniaturized version of a characteristic Lauren casual wool sports jacket, waistcoat and colourful bow tie, then used sandpaper to fray and tear the bottom half of this detailed construction. His *Untitled* work of 1995 is 'not a mechanism that deters sentimental response, but . . . a reaction to what the clothes stand for, their social values and their repression of other, more polymorphous identities'. Townsend (2002: 119) suggests that LeDray has 'epitomized and undermined all that Ralph Lauren spent more than a decade and a slew of money to convey'. LeDray's work with garments as metaphor continued in his installation 'Men's Suits',

FIGURES 8.3 and 8.4 *Ralph Lauren. Fall/Winter 1985. Lauren created a look that evoked old-world class through elements such as ruffled collars and cuffs, and accessories such as jewellery, riding-style boots and hats. (Photos by Niall McInerney.)*

created between 2006 and 2009. Exhibited at the Whitney Museum in late 2010, LeDray creates a men's suiting store in miniature, with an impressive array of hand-stitched garments at half-scale displayed in a dingy resale-type environment. His other works also address clothing as objects that hold memories, as well as contemplating the human labour that goes into tailoring and garment production through his meticulous miniature recreations.

Calvin Klein

Paralleling Lauren's career was Calvin Klein, who began working as a coat designer. Klein often commented that designing coats was a great challenge as they were the least inventive category of clothes. He sold his first samples to Bonwit Teller in 1967, and quickly moved into sportswear design by combining linen blouses with flannel skirts. In 1968 Mildred Custin, the president of the New York department store B. Altman, decided to feature his youthful coats and dresses in the store's fall window displays, and his clothes were first featured on the *Vogue* magazine cover in 1969. His first catwalk show in 1970 included sportswear and separates, followed by his 'Coatless' collection in 1972. Klein received his fits Coty award in 1973, followed

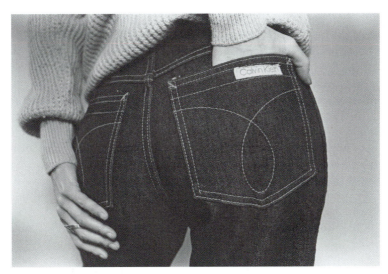

FIGURE 8.5 *The back pocket of a pair of Calvin Klein jeans, Cambridge, Massachusetts, USA, 3 January 1979. (Photo by Barbara Alper/Getty Images.)*

by a second award the next year. The designer's personality was reflected in his garments: Klein was known for being unpretentious, clean-cut and charismatic, with the goal of making practical clothing that consumers enjoyed wearing. Klein's label quickly attracted celebrity clientele as well as wealthy consumers. His high-profile clients included Jackie Kennedy Onassis, Liv Ullmann, Susan Brinkley, Lauren Hutton and Nancy Reagan. The monochromatic and minimalist conservatism that underlines his garments secured the global appeal of his label. His most effective marketing promotion, which created considerable notoriety for his label and appealed to the masses, was for his line of designer jeans. Launched in 1976 as part of his sportswear collection, his advertising campaign in the early 1980s fuelled the craze for a new association with denim that boasted the designer's name on the back pocket. Modelled by then fifteen-year-old Brooke Shields in a series of controversial ads, she wore jeans so tight that her signature line in the commercial boasted: 'You wanna know what comes between me and my Calvin's? Nothing.' Through the television commercials, director Richard Avedon used the American starlet to promote the range in a very suggestive, sensual manner – also inciting major controversy about child pornography and sexualization. However, a new genre had been opened in American advertising culture, promoting the idea that 'sex sells'.

In 1982, the famous American fashion photographer Bruce Weber capitalized on this blatantly sexual advertising by using highly contoured male bodies, wearing only Calvin Klein underwear, in an unprecedented marketing campaign. According to Valerie Steele (2000: 126): 'Weber created the most famous erotic photographs of men ever used in mainstream advertising.' Klein's strategic response to the body-hugging fashions of the 1980s reflected changing social mores and exploited the sexual taboos of the day.

Colin McDowell, in his *The Man of Fashion: Peacock Males and Perfect Gentlemen* (1997: 173–6), argues that Klein – as 'the first to use male sex to sell clothes' – was so successful that it was 'not inconceivable that future social historians writing about America will refer to the first few years of the 1980s as the CK era'. Branding became big business in the 1980s, and designers tried to capitalize on this growing market of 'designer label as status'. Klein, capitalizing on his underwear fame, had his name boldly printed on the waistband of his men's underpants. As jeans were worn fashionably low-slung at the time, the label was brilliantly revealed. The underwear became an international best-seller, and McDowell (1997) points out that the desirability of the garments was sustained by Weber's risqué advertising campaigns and seductive photography. When these fashion images of the male torso began to dominate the urban environment (an enormous billboard advertising Klein was erected in Times Square in 1982), a new form of male sexual iconography was born. The billboard advertisement not only endorsed a new era in male fashion (in both heterosexual and homosexual terms), but more significantly acknowledged that the 1970s health and fitness craze had culminated in the celebration of a well-developed muscular body image of young men in the 1980s.

The conglomerate Phillips–Van Heusen Corporation (PVH) began a new era when it acquired the Calvin Klein Company in 2003, as it recognized that the brand offered incredible growth potential worldwide. Several new licensing agreements were signed in 2005, which further expanded the global presence of the prestigious Calvin Klein brands. This included handbags and small leather goods, men's and women's footwear, and 'ck' – Calvin Klein's bridge label, specializing in women's sportswear – which was distributed in Japan and South-East Asia, as well as through selected American department stores.

From 2016 to late 2018, Raf Simons was appointed Chief Creative Officer for the brand, bringing a more colourful and avant-garde approach to the formerly subdued, monochromatic line. Although the fashion critics received his changes favourably, the line did not sell, and Simons was dismissed by the brand.

FIGURE 8.6 *Calvin Klein, Spring/Summer 1988. (Photo by Niall McInerney.)*

Donna Karan

Donna Karan is one of the most successful American designers of the twentieth century, and the heir to many of the sportswear concepts introduced in the 1930s and 1940s by the first wave of women's sportwear designers such as McCardell, Cashin and their peers. Before starting her own label, Donna Karan designed for another classic sportswear designer: Anne Klein, who hired her in 1968 while she was still a student at Parsons School of Design. After Klein's passing in 1974, Karan took over as head of design (1974–84), presenting her first collection as a wardrobe of casual clothing that could be worn over a knitted leotard. Her collections at Anne Klein, including a 'bridge' line called Anne Klein II designed with former Parson's classmate Louis Dell'Olio, were so successful that she was awarded two Coty awards (1977 and 1982). In 1985, she founded her own label: Donna Karan New York. Building on the concept of a modular wardrobe that would make clothing selection faster and more convenient for working women, she developed the basis of her collection: the 'seven easy pieces' system of dressing. Following critical acclaim and positive feedback from women who embraced the feminine yet professional style, Karan continued to build upon the idea of separates that complemented a bodysuit and black tights – adding a blazer, pleated trousers, or a leather jacket, and a versatile shawl that could be worn as a scarf or a wrap skirt.

Although the seven pieces in the system were subject to change, Karan's philosophy towards designing remained the same. She explained that design was a constant challenge to balance comfort with luxury, the practical with the desirable. By creating a tailored soft look, her garments were intended to suit the lifestyle of the successful working woman – a type of no-fuss fashion. Her garments follow the movements of the body closely: jackets are made without the stiffness of linings, skirts gain greater sensuality. Karan described her objectives as wanting to make comfortable clothing that was easy, simple and sophisticated – clothes that could travel. She diversified the Donna Karan International collection to include menswear and the very successful DKNY Jeans diffusion line, started in 1988. Her clothing image sells an American

FIGURE 8.7 *Donna Karan. Fall/Winter 1986. The black bodysuit, which came in a variety of sleeve lengths and necklines, was a staple of Karan's 'Seven Easy Pieces'. (Photo by Niall McInerney.)*

FIGURE 8.8 *Donna Karan. Fall/Winter 1987. Karan's line softened the silhouette for women's workwear. (Photo by Niall McInerney.)*

lifestyle, a trademark design philosophy. Her flagship store located at 819 Madison Avenue was described throughout the 1990s as the ideal shopping environment. The mood projected was very restful, with a water rock garden, soothing music and seductive lighting. Her work sold through her own retail stores and major retailers, and the company went on to become a publicly traded enterprise in 1996. Five years later, DKNY was acquired by LVMH (Louis Vuitton Moët Hennessy).

Redefining womenswear: Power dressing

Gender issues from the 1960s resurfaced in the 1980s. The women's liberation movement had lobbied for equality in employment in terms of pay, benefits and promotional opportunities. In the 1980s, despite the fact that an equal opportunities act was enacted in many Western countries, women in professional careers used fashion as a political language to illustrate their expectations of power and position in the management structures of large corporations. Ironically, as the more casual, loose-fitting garments popularized by Armani, American sportwear designers, and the Japanese avant-garde designers were embraced by male executives, the fitted tailored suits traditionally worn by men found refuge in women's businesswear. Visually, at least, there appeared to be a role reversal. This style of dress was worn particularly by women who were trying to 'break through the glass ceiling' – a common feminist cliché. 'Hard chic' was a slick, high-fashion look represented by exaggerated shoulders and streamlined silhouettes, meant to minimize natural curves and project equality in corporate environments. It allowed women to look professional, high-powered and successful, without objectifying themselves. In the film 'Working Girl' (1988), young finance secretary Tess (Melanie Griffith) redefines herself by doffing her big hair, gaudy jewellery and short skirts in favour of a more streamlined look typified by her boss, Katharine (Sigourney Weaver), and gets taken more seriously at work and in life. Power dressing for women relied on mimicking the male silhouette, featuring square padded shoulders, narrow skirts or trousers with belts, and tailored blouses that in many ways resembled Arrow brand business shirts. Well-cut jackets exuded a sense of confidence and authority. A neck flounce reminiscent of a bow tie completed the look, along with stiletto heels projecting a no-nonsense approach.

Calvin Klein and Georgio Armani were both advocates of power suits for women, taking a gender-neutral approach to this style. However, it was the female designers who advocated for comfort and functionality that transformed this look. By the late 1980s, led by the popularity of Donna Karan's upscale line, many of the silhouettes presented by her male counterparts were softened in order to give women the option for a more feminine – yet still powerful – silhouette. By creating softer lines and using high-end materials such as cashmere, wool jersey, leather and suede, Karan redefined the look of power dressing. Quoted in the *New York Times* (Weir, 1985), Karan's philosophy for businesswear for women was that 'the clothes shouldn't overpower her, she has to overpower them'. Karan was in good company: other women designers were creating their own independent labels with the same goals in mind of providing women with clothes that were comfortable, practical and flattering, without taking away from women's natural shape. Among her peers who achieved success in high-end sportswear are Carolyne Roehm, Norma Kamali and Adrienne Vittadini, all creating business workwear and stylish sportswear.

Jean-Paul Gaultier's designs for menswear also reflected changing attitudes towards gender representation in the 1980s and 1990s. While the canons regarding suitability of dress for men had altered slightly, Gaultier aggressively contested gender stereotyping by consistently presenting cross-dressing in his menswear collections. His male models wore feather boas, bejewelled bodices, corsets and furs, and skin-tight trousers that did not deny masculinity but offered an alternative vision of male sensual attire. His clothing – both for men and women – could be described as fetishistically obsessed, reflecting a social deviance and defiance. He made body piercing and tattoos acceptable on the Paris catwalk by using models that he had chosen from the street. Famously designing the conical bra for Madonna's Blonde Ambition tour (1990), Gaultier embraced the controversy that came with pairing traditional corsetry with the black pin-striped power suit for her video 'Express Yourself' – both of which challenged the norms of contemporary female dress codes. Often described as the 'bad boy' of fashion, Gaultier's subversive designs had a considerable influence on contemporary twentieth-century fashion. Other designers shared his approach, including Vivienne Westwood, Thierry Mugler, Dolce & Gabbana, and America's John Bartlett.

Fashion as ideological billboard

Social messages conveyed through clothing have the power to display the ideology of the wearer. From humble beginnings, T-shirts have functioned historically as a form of political poster. Like Levi's jeans, the T-shirt transformed itself from a basic working-class utilitarian garment into a postmodernist signpost that advertised and expressed personal interests and individual beliefs. Constructing identity through lifestyle is determined by 'the type of popular cultural products we consume, and the creative uses to which we put these products or commodities' (Kidd, 2002: 109). Just like the T-shirt, new products – like the beanbag (designed by Gatti, Teodoro and Paolini in 1968–9) – spoke to one's emotional and sensual, rather than functional, needs. The quest to define 'self' amongst postmodernist youth culture was paralleled by the popularity and rise of the T-shirt. The new consumerist-led society relied on diversity and changeability, which was precisely what the inexpensive T-shirt offered. Like blue jeans, T-shirts have become cultural icons, and are usually discussed within a paradigm of capitalism, sociability and leisure lifestyles. The visual pluralism that they offer includes expressions of social or political beliefs or affiliations, and likes or interests, and they easily become an advertisement for commercial products or a medium for self-expression. They replace postcards or photographs, depicting the places that one has visited, as well as acting as a souvenir of one's travels. The 'I ♥ NY' slogan by Milton Glazier has been copied by cities around the world, but originated in New York – the home of the quick message. Madison Avenue, famous for its 'ad men', used T-shirts in the 1940s to gain support for the presidential elections. Long before anyone else, they comprehended the potential of clothing as a new form of visual dialogue.

As a graphic tool, T-shirts have become a mandatory means of sartorial protest for the young. Protest campaigns about Civil Rights and the Vietnam War were referenced in the visual arts. Graphic designers such as R&K Brown (1969) in their appropriated *Iwo Jima* photograph, and George Maciunas's (1969) *American Flag* poster protested about genocide committed by American troops in conflicts over the century. In 1968, Japanese artist Hirokatsu, as a reminder of the Second World War, created a poster entitled *No More Hiroshimas*, and Ron Borowski's sardonic photograph of a black American, with an American flag superimposed over his face, read: 'I pledge allegiance to the flag of the USA . . . where all men are created equal'. T-shirts were worn to street marches as a sign of peaceful protest, with their verbal and visual references acting as effective communication tools, bridging language and cultural barriers. Both the hippies of the 1960s and the punks of the 1970s used the T-shirt as a means of protest and propaganda, with perhaps one of the most controversial being produced by fashion designer Vivienne Westwood in 1977. The image of Queen Elizabeth with a safety pin through her mouth was a bold political statement that enraged the British, and was seen as an unforgivable act of rebellion (see Fig. 6.2).

The mass production of T-shirts gathered speed in the 1960s with the invention of plastic transfers, spray paint, and especially Plastisol (1959), a plastic printing ink that couldn't be washed out of fabric. By 1965, marketing professionals had begun to recognize the T-shirt as a medium for exploiting product branding internationally. As a walking billboard, they provided unpaid advertising for companies such as Budweiser, Coca-Cola, Disneyland and, later, sporting companies such as Nike and Slazenger. The use of constant repetition as a tool, adopted by commercial television advertisements to hypnotize viewers, inspired Warhol's silkscreen multiple prints of Campbell's soup tins.

In much the same way that Warhol's screen-printed images were seen as a blatant comment on consumerism and the manipulation of the public by advertising agencies and media corporations, the T-shirt served a similar purpose. The mass production of T-shirts ironically and satirically functioned as a critique of the superficialities of society. Most effectively, they were used as a means of expressing cynicism about the dominant culture, which still continues today. T-shirts can make provocative statements about racism, gender, violence and obscenity. Postmodernist artists used humour extensively to point out the contradictions and complexities of modern life. As a form of self-expression or self-branding, the T-shirt conveys messages to others indicating one's preference for a particular style of music, and acts as a conversational catalyst for like-minded people. Musicians and rock groups use T-shirts as 'memorabilia retailing' for their tours, seen as an important part of the promotional fanfare. Slogans such as 'I'm High on Life', 'The Anti-Everything T-Shirt' and 'Born Free' were popular in the 1960s and 1970s.

Fashion historian Leslie Watson (2003) explains how the 1980s ushered in political correctness and social awareness in London. She notes that designer Katherine Hamnett launched a T-shirt collection called Choose Life – clothes with a social message, including 'Stop Acid Rain', 'Preserve the Rainforests' and '58% Don't Want Pershing'.[2] The last-mentioned shirt was worn by the designer herself when she met Prime Minister Margaret Thatcher at Downing Street in 1984 (2003: 125). Ecological T-shirts were made of cotton that had been grown without the use of pesticides or from recycled materials. It seems that the greater the commitment to a cause, the more blatant the message became.

Fashion can be part of a political platform that is sympathetic to the ambitions of various movements, from environmental platforms to those against racism, sexism, and forms of local politics that advocate national pride and tribalism (Finkelstein, 1996: 76). The highly successful

FIGURE 8.9 *Italian photographer Oliviero Toscani photographs a group of children who are wearing Benetton clothing. Toscani began his collaboration with the Benetton clothing company in 1982 and became known for his controversial advertising campaigns. (Photo by julio donoso/Sygma via Getty Images.)*

Benetton label (est. 1965) was fast-tracked to popularity based on the marketing strategy that individuals use branding to identify with social or political causes. The Italian brand became famous in the 1980s for its luxury-priced sportswear, but mostly due to its advertising. Photographs by Oliviero Toscani were used in Benetton's global advertising campaign, 'All the Colors of the World', run by J. Walter Thompson in the US (1983–92). The initial ads in the 1980s included the key words of the campaign, accompanying a diverse group of models in multipatterned, colourful clothes.

Some of the ads were political, showing US and Soviet athletes together amicably towards the end of the Cold War (1986). These sentiments became associated with the label, which is intrinsically linked with the actual clothing. The consumers were buying a social placebo, signifying that they share a common philosophy and are monetarily contributing to a cause – thereby justifying the expense, as it is akin to making a charitable donation.

By the early 1990s, the ads changed dramatically, relying on visual shock to gain and sustain the viewer's interest. Benetton's advertising in this period rarely showed an image of the product, because the product becomes secondary to the social 'consciousness' that it sells with its clothing. The visual images still focused on human relationships, reinforcing the need for racial equality and compassion, especially for those dying of the much-stigmatized AIDS epidemic,[3] but protestors and critics argued that the events depicted were being commodified. These included a wide range of topics: a newborn baby with its umbilical cord still attached, dead soldiers in the Bosnian war, a nun and a priest kissing. Following much controversy, the J. Walter Thompson agency and Benetton parted ways, and the Joker agency took over. In 2000, Benetton ran a series of ads under Toscani's photographic direction that would have grave financial consequences for the brand: images of prisoners on death row. The result was a lawsuit by the US state of Missouri, and the loss of a lucrative contract with Sears Roebuck department store, who pulled the brand's franchising contract (Kiefer, 2017).

However, the label still actively pushes the limits on acceptable advertising, launching their Unhate campaign in 2011, featuring an interracial homosexual couple kissing. This marriage of fashion – in this case, through its advertising – with social activism leads to a number of questions about the true role of fashion. In a blog about the controversial brand, Kasia Stempniak (2019) asks: 'Did Benetton's advertisements pioneer this modern phenomenon of "brand activism"? Or were Benetton's ads an example of a company commodifying social causes and taking advantage of the ethically murky waters of fashion advertising?' Toscani rejoined the brand in 2017 after a long hiatus, and now disseminates his social messages through a different approach: a schoolroom filled with children from around the world. Toscani recently said in an interview: 'Brands are very important. They've got a social impact and are using public space. You have to say something interesting' (Kiefer 2017).

Quite literally, by the end of the twentieth century, fashion had become seamlessly allied with grass-roots human issues. Global issues such as homelessness, personal welfare and safety created anxieties that were quickly addressed by leading designers, both Western and Eastern. Mendes and de la Haye (1999) elaborate: 'The Italian company Superga created bulletproof clothes, with built-in air pollution masks, acid rain protection and infrared, night-vision goggles. Lucy Orta, a Paris-based conceptual designer, addressed world conflict and the destruction of urban life. Her Refuge Wear range, introduced in 1992, featured multi-functional survival clothes which adapted to form tents and sleeping bags' (1999: 256).

The House of Prada, originally established in 1913, brought out a minimalist range of nylon bags and rucksacks, which became a staple accessory for both men and women in the 1990s.

Even Issey Miyake, inspired by the new trend, designed a man's vest that could be converted into a backpack. Younger Japanese designers such as Hiroaki Ohya created *The Wizard of Jeanz* in 1993, a series of twenty-one books that folded out into clothes. The notion of permanence associated with books, which transfer knowledge from one generation to another, inspired this idea. Louise Mitchell, curator of the 2005/6 exhibition *The Cutting Edge: Fashion from Japan* at the Powerhouse Museum in Sydney, Australia, featured his work amongst others. She explains:

> The *Wizard of Jeanz* is a technical tour de force, a feat of skill that allows a book to transform into a ruffled neckpiece, a pair of jeans or an elegant evening dress. In a similar experimental mood, Shinichiro Arakawa created a series of garments that are framed like paintings but, once out of the frame, put on and zipped up around the body, become real wearable clothes. Transformable themes are also seen in Aya Tsukioka's wrap skirt, with its apron front screen-printed on the reverse with the image of a vending machine similar to the millions found on Tokyo's streets. When the wearer unties the waistband and lifts the apron above her head, she can 'hide' behind this image. The designer's aim is to provoke laughter by creating clothes that encourage the viewer to recognize the need for moments of respite from the pressures of everyday life.
>
> MITCHELL, 2005: 9

One of the roles chosen by artists since the pop art movement has been that of questioning and challenging consumer desires for the new and improved. In art, the T-shirt has been used to reflect the culture of the street and everyday life, and has turned T-shirts with slogans into art objects. Artist Jenny Holzer produced an 'Abuse of Power Comes as No Surprise' T-shirt, while graffiti artist Keith Haring used T-shirts to bridge the gap between graffiti art in the street and the museum. These T-shirts – also Hamnett's protest shirts – were exhibited at the Documenta VII exhibition, held at the Fashion Moda Gallery in East Village New York in 1982. Chris Townsend, in *Rapture: Art's Seduction by Fashion* (2002), remarks that both fashion and art were unified in making the body a billboard for one's beliefs. He elaborates upon artist-driven retailing developed by Fashion Moda – who had its roots in Claes Oldenburg's pop art project *The Store* – as an enterprise allowing young artists to sell their ideas as low-priced editions in the form of the T-shirt. Townsend references a parallel in the early 1990s of the East London shop run by Tracy Emin and Sarah Lucas, selling the 'Complete Arsehole' T-shirt, in which this new self-deprecating irony displays a new approach to art practice 'from the ideological earnestness of the early 1980s to a micro-celebrity culture where individual identity was paramount, even in its mocking erasure' (2002: 47), and noting that fashion, as much as art, could accommodate these two extremes.

Textile artist Miriam Shapiro also claims that young female artists, in particular, are interested in using costume as tent, home, protection and theatrical design. She uses fabric as a metaphor for life – a material that becomes more fragile with age and, as it fades, becomes a reminder of the limited time we have to enjoy life. Miro Schor's work *Dress Book* (1977) is an earlier example of how a dress, formatted as a book, can be used to narrate a story, to act as a diary which records personal feelings and document one's journeys in life. The fragility of the paper can represent vulnerability and the viewer can turn the pages of the dress, reading 'her' like a book. This cross-referencing of similar themes in fashion and art reinforces the importance of identity and meaning to designers and artists alike. Caroline Broadhurst, whose colourless line drawings of skeleton clothes in the late 1980s, illustrate the link well. She explained: 'Clothing holds a visual memory of a person, and it is this closeness to a human being that I am interested in' (Colchester, 1991: 141). Her work communicates the intimacy of clothing, the idea that they have been shaped not just by fashion, but by somebody's life. Undoubtedly, these provocative statements question the role that the visual arts play in today's society. Coupled with technological advancements in textile development, personal notions of insecurity, anonymity and tribal affiliations reinforce the concept that fashion actually came from the street and not the catwalk. More recently, the integration of electronic elements with clothing have expanded the role of technology in fashion, as well as interpretation of the symbolic significance of garments through art installations (see Andrea Lauer's work in Chapter 10).

Street style on the catwalk

In the context of the fashion system, street style is a kind of anti-fashion that begins with a group of people that subscribe to the same beliefs, signified by wearing a shared style. Polhemus elaborates on this concept in *Street Style* (1994) by defining these groups as 'style tribes'. Although this is not a new phenomenon by the 1980s – Karl Lagerfeld has suggested that Mary Quant became the first symbol of street fashion because of the great diversity in her collections – by the 1990s, according to Polhemus (1994: 131), 'the history of street style . . . [had become] a vast theme park'. In the 1980s, nostalgia opened the floodgates for revivalism of many of the past street styles – 'neo-mods, neo-Teds, neo-hippies, neo-psychedelics, neo-punks and . . . neo-New Romantics' (1994: 130). He also argues (1994: 131) that this 'supermarket of style' first emerged in Japan, and that every piece of attire worn 'comes as part of a complete semiological package deal' (see Chapter 6). Collage aesthetics, consisting of a juxtaposition of words and images, multiply meanings and associations, which contributes to formulating a multi-layered 'reading' of the work or a diversification of identity for the fashion wearer.

This concept is perhaps best exemplified by the late 1980s/early 1990s grunge aesthetic, a movement that, like punk, grew out of the music scene and streetwear. 'Grunge' was the word used by the Sub-Pop label to describe the sound of post-punk bands playing in clubs in Seattle and other major US cities in the Northwest, whose metal guitar and grating vocals identified the 'Seattle Sound'. The dress and appearance of its fans and musicians were equally jarring: a mix-and-match, anything goes anti-style that indicated the apathy and indifference of the wearer to outside opinion and fashion ideals of the day. Popular bands emerging from this scene included Soundgarden, Pearl Jam and Nirvana, among others. Nirvana's lead singer, Kurt Cobain (1967–94), was the poster child for grunge: a mop of greasy hair half covering his face, loose flannel shirts tied around the waist, dirty jeans, short-sleeved shirts over long, untied combat boots, and a general look of dishevelment. In film, this look was embodied by Cliff Poncier, the rock-star wannabe played by Matt Dillon in Cameron Crowe's 'Singles' (1992) (the film's made-up band, Citizen Dick, features three of the musicians who would form the band Pearl Jam). The look was further propagated by promo photos and MTV videos of 'Smells Like Teen Spirit' (1991), the band's first hit. Marc Jacobs, creative director at Perry Ellis from 1988–93, is credited with being the first designer to put grunge on the runway for the Spring/Summer 1993 collections; met with disdain by fashion critics, he was fired from his position and left to create his own label. But the momentum of grunge as a popular look had been set in motion, and ready-to-wear was soon inundated with mix-and-match plaid, granny floral dresses, flannel shirts, oversized and cropped clothing juxtaposed in layers, all paired with Doc Martens or Birkenstocks.

FIGURE 8.10 TO 8.13 *Design by Marc Jacobs for Perry Ellis, Spring/Summer 1993. This collection famously brought 'Grunge' to the runway by presenting an orchestrated mismatch of colours, patterns and style. (Photos by Niall McInerney.)*

Through MTV and other media, the Grunge look travelled the globe, resonating with teens and twenty-somethings as a new form of anti-fashion.

Fashion theory in the 1990s reflected upon this mix-and-match approach to fashion as a rehashing of previous styles and eras. Polhemus (1994: 130) insists that: 'Street style . . . [in the 1990s] is characterized by the extent to which it exists within the shadow of its own past.' More critically, social historian Dick Hebdige (1987) sees British street style as 'the decay of the present while viewing the past'. He argues that design uses objects that have been detached from their original sources and reused to transform history into memory. He alludes to the fashion charade of neo-punk, as a ubiquitous look that had no basis in real meaning, and comments that punks now expected to be paid to be photographed. As reflected in the grating guitar riffs and lyrics of Grunge music, cynicism prevailed in the fashion of the 1990s. By the middle of the decade, fashion journalists had become highly critical of the constant rehashing of appropriated styles, as well as the lack of originality and sincerity in design. They, amongst many others, signalled the demise of the haute couture empire. Ailing economies and the Gulf War, with its rising oil prices and halting trade with Arab Emirate countries, contributed to the fall in sales of high fashion and perfume.

A few designers working outside the system avoided the pastiche and overworked design nostalgia, considered overpriced for many who could not see the value in buying 'underprivileged' clothing. Issey Miyake (see Chapter 6), Shirin Guild and Asha Sarabhai are included in this list (Mendes and de la Haye, 1999). Cultural authenticity was applauded in the work of these respectively Japanese, Iranian and Indian designers, who 'reworked their own cultural clothing traditions in a reductionist aesthetic which resulted in modern, functional clothes that were in many respects trans-cultural' (Mendes and de la Haye, 1999: 255). Young Belgian designers took deconstruction – which seemed to emerge most convincingly from the design studios of the Japanese Rei Kawakubo and Yohji Yamamoto in the 1980s – to new heights. All trained at the Royal Academy of Fine Arts in Antwerp, Martin Margiela, Ann Demeulemeester, Dirk Bikkembergs and Dries Van Noten made their mark on Parisian fashion. In particular, Margiela and Demeulemeester specialized in garments that critiqued garment-making itself (see Chapter 7). Exposed seams highlight the fabrication process, lining is revealed, loose threads hang down like tentacles, fabric draws your attention to surface renderings, and the 'objectification' of the garment encourages a reflexive analysis of the work's meaning. Just as postmodernist art envies fashion's media exposure and glitz, postmodernist fashion searches for greater intellectual credibility.

Museum exhibitions of fashion

In 2011, thirty-seven major fashion exhibitions were held worldwide. According to the Fashion Institute of Technology's Valerie Steele (2011), when the Metropolitan Museum of Art in New York first held a retrospective show of the work of a living designer – Yves Saint Laurent in 1983[4] – it was the first time this type of exhibition had been held. The ensuing controversy created amongst the museum trustees led to a decision that all future solo retrospective exhibitions had to represent the work of deceased designers only (a decision that would later be redacted). Ironically, this dictum did not apply to fine artists.

Today, fashion exhibitions attract a large audience and have become major blockbuster shows for museums around the world. Finally breaching the gap between commerce and culture, progressive museum directors and curators now appreciate that the methodologies employed in display and presentation both in the (department) store and the museum share a common objective: that of creating a spectacle. Acknowledging that the fashion industry and the art museum rely on this centrality of display, other links between fashion and art can be assessed. Distinctive fashion garments, designed by both the masters of haute couture and ready-to-wear collections, are now conceived as being both cultural and commercial treasures and command respect in national museum holdings.

Curatorial rationales for fashion exhibitions often reference themes that contextualize fashion within a changing cultural arena, such as 'Radical Fashion' at the Victoria and Albert Museum in 2001–2, which considered the concept of the avant-garde in postmodernist fashion; 'Superheroes: Fashion and Fantasy' at the Costume Institute of the Metropolitan Museum of Art in New York in 2008, which created a vision of fashion superheroes as the ultimate fashion icons; and 'Art and Fashion: Between Skin and Clothing' at the Kunstmuseum in Wolfsburg, Germany in 2011, which considered fashion as a legitimate art form. Recent retrospective designer exhibitions that reveal the aesthetic development and historical narrative of the oeuvre have attracted unprecedented attendances in museums worldwide. The proliferation of retrospective blockbuster shows suggests that we are marking the end of an era for some of the twentieth-and twenty-first-centuries' greatest designers. For the Metropolitan Museum in New York, the Costume Institute's 2010 Alexander McQueen exhibition, 'Savage Beauty', curated by Andrew Bolton, drew more than 660,000 visitors – one of the largest recorded audiences in the museum's history. In 2010, the Petit Palais in Paris held the first retrospective show of Yves Saint Laurent since his death in 2008. Christian Dior's work was celebrated at the State Pushkin Museum of Fine Arts in Moscow in 2011.

In the same year, Jean-Paul Gaultier's travelling exhibition was first displayed at the Montreal Museum of Fine Arts and Yohji Yamamoto's thirtieth anniversary show was feted at the Victoria and Albert Museum in London.[5] Rei Kawakubo's pioneering collections were featured in a solo exhibition at the Metropolitan Museum in 2017, reviewing her major contributions both to fashion and feminism. The 'Fashion Futurist' retrospective exhibition of Pierre Cardin's work at the Kunstpalast Museum in Düsseldorf, and its display as 'Future Fashion' at the Brooklyn Museum (2019–20) also drew large crowds by displaying garments from the vast archives of a lengthy career; the pioneering designer passed away the same year (December 2020) at the age of ninety-eight.

Summary

The changes to the fashion system during the last quarter of the twentieth century were the result of multiple factors. The rise of American luxury ready-to-wear rivalled haute couture for high-end clientele who wanted chic but practical clothing for everyday life. Designers became integral to branding practices, gaining celebrity status while creating 'lifestyle' brands, while the development of e-commerce and strong online presence has provided new consumer markets. Street Style continued to evolve as a major fashion influence, inspired by the post-punk music scene in the US Pacific Northwest, as evidenced in the Grunge collection by Marc Jacobs for Perry Ellis. Fashion, as a representation of cultural movements, gained prominence in museum exhibitions.

Notes

1   Lauren's classic menswear style dresses the main characters in the 1974 film production of *The Great Gatsby* (costume designer Theoni V. Aldredge).

2   Hamnett's T-shirt slogan of '58% don't want Pershing' represented the percentage of Europeans opposed to the deployment of American nuclear weapons – cruise and Pershing missiles – which had been deployed across Europe without consulting the electorate. Ultimately, Hamnett's creation and display of the T-shirt at this highly publicized event with the British Prime Minister, Margaret Thatcher, was along the lines of an anti-nuclear (and somewhat anti-government) protest.

3   Some of Benetton's most memorable images include images of interracial relationships, such as a black mother suckling a white baby and a biracial lesbian couple covered with a blanket and holding an Asian baby. Another ad shows David Kirby, a gay activist dying of AIDS surrounded by family.

4 Curated by Diana Vreeland, former editor of American *Vogue*.

5 Past momentous travelling exhibitions include: 'Giorgio Armani' at the Guggenheim, New York, in 2000, Bilboa in 2001 and the Nueu Nationalgallerie, Berlin, in 2003; 'Vivienne Westwood' at the Victoria and Albert Museum, London, ANG, Canberra, and De Young, San Francisco, 2004–7; and Maison Martin Margiela '20' at the Modemuseum, Antwerp, 2008, Munich in 2009 and Somerset House, London, in 2010.

9

The Corporatization of Fashion

Introduction

Although contemporary fashion has been inspired by fine art, popular culture and social phenomena, its foundation as a lucrative business has prompted the industry to continue seeking greater means of distribution and profit. Though there isn't one specific moment or designer that marks this transition, the global politics and economic shifts in the latter half of the twentieth century led to the current structure of the fashion industry today, from licensing deals to diffusion brands. The most significant changes in the way that fashion is bought and sold to consumers emerged with the commercial development of the internet and the emergence of online shopping as the preferred means of purchasing clothing.

Global conglomerates

Conglomerate corporations grew from the 1960s onwards. Many high-profile designers, including Calvin Klein, Donna Karan, Michael Kors and Perry Ellis, amalgamated with numerous other companies to form giant international networks. Their distribution channels include regional, national and international department stores, mass-merchants, sports-related speciality stores and corporate wear distributors throughout the world. Many of these huge global conglomerates developed from humble beginnings.

For example, a relatively unknown businessman named George Feldenkreis started a small apparel wholesale company called Supreme International in 1967 as an importer of guayabera shirts – a pleated, four-pocket shirt with vertical pleats popular with Latino men. The Miami-based company expanded rapidly, and by the late 1990s had acquired companies including Penguin, Crossings and Perry Ellis, who had established his classic American sportswear in 1978. It changed its name to Perry Ellis International (PEI) after adding John Henry, Manhattan, Lady Manhattan (1999) and Jantzen (2002). New brand names emerged, including Tommy Hilfiger (swimwear) and Nike. Between 2003 and 2005, other companies merged, including Salant, Axis, Tricots St Raphael and Tropical Swimwear. PEI traded throughout the United States, Puerto Rico and Canada, and its largest customers included Wal-Mart, J. C. Penney, Mervyn, Kohl's Corporation and Sears Roebuck.

Not surprisingly, it became harder for individual designers to establish either haute couture salons[1] or smaller ready-to-wear businesses without extensive funding, in order to compete in an increasing global industry. These huge global corporate conglomerates license their proprietary brands to third parties for the manufacture and marketing of various products – footwear, fragrance, underwear, activewear, loungewear and outerwear. In terms of marketing, these licensing arrangements raise the overall awareness of the brands.[2] They use highly sophisticated 'family of brands' promotions to develop and enhance a distinct brand, styling and a pricing strategy for each product category within each distribution channel. They target consumers in specific age, income and ethnic groups. This globalization of fashion has impacted upon the apparel sector in America, as well as other countries, in four major ways. First, department stores and chain store sectors have been forced to amalgamate into a smaller number of stronger retailers. Second, larger retailers have needed to rely more on their own design expertise and to incorporate advanced systems of technology in their businesses. Third, there has been a growth in the importance of establishing strong brand names as a source of product differentiation. And finally, products are being manufactured in parts of Asia, Africa and South and Central America, where the labour costs are lower and mass production is more cost effective.

This manufacturing shift to developing countries was hastened, in particular, by internal problems that gained momentum by the end of the last century. For example, the New York garment district was plagued by Mafia-infiltrated trade unions, which ultimately increased labour production costs and literally froze the trucking industry – which impeded the delivery of goods (Blumenthal, 1992). It is estimated that organized crime cartels were 'costing' the district a staggering $60 million a year by the early 1990s.[3]

Aided by politics, the manufacturing and importation of goods from overseas was opened up by the 1972 visit to Beijing by US President Nixon, who went to discuss issues of the ongoing war in Vietnam with Chinese officials. In exchange for China's assistance, Nixon offered trade concessions, credits and technical assistance. Although the Chinese influence in North Vietnam was somewhat overestimated, the proposed political alliance thawed relations between these two superpowers. From 1973 onwards, trade between the US and China increased exponentially, particularly manufactured garments and textiles for the apparel sector. Other East Asian locales such as Taiwan, Hong Kong and Singapore, developed a sweatshop system after the Second World War to supply wealthier nations with textiles and consumer plastics (Powell, 2014). As the per capita income of those societies rose and sweatshops were eliminated, these operations moved to developing countries such as Bangladesh.

With increased technological communication systems, the world increasingly became a smaller place, where shared ideologies grew, consumer culture dominated, and social belonging no longer adhered to the concept of clothing as an identifying signifier. By the turn of the twenty-first century, the fashion system had changed profoundly and the 'global village' (first mooted in the 1960s by Marshall McLuhan, a Canadian philosopher and writer) had become a reality.[4] Clearly, this homogenization of style did not allow for individual difference, regional bias or cultural flavour; instead, it promoted a uniformity of thinking and taste. But by creating a global aesthetic, has fashion ultimately undermined individual and cultural differences?

LVMH: The super syndicate

From the 1980s onwards, with the growing uncertainty in the global financial markets, fashion designers and others sought to consolidate their business interests by taking refuge with other firms. Of these commodity chains, by far the largest and most influential is Louis Vuitton Moët Hennessy (LVMH), a global fashion conglomerate in which the centrality of branding of luxury goods is the dominant competitive strategy for success. During the 2000s, the luxury market nose-dived, along with the stock market, and conglomerates like LVMH looked to divest themselves of unprofitable companies, and subsume larger, more secure companies under their banners in order to weather the financial storm. By 2011, LVMH had expanded to an international retail network of more than 2,500 stores and 80,000 employees worldwide. It viewed itself as a patron to the arts, committed to supporting young artists and designers, including John Galliano, Alexander McQueen and Marc Jacobs, who seemed to have the versatility and skill to reinvigorate older, more staid labels. Its marketing strategy was based on the idea that haute couture, while not cost effective itself, has had an unparalleled influence on brand profile and publicity. The concept of successful branding, a philosophy upon which the empire was built, resulted in the LVMH group acquiring a unique portfolio of more than sixty prestigious brands. Monsieur Bernard Arnault, CEO of LVMH, a very powerful player in global identity politics, determines the head designers of the fashion houses under his banner. He selectively chose designers who could refresh and yet sustain the branding image of older fashion houses, which needed to meet the forces of an increasingly competitive market. In the 1990s, Galliano revived the House of Givenchy and was then moved on to the House of Dior, leaving the Givenchy position to McQueen, another outstanding postmodernist designer of the time.

Luxury heritage branding

Syndicates of multibrand groups such as the leading LVMH, Compagnie Financiere Richemont and Gucci created empires built on the acquisition of labels, particularly in the 1990s. In the 2000s, they were divesting themselves of some poor performers and investing more in their core brands. A trend emerged over the first decade of the twenty-first century where more profits were being made in luxury goods such as watches, jewellery and perfume than in designer clothing. Luxury heritage brands such as Chanel, Dior and Givenchy have relied on their appeal as labels exemplifying status and prestige, based on a classic timelessness – in historical as well as emotional terms. According to McMahon and Morley (2011: 69), the success of these brands in the twenty-first-century market is determined by 'their ability to develop new design and branding strategies in response to consumer feedback, while retaining the emotional core values of their heritage'. For instance, Karl Lagerfeld's success designing for the Chanel label underlines McMahon and Morley's observation that 'new designers need to create product that identifies and continues to express and repeat elements of the original creator's signature style while imbuing creations with their own creative identity to make the product relevant in the present' (McMahon and Morley, 2011: 72).

Luxury heritage brand labels such as Gucci (revived by Tom Ford in just a few years) and Cartier have a familiar built-in brand stature and 'authentic' strength that immediately attract consumer respect. Consumers can develop a psychological connection with these products as they enhance their own sense of self-esteem, self-concept and self-worth. Kapferer and Bastien (2009) argue that to desire luxury is to desire becoming part of an elevated class. In the contemporary market, as iconic brand 'signatures' rely on this essence of exclusivity or rarity (not offered by counterfeit copies), they must protect the distribution networks by limiting accessibility – exemplified by the practices of De Beers diamonds.

De Beers was established in 1870 with the discovery of huge diamond mines near Orange River in South Africa, with major British investors combining their interests as De Beers Consolidated Mines, Inc. (1888) – essentially forming a monopoly.[5] The De Beers corporation launched a campaign in the 1930s to market this new and abundant commodity as luxury items – mostly through price fixing within their monopoly, and aggressive marketing. Hiring

New York ad agency N. W. Ayer in 1938, which included a push by fashion designers to display and tout the trend, De Beers advertised its diamond jewellery as luxury items photographed on socialites and Hollywood film stars – referenced in company memos as 'a form of propaganda'. Due to US anti-trust laws, De Beers was not allowed to promote De Beers directly, or even show a picture of a diamond; instead of showing the product, the company commissioned works by fine artists such as Andre Derain, or purchased paintings by Dalí and Picasso, accompanied by clever copywriting (Sullivan, 2013). It wasn't until 1947 that diamonds were advertised as a sign of love and romance, with Hollywood films as the vehicle to propagate this new idea. The company went so far as to send representatives to high schools around the US to explain how diamonds represent 'indestructible love' and that a diamond ring is the proper culmination of courtship as an expression of eternal love through marriage (Friedman, 2015). This idea was immortalized in an Ayer slogan authored by Frances Gerety that De Beers still uses today: 'A diamond is forever' (Sullivan, 2013), indicating the longevity of its worth as a symbol of love, and also reinforcing the concept that diamonds should never be resold.

Beginning in 1967, the De Beers concept was marketed with equal success to consumers in Japan through the campaigns devised by J. Walter Thompson (the same agency who worked with Benetton in the 1980s; see Chapter 8). The ads showed Japanese models wearing European dress and involved in activities – driving, biking, playing sports – with conspicuous foreign

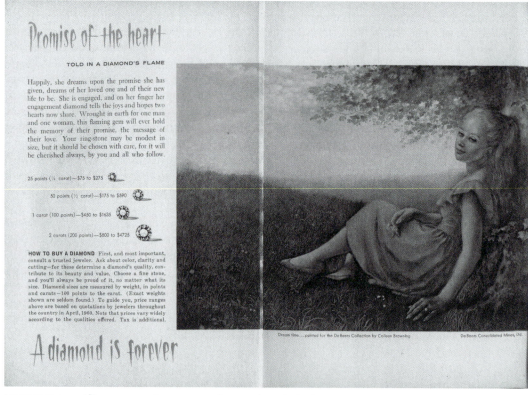

FIGURE 9.1 *Advertisement by De Beers diamonds with the famous tagline 'A diamond is forever' coined in 1947. August 1960,* Reader's Digest *magazine. (Photo by SenseiAlan.)*

imports, representing Western ideals of upper-class life. Within a short period of time (1967–81) the diamond engagement ring had successfully replaced traditional non-material Japanese matrimonial traditions, such as bride and groom sharing rice wine from a wooden bowl, as a symbol of modern Western values (Epstein, 1982). By the early 1980s, profits from the Japanese market were second only to the American market.

In addition to advertising, luxury brand marketing in the fashion sector by the 1990s became inherently linked to the flagship store experience. The brand headquarter store was the symbol of the brand, and as such was required to be architecturally unique and designed by a famous postmodernist architect. The prestige and status associated with the architectural brilliance is transferred to the products and to the customers themselves. As the Japanese are among the world's biggest luxury consumers, Tokyo is a key location and Prada is one of the leading firms represented by cutting-edge architectural design there. Its flagship store in Aoyama, Tokyo, designed in 2003 by Herzog and de Meuron, is a strikingly unconventional, five-sided, six-storey glass crystal with signature diamond-shaped glass panes that resemble bubbles from the outside of the building. The Maison Hermès in the Ginza district of Tokyo designed in 2001 by Renzo Piano uses extensive areas of glass square cubes, inspired by traditional Japanese lanterns, as a curtain-walling. The density of the glass sound-proofs the interior, and at night the entire building glows and has pixilated windows of blue dots that make the people inside appear as if they are on a television screen. Christian Dior's Tokyo store designed by architects Kazuyo Sejima and Ryue Nishizawa has floors of different heights, and Puma House designed in 2011 by NENDO is made up of multiple staircases used as display stands throughout the interior of the building. It symbolizes movement and the relationship between fashion and sport. Rem Koolhaas designed Prada's New York flagship store and also its 'transformer' shape-shifting building in Seoul, which was designed as a unique temporary structure that could be picked up by cranes and rotated to accommodate a variety of cultural events. Other outstanding flagship stores include Fendi in Beverly Hills designed by Peter Marino and Alexander McQueen in Los Angeles designed by Pentagram.

Franchising, licensed copying, diffusion lines[6] and the process of branding were initiated well before the twenty-first century. More recently, marketing strategies have been reinvented, changed, modified or consolidated. Bridging the gap between the expensive, high-fashion garment and affordable mass production lines relied on the media landscape, and its role was critical to the fashion system. The 'signature label', inherent to the two-tiered system of couture and ready-to-wear, had been exploited by a succession of designers since the early 1900s, as noted throughout the book, but became even more important in the twenty-first century to reinforce quality and authenticity and to develop brand loyalty. To summarize, Power and Hauge outline the five key operational rationales adopted by most successful firms, which include the use of brand building: first, as a strategy to differentiate your product from your competitors; second, as an umbrella that focuses on the firm/syndicate and its image rather than on individual products; third, as a means for firms to diversify into product and service provider areas outside the core business; fourth, as a vehicle to allow for flexibility or change in managerial or designer structures; and, finally, as a platform for co-branding or linking brands together (Power and Hauge, 2006: 8–10).

The designer as product

Just as actors, sportspeople, musicians and models have become global celebrities, so have the fashion designers themselves. In the past, individual designers sometimes shunned their own fashion shows because they were too private, camera-shy or aloof to attend. Traditional French haute couture relied on intimacy, privacy, select customers, elite venues and extreme subtlety in business transactions, and certain designers – such as Balenciaga – preferred to stay in the shadows. This not only hindered image profiling, but often restricted sales as well. In today's market, the presence of a designer will not only boost sales at collection showings, but at store openings and perfume launches as well. Their image becomes synonymous with their product. In turn, the 'designer as product' maximizes brand awareness. Armani will appear on stage dressed down in white T-shirt and jeans. This downmarket image not only advertises his diffusion line, Emporio – created for a younger clientele – but also reinforces that the white, single-pocket T-shirt is the ultimate universal casual statement for men – in fact, the best-selling line since the Second World War.

Reinforcing the designer label's image, Calvin Klein became the master of image creation and – like a chameleon – metamorphosed his image from the suave man about town to the sophisticated and more mature suited businessman. Yohji Yamamoto continues to wear understated black – historically the symbolic colour of intellectual pursuit – and signifies his perceived reluctance to promote his creative work as commercial enterprise. Tom Ford and the late Karl Lagerfeld, both always immaculate, exude a confidence through their self-assured manner, which mirrors their success in the industry. For designers, remaining in the public eye is central to the marketing success of their fashion goods.

Haute couture collection showings cost a designer hundreds of thousands of dollars, which is never retrieved in sales; however, the opulent displays generate pages of free advertising, keeping the designer's name constantly in the media. The post-war French haute couture firms became corporate entities as they were only able to survive with massive financial investment and management. Dior's business, for example, was backed by a textile magnate and run by a business manager, while the designer himself was allotted a share of the profits.

Licensing is a very effective way of reaching a mass consumer audience with little effort or expense on the part of the designer. The licensing of many additional types of products has become a major source of income. When a designer agrees to let a manufacturer use his or her name on a product, the designer receives a royalty (usually between 7 to 8 per cent of the gross profits). This could include goods such as sunglasses, millinery, textile goods (towels, sheets, etc.) or other household items. Pierre Cardin was the first designer to sign a licensing contract to mass-produce ready-to-wear for a vast audience in 1959 (see Chapter 5). Significantly, by doing so he established the commercial mechanism by which the industry thrives today. At the time, this outraged the *Chambre Syndicale de la Couture Parisiènne*, a syndicate of haute couture designers whose main aim was to uphold the exclusivity of individual design. As retribution, he was denied membership of the elite group for a while (which meant that he couldn't show his collection as part of the Syndicale's Paris Fashion week), despite the fact that his garments had become headline news as trendsetting design. His aim was to produce fashion for everyone, not just the rich, and he soon began to make brand-name furniture and later gave his name to over 900 products, including carpets, floor tiles, frying pans, restaurants, cars, boats, olive oil and mattresses (*The Age*, Melbourne, 1 August 2003). He became a global billionaire through licenses that carry his name in ninety-seven countries, including New Zealand, China, the United States, Canada and Russia. Undoubtedly, Cardin was a world leader in developing an individual brand-name portfolio.

By the 1980s, the royalties gained from the licensing of fashion labels, as well as the sale of perfume, cosmetics and other fashion products, became the main source of profitability for many designers, including Yves Saint Laurent. For many of these products, the value resides only in the name of the product; otherwise the item has no social currency. In contemporary society, class differences are no longer visually conspicuous. Multinational corporations have globalized fashion and fashion products to such an extent that branding has become essential to create an illusion of status – to create a difference in objects which otherwise appear to be very similar.

In the last chapter of *20th Century Fashion* (1999), Mendes and de la Haye provide an exceptionally detailed account of the proliferation of designers and fashion styles that brought the twentieth century to a close. From futuristic clothing inspired by technological advancements to the plurality of ethnic styles and historical revivals, the 1990s produced eclecticism unrivalled since the 1890s. They recount the changing names of de facto head designers in the leading couture houses, such as McQueen at Givenchy, Galliano at Dior, Lagerfeld at Chanel and Ford at Gucci. By 2006, McQueen had moved to Gucci and Tom Ford to Yves Saint Laurent. In each case, the designers are assessed by their ability to appropriate the details, themes or 'looks' of the *maisons*, and to capture the essence of the original designer's work.

Yet one of the most significant trends, according to Mendes and de la Haye, was the move from ready-to-wear – which has become more expensive – to diffusion lines aimed at global audiences. Just as haute couture was used to advertise and promote a designer's ready-to-wear lines, now ready-to-wear lines are used to promote diffusion lines. The cheaper diffusion lines were not widely advertised in the 1980s, but by the 1990s they were being paraded down the catwalks. America again took the lead in this new marketing venture, and when Donna Karan brought out her diffusion line, DKNY, it became an immediate success. More often than not, these lines were simple, conservative and inoffensive – a 'fashion understatement', but they have since expanded into formalwear. According to Frankel (2001: 56), designer Issey Miyake doesn't approve of diffusion lines, which he says are insulting and patronizing to the wearer. He says, 'I don't want people to think of my clothes in terms of money, to feel they can only afford second best.' Instead, he claims that, with his Pleats Please line: 'I worked on how to keep the price down.' For Miyake, it seems, success translates as more than making money; he focuses on the relationship of the wearer with the clothes.

Even Cartier Jewellers (established in 1889 in the Rue de La Paix in Paris), which had sold jewels to the crown heads of Europe, succumbed (in 1973) to producing a diffusion gift line called Les Musts de Cartier, which included spectacle cases, leather goods and luxury lighters that could be purchased for two hundred dollars. Not only did this strategic move stabilize the company's financial affairs, but it also revived the luxury goods market. The directors did not see it as a democratization of the brand name, but as an opportunity to provide the public with greater access to luxury goods without detracting from the prestige of the Cartier name.

Fashion as philanthropy and installation

With so much profit inherent in the business practices of the corporatized fashion industry, there was a counterpoint with philanthropic endeavours. In the 1980s, monster fashion shows were organized, often to benefit charities. Bruce Oldfield's show raised funds for a children's orphanage and Karl Lagerfeld's for the Cancer Appeal, while Chanel gave money to support the Metropolitan Opera. Fashion Aid was held in the late 1980s, with the proceeds used to send food to Africa. A variety of designers also participated in the prestigious Street to Couture show in the Royal Albert Hall in London.

By the early 1990s, politics had become an overt part of the fabric of fashion design. Not only did fashion respond directly to current events, but many designers incorporated philanthropy as part of their corporate profile. According to Casadio, Moschino launched Project Smile in 1993 to raise funds for HIV-positive children. An auction, 'Art in Love', took place in collaboration with Sotheby's at the opening of Moschino's New York boutique. Artists such as Julian Schnabel, George Condo, Donald Baechler, Arman and John Baldessari donated works to be sold. The profits were given to Hale House, an organization providing support for children of alcoholics and drug addicts in Harlem (Casadio, 1997: 125).

In a more overt way, Ralph Lauren employed his Polo collection to raise funds for cancer care and prevention. This marketing technique, which utilized text written across the wide display windows of his stores worldwide, functioned as a sidewalk drawcard and proved to be effective in persuading buyers to enter his shops. Most designers adopted this philanthropic trend throughout the 1990s, as it not only supported humanitarian causes and gained goodwill, but could also be used as an effective tax deduction. Within a wider context, Hauffe argues that corporations use sponsorship of the arts to enhance their image as consumers began to demand a greater sense of corporate social responsibility, and that dedicating the proceeds to humanitarian causes ultimately leads to the restoration of public approval for decaying reputations (1998: 172).

Utilizing the art world as a bridge to corporate identity, a number of corporate fashion houses are funding their own museums in order to raise the public profile in a way that supersedes endowments or sponsorships. Prada has established the Fondazione Prada in Milan and Cartier the Foundation Cartier pour L'Art Contemporain in Paris. This indicates the financial power and growing cultural influence that the globalized fashion industry wields. The art industry now seems to be envious of fashion's ability to be more than a rhetorical device, or a cultural object, used by artists to comment on the seduction of popular culture in our society.

Collaborations between fashion and art shifted from low-scale displays of artwork in fashion outlets to large-scale installations in the late 1990s. Fashion designers such as Tom Ford (when at Gucci – part of the Pinault-Printemps-Redoute retail group, now Kering) collaborated with the American performance artist Vanessa Beecroft to produce Show 2001 at New York's Guggenheim Museum of Art. Twenty models stood as a static display, frozen in time, on the ground floor of the museum wearing Gucci heels, thongs and tops (and some nothing at all) with fixed stares returned to the audience, who in turn became the subject of the gaze. Beecroft's photograph documenting the work comments not only on the notion of sexual fantasy, but parodies the coldness and cruelty often seen in Helmut Newton's fashion photographs. This human installation became a historically significant event in 'an evolution of supportive relationships that runs from such involvements as Schiaparelli's costuming of films by Man Ray, and Buñuel and Dalí, and her provision of mannequins for the 1938 Surrealist exhibition in Paris' (Townsend, 2002: 96–8).

Perhaps designers are using fashion more effectively to communicate ideas and emotions to an audience, the majority of which has lost touch with meaning in art practice. Wearing fashion involves the audience's participation in the communicative process, an experience that the art object in its traditional museum context does not allow, although interactive installations have been a sub-genre in the art world since the 1970s. Perhaps this is one reason that presentations of fashion collections have become more like art performances, and fashion photography.

Perfume: A licence to make money

With a sizeable profit margin, perfume makes hundreds of millions of dollars' profit annually. What is perfume's appeal? As a status item, it is more affordable to a mass-market, and it allows a 'cheap' entry into a designer lifestyle. Perfume literally provides a touch of luxury to the mundane life of a middle-class consumer. Paul Poiret, an astute businessman, was the first to create his own scent before the First World War, naming it after his daughter Rosine. Recognizing that the packaging is as important to the consumer as the scent, Poiret had his perfume bottles uniquely hand-blown from Murano glass in Italy. Chanel No. 5, launched in 1921, is one of the most famous perfumes in the world; in her streamlined approach, Chanel chose a sleek geometric art deco bottle that has never been redesigned. One-third of the early couture firms developed lines of perfume, whose names have far outlasted the couture houses. Long past the time when the houses of Patou and Lanvin ceased sell clothing, their names were immortalized by their perfume labels. With a 60 per cent pure profit mark-up, these sales can keep a business afloat, and often not only outstrip its couture lines, but its prêt-à-porter lines as well. During the Second World War, American soldiers returning from service in Europe were known to buy the women in their lives either silk stockings or perfume, or both. In most cases, when they entered a French *parfumerie*, the only name they recognized was Chanel No. 5. Perfume sales soared for Chanel in the 1940s and 1950s; today it is still the top-selling brand, with a bottle selling every thirty seconds. It was originally created by Ernest Beaux, and it was the fifth sample Beaux asked Chanel to appraise – hence the name. By the 1960s, the three leading couture houses, Chanel, Dior and Yves Saint Laurent, were also the top-selling perfume establishments.

Even though males had been wearing scents for centuries, masculine colognes – tending to have more citrus and woody notes than women's perfume – became huge marketing products in the 1970s. By the 1990s, perfume sales had reached $7.5 billion and celebrities of all kinds were marketing their own scents. However, without the networking of internationally branded names afforded by the fashion designers, the majority of the new perfume lines went out of business. Only one in five perfumes remained on the market after three years. Calvin Klein developed unisex scents, bringing out ck one in 1994, and continued his success with three other lines of perfume: Obsession, reported to contain 200 ingredients; Eternity, the sales of which outstripped those of his clothing line; and Escape, which was launched at Macy's, New York's middle-class department store, in the 1990s.

The death of haute couture?

By the mid-1990s, it seemed that French haute couture was no longer sustainable. London journalist Juliet Herd (1991) wrote of the unbridled indulgence that sounded 'the death knell of haute couture' at the start of the 1990s. This 'extinction of the Paris couture industry' was reaffirmed by Pierre Bergé, the high-profile head of Yves Saint Laurent, when he stated that 'Haute couture will be dead in ten years' time' (Herd, 1991). The French prime minister, who believed the French fashion industry 'needed an overhaul' in order to survive, called a summit meeting to discuss the troubles of the ailing $3.3 billion export industry. It seems that the exclusivity of the Chambre Syndicale, the industry's powerful authority, prevented the inclusion of the younger, more avant-garde designers in the 'club', and that wealthy young clients were turning to ready-to-wear as haute couture 'seemed to be running out of ideas'. Herd argues that 'the lack of originality among top designers was highlighted at the French collections', where one fashion expert observed that 'many top couturiers appeared to be wandering up blind alleys, uncertain of their role'. Significantly, there were twenty-one haute couture houses in Paris at this time, according to the Chambre Syndicale, which regarded haute couture (and not ready-to-wear) as the backbone of their business.

Similarly, the 7 November 1991 issue of *L'Express* asked a pointed question: 'Who broke the desire machine?' Historian Chenoune (1993: 316) argues that: 'Many people have begun to feel that the current *fin de siècle* is marked by an unhealthy atmosphere' and that the problems of 'Aids, unemployment and economic recession are complicated by the political upheaval and ethnic nationalism resulting from the recent collapse of communism and the Soviet empire'.

Placing this phenomenon within a social and historical context, could it be that Western fashion had exhausted its endless appetite for change by the 1990s? In their constant search for novelty, some designers looked back to previous historical periods, while others found a need to react to or contradict that which had gone immediately before. This lack of direction seemed to be broadcast in the growing superficiality of styles that led Suzy Menkes, former Fashion Editor of the *International Herald Tribune*, to comment on the bankruptcy of innovation and new ideas (Menkes, 2000).

Crane (2000: 143) suggests that, by the late 1980s, there were two groups of couturiers: 'one group included older designers . . . who produced collections that often consisted of restatements of ideas and motifs from the history of designer fashion'[7] and who took 'few risks, varying their collection just enough to keep in step with the times'. The other group, she adds, consisted of younger designers whose work was more unconventional and 'who were recruited especially for their originality or the entertainment value of their designs'. In other words, they were hired because of 'their skill in attracting the attention of the media'. When the selling of haute couture garments is no longer a priority, the more outrageous the collections are, the more publicity is generated for the designer brand – which, in turn, sells more profitable auxiliary products. Large-scale fashion shows called 'Défilés' were held in Paris, in which the big names – including Mugler, Lacroix, Gaultier and Lagerfeld – created spectacular designs; however, few were ever transformed into real fashion (Lehnert, 1998: 171). Bernard Arnault, the financier behind Dior, Givenchy and Lacroix, tactfully described couture as 'the research and development laboratory of Paris style' (Steele, 1999: 288).

Gucci set an example for reinventing an established fashion house by hiring a new young American or European designer as the new 'image-maker' – a move simultaneously employed by Givenchy with the appointment of McQueen in 1996. In less than five years, Ford single-handedly transformed Gucci – seen as a tired old status label – from a $250,000 business facing bankruptcy to a $10 billion asset. In 2004, the *New York Times* described him as 'the ultimate *fin de siècle*' designer. Ironically Ford, who began his career on Seventh Avenue, underlined the continued importance of the interplay of commerce and culture when he explained: 'You know, I started in New York, and really if the collection you designed didn't sell, you were fired the next day.' He added: 'I don't pretend to be anything other than a commercial designer and I'm proud of that' (Frankel, 2001: 132). Starting his own line in 2005, Ford became involved in advertising campaigns, store designs and the packaging of eleven merchandising lines. He has revived the 1960s, 1970s and 1980s look in his collections, of which half of the company's sales are in Asia.

However, other staid couture houses could not withstand the costs of producing bespoke clothing. Yves Saint Laurent haute couture was losing $20 million a year when it closed its doors in 2002. There were only eleven elite haute couture *maisons* remaining in Paris, as few clients were willing to pay in excess of $90,000 for a made-to-measure garment. Saint Laurent had 120 remaining regular customers, including France's first lady, Bernadette Chirac. Bergé, the company chairman, finally admitted: 'Let's not kid ourselves – haute couture is finished and it's better to get out before it disappears completely' (quoted in *The Australian*, 2 November 2002).

Despite these negative predictions for the future of haute couture, the Paris-based institution is still thriving, with many labels such as Dior and Chanel still setting trends for the ready-to-wear industry. The renewed interest in a more sustainable model for the fashion industry has encouraged these industry leaders to embrace the one-off as one potential solution for the over-consumption of fashion in the twenty-first century – at least for clients who can afford a 10,000 USD price tag. Haute couture labels including Vionnet, Schiaparelli and Balenciaga have been resurrected and are presenting new collections based on iconic elements of their respective namesakes. Small independent couture houses have been quietly building a roster of international clients without large advertising budgets, allowing them to experiment more with ideas and create conceptual work, such as Viktor & Rolf (see Chapter 7) or work with new technologies, such as Iris van Herpen (see Chapter 11). Arguably, couture houses stay afloat with the combination of bespoke garments, ready-to-wear lines, and its more lucrative perfume and beauty lines, but this model has been in use since the 1920s. From a financial standpoint, it could be argued that haute couture is, in fact, a better investment than luxury ready-to-wear, gaining in value as artwork would do following a well-known artists' death. From a sustainability standpoint, haute couture also offers an alternative to fast fashion, which is intended for quick use and a 'disposable' mind-set (see Chapter 10), couture is crafted with care to last for decades and become heirloom pieces that can be passed down for generations.

Counterfeit chic

For many, the media's constant bombarding of the public with advertising imagery reflects the malevolence of mass consumerism.[8] By using manipulative devices, advertising seduces the buyer of limited means to purchase imitation 'status' luxury products including pseudo-designer labels and perfume brands. This fuels the production and sale of 'knock-off goods', or cheap fakes, by Asian manufacturers, amongst others. An article in *Bazaar* (April 2005) argued that China was the main source of counterfeiting; however, in the aftermath of negotiations by the United States–China Joint Commission on Commerce and Trade in 2004, the Chinese government announced the formation of a new counterfeiting task force to attack the problem.

As evident from the beginnings of haute couture, issues with copyright infringement plagued high-end designers from C. F. Worth to Madeleine Vionnet (see Chapters 1 and 3), continuing to the current day. In 2006, Louis Vuitton – one of the most pirated brands in the world – had forty full-time lawyers and 250 freelance investigators, and spent 15 million euros to fight counterfeiting. In the same year, LVMH, Prada Holdings, the Burberry Group and Pinault-Printemps-Redoute's Gucci successfully sued a Silk Alley landlord in Beijing, China for copyright infringement. Despite the court ruling, newspaper journalists rationalized that it would not increase the sale of the luxury goods, as buyers in the counterfeit market usually could not afford 'the real thing' anyway.

According to Indicam, an anti-counterfeiting coalition based in Italy, worldwide production of counterfeit goods has reportedly jumped 1,700 per cent since 1993, and according to the ACG, the number of fakes seized in the European Union has increased tenfold between 2000 and 2005 (Thomas, 2005: 75). In the United States, law authorities (in a report to the US Congressional House Committee on International Relations, 2003) argue that they are now recognizing the connection between the financing of terrorists and intellectual property crime.

Undoubtedly, one main concern relates to the negative financial impact this is having on legitimate businesses. In France, where anyone found guilty of producing, importing or exporting

FIGURE 9.2 *Louis Vuitton Spring/Summer 2005 ready-to-wear fashion collection, by designer Marc Jacobs. Counterfeiters study authentic designer goods carefully in order to make imitations of these luxury items. (Photo by Stephane Cardinale/Corbis via Getty Images.)*

fakes as part of an organized gang can receive up to five years in prison and a fine of €500,000, even tourists passing through France with counterfeit goods bought elsewhere risk a maximum fine of €360,000 and up to three years in jail. Similar fines exist in Italy as well. The targeting of the consumer, rather than the producer, might be the most effective solution to this ever-increasing problem of fashion piracy. Michael Kaplinger of the World International Intellectual Property Organisation adds that 'While digital technologies have revolutionized the way in which we create and do business, those same technologies have fuelled a dramatic escalation in IP-crime' (Kaplinger, 2008: 2).

E-commerce and online shopping

The direction of fashion in the twenty-first century has been largely shaped – as most things have – by the internet and the development of e-commerce as a viable alternative to in-person shopping. Department stores were revolutionary in the nineteenth century for combining ease and splendour for shoppers by bringing together all the items one needed to purchase in a single location, and surrounding those essentials with luxury goods to tempt the consumer into overspending (see Chapter 1). Department stores coaxed bourgeois customers to indulge in impulse purchases by offering items on credit to shoppers, as well as easy exchanges or returns for unwanted merchandise, while constantly refreshing shelves with new and exotic items. Consumers revelled in the grandeur of the atmosphere at the Bon Marché, Harrod's, Selfridge's and other retail destinations, which provided them with not only an opportunity to purchase but also to model their new clothing in society; the court life of the Bourgeoisie, so to speak. Middle-class America mirrored this practice in the nineteenth century through the development of department stores that were established throughout the country, such as Macy's or Lord & Taylor's, known for offering service as well as competitive prices. The social aspect of being seen and served at a department store also mimicked the lifestyle of the upper classes, fostered by solicitous customer service by salespeople whose salaries were heavily dependent on commission. Many of these essential retail elements are still inherent in the way people shop today, but the means of delivery have changed.

Even before the internet connected real and virtual life, people were beginning to shop from home using technology. Home shopping channels such as QVC were increasingly popular, and the mail-order catalogue sector for apparel companies had a robust customer service aspect. These services, however, were still conducted via telephone, and as such were not technically e-commerce, which is defined as electronically buying or selling products online through the World Wide Web.

The shift to having products and services available online happened several decades after computer networking was developed. The technical foundation of the internet was initiated in 1966 as ARPANET (Advanced Research Projects Agency Network) by the US Department of Defense, which established an interconnected network of computers in 1969. Set up and utilized primarily for research, the main users were scholars and scientists communicating between university campuses and government agencies across the US and Europe. Eventually, this system became known as the 'Net' from internet – the network infrastructure supporting the connection between computers that relayed information. Up until the mid-1990s, the general public did not access the information that was available on these shared networks.

In order to make the Net more accessible to laypersons, a software overlay was developed, a concept developed by British researcher Tim Berniers-Lee at CERN (Switzerland) in 1989–90

(Press, 2015). Named the World Wide Web and referenced simply as 'the Web' (accounting for the 'www' in front of any site that resides there), the network was imbued with a user-friendly software interface (a browser) allowing for a broader spectrum of users. However, commercial traffic over the internet was still illegal until 1991. The lifting of the non-commercial use ban by the NSF (National Science Foundation), as well as the development of the Web, opened up use of the Net considerably.

When the Web went public in 1994, there were only a handful of e-commerce sites to visit. The '.com' following many sites is short for 'commercial' and indicated sites intended for this use (the generic top-level domain name ended with '.net'). These were not flashy, animated sites to which users have grown accustomed, but simple text-only pages executed in HTML (Hypertext Markup Language). Shoppers could access 'computer stores' which featured icons that looked like buttons to navigate the site, often with instructions such as 'scroll down' or 'click here' to help introduce users to the functionality of the site. The first successful e-commerce site was Amazon, founded by Jeff Bezos in Seattle in 1994; still growing as a tech giant today, Amazon.com was among the first successful online locations to purchase products (primarily books, in those days). Founded the same year, online auction site eBay was also an early revolutionizer in e-commerce by allowing users to sell and purchase items online, opening up opportunities for anyone to become a merchant simply by creating an account.

It should be noted that, just as department stores and ready-made clothing were met with much hesitation and scrutiny by nineteenth-century patrons, online shopping also seemed like a mysterious and dubious replacement for the department store experience to internet users. Technically speaking, the biggest obstacle in e-purchasing was not online access, but security issues with sending payment information and other data over the Net which could be intercepted and exploited. Print publications and cable TV commercials warned consumers about the 'dangers' of online shopping, playing on fears of credit card exploitation.

The first successful example of encrypted e-commerce took place in 1994, between the startup company NetMarket, a website run by 21-year-old Dan Kohn in Nashua, NH, and one of its employees Phil Brandenberger. (At the time, users needed to download and run the Unix-based browser X-Mosaic to access the site.) Logging in to his workstation in New Hampshire from Pennsylvania, Brandenberger purchased a CD of Sting's *Ten Summoner Tales* via credit card on NetMarket, running the data encryption program PGP (Pretty Good Privacy). As the first encryption-protected transaction, this was a crucial step towards establishing secure online purchasing protocols.

This advance in e-commerce was reported on 12 August 1994 in *The New York Times* in an article by Peter Lewis, entitled 'Attention Shoppers: The Internet is Open', describing online retail as 'a new venture that is the equivalent of a shopping mall in cyberspace' (Lewis, 1994). Even the title of this article references the department store mentality, as it is a spoof of K-Mart 'blue light' specials: promotional discounts were announced through overhead speakers in stores, with blue strobe lights locating the items, a practice developed in 1965 and continued through 1990 at over two thousand K-Mart store locations. This relational device comparing in-person shopping to online shopping would persist throughout the first decade of e-commerce as a way of acclimating consumers to a new way of purchasing products. Ultimately, this early foundation for data encryption was critical in coaxing the general public to spend their money online in a strange and unknown place.

This inevitable shift to online retail or 'e-tail' (from electronic retail; coined in 1995) had to offer something to shoppers to make up for the absence of customer service, and this would come in the form of cost savings and customization. Consumers were easily able to research the

FIGURE 9.3 *A television monitor plays a short cable TV commercial warning consumers of possible internet fraud, 4 August 2000 at the Niles, IL City Hall. The 30-second cable spot delivers a stern warning for internet shoppers, 'Ask yourself, "Do I want a chance . . . at becoming a fraud victim?"' (Photo by Tim Boyle/Newsmakers.)*

products they wanted to purchase online, requiring merchants to display more transparency and accountability for price markups. The shift of e-commerce to a growing number of consumers, rather than a few tech-savvy shoppers seeking specialized items, happened in tandem with the globalization of the mid-1990s. As fast fashion became a phenomenon in clothing due to its affordability, the search for bargains became easier to conduct online. Search engines such as Yahoo (founded 1994) and Google (founded 1998), offered their technology for free by generating revenue through ad sales, and were developed in order to help users find what they were looking for faster and more easily. Ironically, the initial developers of the Net – who were running newsgroups, chat rooms or forums using IRC (Internet Relay Chat) to share information – were determined to keep internet culture as non-commercial as possible, but advertising and e-commerce soon changed the nature of cyberspace.

Despite the uptick in e-commerce, online shopping was relegated to the home or work computer due to networking and portability constraints until the first decade of the twenty-first century. The development of 4G computing and smart phones from 2007 onwards made the internet portable, exponentially increasing the penchant for online shopping. By 2017, 80 per cent of cell phone users were using smart phones, and more than 50 per cent of these were connected via 4G/LTE (Deloitte, 2017), making mobile purchases more convenient. As shopping became easier, faster and less expensive, e-commerce contributed to increased sales and production of fast fashion, most of which was globally outsourced to the inexpensive labour force in developing countries (see Chapter 10). While the percentage of online apparel purchases was still lower than the offline rate at 38.6 per cent (DigitalCommerce360.com, 2020), store closures resulting from the COVID-19 global pandemic is approximated to have accelerated the online shopping adaptation and growth by two to three years, according to Barbara Kahn, marketing professor at the University of Pennsylvania's Wharton School of Business (Lufkin, 2020).

Amazon, one of the founding fathers of e-commerce, continues to increase its dominance in consumer purchasing by extending its reach into the fashion realm. According to Amazon's Fashion President Christine Beauchamp, shoppers have purchased over a billion fashion items worldwide via mobile device (Phelps, 2020), prompting the online giant to create its Luxury Stores. Premiering in fall 2020, Amazon partnered with luxury ready-to-wear brands such as Oscar de la Renta to provide customers with a strong mobile application that will allow users to shop via brand or garment category, with an option to virtually try on their selections through its View in 360 tool. Although the shopper is still viewing the clothing on a model rather than oneself, it allows the user to choose their model by size, height and body proportions to improve accuracy.

Fit has proven to be the largest obstacle of online fashion for merchants, resulting in a much higher return rate than its brick-and-mortar counterparts. To this end, virtual tools helping shoppers visualize their garment purchases are crucial to helping brands build a loyal customer base. The shift for fashion companies from department store wholesaler to online partner requires brands to reassess and redefine their marketing and customer service practices; on one hand, Amazon offers increased autonomy for their fashion partners, and new inroads to a broad consumer group for existing and emerging labels. However, this autonomy brings a host of additional issues: brands partnering with them now have to launch and maintain direct-to-consumer e-commerce, particularly with regard to the high rate of online purchase returns, which could prove to be more cost prohibitive than the in-person business model dominating retail from the mid-nineteenth to early twenty-first centuries.

The revolution in online shopping has left once-revolutionary department stores, whose existence threatened the small shops of main street in the nineteenth century, at a cultural and financial disadvantage. Although the existence of brick-and-mortar retail was in jeopardy prior to the COVID-19 pandemic, quarantine orders and the global economic downturn toppled the financially precarious existence of stores. Despite those buyers who craved the in-person shopping experience, prolonged store closures and consumer fears of contracting illness had deleterious effects on department stores and fashion retailers. In 2020 alone, retailers filing for bankruptcy include the Ascena Retail Group, Inc. (parent company of Ann Taylor, Lane Bryant, and others), as well as J. C. Penney Co., Neiman Marcus Group Inc., Brooks Brothers Group, Inc., and J. Crew Group Inc. The oldest department store in the US, Lord & Taylor, closed its flagship store in New York in 2019 after being acquired by Le Tote; unable to regain losses, the new owners filed for bankruptcy in 2020, announcing closures for all store locations (see Chapter 11). Rent the Runway also announced permanent closures of all locations in August 2020, followed by Tapestry, parent company of high-end labels including Kate Spade and Coach, announcing store closings in the same month. Ironically, Amazon – whose success as an online shopping superstar fostered store closings – is increasing its brick-and-mortar locations in the wake of retail's collapse with 'Amazon Go' and other physical locations. But as consumers increasingly shop and live their lives online, fashion's changing existence from physical to virtual space leads to new questions about its role.

Summary

Business strategies in the last few decades of the twentieth century led to new practices in the organization of branding. Global outsourcing and communications linked through technology led to inexpensive production, making fashion a powerful part of the global economy. The globalization of the fashion supply chain and the development of multibrand conglomerates led to an increase in licensing, which in turn led to rampant counterfeiting. The globalization of fashion simultaneously created mega-conglomerates, while also fostering the individuality of smaller brands. Despite the grim outlook for the future of haute couture, this sector of the fashion world has managed to reinvent itself by hiring young designers and embracing ready-to-wear, beauty and perfume lines to provide revenue.

Notes

1 In Paris, only four new couture houses opened between 1970 and 1995.

2 The first known license was created by Schiaparelli in 1940, but licenses were more consistently created by Dior in the 1950s. Pierre Cardin also worked extensively with licensing deals from the late 1950s onwards.

3 Carlo Gambino assumed mafia control of the garment district in 1957, and took over the Consolidated Carriers Corporation, the largest and most important trucking business in the area. As distribution costs soared, America's $2.5 billion fashion industry suffered. As a result of these corrupt practices, from 1955 to 1992 business shrank by 75 per cent, costing New York some 225,000 jobs.

4 Marshall McLuhan became famous for his books entitled *The Medium is the Message* (1967) and *Culture is Our Business* (1970).

5 Sullivan, Epstein and Friedman both refer to De Beers as a 'cartel'.

6 A diffusion line is a cheaper production line of apparel, which is marketed to a wider audience at lower prices.

7 In 1992, 75 per cent of the couturiers were over fifty, and four were over seventy (Crane, 2000: 143).

8 In literature, as in the arts, writers criticized consumerism and media manipulation. John Kenneth Galbraith wrote *The Affluent Society* and Vance Packard wrote *The Hidden Persuaders*, *The Status Seekers* and *The Pyramid Climber*.

10

The Sustainability of Fashion

Introduction

This chapter will reinforce the need for a more sustainable approach to fashion, looking at multiple factors that impact the global industry. Outlining the social, economic and environmental effects of current and past practices, changes to the current system will be discussed in conjunction with consumer attitudes towards fashion. Sustainable alternatives, including use of chemical-free organic fibres and textiles, nontoxic dyes, and biosynthetic alternatives to natural fibres and leather, will be charted alongside technological advances. New strategies introduced and developed to foster sustainable textile production, including those that impact both developed and developing countries, will be discussed. In terms of waste, a symbiotic liaison between the designer, patternmaker, manufacturer and consumer. Recycling and vintage clothing is also considered as another form of sustainable fashion consumption.

The origins of disposable fashion

In order to recognize the major shifts in the ready-to-wear apparel industry, it's helpful to lay out a timeline. Many issues with regard to manufacturing in the fashion industry today have stemmed from the technological advances made during the industrial and post-industrial eras. Up to the nineteenth century, clothing production was a slow and difficult process, requiring significant capital; expensive wardrobes were, in fact, a form of both social and financial currency primarily reserved for the upper classes. Advances in fibre processing, spinning and weaving hastened the production of cloth, but the cutting and assemblage of garments was still a laborious process performed by hand. The invention of the sewing machine and the development of an organized manufacturing system sped up the process of garment making to create mid-priced clothing that developed into the ready-to-wear industry, but at a human cost to the labour force (see Chapters 1 and 4). Various consumer price points developed within ready-to-wear sector, from luxury designer items to discount clothes copied from top names in fashion.

The ready-to-wear industry was cultivated in the US, developing into a thriving economic sector during and after the Second World War. According to the US Department of Labor, up to the 1960s, 95 per cent of American clothing was made domestically, and the average household spent nearly 10 per cent of its income on clothing and footwear, buying approximately twenty-five new items per household annually (Bureau of Labor Statistics, 2012). In comparison, the 2000s have seen domestic clothing production in the US drop to only 2 per cent, and households spend only 3.5 per cent of its income on a growing number of apparel items, indicating that people are buying more apparel items for less money.[1] Given the rate of inflation over this fifty-year period, one wonders: how have clothes become cheaper as the price of everything else continues to climb? This can only be possible through a decrease in the retail and manufacturing price of clothing, which is dependent on a number of factors.

As the ready-to-wear apparel sector gained momentum during the early twentieth century, the industry was firmly planted in New York, where it was crucial to have proximity between manufacturers and design offices in the garment district. However, this started to shift in the 1970s as countries in Asia and Latin America established textile mills and garment factories (see Chapter 8). The shift from maritime to commercial jet travel also sped up shipping and made global production much more expedient. In a bid to economize manufacturing costs, many designers and design firms moved their manufacturing off-shore to China, Bangladesh and other developing countries, whose labour laws were not as stringent as the US and whose factories could handle large-scale production runs for mass-produced garments. To an extent, this prohibited smaller firms that only wanted short production runs from accessing similar services. Off-shore production often led to problems with quality control, counterfeit or copied designs, and ethical considerations, including underpaid and exploited labour, child labour and unsatisfactory working conditions, many of which could not be controlled by the designer. The North American Free Trade Agreement (NAFTA) of 1994 eliminated many of the last financial barriers of overseas manufacture, including import taxes on clothing. Following this development, retail chains such as The Gap and J. C. Penney transitioned away from domestic clothing manufacture in the 1990s, focusing instead on design and marketing; luxury ready-to-wear labels followed in the decades to come. Global manufacturing practices became even more cost-effective with the public availability of the World Wide Web (1995) and email (see Chapter 9), which replaced costly telephonic and fax communication. As a result, ready-to-wear became less expensive and more plentiful, but declined in fabric and sewing quality.

The ability to create this global supply chain, in which design houses collected bids on production and sourced the least expensive manufacturer regardless of location, was due to the availability of petroleum. Much of the world's oil supply comes from the Middle East; treaties made in the early twentieth century between the West with Middle Eastern countries, and the formation of OPEC (Organization of Petroleum Exporting Countries), ensured that European and American businesses had plenty of fuel to power vehicles. Not only did this available petroleum provide cheap transportation for global shipping, but it provided the base for many of the synthetic fabrics that dominate fast fashion today, including polyester, spandex and other inexpensive lab-made thermoplastics. In terms of retail, these developments allowed the apparel industry to offer a wider variety of goods to a younger demographic and lower class of consumer with less disposable income. Conspicuous consumption following the Second World War was represented not by bejewelled and expensive materials, but rather by a sheer abundance of mass-produced consumer goods.

The era of consumer culture provided new directions for fashion as well. In the 1950s, department stores such as Macy's bought couture originals from Paris and, in agreement with the designer, produced lower-priced copies of the garment for middle-class consumers (Tortora and Marcketti, 2015: 516). Licensing deals also provided designer labels on less expensive clothing. By lowering the price of fashionable clothing, consumers experiencing post-war financial stability could shop more often. In 1960s London, boutiques such as Biba attracted large groups of young shoppers (see Chapter 5) with limited spending capacity by changing styles frequently and piling clothing on tables, creating visual abundance. Pricing garments within the salary range of the average working girl in London was the guiding principle of

Hulanicki's merchandising philosophy; customers returned weekly or monthly to replenish their supply of affordable, stylish clothing.

Although clothing produced for Macy's or Biba was hardly 'disposable' (fabrics were primarily still natural, or manufactured from natural materials rather than synthetic materials) the idea of cheap, disposable fashion – as well as disposable art – became manifest in the notions of postmodernity. It was the message and not the medium that was of primary concern. Fads or 'short-lived' fashions challenged the concept of permanence, classic styling and practicality. Neo-Dadaism, as it was called in artistic circles, reignited an interest in Duchamp's early work. This renewed interest in conceptual art was initiated by Duchamp's first exhibition in New York in the early 1960s (which included his famous 1917 ready-made, a urinal entitled 'Fountain'). After it had been rejected by mainstream institutions, the exhibition was held at Alfred Steiglitz's Gallery at 291 Fifth Avenue. In 1963, the first great Duchampian retrospective was held in Los Angeles, and it reinforced the notion of the ready-made, which not only influenced the development of pop art but also helped to consolidate interest in conceptual art. It evolved around the Fluxus movement and was inspired by a number of post-war artists who, in the 1950s, effectively exhibited nihilistic work that questioned the nature of the art product itself. New York artist Robert Rauschenberg exhibited 'Erased De Kooning Drawing' (1953), which was a piece of blank paper. In 1957, Yves Klein declared that his paintings were now invisible and to prove it he exhibited an empty room. It was titled 'The Surfaces and Volumes of Invisible Pictorial Sensibility'. The birth of the conceptual art movement, which dated from approximately 1967 to 1978, formally acknowledged that the idea or conceptual process was more important than the end product, or artefact. It was the means, rather than the end, that mattered – an idea stated by Sol Lewitt in his 'Paragraphs for Conceptual Art' in an article for *ArtForum* (Summer 1967). Joseph Kosuth's experimental work 'One and Three Chairs' (1965), which included a physical chair, a picture of a chair, and the dictionary definition of a chair, printed and mounted on the wall, also hearkened back to many of the Dada and Surrealist concepts of the 1910s and 1920s. Arguably, an end art product was not necessary at all, and the event or the art process could be recorded for history through photography or video.

By the end of the 1960s, 'happenings' – which were seen as a type of art 'performance' – gathered strength, and they became integral to the anti-materialistic views of the hippie movement. They embraced social change and emancipation for women, students and children. They were tied to 'the extraordinary productions of pop concerts – from the Rolling Stones to The Who, from Roxy Music to Alice Cooper – the new performance became stylish, flamboyant and entertaining' (Goldberg, 2001: 154). Contemporary performance art evolved from these conceptual beginnings. Art could be ephemeral and transient. 'Live gestures have constantly been used as a weapon against the conventions of established art' (Goldberg, 2001: 7).

Considering these contemporaneous movements, it is more than coincidence that paper dresses were very much a fashion fad between 1966 and 1968.[2] With paper dresses, the purchaser could use scissors, crayons, paint and stickers to customize the garment. Paper clothing had all the attributes necessary to be truly democratic fashion – it was affordable, accessible and appealed to the young. In *Art History*, Whitely (1989: 82) discusses how the low cost of manufacturing and printing paper garments was in keeping with the pop art sensibility of 'enjoy it today; sling it tomorrow' consumerism. He adds that, at a time when fashions changed so rapidly in order to be up to date, it didn't matter if the fashion consumer purchased inexpensive, flimsy garments because by the time they were worn out, they were also out of fashion. Commenting on the New York City Boutique Paraphernalia, where designer Betsey Johnson started her career, Warhol characteristically quips: 'Almost everything in the store would disintegrate within a couple of weeks, so this was really pop.' In the 1960s, people's expectations were that disposability was the way of the future (Healy, 1996: 28), and as paper could not last for more than one or two wearings, this contributed to its up-to-the-minute fashionability.

In the world of science and technology, society was increasingly developing a throwaway mentality. NASA had considered paper clothing for space travel, and the Scott Paper Company released a psychedelic paisley dress in 1966 as an advertising gimmick to promote a new line of table napkins in the United States. They offered readers a paper dress for $1.25 and, in less than six months, 500,000 dresses had been sold. The dress was very fragile and light-sensitive, as the material was made from binding wood pulp and rayon mesh. Mars Manufacturing Corporation, America's leading producer of paper dresses, used the wonder fabric Kaycel, as it was both fire- and water-resistant, and the dresses were labelled 'Waste Basket Boutique'. France produced the

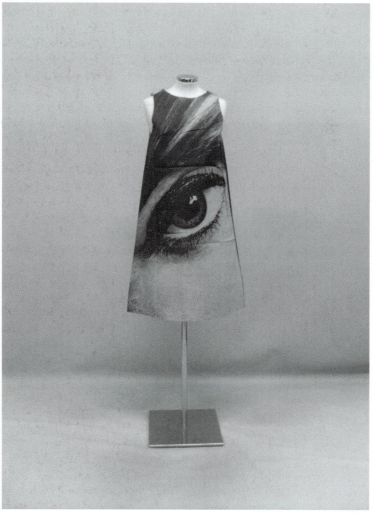

FIGURE 10.1 *'Mystic Eye' Paper Dress by Harry Gordon, 1967. The photographic eye is that of Audrey Hepburn. Collection of the Peloponnesian Folklore Foundation, museum no. 2006.6.90. (CC-BY.)*

paper bikini, designed to disintegrate upon contact with water, and Dispo in London sold throwaway paper dresses that could withstand three washes and three ironings. Campbell's brought out the Souper Dress – a sleeveless paper shift which featured repetitive Campbell's soup cans (à la Warhol) as a promotional piece of fun clothing. American graphic designer Harry Gordon designed a series of poster dresses (one was a close-up shot of an eye with long eyelashes), with images screen printed on to an A-line mini dress that fastened at the shoulders with Velcro straps.

The designer Paco Rabanne was commissioned by Scott Paper to make paper dresses to complement his better-known plastic and metal creations designed for the Paris catwalk. Alexandra Palmer (2001: 85–105) explains that paper clothing, which appeared to be nothing more than a very short-lived fad, had a considerable impact upon the fashion of the day. She offers an extensive catalogue of the large variety of garments worn by both ordinary people and an array of celebrities. Among others, she lists the Beatles' custom-made neon orange jackets worn on their Los Angeles visit, the paper saris of Air India's hostesses, plus numerous garments worn by the rich and famous at high-profile paper balls and dinners, some of whom traded their couture garments for paper clothing. Palmer explains that widespread public interest in paper garments was furthered by these examples of high society in disposable garments, stating 'the highly fashionable Mrs Kennedy' and 'the Duchess of Windsor, who was on the "Best Dressed" list, wore a paper dress thus providing a role model for older and more conventional women to wear them' (2001: 85–105).

The mission of the pop artists was to take art out of the galleries into the streets, the main objective being to make art part of life, as it had been until the eighteenth century when national museums became the repositories of formerly private collections. In terms of cultural significance, this was the main contribution of the paper dress. With its novelty value, it became a metaphor for the concept of disposability in a modern industrialized society, who rejected the 'make do and mend' sensibilities of the previous generation.[3] By rejecting this wartime ethos and reinforcing the potential for the successful substitution of materials and clothing with new ones, it attested to the unlimited possibilities for fashion within the new technological world.

This mind-set of clothing as a disposable item formed the foundation for today's fast fashion industry. The term 'fast fashion' is a reference to the turnaround rate of new styles from catwalk to runway, as much a by-product of the internet revolution as the globalization of manufacturing and inexpensive labour. Consumer expectations for a constant supply of fresh looks has resulted in a rehashing of previous styles, and fashion presents as many as twelve 'seasons' per year, rather than the two main collections (Spring/Summer and Fall/Winter) that previously defined major showings. A vicious cycle is created by the availability of cheap clothing and consumer spending habits, in which clothes quickly fall out of fashion and fall apart at the seams, headed for the trash heaps sent to landfills in the developing world.

Industry issues: Waste, pollution and labour

The immediate issues plaguing the fashion industry in the twenty-first century include negative environmental impact as well as issues with fair trade. Industrialization as a whole was catastrophic for the earth's natural ecological balance, emitting carbon-filled steam-powered smoke from trains and factories, as well as chemical waste, into the air and water. Petroleum-based vehicles such as cars, trucks and airplanes have greatly accelerated the rate at which the planet is degrading, leading to various social and political movements striving to affect change.

Ethical issues mentioned earlier in this chapter include underpaid and overworked labour forces, whose working conditions resemble those of the immigrants who first worked in the apparel industry in New York City (see Chapter 4). Ultimately, these social and environmental issues are overlooked time and again as the spending inherent to consumer culture continues to spark demand for inexpensive goods, including fashion.

The fashion industry has the second-largest carbon footprint of any industry on the planet, second only to the petroleum industry (Quantis, 2018). One of the major issues with environmental impact comes from fibre sourcing and textile manufacture. The industry has relied on the production of textiles made from raw fibres such as cotton that are cultivated in fields where considerable amounts of water are needed and chemicals used, despite the fact that insecticides pollute both the air and water. The World Wildlife Fund has estimated that it takes 8,500 litres (2,245 gallons) of water to raise 1 kilogram (2.2 pounds) of cotton lint – enough to make one pair of blue jeans (Kaye, 2011). Energy is expended in the spinning, weaving and knitting processes, and along with the transportation and distribution of the raw and finished products, this increases greenhouse gas emissions.

Other natural fibres have been flagged for being problematic as well: protein-based fibres such as silk and wool are cited by animal rights activists as a form of animal cruelty. Silk production of *Bombyx mori* moths includes boiling the unhatched larvae in order to reel off the filament from the cocoon, killing the moth; this breed-to-kill method is sometimes rejected in favour of 'Ahimsa' or 'Peace' silk, made from silk staple fibres after the moth has hatched. In addition to fur and leather, which often results in the slaughter of animals simply to obtain their hides, the shearing of wool from sheep is also considered harmful to the animal by organizations such as PETA (People for the Ethical Treatment of Animals). Cellulosic (plant-based) fibres such as linen (made from flax) or fibres such as hemp are increasingly used as a more sustainable alternative to cotton, but also require intense amounts of water and pesticides if grown conventionally, as well as human labour to break down the bast fibres for spinning.

Perhaps the most environmentally problematic aspect of contemporary textile manufacture is in the dyeing and finishing of fabric. Textiles and fibres were dyed with natural sources for thousands of years until the mid-nineteenth century, when Englishman Henry Perkin accidentally discovered aniline dyeing through a failed chemistry experiment in 1856. As a young medical student, Perkin was attempting to synthesize coal tar – the unwanted runoff produced by all those coal-powered factories and steam engines in the industrial era – into quinine, as a potential cure for malaria. Dropping a piece of fabric into the solution and leaving it overnight, Perkin returned to find a brilliant purple colour had stained the cloth, and the synthetic dye industry was born. Aniline dyes quickly replaced natural plant-based dyes such as madder, indigo or safflower; requiring massive amounts of water and polluting local waterways with chemical runoff, aniline dyes were also inferior to natural methods as they were not colourfast. Synthetic dyes contained highly toxic chemicals and pesticides such as arsenic, and the popularity of the first man-made fibre, rayon (first discovered in 1888) led to vast amounts of chemical pollution. Subsequently, finishing processes were developed to extend lifespan and improve performance of aniline-dyed textiles. Other finishing processes developed in the twentieth century – such as water repellency, wrinkle or stain resistance – are also water-intensive, and include chemicals that deposit pollutants into local waterways.

Following the Second World War, production of thermoplastic fibres such as nylon, polyester and spandex made of petroleum-based polymers, seemed like revolutionary fabrics. These were used for foundation garments and swimwear of the 1950s, coloured tights of the 1960s, leisure suits and tube tops of the 1970s, bodysuits of the 1980s, and skinny jeans of the 1990s and

2000s. However, these garments require hundreds of years to biodegrade. Clothing made with synthetics do not hold up over time, and are considered disposable due to how inexpensively they can be purchased. For eco-conscious consumers, these are often donated to second-hand clothing organizations or deposited in clothing banks; however, given the number of garments received and the poor quality of textiles used, discarded garments are most often resold by large-scale recyclers to developing countries. In Africa, mountains of plastic and polyester/synthetic throwaway apparel are being used for landfill, but they have already reached capacity for purchasing disposable clothing from the developing world (Dowsett and Obulutsa, 2020). The bulk of recycled clothing – those that consumers will donate to Goodwill or deposit clothing in bins in an effort to be eco-conscious – end up being incinerated to save costs for developed countries. As of 2016, New York City spent over 20 million USD to export textiles to landfills and incinerators (Wicker, 2016). Some of this has been diverted by programs such as Re-FashioNYC, launched in 2011 and run by the Department of Sanitation, but it equals a small percentage of the total waste.

While there has been a resurgence in recent years of the rediscovered art of hand dyeing and fabric printing using natural vegetable dyes or azo-free dyeing, these craft-based techniques are too labour-intensive and expensive to offer a solution to the global industry. According to textile conservator Sarah Scaturro (2008: 469–88), technology plays an ambivalent role in the environmental debate, as it acts as both a destructive and enabling force. Scaturro argues that it heralded the built-in system of redundancy through efficient 'fast fashion' products, which led to 'a profusion of detrimental textile manufacturing by-products and waste entering the ecosystem' as well as 'a vast amount of energy needed to make and take care of all the clothing produced'. As a more positive facilitator, she believes that, in the future, technology can serve to improve methods of clothing creation, consumption and disposal. 'This tension between technology, as a positive or negative factor in the sustainable reality of a culture's resources, is at the core of any discussion on technology and environmentalism' (Scaturro, 2008: 474). It seems that there are no easy solutions. For example, she points out that while the organic fibre advocate organization Organic Exchange is committed to increasing the production of organic cotton by 50 per cent a year in the United States, the reality is that organic cotton does not produce the same yield or volume that conventional cotton can, making it more costly, and there is virtually no reduction in the harm that occurs during the subsequent dyeing and manufacturing process. It would seem that an international standard is required that oversees the entire production cycle not only of cotton yarns[4] but fabrics generated from renewable sources.

Sustainable alternatives

Environmentally-conscious designers and textile engineers have been forging the path to a more circular fashion economy, with the goal to eliminate waste. Considering the current cycle as a linear one – buy, use and quickly discard – apparel items have little reuse or recycling. As of 2019, only 1 per cent of clothing is recycled, and what doesn't end up in landfill is incinerated, also causing environmental harm. Since the early 2000s, sustainable alternatives to water-intensive and synthetic fibres have been explored as viable alternatives for environmentally-friendly textiles and apparel. Decreasing fashion's carbon footprint, innovative companies are developing biosynthetic fabric and fibres, made from polymers created from renewable resources. Now commercially available, first generation biopolymers from starches and sugars in foods such as corn and beets can replace nonrenewable petroleum-based fibres, and even be processed

FIGURE 10.2 *Rachel Marx walks the runway in a biosynthetic leather coat from the Stella McCartney collection as part of the Paris Fashion Week Womenswear Fall/Winter 2020/2021 in Paris, France. (Photo by Peter White/Getty Images.)*

on the same equipment to create a product that mimics the qualities of synthetics (Aboutbiosynthetics.org, 2017).

Viable biosynthetics present the next revolution in textiles. Bolt Threads, based in Emeryville, CA, has created a faux leather called Mylo, made from mycelium, the network of cells in mushrooms. The resulting fabric is a leather alternative used for handbags and clothing. The company has also engineered Microsilk, which mimics the silk fibres spun from spiders, by engineering proteins and fermenting them in yeast, sugar and water. Sustainable fashion frontrunners Stella McCartney and Adidas, in collaboration with Bolt Threads, used Microsilk in the Autumn/Winter 2019 collection for the Infinite Hoodie and Biofabric Tennis Dress, both of which are biodegradable, representing the potential to create a circular fashion economy. In addition to lab-grown leather alternatives, McCartney's label also uses recycled polyester to replace luxury products such as Brazilian calf leather, which harms both the planet and the animal world. More recently, McCartney worked closely with Bolt Threads to develop a new collection of garments made of Mylo (Farra, 2021).

Additional leather alternatives such as Technik-leather, utilized by Los Angeles-based Vicki von Holzhausen for her handbag line, improve upon the old synthetics such as PVC by using recyclable polyurethane. Other biosynthetics with a leather-like quality include the Spanish Piñatex, made from the fibrous waste from pineapples, already in collaboration with H & M and Hugo Boss. Some biosynthetic fabrics have even been proposed as carbon-negative: New

York designer Charlotte McCurdy has created a bioplastic made from algae powder, which draws carbon out of the atmosphere. This concept is also the guiding principle of PostCarbon Labs, a London start-up founded by co-founders Dian-Jen Lin and Hannes Hulstaert: the team created a photosynthetic algae layer which can be applied to any clothing to produce as much oxygen as a small oak tree.

Other lab-made fabrics utilize food waste to create alternative natural fibres. Due Di Latte, founded by Italian fashion designer Antonella Bellina, creates 'milk fibre' by using the whey from expiring dairy products and spinning it at high velocity into a silky staple fibre. Her research was inspired by that of 1930s Italian chemist Antonio Feretti, who used casein from milk to produce a wool-like fibre he called Lanatil; Feretti's invention didn't sustain popularity due to issues with tensile strength and odour issues, but Bellina built upon his initial experiments to create a product that is washable and pliable, as well as hyperallergenic and antibacterial. The company Orange Fiber uses citrus waste from Sicily's juice industry to create a silky cellulosic fibre that can be woven into a silky sustainable fabric, or blended with other fibres. First presented at Expo Gate in 2014 by Polytechnic Milan graduates Adriana Santanocito and Enrica Arena, Orange Fiber is in use for a capsule collection by Ferragamo and the H & M 'conscious' collection (2019).

Dyes have undergone a revolution as well. According to the World Bank, textile dyeing is responsible for 20 per cent of industrial global water pollution. Companies such as UK-based Colorifix seek a correction of both water usage and synthetic dye replacement by engineering colours found in nature. Recreating the DNA sequence of any natural pigmentation source, they extract the colour sequence and replicate it through live microorganisms. As of 2020, the company is working with fast fashion giant H & M to create more sustainable clothing. The French company Pili is also reducing its carbon footprint by using agricultural waste to produce bioengineered organisms whose enzymes work at room temperature without toxic solvents. Striving to create a more environmentally-friendly dye for blue jeans, San Francisco-based Tinctorum is engineering bacteria that mimics the Japanese *Polygirum tinctorum* indigo plant, replacing harmful chemical dyes and runoff.

Returning full circle to the idea of paper clothing – the original 'disposable fashion' – the Swedish-based company Pulp It is creating a nonwoven paper fabric from wood pulp and other bio-based materials in conjunction with London's Centre for Circular Design. Finished with natural dyes and assembled into garments using ultrasound to fuse the layers together, pleating is added for stretch; customers can customize garments with laser-etched designs and choose colours, patterns and silhouettes.

In addition to solutions for more sustainable and biodegradable materials, much of the excess waste in fashion can be eliminated by altering garment design. Pattern-making is integral to the design process as technical and aesthetic considerations must be considered simultaneously. In today's fashion production, pre-consumer fabric wastage equates to 15 to 20 per cent in traditional cut-and-sew methodologies. When methods are informed by environmental concerns, designers look back to historical precedents, including fully fashioned knitted garments that have no cutting, tube-knitted seamless garments informed by advanced technology (Miyake's APOC) or one-size-fits-all made from uncut rectangular lengths of fabric. When there are fabric off-cuts, this material must be able to be recycled, and this could include using it for quilts, as fibre, or as rags to make rugs, blankets, stuffing or other small craft items. This would allow all off-cuts to be made into new fabrics. Chemical companies like Wellman USA, an early leader in synthetic fibre recycling, and Japan's Teijin, which introduced Eco-Circle, have established successful polyester-recycling technology schemes.

In general terms, waste reduction is preferable to recycling or disposal, because 'recycling can impact negatively on the environment through transportation (fuel, emissions) and reprocessing (in particular, water, energy and chemical consumption)' (Gertsakis and Lewis in Rissanen, 2005: 3). Historical precedents established in fashion history present more sustainable constructive methods than are used today. These included ancient traditional and national costumes such as the Greek peplos made from two large rectangular pieces of fabric pinned at each shoulder, the Japanese kimono, which was made from eight rectangular pieces of fabric sewn together, and the Indian sari, which wraps around the body. Madeleine Vionnet and Madame Grès, renowned as masters of drape in the early decades of the twentieth century, were admired for their genius in manipulating cloth rather than cutting it; Zandra Rhodes's textile designs determined the shape and form of her garments in the 1970s and 1980s; Hishinuma's experimental use of triangles in the 1980s fitted together to form a modular unit as a means of preserving fabric; Miyake's APOC vision introduced in the 1990s used a tubular knitting system as a means of revolutionizing and simplifying garment construction; and the label MATERIALBYPRODUCT was created by Australian co-designers who developed a new system of pattern-making in the 2000s where the off-cuts are used as a decoration or extension of the main garment.[5]

Technology also provides potential solutions to the problem of waste. Mycotex, a sustainable fabric made from mushroom roots by research group NEFFA in The Netherlands, uses living organisms and 3-D pattern imaging to create seamless, fully fashioned garments that will biodegrade once no longer wearable – simply bury in the ground and let it decompose. Also working with the idea of reducing fabric waste and streamlining garment construction, the Australian design team Donna Franklin and Gary Cass partnered to develop Micro'be': a seamless biosynthetic garment created with bacteria from fermented wine (2012). The project team then went on to create a 'Beer Dress' from Nanollose Microbial Cellulose, inspired by the flower of the hop plant. Diana Scherer, a Dutch artist working with plant roots to create a lacelike fabric, displayed her biodegradable dresses at 'Fashioned From Nature' at the Victoria and Albert Museum (2018–19), exploring the possibilities for natural cloth production without the labour and greenhouse gases created by textile factories.

Green is the new black

In 2008, fashion writer David Lipke posed the question 'Is Green Fashion an Oxymoron?' in *Women's Wear Daily* (31 March 2008). Lipke's article ponders how 'an industry driven by disposable trends and aesthetic whims can reconcile itself to an era of conservation'?

Fashion, as a 2.5 trillion-dollar industry, has been slow to embrace changes that would threaten its viability as a financial heavyweight in the global economy. While the 'Green Designer' exhibition was held as early as 1986 at the Design Centre in London and the label Esprit led the way with its inaugural Ecollection in November 1991, 'fashion as a design discipline has been late to investigate the theoretical greening of the design production loop, lagging behind industrial design and architecture' (Thomas, 2008: 526). Yet, interestingly, consumer activist group campaigns have tended to target fashion events more than other disciplines. Marketing strategists realize that, in the postmodernist age, when social and political commentary has become associated with both art and sartorial design, consumers now demand accurate and truthful labelling (provenance) and information relating to fair payment and healthy working conditions (fair trade) in order to make informed and conscientious decisions regarding their choice of clothing. For some, shopping has become an ethical minefield. According to Thomas,

FIGURE 10.3 *General view at the MATCHESFASHION.COM X KATHARINE HAMNETT LFW Spring/Summer 2018 event at ICA on 17 February 2018 in London, England. Hamnett's T-shirts functioned as billboards for social justice. (Photo by Darren Gerrish/WireImage.)*

'potentially, there is an ideological connection between ethical trading and ethical fashion, thus conferring on both an altruistic intent and political stance' (2008: 532).

The dichotomy still remains that fashion, throughout history, has been driven by a desire to establish social class differentiation and status within a group through conspicuous consumption, but the desire to ally oneself voluntarily with an ideology has proved to be a stronger incentive in the twentieth and twenty-first centuries. In the 1970s, in particular, environmental concerns, including the energy crisis and the inhumane treatment of animals, led to major changes in the textile, fur and cosmetic industries. Subsequently, it became very fashionable to wear multilayered natural materials, such as wool, cotton and hemp, fake fur coats and to don natural complexions. Mixing art and politics, artist Katharine Hamnett initially exhibited her 'environmental' T-shirts (see Chapter 7) in the 1980s, and has continued with garments donning activist slogans such as 'Make Trade Fair' and 'No More Fashion Victims'. She then turned to fashion design and today creates 'fashionable' clothing, adhering strictly to environmental and ethical guidelines.

Other designers have used their celebrity to promote causes. From the 2010s to the present, Vivienne Westwood has been openly committed to being an activist for environmental and social causes, taking on big oil to protest fracking and promoting change in order to defend mother earth. In 2020, Stella McCartney released her 'A to Z of Stella McCartney' – a manifesto outlining the commitment of her label to using sustainable materials and upcycling fabrics. Determined to promote a zero waste fashion industry, protect natural resources, and defend

FIGURE 10.4 *A model presents a creation made of fur-free-fur by Stella McCartney during the Women's Fall/Winter 2020–21 Ready-to-Wear collection fashion show in Paris, on 2 March 2020. (Photo by ANNE-CHRISTINE POUJOULAT/AFP via Getty Images.)*

animal rights, McCartney's Fall/Winter 2020 Collection included fur-free-fur (made from corn) and biosynthetic leather. Models were led down the catwalk in Paris by a giant dancing cow holding a non-leather purse.

In her essay 'Clothes That Connect' (2007), Kate Fletcher accurately predicted that in order for eco-fashion to be sustainable, its clothing must be fashionably stylish as well as environmentally correct. In the same decade, American academic Theresa Winge postulated that eco-fashion has now become depoliticized – no longer associated with anti-war campaigns and anti-mainstream activities as it was in the 1960s and 1970s – and less stereotyped as a commodity fetish by celebrities, including actors George Clooney and Julia Roberts and photographer Annie Leibovitz, who were among the first to promote sustainable fashion as an aesthetic life choice 'on the red carpets and in the pages of magazines' (2008: 513).

Since the mid-2000s, sustainable fashion has attracted a much wider audience. As a popular theme targeted by magazines, journals, websites, special events, educational institutions and corporate and commercial bodies, the industry seemed to become suddenly consumed with its own practices and the deleterious effects of over-production. For example, in 2006 *Vanity Fair* magazine brought out its 'Green Issue' outlining the designers who had presented eco-fashion on the runway.[6] Smaller niche magazine publications endorsing eco-fashion from the mid-2000s include the *New Consumer*, *The Ethical Consumer* and *Ecology* (United Kingdom), *Organic Style* (United States), *Green* and *GreenPages* (Australia) plus other mainstream magazines that contain photographs and articles featuring celebrity activists with environmental issues such as *Elle*, *Glamour* and *Marie Claire*. Numerous academic book publications and journal articles have proliferated, including the international journal *Fashion Theory* (Bloomsbury), which in 2008 dedicated a special issue to eco-fashion with writings from scholars around the world discussing the complexity of sustainability issues in fashion. Subsequently, a range of sustainability-based themes have dominated fashion textbooks, from sourcing eco-friendly fibres and ethical production to zero waste fashion design.[7] The ethical and sustainable magazine *SIX* was launched in 2011 to celebrate the designers, individuals, independent brands and companies that are creating a more ethical and sustainable future for the fashion industry. The 2010s witnessed the flourishing of online sources for both professionals and consumers. Ethical Fashion forum (www.ethicalfashionforum.com) outlines how to combine sustainable practice with commercial success in fashion, and fashion-conscience.com operates vending portals that offer different interpretations of ethical fashion, subcategorized as vegan, sustainable, ethical and by natural materials. Consumer education has also become widespread, with websites such as The Good Trade (thegoodtrade.com) providing consumers with a portal that hosts a daily newsletter, blogs by guest specialists, and a section devoted to 'Zero Waste'. Although consumers are still motivated by cost efficiency, there is a growing movement among Millennials to make more socially-conscious fashion purchases, and this demographic is seeking out companies who are transparent about their practices. Social media influencers have played a major role in the popularization (or boycott) of certain companies based on ethics related to materials or practices that do not fit a sustainable profile.

Exhibitions, trade fairs, global forums and eco-friendly design competitions and awards have attracted considerable local, national and international interest over the first decades of the twenty-first century. The Museum at FIT (Fashion Institute of Technology) in New York generated awareness in the heart of the garment district through their exhibition 'Eco-Fashion: Going Green' (23 May to 11 November 2010). Organizers Jennifer Farley and Colleen Hill explored multiple themes related to sustainable clothing, including synthetic and natural fibres, textile manufacturing, ethical treatment of workers in garment production, and animal rights. Repurposed/recycled garments by high-end labels such as XULY.Bët and Martin Margiela were displayed alongside organic cotton garments by Edun. Handmade patchwork clothing from the 1960s and 1970s by groups such as the Appalachian-based Mountain Artisan cooperative were displayed side by side with luxury designer Giorgio di Sant'Angelo, demonstrating the universal appeal of repurposed garments. Contemporary handmade garments by designers such as John Patrick and Carlos Miele, both of whom work with indigenous artisans in Peru and Brazil respectively, indicates the continuing concern with environmental and ethical issues specific to the textile and apparel industries.

The Shanghai International Fashion Culture Festival in 2009, which included the 'Green Fashion' International Clothing and Textile Expo (covering a vast area of 50,000 square metres in its International Expo Centre), was one of many large-scale trade shows that incorporated a sustainable platform. Since then, a number of sustainable fashion weeks have been launched in cities around the world, starting with the inaugural event in Helsinki, Finland founded by Evelyn Mora. Inspiring similar events founded on green principles, sustainable fashion weeks began in Vancouver, Seattle and San Francisco, and Eco-Fashion Week in Australia (est. 2017). The first carbon-neutral fashion show was held by designer Gabriela Hearst in New York in 2020; in Copenhagen, chief executive of Danish Fashion Week, Cecelie Thorsmark, pledges a more sustainable fashion week by 2023. Moving forward, the business model for the industry needs to change in order to remain both profitable, and this includes educating the next generation of financial leaders to consider a more holistic approach – a concept that has been trending

FIGURE 10.5 *A hand-painted dress by John Patrick on display at the Museum of FIT for the exhibition 'Eco-Fashion: Going Green' (2010). (Photo by SCOTT MORGAN /Patrick McMullan via Getty Images.)*

since the mid-2000s. In design education, several programs have developed an area of specialty in sustainable fashion, from Central Saint Martin's and the London College of Fashion, to FIT and Cornell University in New York. In business education, one UK MBA business degree, in conjunction with the conservation charity World Wildlife Fund, has incorporated sustainability at its core, entitled the 'One Planet MBA' at the University of Exeter (Morgan, 2011). The program includes modules on corporate social responsibility and a circular economy design challenge for graduate students, solving real problems for organizations.

Corporate social responsibility has influenced many fashion distributers and corporate retailers, including the Arcadia Group and Marks & Spencer, whose marketing campaign 'Look behind the label' highlighted its use of fair trade cotton and food products, becoming 'its most successful consumer campaign ever' (Attwood, 2007, in Beard, 2008: 452), and the company aims to be carbon neutral by 2012. Walmart, the largest retailer in the world, became the biggest US producer of organic cotton in 2009. As well, in 2011, H&M launched its first eco-collection called Conscious made from recycled polyester, organic cotton and Tencel, a natural man-made fibre; H&M caused a buzz when it partnered with the French fashion house Lanvin for its Waste collection, but seemingly, 'the line of dresses and bags were at too high a price point for many of its customers' (Kaye, 2011; Leon Kaye is the founder and editor of GreenGoPost.com); individual designer houses such as YSL adopted the strategy of upcycling pre-consumer waste; and Issey Miyake opened his newest concept shop Elttob Tep (Pet Bottle spelled backwards) in Ginza selling innovative fabrics created from recycled plastics.

Vintage clothing as recycling

Historically, recycling has been embedded in the fabric of society. Throughout the ages, garments were passed from mother to daughter, father to son or to other family members or friends. Worn parts were patched or cut off, clothing was resized and – in some cases – stylistically modified or redesigned. The 1970s back-to-nature era saw the mushrooming of second-hand clothing or charity stores opening in towns and cities across the Western world. Driven by a global energy crisis, these outlets allowed buyers, often of limited means, an opportunity to be seen as environmentally conscious. Many of these clothes that were recycled or 'upcycled' were originally made from 'good' materials as the integrity of the fabric prolonged the life of the garment, and their construction was based on quality craftsmanship. Garments originating in the 1920s and 1930s, for example, were valued for their uniqueness, their hand-beading and embroidery and for their ability to be easily transformed into contemporary pieces. It was a nostalgic decade, very much in keeping with postmodernist trends, which appropriated not only fashions from the past, but also classic films and furniture became popular modes of consumption as well. In humanistic terms, this heralded the reemergence of emotional connectivity – of acknowledging that clothing with links to the past can have an in-built memory. This tenet is now widely accepted and has proved to be an incentive for contemporary designers such as Yamamoto and Margiela. Yamamoto's famous quote that he liked clothes that were old and worn and that throwing out an old coat was like throwing away an old friend (see Chapter 6) is testament to this statement.

The sustainability movement in the 2000s has seen a proliferation of chain vintage stores such as Buffalo Exchange, with outlets in thirty-five cities throughout the US where shoppers can exchange or sell their clothing; however, most customers are limited by the denial of most fast fashion items. The UK-based Retold, founded by Clare Lewis in 2018, sells mid- to high-priced vintage items in both pop-up stores and online. ThredUp and Swap.com offer more affordable vintage options both online and in a limited number of brick-and-mortar locations. Online-only retailers such as Brooklyn-based Etsy offer a combination of new and vintage items. Many vintage resale businesses are heavily reliant on Instagram feeds and other social media to advertise their wares, such as Cassie O'Neill's Darling + Vintage; others scaled up their business by combining brick-and-mortar and web-based business with social media, such as One Scoop Store founded by Holly Watkins in the UK. Other businesses work as a central repository for smaller venues, such as Imparfaite, which works with over 350 stores across France and offers daily drops or curated collections for members. Online forms of exchange continue to emerge as viable alternatives to the purchase-and-discard practices of fast fashion, as well as those that seek second-hand luxury items. Many shoppers turn to resale sites like Designer Exchange (founded 2013) or Rewind Vintage, where experts authenticate designer items, providing the seller with cash. For high fashion items, the San-Francisco-based RealReal has luxury consignment locations in Los Angeles and New York; Vestiaire Collective, Poshmark or Tradesy offer deals on pre-owned designer clothing as well. Other options include HEWI (Hardly Ever Worn It) London, which functions as an auction site for buyers who want anonymity similar to eBay's model; or Vide, which functions as a middleman between buyer and seller.

As the repurposing of textiles and the recycling of clothing has become the most responsible practice in eco-fashion in the twenty-first century, it is not surprising that online media now plays an important part in disseminating and sharing information, including blogs and social media networks associated with reconstructive sewing methods and distribution outlets or websites. Some vendors will operate smaller stores within these sites, reselling items sourced from local outlets. These online vending options, facilitating the global distribution of old clothing, are the antithesis of today's fast fashion where newness and expendability have been canonized and ideals of novelty and profit firmly embedded in the industry's agenda. Fashion's inherent consumerism has increased exponentially since the Second World War, fuelled by the media, but is now being questioned following tragic world events and the global economic downturn experienced since 2000. Have these events forced some sectors in society to reevaluate their ethical standards, value systems and environmental concerns? Is the world developing a growing social consciousness?

According to Alexandra Palmer, the revival of second-hand clothing, in most cases, has little to do with environmental concerns. She argues that few 'vintage whores' (Palmer and Clark, 2005: 197) are motivated solely by altruistic motives, such as a concern for sustainable fashion, and are drawn in part to the aura of the clothing in its past life, its history concealed beneath the surface of the garment. Vintage wear also appeals to the younger generation for financial or economic reasons because it allows for a fast turnover of clothes in one's wardrobe. Historically, clothing was often used as barter, and this practice has been reinstated in modern society. This act of bartering, where one item is exchanged for another, has long been an inherent part of everyday life in the markets of Zambia and other parts of Africa, amongst other cultures, where nothing is wasted and the concept of reusing and modifying is indicative of the cultural ethos.

Other sustainable approaches

Individual designers have responded to the global issue of waste by adopting a more responsible design methodology that can be formulated within existing technology. By using more holistic approaches, their work reflects sustainable practice in terms of textile development, minimizing fabric waste, manufacturing methods, and aftercare and disposal with an emphasis on innovative research to develop new products. Large footwear corporations, amongst others, in order to build a successful brand identity, have embraced eco-design as an effective marketing strategy. Nike, for example, recycles used rubber trainers for playground surfaces (Delong, 2009: 109). While some designers recycle old products or use only organic materials, others are concerned more with design integrity, insisting on the evolution of an idea rather than responding to consumerist demands.

Eco-consciousness is fundamental in the work and philosophy of both established and emerging international designers in their quest to reduce the fashion industry's environmental footprint. The list of designers involved in sustainable design is growing exponentially, but some of the early pioneers are worth noting here. Eileen Fisher, who established her brand in New York in 1984, has been a sustainable fashion industry leader, working with both garment design and sustainable natural materials for her upscale ready-to-wear label. British designer Jessica Ogden has built a brand since the mid-1990s with the premise of recycling vintage or found garments. Russell Sage revamped trademark fabrics like Burberry into streetwear-inspired garments before moving his focus to interior design. Katherine Hamnett's use of organic cotton and eco-awareness statements printed on her T-shirts remains a staple for fashion spending that is both ethical and functions as ideological statement (see Chapter 7). Americans Susan Cianciola, who used vintage fabrics for one-off garments, and Miguel Adrover, presented a 'garbage collection' using unusual recycled products; and Yeohlee Teng, who produces one-size-fits-all garments and fights to preserve local rather than overseas production by producing nearly every garment she sells right in the Garment District in New York City. Luxury eco-brands are limited, with the exception of Stella McCartney and Ciel in the United Kingdom, Fin in Norway and Linda Loudermilk in the United States. However, as biosynthetic alternatives begin to mimic high-end fabrics and offer sustainable solutions, luxury ready-to-wear is participating in trying out these new materials (see 'Sustainable Alternatives' section in this chapter).

Sustainability of craft, or the incorporation of hand-worked techniques, now referred to as 'slow design' (aka 'slow fashion') has become central to the philosophy of eco-conscious designers. Brown's *Eco Fashion* (2010: 13) states that 'these traditional craft skills have become more valued and used, and eventually incorporated into the fashion industry through partnership with high-end designers'. Brown cites examples of fair trade, community-based liaisons that have produced 'Indian embroidered sundresses, African beaded jewellery and Peruvian knitted sweaters'. With the eradication of traditional craft talent in the developed nations of North America and Western Europe, she argues, a greater appreciation has developed for the indigenous and inherited craft expertise in communities around the world. She provides specific examples of this practice:

Noir in Denmark is in partnership with Ugandan farmers and supports their development and production of organic long-staple cotton. Carla Fernandez of Taller Flora works with Mexican artisans, reinterpreting their techniques into highly sophisticated designs while learning from their knowledge: a truly collaborative process. With every design and every stitch, Alabama Chanin honours the women of the south of the USA, their history, their struggles and their everyday skills sets. Her work is a labour of love.

BROWN, 2010: 13

African designer Lamine Kouyate, with his label XULY.Bët, deconstructs and reconstructs recycled clothing 'by applying stitches on the outside of his garments to focus attention on the (frayed) edges where threads hold garments together' (Rovine, 2005: 215). According to Rovine, 'The garments incorporate visible seams, like healed wounds that have left their mark (by using red thread), the past lives of clothes that have been re-shaped into new forms' (2005: 219). Kouyate incorporates torn pockets and discoloured collars along with the old collar labels of used shirts and pant waistbands to visibly exaggerate the links with the garments' past lives and as a way to 'document the changing identities of these garments . . . and their attraction lies in the imaginative potential of their former life' (Rovine, 2005: 221).

Rebecca Earley from the Chelsea College of Art, London, transforms and reinvents discarded blouses from charity shops. She employs upcycling techniques, using heat photograms and overprinting the surface of the reshaped garments. Stains are covered with the reactive overlaid dyes, and when it completes its second life, the garment can be transformed a third time into a quilted waistcoat. Kate Goldsworthy, who worked with Earley as a student and became Co-Director of the Centre for Circular Design in 2008, developed a method of bonding a lining made of recycled polyester fleece to the original textile without the use of adhesives or bonding agents to produce the textile for the waistcoat. Laser etching creates a delicate lacelike effect, with melted transparent materials digitally controlled to facilitate the process of fusing (Brown, 2010: 164). Goldsworthy works with Swedish-based Pulp It on their paper clothing project (see 'Sustainable Alternatives' section in this chapter).

Ethical concerns

Fashion, in the second decade of the twenty-first century, finally found its consciousness, and its designers, models and business entrepreneurs alike have joined global musicians to attempt to make the world a better place. This was not an overnight realization; it began in the 1970s and 1980s – a time when unethical practices were publicly highlighted in fashion and associated industries with attention on the wearing of fur, feathers and animal skins and the inhumane and barbarous treatment of animals, as well as their use in the research and development units of cosmetic companies. Ethical practice includes the culture of advertising and, in particular, the exploitation of child models to promote a prepubescent sexuality in fashion advertising, which fulfils a cosmetic function, distorting social values and attitudes. Over the past few decades, socially responsible practices drew attention to the rise of racial discrimination in modelling and the very limited number of African and Asian models used. While projecting an image of multiculturalism, American *Vogue* included only a handful of black celebrity faces on its covers between 2002 and 2009.[8] Fashion photographer Nick Knight made particular reference to this commercially driven racial favouritism in his film *Untitled* (2008) featuring Naomi Campbell. As well, the promotion of an unattainable body image – a trend impacting greatly upon young people worldwide – has led to a disturbing increase in anorexia and bulimia in today's society. A number of designers have attempted to counteract stereotypical and idealized gender and body images through their styling. In Italy in 2006, fashion agents signed agreements not to use underage or underweight models for runway shows.

Greenwashing, a term coined in 1986 by environmentalist Jay Westerveld, was adopted to describe a cover-up marketing ploy often used by individuals, companies and organizations to downplay the unethical practices that proliferate in big business, including the fashion industry. From a sustainability standpoint, this includes a lack of transparency about materials as well as ethical garment production, including the use of child labour. Labelling inconsistencies and misleading classifications confuse the buyer and often compromise provenance. Sandy Black, in *Eco-Chic: The Fashion Paradox* (2007), reports that those buying fair trade cotton may not necessarily have an organic product, and some companies blur the component content of blended fabrics.

As global production in developing countries has been revealed to have significant labour issues, these have become a major point of contention. Workers' wages in developing countries are difficult to contextualize, and Western designers are often misled into believing that workers are being paid a reasonable sum for their production practices. Even when employee pay is shown to be below the local living wage, economists will argue that sweatshop workers are better off receiving low wages than being unemployed. However, working conditions in developing countries often resemble those of the sweatshops in Europe and America in the nineteenth century (see Chapters 1 and 4). Labour laws differ from one location to another, and employees often work long hours (more than 10 hours per day) in unsafe conditions. The Rana Plaza tragedy of 2013 in the Dhaka District in Bangladesh – a major garment producing location globally – proved that working conditions are still as unsafe as they were in 1911, during the Triangle Shirtwaist factory fire in New York. More than 1,100 garment workers perished in the collapse of the crumbling structure of the factory in Rana Plaza, acting as a wake-up call to some companies to rethink their manufacturing practices. Consumers were made more aware through documentaries such as *The True Cost* (2015), which focus on the environmental and ethical problems created by mass consumer culture, and fast fashion in particular.

It's not only fast fashion that has issues with production. Australian journalist Elisabeth Wynhausen (2008: 28) tried to map the supply chain or trail of a designer garment. She found that manufacture took place in China if more than 300 garments in one style were required (otherwise a surcharge was imposed), as US orders of one style were often in the tens of thousands. The garment designs, often samples made from samples or photos of garments seen in New York shop windows, were handed to the trading houses in Hong Kong, which acted as the intermediaries between foreign buyers and Chinese factories. A shirt could be made and delivered to any major city worldwide for approximately one-half of the cost of making it on-shore. For smaller orders, local factories with in-house machinists were used, but a certain amount of outsourcing or subcontracting to sweatshops was also used, where migrant workers were unlawfully paid below minimum wage, contrary to restrictions imposed by the Australian government. A number of unscrupulous employers get work done outside their factories without registering with the Australian Industrial Registry, a requirement under the federal clothing trade's award. While unsustainable levels of clothing production and consumption may exist in the developed world, a more far-reaching problem is 'the negative economic, social and environmental effects (that) tend to fall upon developing countries where an ever-increasing proportion of clothing is produced' (Rissanen, 2005: 7). With an estimated 30 to 50 per cent of British, European and American fashion manufactured goods now being produced off-shore, the subsequent exploitation of local and national factory and industry workers in terms of health and working conditions has led to concerns about the treatment of garment factory workers in locations such as the Pearl River Delta in China and the ghettos in India. This exploitation includes the use of very poorly paid sweatshop labour, using dangerous chemicals to produce textiles and clothing and the use of limited fossil fuels (already exhausted) to sustain the supply chains, leading to the gradual degradation of the environment.

Due to the growing awareness of these collective problems, the 2010s witnessed the rise of fashion labels that were committed to both sustainable materials and ethical treatment of workers, displaying a high level of transparency in their production practices. Companies such as Reformation in Los Angeles, CA maintains all its design, garment production and photography in-house at its headquarters. Local production decreases the company's carbon footprint and also ensures fair treatment of its workers, who are protected under US Labor laws. Sézane, founded in Paris (2013), incorporates fair labour standards and produces two-thirds of its garments in Europe. Other companies focus on bringing fair trade to artisans, such as the brand Indigenous, working with textile workers in South America. Although not all brands are willing to be transparent about their manufacturing practices, the industry at large is slowly moving towards a consumer-driven demand for ethically made clothing.

Many of the persistent issues stem from lack of enforcement across borders. It seems that there is 'no single organization or government body to regulate any specific "code of conduct" for the fashion industry although there are several trade associations with schemes set up to monitor and encourage ethical practices amongst commercial firms such as Ethical Trading Initiative in the UK, Solidaridad and the Clean Clothes Campaign in the Netherlands, Fair West in Australia or the Fair Labour Association in the USA' (Beard, 2008: 450). Regarding other problems such as 'counterfeit chic' (see Chapter 9) and the theft of creative intellectual property, some fashion industries are attempting to establish both formal and informal ethical codes. For example, in New York, Diane Von Furstenberg, former chairwoman of the Council of Fashion Designers of America (CFDA) from 2015–19, sought greater government regulation of intellectual property design and fair trade policies. Despite highly globalized consumer markets and fashion conglomerates (see Chapter 9), individual designers have fought to retain financial independence, allowing them to maintain a moral responsibility towards worker exploitation and providing protection for their own intellectual property. However, due to the limited supply of eco-friendly material, products often display an inflated exchange rate. For the limited, yet expanding, eco-conscious consumer base to become part of the mainstream or dominant culture will take time and money. Luxury sustainable goods offered by leading style labels help to reinforce the notion that eco-fashion of the twenty-first century represents a commodity that has an appeal to a much broader consumer market than its counterpart of the past.

It also underlines the fact that guilt doesn't sell fashion, desire does. Those desires were catered to in the department stores of the nineteenth century that flourished as the Bourgeoisie craved a glamourous service-centred lifestyle, mirroring the aristocracy. But as streetwear infiltrated couture, and brick-and-mortar stores were relegated to mere showcases for purchases made online (see Chapter 9), the system upon which fashion was built began to crumble. Desire and beauty, as well as the ebb and flow of the global economy, has shifted fashion's tide. Now in the wake of the COVID-19 crisis, the closing of retail locations and ensuing global recession has created a backlog of inventory, as well as looming questions about how the industry will change moving forward. Current CFDA Chairman Tom Ford (since 2019) sent a letter to all membership applauding fashion's immediate response to the shortage of mask and personal protective equipment (PPE) donated for health care workers in the early months of the pandemic (Foley, 'Tom Ford Writes CFDA Members,' 2020). Discussing the uncertainty of fashion's future, and ensuring support for designers going forward, Ford focuses on the uncertainty for fashion in the wake of the pandemic. The June/July 2020 issue of *Vogue* featured interviews with top designers including Marc Jacobs, Donatella Versace, Miuccia Prada, Tory Burch, Olivier Rousteling (Creative Director, Balmain), Natacha Ramsay-Levi (Creative Director, Chloe) and Tom Ford himself, asking each what the future of fashion will look like (Leitch, 2020). Most designers agree that flying to different locations for collection showings and photo shoots is an antiquated practice adding unnecessarily to the industry's carbon footprint, and that designers going forward need to rethink production from a less-is-more perspective. These changes, if embraced across the industry as a whole, will already bring significant changes to the environmental problems it has created.

Summary

The latter half of the twentieth century witnessed a significant change in the pricing and availability with the development of licensing, diffusion lines and fast fashion, accelerating the rate at which consumers in Western cultures were buying and discarding garments. Industry production and consumption waste, in turn, created environmental as well as ethical issues. In response, the fashion industry has slowly embraced the growing sector of sustainable fashion, vintage upcycling and recycled clothing and materials, moving towards creating a circular industry rather than a linear one depleting resources.

Notes

1 Statistics from 2012, Bureau of Labor Statistics, U.S. Department of Labor, *Occupational Outlook Handbook: Fashion Designers*, available online at: https://www.bls.gov/ooh/arts-and-design/fashion-designers.htm (accessed 6 July 2020).

2 Several museum collections with contemporary fashion include paper dresses in their collections. The Victoria and Albert Museum in London holds paper dresses in its collection, categorized under 'Subcultures'.

3 The term 'Make do and mend' was the title and slogan in a pamphlet issued by the British government during the Second World War, providing housewives with practical ways to restore and repair worn-out garments, or refashion new garments using materials from older ones – known now as upcycling. For an example and more on this topic, see the British Library timeline: https://www.bl.uk/learning/timeline/item106365.html (accessed 10 December 2020).

4 While sustainability advocates focus on water and fossil fuel scarcity, cotton, which requires large amounts of both resources, has faced a global shortage (Kaye, 2011).

5 Liliana Pomazan (English and Pomazan, 2010) describes this process: through this innovative technique, at least two garments are simultaneously cut from one length of cloth, one from the positive pieces and one from the negative. Depending on the design, the negative (anti) may be patched with other fabrics to complete the garment, or they may be left open and worn over the classic (positive) garment, almost as an accessory, or used as a diffusion line called 'waste collation' (2010: 220).

6 Nielsen Global Online Survey on internet shopping habits (Grail Research, 2009). Eco-aware designers who were referenced included Armani, de la Renta, McCartney, Betsey Johnson and Tom Oldman.

7 Textbooks on sustainability and sustainable practice include: Fletcher, K. and L. Grose (2012), *Fashion & Sustainability: Design for Change* (Laurence King Publishing,: London); and Gullingsrud, A. (2017) *Fashion Fibers: Designing for Sustainability* (Fairchild Books: London and New York).

8 Halle Berry, December 2002; Liya Kebede, May 2005; Jennifer Hudson, March 2007; and Michelle Obama, March 2009.

11

The Digitization of Fashion

Introduction

Trends in fashion are no longer solely determined by styles on models who stroll down the runway or appear in print. As we increasingly live and shop online and develop avatars representing us in the cyber-realm, fashion and its ideals have become absorbed into the virtual world. Cultural shifts pertaining to the way in which fashion is experienced, created and perceived have developed from major changes in retail via e-Commerce, virtual couture, use of digital technology to create or embellish garments, and development of smart textiles. Social media has become a major player as a commercial and cultural phenomenon in the popularization of micro-trends and the role of the influencer. Movements for social equality have led to changes in gender expression, beauty ideals and an increasing demand for inclusivity in the fashion system.

Virtual couture

In tandem with problems created by mass production and global outsourcing, the new sector of virtual couture has gained popularity, and lucrative partnerships have been formed between fashion and technology. These include dressing avatars in digital brand-name clothing, customizing clothing through fashion and styling apps, and embedding technology itself into smart garments that communicate with other devices to perform a function. Developments in computing technology allowing online access from smart phones made shopping into a portable, online experience, and use of Virtual and Augmented Reality presents fashion in new ways that appeal to young consumers. By turning fashion into a digital phenomenon, the way that clothing is perceived, presented and marketed has determined a new course for the future of the industry.

As smart phones and alternate digital realities have made the cyber-realm more easily accessible, fashion itself has become a digital phenomenon. Virtual Couture encompasses many aspects of the online fashion phenomenon, including online fashion shows and digital fashion; as well as Virtual Reality (VR), Augmented Reality (AR), and Mixed Reality (MR) experiences that enhance apparel through digital means. Ultimately, all these modalities continue evolving to satisfy many of the needs and desires that fashion itself fulfils: a new kind of conspicuous consumption that provides wearers (digital or real) the opportunity to project an image to the viewer through their attire. Enhanced by technology, modelling a new outfit online allows for fantasy to supersede reality by using avatars or idealized versions of oneself, or by digitally donning luxury designer clothing.

Arguably, the fashion industry's model may be drawing upon other digital practices, such as gaming and the development of avatars as a virtual identity. Fan games such as Fortnite, Star

Trek Online, World of Warcraft and Call of Duty incorporate 'virtual goods' available for purchase in online communities and games, including clothing and accessories for custom-designed avatars. These accoutrements can be bought using real or digital currency, monetizing the game; more often, these are earned by fulfilling a quest or completing a level. Although gamers may not be fashion-conscious in real life (IRL), they spend hundreds or thousands of hours gaming to outfit their virtual personas as a representation of their skills. In this context, the avatar's clothing represents a status symbol for the gamer: displaying connection, abilities or alignment within the gaming realm.

Considering the avatar as a foundation for virtual couture, the interdependent relationship between fashion and gaming culture becomes clear: just as gaming adapted the idea of buying or earning avatar styling and customized accessories from the physical world, fashion also borrowed back from the gaming industry to build a virtual world for trying on clothes. Some early examples of this phenomenon were embedded in pop culture, such as the cult classic film *Clueless* (1995) in which teenaged protagonist Cher (Alicia Silverstone) uses software on her PC desktop to model several ensembles on an image of herself – her 'digital twin' – before selecting her clothes for the day. This concept of selecting and modelling clothes on an avatar is still present in games today; in some apps, users can create a digital twin to model their clothes, the gaming equivalent to 'skinning' avatars. The Genies app – an avatar-to-avatar-communication platform via mobile device – specializes in creating customized avatars resembling caricatures; as of 2020, users can choose from over a million mood-expressions and luxury clothing options to send messages in real time via SMS. Partnering with Gucci for its custom luxury avatar apparel (at a cost of $10 M to Gucci), users can outfit their Genies with pieces from the real-life collection, as well as purchase items they see on other users.

Other partnerships between high fashion and gaming include Louis Vuitton and League of Legends. The real-life capsule collection was replicated as digital skins that went for $10 USD per piece. Moschino entered a similar partnership with SIMS, in which – typical of Moschino's playful aesthetic – the real-life clothes featured pixelated digital images, emphasizing the overlap between real and digital worlds. Other companies have offered their real-life garments as downloadable content (DLC), such as the lifestyle brand 100 Thieves, who partnered with Nintendo's Animal Crossings to offer digital versions of every apparel item they've ever featured in their Instagram drops. And of course, celebrity-backed games are ever-popular, including Kim Kardashian Hollywood, which has partnered with several high fashion brands including Balmain, Karl Lagerfeld and Roberto Cavalli since 2014 to offer avatars luxury wardrobes; in the case of Lagerfeld, this was intended to drive users to a real-life launch. Fast fashion has also partnered with gaming: ASOS X SIMS (EA) allows users to create a virtual ensemble, then purchase and wear it IRL.

In addition to working with developers to incorporate digital clothes into games and outfit avatars, fashion houses have developed their own apps, such as Gucci Arcade or Fendi's Mini Game on the WeChat network in China (2019), in which users collect items as they advance through various levels. Apps such as Drest – created by Net-a-Porter alumna and former *Harper's Bazaar* editor Lucy Yeomans – allows users to dress avatars of real-life supermodels such as Natalia Vodianova, Irina Shayk, Imaan Hammam and Doutzen Kroes. The app presents daily style challenges, in which users become fashion editors to compete for in-game currency, which can be used to purchase virtual luxury garments for the avatars. Drest is affiliated with more than 160 brands, including Valentino, Stella McCartney, Burberry, Prada and Gucci. Other apps, such as Ada (named after the mother of computer programming, Ada Lovelace), allow users to dress avatars in luxury garments and photograph them in palatial environments, then share the photos on social media. Users and viewers can purchase the designer clothing IRL from Ada's affiliates. This is similar to the app Covet, in which users style 'paper dolls' and then purchase physical garments from the app's partners. The goal of these apps is to make the glamour of the fashion industry – from luxury brands to model avatars – accessible to everyone, albeit virtually. Is this the true democratization of fashion?

Technology and sustainability also find harmony in digital clothing, since they don't add to the world's landfills when out of fashion. In November 2018, Norwegian streetwear retailer Carlings released its first digital clothing collection, selling out in the first week on Instagram. Users upload a photo of themselves which is then manipulated to make it appear as though they are wearing the collection, then share their avatars on social media. Inspired by Fortnite and 'skinning' (dressing your avatar in a digital game), the apparel is genderless and priced within the range of young consumers at €10 to €30 ($11 to $35 USD). Also founded on the premise of using technology to conserve resources, New York-based digital agency Neuro Studio's Solventus 2019 collection utilized 3-D scanning of human models to create digital designs for bespoke clothing, which was then 3-D printed with recycled materials. Part of the draw for consumers is the ability to customize their clothing, involving them the design process – a concept that athletic apparel company Nike has been implementing in a literal sense with their line of Adapt BB trainers, which uses biometric data from the wearer to alter the fit of the shoes.

As avatars are styled and shared on social media, they take on a life of their own. Popular avatars become celebrities in and of themselves for beauty and fashion campaigns, such as Final Fantasy's Lightening for Louis Vuitton (2016), or Miquela Sousa (known by the handle @ lilmiquela), becoming computer-generated influencers. Users also become their avatars: the virtual persona comes to life when gamers dress as their favourite digital personas IRL for annual events such as Comic-Con International in San Diego, CA. Fantastical costumes are developed based on digital wardrobes, opening the door between these two worlds. The digital and physical worlds become interconnected and interchangeable. As futuristic as this sounds, this relationship of the real and the imagined is reminiscent of the role of fashion in the early twentieth century, when Poiret created Orientalist ensembles that brought theatre to the salon, and Delaunay created Simultaneous dresses that converted wall paintings to wearable art (See Chapter 2).

Other developments in virtual goods include digital-only clothing that do not have a real-life equivalent. In April 2019, the first digital-only couture was sold for $9,500 USD. 'Iridescence' is a custom-fit digital-only couture garment designed by The Fabricant, an Amsterdam-based Digital Fabric House, and AR artist Johanna Jaskowska (Roberts-Islam, 2019). The dress was auctioned for charity and sold on the blockchain using crypto-currency. Designers of virtual clothing, however, need a different skill set than traditional fashion designers; even if the artistic vision and design is based on physical textiles and garments, the ability to create successful 3-D modelling lies with software engineers rather than dressmakers or tailors. The Fabricant uses both traditional pattern-making software alongside 3-D modelling in order to create custom garments for avatars.

Where does this position the traditional world of couture, which distinguished itself by using luxury textiles to create skillfully handmade garments? Will there be a job in the near future for 'digital tailors' and will there be libraries of digital fabric? Perhaps the exclusivity that haute couture sought to represent at its core foundation is finding renewed strength in the virtual world with bespoke digital couture, while the availability and price point of ready-to-wear is replicated through skins for avatars. Ultimately, any fashion company looking to supply virtual goods has to build brand familiarity with a new generation of Gen Z consumers who increasingly shop and dress virtually, and either cannot afford or do not place the same value on real-life luxury apparel. This shift away from physical objects has only been amplified by the economic downturn looming as a result of the 2020 global pandemic, as well as the increased amount of time spent living life online.

The ultimate in experiencing virtual fashion, however, may be manifested through VR, AR and MR. VR involves being immersed in a 3-D rendering of an alternate space; in fashion this can be virtually trying on clothes, or wearing VR goggles to experience a fabricated reality. AR is generally defined as image enhancement through a filter (goggles or a phone), while MR is a combination of real-life elements and virtual elements, such as overlaying computer images onto the physical world using goggles and an app. Matthew Drinkwater, Head of Innovation Agency at the London College of Fashion, has been experimenting with the 'Magic Leap' MR goggles that overlay digital imagery onto real objects. Drinkwater's vision for the future of fashion predicts that modelling a new outfit will become a virtual experience, in which a photo-realistic avatar is created by a smart phone and the viewer dons MR glasses to view the avatar in different ensembles, also photographed in 3-D. Drinkwater predicts that there will be an AR cloud that our avatars can inhabit, and in this augmented world fashion will be experienced as a digital overlay, allowing appearances to shift and change based on the filter applied by the viewer – technology that will present your avatar to the world in your digital clothing of choice. Popular culture has already been exposed to this concept in various computer-generated (CG) versions in streaming content series such as 'Upload' (Season 1, Episode 3), featuring AR mirrors in which wearers can view themselves in virtual clothing, also set in an entirely VR world representing the afterlife.

The use of technology to create garments bridges the worlds of art and fashion, bringing together multiple disciplines that enhance the capability of clothing. Andrea Lauer, Professor of Digital Storytelling at Princeton University, is an artist and technologist experimenting with AR and clothing as a metaphor of human interaction. Lauer's work is inspired by science and engineering, manifested in handmade clothing that comes to life through AR, such as her work 'From Above, The Cinderella Effect' (2018). The work features an oversized shirtdress with digitally printed constellations in bird silhouettes. When viewed through an AR app on a mobile device, the birds encircle the viewer who becomes the embodiment of a constellation of sparkling stars. She further investigates this concept through her work 'Under One Sky' with astrophysicist Janna Lavin, whose study of black holes contributed to the understanding of the shape of time-space dimensions. For the MAX Space Festival in San Francisco, Lauer created a flight jumpsuit inspired by her conversations with Lavin: viewers witness a recreation of the 1919 solar eclipse as witnessed by Sir Author Eddington, digitally printed as a repeat pattern on the textile, while viewing the garment through a specially designed AR app called RISEN. This historic event brought Einstein's theory of general relativity to the English-speaking world and to a new audience 100 years later.

Lauer's work, in addition to carefully referencing traditional garment forms, uses technology to connect the viewer with the wearer in new ways by altering the role of each: the body of the wearer becomes a portal to celestial phenomenon, which the viewer is experiencing through a specialized lens, simultaneously transforming them both through the display of clothing. In earlier works such as 'Torsolovely' (2008) Lauer experimented with this relationship between wearer and viewer through sensors recording sound and touch. Inspired by a garment used by Agnes Richter, a nineteenth-century mental patient who sewed her memories into her clothing for lack of pen and paper, Lauer reinvented this concept to relate to her own experience. Creating a Victorian-style jacket, Lauer added sensors carefully placed on the garment to create a topographical map of her body. The interactive piece mapped touch, sound and smell brought to the work by viewers, and this viewer data was recorded to create a 'memory composition – a collage of recorded sound . . . released into the world' (Lauer, n.d.).

FIGURE 11.1 *Andrea Lauer. Gallery view, 'Under One Sky' (2019) and 'From Above: The Cinderella Effect' (2018), exhibited at the MAX Space Center. (Photo courtesy of the artist.)*

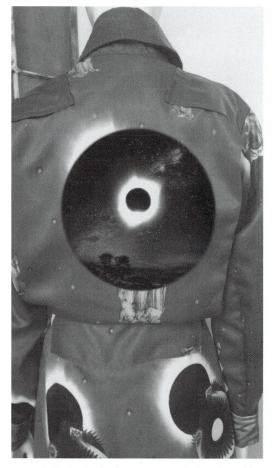

FIGURE 11.2 *Andrea Lauer. 'Under One Sky' (2019), detail. Janna Levin's Black Holes Blues and Other Songs from Outer Space, Custom AR app, 3-D animation, digital printing on recycled polyester, reflective fabric. (Photo courtesy of the artist.)*

FIGURE 11.3 *Andrea Lauer. 'From Above: The Cinderella Effect' (2018), detail. Digital printing on recycled polyester, AR app. Lauer's garment flutters with printed and animated birds activated by the app through the viewer's mobile device. (Photo courtesy of the artist.)*

Heidi Boisvert, Director of Emerging Media at NYC College of Technology, City University of New York (CUNY), also experiments with interactive performance works to map human interaction. Informed by her background as a game designer, Boisvert's '[Radical] Signs of Life' (2013) is a large-scale multimedia experience designed for audience participation during a live dance performance, in which biophysical sensors are applied directly to the dancers' bodies to record the biometric data from their movements. An adaptation of Conway's 'Game of Life', the performance is set up as a live video game with the goal of survival: the stage is divided into territories, and as dancers move through various sections, they edge other dancers towards starvation or loneliness. The dancers' biometric data is fed into a biological algorithm projected as 3-D imagery on screens facing the audience; Boisvert explains on her website that 'as the audience interacts with the images produced, they enter into a dialogue with

FIGURE 11.4 *Andrea Lauer. Torsolovely, 2008. Lauer's sketch incorporates garment elements from Victorian clothing, the origins of her inspiration, as well as displaying the zones that occupy the electronic elements of her interactive garment. (Photo courtesy of the artist.)*

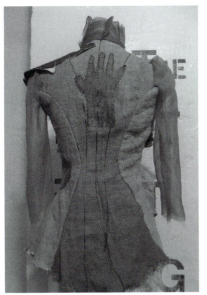

FIGURE 11.5 and 11.6 *Andrea Lauer. Torsolovely, 2008. Electronic elements of interactive garment, outlined to inform the viewer as to where and how to activate the piece (left). The finished garment (right). (Photos courtesy of the artist.)*

FIGURE 11.7 *Heidi Boisvert. [Radical] Signs of Life (2013). Boisvert created a live interactive 'game' by using game-based rules and sensors to map dancers' movements. (Photo courtesy of the artist.)*

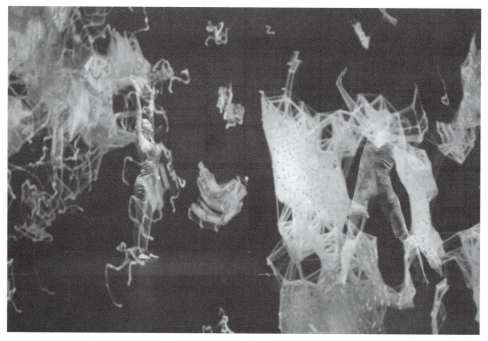

FIGURE 11.8 *Heidi Boisvert. [Radical] Signs of Life (2013). Dancers in the live performance respond to projected images, created by viewers interacting with a dynamic database. (Photo courtesy of the artist.)*

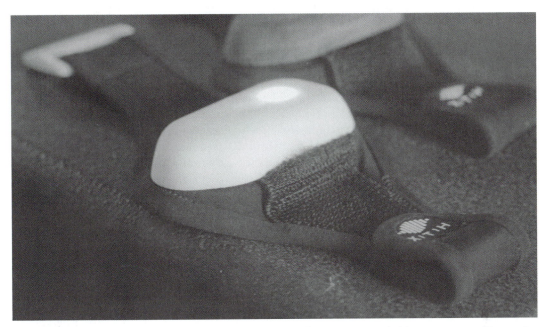

FIGURE 11.9 *Heidi Boisvert. XTH Sense. Boivert is the co-creator of this open source biocreative instrument that allows users to connect with other devices to map biometric data such as temperature, blood flow and heartbeat. (Photo courtesy of the artist.)*

the dancers' (Boisvert, n.d.). using rule-based choreography corresponding to a database of phrases. Boisvert's work contemplates the newest developments in wearable devices and interactive garments, which blur the boundaries of bio-memory and bio-data. Her work contemplates questions of appropriate uses of technology and the body, as well as data privacy issues.

Technology in fashion: A brief history

The functionality of physical garments as portable technology is gaining recognition as an important sector in both technology and apparel industries. As the closest thing to our bodies, garments and accessories have the potential to regulate biorhythmic functions and alert the user about risk, as well as protect the wearer against harmful elements. But as fashion gets more directly involved with the development of smart textiles, aesthetics and connectivity are driving the direction of interactive garments.

Twentieth-century DIY examples of smart textiles show LED wires attached to prefabricated garments, lighting up various body parts in a dark space for dramatic effect. However, the concept of luminescent garments is much older than the invention of electricity. In the Ancient Near East, metal bracteates were attached to clothing and placed on larger-than-life statues of the gods, carefully placed within temples to reflect the sunlight at a precise moment during the equinoxes, whose effect must have been blinding to viewers. In the medieval era, 'cloth of gold' was made popular in Europe through the plundering of the Crusaders, who brought home booty from the Islamic world. These gold-ground silk textiles were offset with polychromatic yarns, executed as velvet or compound weaves to produce complex designs; the gold was usually flat strips of foil wrapped around a silk core yarn that floated on the face of the cloth. Often donated to the Church, these textiles are represented in religious paintings as the mantle of Mary; as the Islamic originals were often inscribed with allegiances or blessings for the ruler in Kufic Arabic calligraphy, these inscriptions also appear on the edges of textiles in medieval paintings as what historians call 'pseudo-Kufic'. Multiple examples of cloth of gold exist in Church treasuries and museums around the world. Renaissance weavers in Italy and France soon adopted these weaving methods to reproduce this luxurious cloth, which became the dress of royalty across Europe. Throughout the Early Modern era, the most coveted objects gifted from Islamic nations to the West included silk textiles with metal-thread accents. Although it wouldn't have been on the minds of the early modern wearers, cloth of gold would have been the perfect fabric for an illuminated garment, because metal is conductive – the first requirement for creating an interactive smart textile.

In the modern era, the concept of adding electronic power to clothing dates back to the invention of electricity itself. In the early 1880s, ballet dancers appeared on stage with battery-powered electric light under the layers of their tutus, reportedly with a light bulb on their foreheads. This caused such a sensation that by 1884, a new way to light your home or business was advertised: Electric Girls (*The New York Times*, 26 April 1884). The Electric Girl Lighting Company advertised the hire of young women outfitted with electrical wiring in their clothing and a light bulb that sat on their foreheads, illuminating at 'fifty candle power', enough light to replace a chandelier. The company proposed to clothe and feed their employees, and customers could choose the 'style of girl' they wanted to light their entryway. This trend went beyond the illumination of dark spaces by servants. The House of Worth created an evening gown for Mrs Cornelius Vanderbilt II [nee Alice Gwynn] for the famous Vanderbilt Ball of 26 March 1883, with a hidden battery that illuminated a hand-held torch. The electrical components seamlessly integrated with the heavily embellished bustle gown, beaded with starbursts and lightning bolts on gold satin with silver tinsel fringe and pearls. The overall effect must have been impressive, even amongst the outrageously costumed guests.

The inventors that brought electricity to the public were cognizant of its potential for the fashion industry. Gustave Trouvé, French inventor of the outboard motor and the first electric-powered vehicle, showed a battery-powered electric sewing machine in 1881 at the first International Electrical Exhibition in Paris, improving upon the foot-treadle model. Trouvé went on to create his 'photophore': an electric headlamp oriented by gestural movements; then 'bijoux electriques' and 'luminous electric jewels' based on the same concept – the original wearables, displayed by fashionable Parisians as tie pins, and on stage by dancers in the Folies Bergère. American inventor Thomas Edison's five page 'to do' list of 3 January 1888 included 'artificial filaments' as well as 'artificial silk' (rayon) at the top of page two, presumably to create conductive cloth; as well as 'surface switches' which may be comparable to today's touch sensors. (Edison, 1888; via PBS.org) Nikola Tesla, who worked with Edison in 1884 before the two parted ways to become rivals in the race to the patent office, invented the AC (alternating current) electrical system, the most significant contribution to our tech-powered world. Pitted against Edison's DC (direct current) system, Tesla partnered with Westinghouse to power the World's Columbian Exposition in Chicago in 1893, then demonstrated the first AC water-powered (hydroelectric) power plant at Niagara Falls, NY. In addition to providing the

FIGURE 11.10 *Mrs Cornelius Vanderbilt in her 'Electric Light' dress on 26 March 1883. Created by the House of Worth, in the collections of the Museum of the City of New York. (Image in public domain.)*

dominant method of delivery for electric power, he founded the Tesla Coil, the foundation for wireless technology. Tesla's philanthropic vision was to provide free electricity for everyone; this ideal was defeated by Edison and Marconi, whose commercial enterprises would prevail. Without electricity, conductive elements and wireless technology, there would be no smart textiles today.

Not surprisingly, the connection between technology and garments is picked up again during the future-obsessed 1960s. As Courrèges, Cardin, and Rabanne created Space Age couture which mimicked the look of aeronautical garb (see Chapter 5), more functional tech clothing was being explored by designers and engineers. A major exhibition featuring the relationship between clothing and technology was 'Body Covering' (1968) at the Museum of Contemporary Craft in New York. The exhibition featured technical advances in textile technology, such as climate-control fabrics that formed the basis for many of the fabrics dominating athletic attire and outer wear today; as well as technical textiles from scuba suits to space suits. The catalogue also featured an early example of an electrically heated garment wired with nichrome powered by rechargeable silver cadmium batteries, powering the garment in freezing temperature up to four hours (1968, Alphabet designs and Vicky Cooper, garment design, NYC) as well as a cooling garment inset with flexible tubing to hold water, acting as the cooling agent through heat transfer (B. Wilson and Co., Hartford, CT). The exhibition also featured Gernreich's loose, unisex printed clothing, redefining the range of movement through garment design, Rabanne's moulded and soldered metal garments hypothesizing upon a fictionalized future, and Cashin's layered approach to body temperature control, as revolutionary advances in fashion technology.

However, the relationship between garments and technology was foreseen by the ground-breaking experimental works presented by NYC artist Diana Dew, who had studied both fashion and engineering (Albanesi, 2020). The Body Coverings exhibition included Dew's 'Movie Dress' with illuminated film cells set in a leather shift, and leather 'Motorcycle Jacket' with incandescent lights, both powered by independent battery packs; and a 'Speaker Belt' with alarm and radio features. A former model in her twenties when she created these works, Dew sold her creations in Paraphernalia, the Soho boutique in which Betsey Johnson got her start; and were popular among the It crowd frequenting Max's Kansas City, where Warhol and other artists congregated. In a 1967 interview with *Time Magazine*, Dew described her electric-powered apparel as 'hyperdelic transsensory experiences' (Gerald, 1967). The dresses were programmable so the user could have flashing lights (up to 12 pulses per second), steady light, or a combination in sequence; the electronic components were removable so the clothes could be laundered. Dew stated in the *Time* article that she was expanding to include flashing ties and apparel wired to play music; this led to her custom designs for several NYC rock bands, including the Blues Magoos, who toured with The Who in 1967 wearing light-up suits that pulsed in time to their music. Dew was not alone in these pioneering efforts; fashion designer and Warhol Factory fan Joan 'Tiger' Morse also created light-up clothing, often in collaboration with Dew, and sold them in her boutique Teeny Weeny on

FIGURE 11.11 *Diana Dew. Detail, light-up dress (1967–8). Video still, PBS Antiques Roadshow. Dew's light-up garments were created with portable battery packs worn around the waist under the garment that lasted several hours. (© PBS.)*

THE DIGITIZATION OF FASHION 241

New York's Upper East Side; she is featured in Warhol's 1967 film **** (Four Stars) as Reel 14. These early garments were not foolproof, however; anecdotes about Dew's electric dresses include girls whose dresses exploded as they were flashing the night away at Max's, and one of the band members of Blues Magoos reported that he received electric shocks while sweating in the suit. Despite these hiccups, Dew was well ahead of her time and eventually sold her technology to the US military, after which her pioneering efforts were forgotten.

Fashion and technology in the twenty-first century

Twenty-first-century advances on the relationship of garments and technology is still informed primarily by advances in technology. Developing interactive garments begins with research and development among several fields, primarily software and hardware engineers in collaboration with textile and fashion designers to create 'smart' or interactive textiles. Smart textiles are generally defined as being one of three types: passive smart, active smart or very smart (aka supersmart) (Kettley, 2016). Passive smart textiles contain a sensor that responds to its environment in a consistent and unchanging way, such as an anti-microbial textile. Active smart fabrics have reflexes and exhibit behaviours through actuators controlled by an integrated button or panel, and may incorporate a microprocessor, such as a garment lit with LEDs that cycles through a pre-programmed sequence of colour changes. The active smart type can also function through closed and open switches activated by touch or other environmental stimuli. Very smart textiles have a range of behaviours determined by the use of processing their own performance as well as external stimuli, usually aided by conductive fibres. Some very smart textiles are self-adapting learning systems, sensing themselves and responding to the environment; or embedded with integrated systems including a processor. One of the most important identifying features of any smart garment, however, is in its ability to function in tandem with the wearer's movements and communicate using sensors. These can be attached as hardware devices, embellished or printed on the surface of the fabric using conductive elements, such as silver thread or pigment; however, these create a clunky interface. Textile engineers worked with technology specialists to develop yarns made from a metal alloy mixed with natural or synthetic fibres, which could then be woven or knitted into conductive cloth. The next wave of smart textile development embeds the sensors in active or very smart garments in the conductive cloth, meaning that the fibres or yarn used to make the textiles can be connected via Bluetooth or wireless technology to report back to its source.

Although this field is constantly changing as new technologies are developed, the involvement of fashion and textile designers marks a new era for wearable technology. Product development in this field involves a collaborative design process to create a prototype that can be mass produced, then refined through iterative generations of the product. Global fashion companies such as Levi's, Adidas and Saint Laurent have partnered with engineers at Google for their Jacquard project, part of the tech giant's Advanced Technology and Projects (ATAP) division. The approach to the role of fabric in their products is that it can function as a touch sensor by adding conductive threads to the surface of the cloth. Google Project Jacquard's founder, Ivan Poupyrev, cites the ability to add interactive components in clothing is the first step to making computing invisibly integrated in everyday materials. The challenge was creating conductive yarn that could also be scalable and mass produced on an industrial loom. The computing components are shrunk down to the size of a button, which can be embedded during the manufacturing process or added as an embellishment. Designers and tailors can then create the garments they like using the smart textiles. By creating a range of products with interactive capability, the wearer has the ability to use the features however it suits their lifestyle. The first collaborative garment design in this project was the Commuter Trucker Jacket, created in partnership with Levi's and available to consumers in 2017. The classic denim trucker jacket was redefined by the Jacquard tag, a microprocessor the size of a thumb. The Jacquard tag is connected through a port in the sleeve cuff, receives signals from the touch surface of the jacket, and transmits them via Bluetooth to an app on a mobile device. The user, idealized as a young urban tech professional commuting to work on a bicycle, can connect with their mobile device by swiping the left jacket sleeve to answer a call, select music, or respond to notifications. The first generation was primarily marketed for men, but the second generation produced in 2019 included women's sizing and styling, as well as customizable options such as a Sherpa lining. The functionality remained much the same. Although the production is scalable, the price tag for this denim jacket is still in the luxury range: in 2017 the MSRP was $350 USD, while the 2019 iteration was $198 USD. Poupyrev acknowledges that the company will have to partner with labels in lower price ranges in order to increase sales, which ultimately brings the final price tag lower due to economies of scale.

Other Google collaborations include the Cit-e backpack developed with luxury label Saint Laurent, which can control music, drop pins while moving, and take pictures. The Jacquard tag is connected to conductive fabric on the strap and functions using gestures, communicating via Jacquard mobile app. Like other wearable technology, there is a haptic element incorporated in the device's communication: either a gentle tapping or flashing lights will send notifications as selected in the app. Moving further into the virtual world, ATAP's project with Adidas GMR is a joint venture partnering Google Jacquard with EA SPORTS FIFA Mobile. By placing the tag on the bottom of athletic shoes for real-life soccer players, a digital twin is materialized in the game that collects biometric data for the player's avatar profile. The premise of this relationship is based on the Jacquard tag's machine-learning algorithms, which measure kicks, speed, shot power and distance to sync the skills of the athlete with the player.

Smaller companies have also proven formidable forces in the push to integrate fashion and technology. Loomia, founded by MIT graduate Madison Maxey, created a modular system that functions with their patented LEL (Loomia Electronic Layer). The technology is used to create soft circuits that can be used in various textile applications, combining a touch sensor with lights and a heating element. Unlike the early experiments of the 1960s by Dew and others, the LED light feature is integrated safely into the flexible textiles, and can function as a safety element for outerwear, while the heating feature maximizes comfort without creating bulk. Both features are controlled by switches, making this an example of an active smart textile. The LEL is programmable, and has the capability to function as an antenna, or patterned to carry power and data on several channels to work with multiple control modules and sensors. Significantly, the company continues to prototype e-textiles to scalable production, and offers a washable product that is cost effective. In 2019, Loomia introduced a heated jacket that uses LEL with an outer layer to create a stylish winter coat.

Fashion designers are also approaching technology as a tool for redefining both ready-to-wear and traditional couture. Turkish-Cypriot London-based designer Hussein Chalayan Dutch and Amsterdam-based designer Iris van Herpen present work that is the avant-garde of future fashion. Both designers use new technologies such as 3-D printing, laser-cutting, LEDs and microcontrollers to realize new and highly conceptual forms, merging art, garment design and engineering. These designers work with collaborative teams of specialist in order to realize their visions.

Hussein Chalayan

Hussein Chalayan recontextualized the notion of the fashion 'spectacle' from one that was based on aesthetics to one that was based on technology. Like other postmodernist artists, his cerebral work became allied more with multimedia, which offered new possibilities and new realities. His experimental work embraced avant-garde expressions ranging from sculpture to video and from architecture to performance.

In his earlier work, while investigating the theme of longevity and antiquity, he appropriated elements of Turkish costume and textiles drawn from his knowledge of his own cultural origins in Cyprus. Replicating age and decay, the garments from his graduate collection in 1993, The Tangent Flows, were buried in the garden with iron filings and took on the archaeological patina of centuries past. He referred to three of his key garments as 'monuments to ideas' as a way of linking the past with the future: the first, a dress from his Geotropics collection (Spring/Summer 1999), where a form resembling a small chair wrapped itself around the contours of the body, becoming part of the garment; the second, the Airplane dress from his Echoform collection (Autumn/Winter 1999–2000) featured moving flaps; and the third, a remote-controlled dress made from materials used in airplane construction with solid moveable flaps from his Before Minus Now collection (Spring/Summer 2000), displayed a tulle underskirt when the flaps were raised. All of these garments related to his underlying themes of iterant existence and cultural displacement, flight and migration. According to Suzy Menkes (2005), his technical wizardry 'was designed to express refugees in flight, camouflaging their possessions' and were inspired by 'events in Kosovo and by Chalayan's childhood memories'. Chalayan partnered with Swarovski to create a crystal dress lit from underneath by laser diodes for his Spring/Summer 2008 collection; as the lasers were reflected through the faceted crystals, they created light prisms emitted from the body. Chalayan likened the effect of the models rotating 360 degrees on a darkly lit catwalk as a reference to celebrity admiration.

Moving away from cultural meaning and memory, his later work, from 2006 onwards, centred on the dynamics of flight and notions of transformation and interaction, and became dubbed 'tech-couture'. His construction-garments became increasingly high-tech, relying on microchips inserted in the garments to mechanically program movements of different plates or sections of the clothing. Fascinated by movement, his garments used power packs of batteries attached to microprocessors to activate the transformation of hems, lapels and headwear – in other words, an entire morphing of the garment. His Airborne dress brought the latest technology – 15,000 flickering LED lights combined with Swarovski crystals – to create a dazzling display in his Readings collection (Spring/Summer 2008).

Other collections included crystal skirts that became video display screens for projections of coloured lights or images of fish swimming underwater, hats that lit up like table lamps and full skirts that could imitate being blown about in the wind. Undoubtedly, Chalayan has been instrumental in completely recontextualizing fashion within an intellectually broader sphere by fusing fashion, art and science. In 2009–10, at the Art of Fashion exhibition held at the Museum Boijmans Van Beuningen, the Netherlands, Chalayan's installation *Micro Geography* encapsulated a fully clothed rotating figure in a vertical tank of water that projected cross-sectioned images on a number of video screens. In the museum video interview complementing the exhibition, Chalayan commented that he had created a 'mini life' that referenced the concept of the 'gaze', much like CCTV footage – a form of documentation that became part of the visual culture. Working as a postmodernist artist, he described the installation as having layers of different meaning, yet he did not offer any possible translations.

Much of Chalayan's experimental work includes an element of performance, captured on film or performed on stage and exhibited in museums, crossing the boundaries between art and fashion. Since 2003, he has directed projects including the short films *Temporal Meditations*, *Place of Passage* and *Aesthetics*, and in 2005 he represented Turkey at the 51st Venice Art Biennale, the world's foremost international art exhibition. In 2015, Chalayan collaborated with choreographer Damien Jalet on Gravity Fatigue, a dance performed at Sadler's Wells. The collaborative work combines Chalayan's approach to clothing as metaphor for the human condition by working with 'gravity as a currency for perception of reality': dancers wear ultra-elasticized garments that wrap, hang and stretch as the dancers test the laws of physics on stage, while others wear sculptural tops with softly draping skirts and isolate movements, playing with concepts of fluidity and immobility. Chalayan's techno-couture is coupled with a ready-to-wear line that echoes elements of his more experimental show-stoppers.

FIGURE 11.12 *Hussein Chalayan's 'Readings' comprises of crystals and over 15,000 flickering LED lights displayed at the Design Museum on 21 January 2009 in London, England. (Photo by Dan Kitwood/ Getty Images.)*

Iris van Herpen

Iris van Herpen uses technology in a different way, but to similarly staggering effect. Having founded her couture house in Amsterdam in 2007, the Dutch designer creates bespoke designs for celebrity clients including Beyoncé, Cate Blanchett and Scarlett Johannson, with a focus on women's empowerment and conscious design. Having been trained in classical ballet, van Herpen's approach is informed by range of movement and the ways in which the body inhabits space. Inspired by nature and natural forms, her works are created using 3-D printing or laser-cutting combined with handwork such as embroidery, lace and draping, creating garments that express the couture tradition as it has evolved over time.

The designer's early work (2009) demonstrates a close examination of textiles and its relationship to the body. Her Mummification series references the ancient Egyptian practice, combining geometric designs and delicate materials that are wrapped and frayed, creating a modern inquiry probing the relationship of life and afterlife. In her 2010 Synesthesia collection, she explores the overlap of sensory perceptions through her use of laser-cut leather garments coated with foil. Based on the premise that clothing in the future would incorporate or supplement sensory perception, van Herpen created an optic puzzle for the viewer through her constantly shifting light forms in the delicate garment forms; while the wearer has a haptic experience through elements such as hypersensitive, vibrating instruments and extra receptors.

Van Herpen's couture collections are collaborative and centre on themes based on the natural world, such as her 2011 Crystallization collection. Drawing inspiration from water in its liquid and crystallized forms, van Herpen designed a series of garments in collaboration with Benthem Crouwel Architects that gave the illusion of being immersed in water, with the splash surrounding the wearer like a moment frozen in time. Different movements of water are explored throughout the collection, from waterfalls to ice crystals. Each work is designed on the computer using 3-D printing software, cut out of PETG clear acrylic sheets, and manipulated by hand using heat and pliers to create the splash. Delving deeper into her title, the series itself is a metaphor for ideas that are crystallized in the mind of the artist as concepts are formed and translated into objects.

Van Herpen's other collections also include interdisciplinary explorations, alluding to the tension between soft and hard objects, and between technology and the natural world. Her collections Hybrid Holism (2012) and Voltage (2013) led her to collaborate with Canadian architect Philip Beesley, shown in concurrent solo exhibitions at Toronto's Royal Ontario Museum (ROM). Beesley and van Herpen are inspired by New Zealand artist Carlos van Camp, known for his experiments with the Tesla Coil, leading to their collaboration for some of the garments in the Magnetic Motion collection (2014). Her more recent collections return to forces in nature as experienced by the body, such as Hypnosis (2017) and Sensory Seas (2020), both of which are made from natural materials assembled to create visual and psychic phenomena based on sound waves, and ongoing collaborations with Swarovski since 2009, including the Biomorphism installation with Rhea Thierstein at the Kristallwelten store in Vienna (2019).

Ultimately, there are a range of technologies being developed to create and revolutionize fashion. The question of their long-term viability lies in the difference between necessity and experimentation, begging the question: when will wearable computing cross the line from a novelty item to a second skin?

FIGURE 11.13 *Iris Van Herpen, 'Crystallization' Dress, Fall/Winter 2011–12. Van Herpen's couture piece was made using hundreds of digital photographs that were 3-D printed from resin, heated and manipulated by hand to create the splash effect – a moment crystallized in time. (Photo by Victor Boyko/ Getty Images.)*

FIGURE 11.14 *Iris Van Herpen, Haute Couture Fall/Winter 2017–18. The 'Aeriform' Dress was made in collaboration with Philip Beasley. Laser-cut metal was manipulated into dome shapes, and assembled by hand. (Photo by Victor VIRGILE/Gamma-Rapho via Getty Images.)*

Fashion as future and fantasy

For many designers and theorists, envisioning dress was crucial to envisioning the future. The unifying fascination among art and philosophical movements of the early twentieth century – emphasizing machinery and technology as the means to reconstructing the world order – led to an aesthetic that represented progress through symbolic representations in dress, evolving into silhouettes still associated with futuristic fashion. How much of this came from art, how much from fantasy and science fiction literature, and how did this play into both couture and ready-to-wear fashions?

Throughout the twentieth century, clothing regularly played a role in the conceptualization of the future. The visual arts and philosophies of Russian Constructivism, Italian Futurism and the German Bauhaus all renounced the hierarchy of fine and applied arts in favour of the functional art object, including dress – which, as with earlier revolutions, played heavily into representing ideology. In post-Imperialist Russia, Popova and Luibov designed unisex jumpsuits with boldly coloured prints fashioned into streamlined garments, representing the break from excess and luxury in favour of the simplicity and equality represented by Communism (see Chapter 3). At the Bauhaus, the esoteric colour philosophies of Kandinsky, Klee, Itten and Josef Albers established colour as its own visual language, also reflected in the costumes of Schlemmer's experimental triadic ballet, and textiles in the weaving workshop led by Stolzl and Anni Albers (see Chapter 2). Industrial materials and forms were primary modes of expression utilized to express the new role of dress and textiles as a forward-thinking artistic medium, incorporating fibreglass and cellophane in woven fabrics for various uses. Ultimately, these styles reflect the shift from ornamental to functional clothing, while retaining the symbolic power of garment forms. Abstract patterns with geometric shapes dominated these experimental forms, setting a precedent for futuristic dress. This is also reflected in Sonia Delaunay's brightly coloured geometric garments, cut loosely to allow for maximum movement as with her Simultaneous/Orphist paintings: the painting comes to life on the body, expressing the dynamism of modern machines (see Chapter 2).

In her essay 'Fashion and Futurism: Performing Dress,' Eugenia Paulicelli analyses the changing world view in the first decades of the twentieth century as reflected – and projected – in the role and appearance of dress in Italian Futurism. Paulicelli points out that styling and the projection of a public persona led to the development of preferred garment forms and colour symbology (2009). The futurist suit design by Giacomo Balla in his *Futurist Manifesto for Male Dress* (published in Italy under the title 'Il Vestito Antineutrale' in 1914) focuses on the asymmetrically cut 'Anti-Neutral Suit' incorporating the red, green and white of the Italian flag. The colours represent not only nationalism, but the conviction that change will come only through revolution and war, evident in Marinetti's Futurist manifesto (1909). The political undertones are quite literal: the 'bellicose' vivacity of this brightly coloured style represents the courage of the Interventionists, contrasted with the neutral colours representing the cowardice of Isolationists, wishing to project neutrality itself by not entering the First World War (Paulicelli, 2009: 194–5). The look of modernity for menswear in particular manifested in asymmetrical suits cut close to the body with minimal decorative features, a model that plays a recurring role even in Science Fiction (Sci-Fi) costume design today, while colour plays a more symbolic role than the seasonal palette of the fashion designer. Colour and form in dress are extracted from broader philosophical contexts, and associated with modernity which is represented by speed, machines and the desire for newness. The unifying concern for all these early twentieth-century movements was the democratization of fashion, an element of fashion's future discussed earlier in this chapter in 'Virtual Couture' and throughout the book. These three main elements of form, aesthetics and availability remain the relevant factors for clothing that designers envision for the future of fashion.

In Paris, the Interwar years were dominated in fashion by Schiaparelli's whimsical and provocative designs. Schiaparelli's timely and shocking designs were noted by the press: at the height of her career in 1937, fashion journalist and former editor of British *Vogue* Alison Settle wrote: 'her clothes were universally sought as the perfect expression of the ideas of her age . . . She has for years been quicker to see into the future than any other designer . . .'[1] Her fascination with the future is manifested in the Zodiac (Cosmique) collection of Winter 1938/9: the celestial bodies and horoscopes play with the human preoccupation with connecting to future events through astrological divination, perhaps resonating with patrons who sensed the global unrest that led to the Second World War later that same year. Schiaparelli's padded shoulders and slim skirt suits created an angular silhouette echoing the aerodynamic quality of fighter planes, while also playing with Surrealist concepts of dream-symbolism through motifs and accessories (see Chapter 2). The future is ultimately imagined as an inversion of the present, thus leading to asymmetrical angles countering the natural symmetry of the body as a metaphor; and through the juxtaposition of unusual materials and motifs, such as Schiaparelli's insect jewellery, prompting a visceral response from the viewer.

Following the Second World War, Americans in particular were fascinated by the extra-planetary world and the possibility of extra-terrestrial beings. The space suit and helmet were iconic representations of explorers who sought to discover the new frontier, while futuristic storylines were represented in comic books, film and later television wearing angular, sculptural clothing fitted close to the body. These iconic costumes were popularized through film and television in productions such as *Buck Rogers* (movie and TV serials between 1933 and 1951, respectively), *Space Patrol* (1950–5), *Flash Gordon* (1954), *Science Fiction Theatre* (1955–7), and *The Twilight Zone* (1959–64). Following the success of these series, *Lost in Space* (1965–8) and *Star Trek* (1966–9) further documented how costume designers envisioned the future. Popular films such as Stanley Kubrick's *2001: A Space Odyssey* (1968), with costumes designed by Hardy Amies, already echoed the Space Age couture of Courrèges, Rabanne and Cardin. Materials contributed to the 'otherness' of futuristic dress as imagined by designers and artists: metal, plastic and other industrial materials provided an edge to the softness of conventional textiles, evoking the machinery that defined the Industrial and post-Industrial eras. Clothing and its relationship to the body became more decorative than functional, and revealing the movement of the physique beneath garments became a common theme that echoed the interest of early twentieth-century modernists.

The nature of fashion as a reflection of cultural and social movements is all the more relevant when considering the connection between dress and fantasy, representing not only the world in which we live, but other worlds in other timelines. Sci-Fi literature, recreated in film and television, become the main medium for human musings on the world of tomorrow. In turn, elements of Sci-Fi have infiltrated haute couture regularly since the white boots and visors of Courrèges, the wool and vinyl ensembles of Cardin's Cosmos collection. Rabanne's metal dresses were featured in the futuristic cult classic *Barbarella* (1968), and subsequently he created a ready-to-wear line of clothing with the same name. Concurrent with the Space Race, popular TV series such as *Star Trek* explored asymmetry and bright colours as a harbinger of future fashion.

Focused on alternate realities, fashion plays an important role as the visual representation of characters and storylines taking place in utopian, dystopian or post-apocalyptic worlds.[2] However, most Sci-Fi literature, film and television is the medium for human musings on the world of tomorrow. In film, a return to the theme of bioengineering – popularized by the original *Blade Runner* (1982) based on Philip K. Dick's *Do Androids Dream of Electric Sheep?* (1968) – provides *Blade Runner 2049* (2017) with a wardrobe of juxtaposed materials and garment styles for humans and 'replicants' (humanoid robots). Costume designer Renee April mixes streetwear with elements of historic dress to help the viewer relate to the lives of the characters with a visual – wet fur representing misery for the replicant, and plastic as a protective layer that also allows for transparency – but consciously stayed away from the stereotypical materials and garment forms that dominated Sci-Fi costuming in the 1960s and 1970s. For the four-part film series *Hunger Games* (2012–15), costume designer Trish Summerville reflects on the translation of costume from literature to film, and her use of materials such as laser-cut gilt leather (perhaps inspired by van Herpen's work). In addition to outfitting and designing specialty pieces in collaboration with others, couture pieces from McQueen and Korean designer Juun J also feature in the films. Popular streaming series also predict fashion for the future as a combination of fantasy and function. Most futuristic clothing in media now reflects the type of environment – both social and physical – in which we may be living during the coming decades. Storylines focus on new cultural sub-groups and survival stories, and costume design reflects these two main themes in the fitted jumpsuits of Earthling flight crews and Martian armour for characters in *The Expanse* (2015–20). Reflective materials and neutral tones still dominate futuristic wardrobes, with a few exceptions, such as the brilliantly contrasted power-sari wardrobe of Shohreh Aghdashloo's character Christjen Avasarala in *The Expanse*, designed by Joanne Hansen. The Belters, a rebellious faction, sport modified mohawks and tattoos on their necks and faces – tribal references that were also utilized by 1970s punks. In other stories, historic details such as nineteenth-century Victorian detailing weaves its way into futurism in unexpected ways in Sci-Fi literature, such as the conservative upscale neo-Victorians in Neil Stephenson's *The Diamond Age* (2000) who are impeccably dressed in real textiles, contrasted with Thetes, who have never seen thread before and wear composite materials formed in a machine.

Sci-Fi literary and film references are reimagined by fans through Cosplay and underground fashion as well. Steampunk fashion of the 1980s to 1990s held its first convention, 'SalonCon' in 2006. Based on an alternate history and social structure that is refl ected in the garb of its characters, Steampunk exhibits a strong Victorian influence, while its variants – Diesel Punk and Cyber Punk – delve into alternate universes for inspiration. Although costume parties always held a strong appeal for fantasy-based social interaction, Cosplay takes this to another level. DIY enthusiasts create their own smart garments with programmable LEDs through kits purchased at Adafruit or other companies providing components for flexible circuitry, and transform themselves into real-life avatars and superheroes from comic favourites. Comic-Con International, held annually in San Diego, CA since 1970, draws millions of fans each year to meet authors dressed as their favourite characters and has expanded to encompass popular video games and Sci-Fi literature. The unifying factor throughout contemporary Sci-Fi costume is that clothing still represents various cultural and socio-economic factions in society, with fashion functioning as an i dentifier.

Representation and inclusivity in fashion

Many of the aspects of fashion that propelled the industry into trillion dollar status are now in need of reconsideration. These include more diversity in the creative and business ranks, representation of a broader demographic in advertising, clothing that transcends gender constructs, and the reconstruction of idealized forms of beauty. Throughout the twentieth century, the industry experienced a shift in leadership for ready-to-wear: new business owners emerged from the immigrant labour pool working in garment and textile construction in the previous century. The Interwar and post-war years led to a flourishing of American design at all price points, and Black designers such as Zelda Wynn Valdes and Anne Cole Lowe began to work outside their communities. Yves Saint Laurent broke with Paris convention by showing his garments on a diverse group of models in the 1960s, a practice that paved the road for several other high-end designers such as Gianni Versace to seek a more inclusive representation of idealized beauty. The 1973 Battle of Versailles notably included Stephen Burrows in its line-up of American designers, and the outgrowth of the civil rights movement included a strong media platform for alternative, if parallel, forms of beauty and fashion. However, a major milestone was made in the 1980s with the induction of Patrick Kelly in the *Chambre Syndicale du Prêt-à-Porter* – the first American member. In memory, the 'Kelly Initiative' was created in June 2020, when 250 Black fashion professionals signed a petition calling for active inclusion of Black talent across all sectors of the industry. In the same month, Editor-in-Chief of *Teen Vogue* Lindsay Peoples Wagner, who authored the *New York Magazine* article 'Everywhere and Nowhere: What It's Really Like to Be Black and Work in Fashion' (Peoples Wagner, 2018) also co-founded the Black in Fashion Council, whose intention for active change includes demands for accountability for equal opportunity by issuing annual index scores for fashion corporations. This demand for a systemic change in the industry also includes equity for LGBTQ+ community members and people of colour.

Other areas of fashion have been shifting towards a more inclusive environment by reforming gender expectations in dress. Arguably, the boundaries for fashion determined by the sexes have been an issue for debate for centuries; in the context of this study, Sarah Bernhardt's famous photograph wearing trousers in her studio was considered scandalous (see Chapter 6). The first decades of the early twentieth century sought to remove the limitations of nineteenth-century dress by 'liberating' women from the corset and other Victorian trappings, while the post-war New Look reintroduced these conventions for a new generation of women. Menswear was also transformed by advances in fashion, such as the self-folding collar and introduction of the sack suit and drape suit, which allowed more freedom of mobility. Ultimately, the latter half of the century witnessed more uniformity in dress for both men and women as essentials such as blue jeans and T-shirts made their way into the wardrobes of both men and women. Gernreich's experimental unisex clothing also appealed to the cause for equality of the sexes. Hippies embraced Eastern forms of dress that issued the same basic elements of a tunic and loose pants for both men and women. As pantsuits and trousers for women became acceptable throughout the Women's Liberation movement of the 1960s and 1970s, men also experimented with dress and sexuality – from Glam celebrities cross-dressing, to the adoption of heeled platform and tightly fitted bell bottoms that accentuated the male form. In 1980s couture and high-end ready-to-wear, barriers for men were broken by the use of brightly printed silks and suits by Versace, who also utilized leather and metallic *oroton* for women's dresses – playing with traditional expectations through colour and materials. In the 1990s, Alexander McQueen sent men down the runway in skirts while women were shirtless, creating an intentional blurring of identities. Several twenty-first-century exhibitions have embraced contributions of gay fashion designers and the evolution of fashion in LGBTQ+ communities. In 2013, the Museum at FIT exhibited 'A Queer History of Fashion: From the Closet to the Catwalk' (13 September 2013 to 4 January 2014), examining both the role of fashion in LGBTQ+ communities as well as the community's contributions to fashion as designers and industry professionals. As the Gay Pride movement took root, the industry embraced a more open expression of individuality and adopted garments forms that identified the wearer with these subcultures.

Advertising and model choices have been highly influential in shaping consumer demographics, while also excluding large segments of society who did not fit the image presented. As the fashion image for women changed mid-century from the couture glamour icon to the girlish waif representing youth culture, a new beauty ideal was formed. The decades from the 1960s, which introduced Twiggy and Jean Shrimpton as 'It' girls, to a sexualized Brooke Shields in the 1980s, to Heroin Chic dominating the runway in the 1990s, evoked major problems among adolescent girls, inspiring movements for change. As digital photography replaced film in the 2000s, Photoshop became a powerful tool to rework reality into fantasy. The effects of these photoshopped images rendered on young women idolizing models in fashion magazines led to a rise in eating disorders, depression and drug use. The new ideals include more athletic models who replace the underfed waif, as well as plus-size models communicating to the growing consumer demographic in this area. The 2010s have witnessed a gradual recreation of the industry standards to one that represents a broader ethnic and racial demographic, including women in hijab for modest fashion, representing a rapidly growing sector of the global industry.

Summary

The Fashion industry is constantly in flux, incorporating new technologies and ideologies as society changes. The development of e-commerce created new experiences for consumers to shop without the ceremonial aspect of visiting upscale department stores, making shopping more practical and economical. While real-life clothing is going online, its virtual counterparts are also finding new modes of expression through virtual fitting rooms and photo-realistic digital twins. Fashion borrows much of its inspiration from online gaming, as luxury brands create skins for avatars that allow for a virtual experience of high-end fashion. Social media contributes to the popularity of digital fashion by providing a new arena in which fashion can be experienced and regarded, without the cost and waste of having an extensive wardrobe. Virtual couture is not limited by the parameters of physical garments, borrowing from Sci-Fi to present fantastical fashion that feeds the imagination. In real life, smart textiles and the increasing viability of garments that function in tandem with wireless technology offer a new future for fashion as more than a visual phenomenon. Lastly, as social justice movements evoke change in the current system, a new industry will evolve that is more inclusive, creating broader clothing options for a wide range of consumers.

Notes

1 Alison Settle, *Clothes Line*, Methuen and Company Limited, London, 1937, p. 14.

2 The cult classic Star Wars films take place in the past, not the future, and the costumes in the original trilogy drew much of their inspiration in form and colour from Eastern elements, from Japanese Samurai armor (Chewbacca; Han Solo) to wrap-coats resembling the cloaks of Buddhist monks (Luke Skywalker, Obi-Wan Kenobi).

Conclusion

A Cultural History of Western Fashion: From Haute Couture to Virtual Couture presents the view that the contemporary fashion industry, established in Europe and the US, is the product of two opposite approaches to clothing. Haute couture was established in the mid-nineteenth century to create exclusivity for its patrons through custom-made garments, while the ready-to-wear industry was built upon the concept of clothing as a commodity that should be available to all social classes. This process first began with the Paris-based couturier Englishman Charles Frederick Worth, known for his exquisite creations which he sold to the royal heads of Europe. Scandalously, Worth also reproduced similar, but less expensive, lines for the middle-class American market. When other designers, such as Paquin, Poiret and Vionnet, followed suit in the early 1900s, this trend paved the way for the subsequent rise of prêt-à-porter – or ready-to-wear – clothing.

Early couturiers were seen as 'artist-geniuses', acquiescent to their upper-class clients, with their astute business dealings remaining invisible. Some designers, such as Poiret, went to great lengths to promote this myth. As social class distinctions began to blur when monetary status outstripped class status, it became clear that the focus of fashion would undeniably shift. Yet even before the turn of the twentieth century, a number of the most prestigious British and European haute couture designers recognized the unlimited middle-class market of fashion consumers in America, as well as in Europe.

Ready-to-wear styles were initially less expensive versions of couture fashions, copied by imitation houses and sold in department stores to middle-class consumers – thus resulting in a need for new fashions every few years, so the ultra-wealthy could continue to distinguish themselves from the lower classes. Beginning with the widespread use of the sewing machine from the 1850s, and coupled with technological improvements in manufacturing during the 1910s and 1920s, key fashion designers were able to respond to modern life in ways that defied convention. Standardization – a prerequisite of machine technology – equally applied to fashion design. Standardized sizes, colours and styles became the most cost-effective means of production. This explains why Chanel's standardized 'little black dress', for example, was initially compared to Henry Ford's 1925 Model T in American *Vogue* (October 1926) for its practicality, minimalist styling and sleek, modern lines. While Chanel, Patou, and other Parisian couture houses in the 1920s chose to offer ready-to-wear lines and sportswear in addition to bespoke clothing, American ready-to-wear design was developing its own sense of style. Through the retail efforts of Lord & Taylor's Dorothy Shaver and public relations promotions by Eleanor Lambert, designers such as Claire McCardell and Bonnie Cashin were able to formalize sportswear as the representation of the ideal American lifestyle. Following the Second World War, American design grew into a genre that was distinctly different from the French couture model, both in business and aesthetics.

Closely aligned with the art world, Schiaparelli approached high fashion as a sounding board to critique itself, mirroring practices of the Dadaists and Surrealists. While she collaborated with many of the Surrealist artists in the 1930s, including Salvador Dalí and Jean Cocteau, this critique of elitist practice later became fundamental to postmodernist discourse, and from the 1960s onwards was underlined by the adoption of popular culture, in its many forms, into all of the visual arts. As fashion parodied art, and art attempted to parody life, fashion became more closely aligned with streetwear and popular culture. While Andy Warhol utilized mass production elements to create Pop Art, fashion also referenced popular Hollywood films, music and media advertising as a common language that bridged differences in social class. In a world of 'high tech', changes or fashion fads proliferated, and the notion of disposability became part of dress. In these circumstances, haute couture quite literally priced itself out of the market. Lifestyle dressing appeared in the 1970s and 1980s, and the United States became the centre of sportswear production. Dressing down rather than dressing up became the new vogue, further contributing to a visual levelling of social class distinction.

The rise of street style, dictated by the lower classes and quickly adopted by couturiers, first became apparent in post-war youth subcultures, and this niche marketing was to impact greatly on the fashion industry in terms of design, marketing and manufacturing. Views held by a number of prominent writers argued that contemporary anti-fashion was crystallized in the lifestyle promoted by the American hippie movement, initially informed by American anti-establishment trends. However, British punk fashion in the 1970s in England was also founded on extremist political views, social alienation and isolation, and anger stemming from growing unemployment amongst the young, creating a nihilistic sentiment seen in dress, behaviour and attitudes unsurpassed since the hostility and violence generated by the 1920s Dadaists in Berlin. Codified by Vivienne Westwood, punk smashed fashion codes and demolished canons of tasteful dress. This deviance of fashion often responded beyond local or national issues and extended to radical feminist ideologies, unconventional sexual mores and attitudes, racism and gender-related issues, political corruption, and environmental and global concerns. Fashion's response to these sociopolitical issues in the 1970s, 1980s and 1990s emphasized the effectiveness of fashion as a visual arts tool to communicate socio-political ideas and to incite revolution. Arguably, when Paris catwalk designer clothes succumbed to the voice of street style, the final step in the process of democratization in fashion was realized.

The term *anti-fashion* has been used to show that fashion and its counterpart have often fed into one another, creating a symbiotic relationship. Change is an inherent part of the fashion system, and anti-fashion – in terms of reacting against the fashion norm – simply completes the fashion cycle. Interestingly, even the adoption of ethnically non-European dress in the 1960s and 1970s was seen as a form of anti-fashion because it questioned Western mainstream directions. This cross-cultural trend was reconfirmed in the early 1980s when the 'second wave' of Japanese designers stormed the Paris catwalks with their version of street style fashion. Using a divergent approach, Yohji Yamamoto and Rei Kawakubo totally deconstructed style, image, methodology, presentation and display in both their work and marketing strategies; while their contemporary Issey Miyake promoted a slow, deliberate approach to fashion. Ironically, these Japanese designers led the way towards invigorating a flagging European fashion industry that had become entangled in the web of appropriation and pastiche. Instead, their work has generously contributed to a more subjective, humanistic and retrospective response to societal mores. Meaning and memory – both of which have come to play an inherent part in clothing design – have contributed to the broader idea that fashion has finally become something more than just a second skin.

The final chapters in this volume examine issues that fashion needs to address in the twenty-first century. Rapid production and turnover of new styles, proliferate use of synthetic materials, and global outsourcing have resulted in issues ranging from human rights abuses in sweatshops to environmental issues affecting climate change. While some designers such as Stella McCartney are leading the way to a more sustainable model, the ready-to-wear fashion industry at large is due for an overhaul. Consumers play a large in role in this reshaping of fashion, as over-consumption and over-production are inextricably linked. Couture, conversely, has found renewed relevance in the idea of the one-off as a more sustainable model. Designers such as Iris van Herpen embrace the notion that couture can exist as a vehicle to explore artistic forms inspired by nature, while collaborating with other discipline experts to utilize technology as a tool. Hussein Chalayan also uses technology in garment-making to advance his conceptual themes, focusing on identity and perception of the 'other' in what is now a global community.

If the twenty-first century is characterized by one predominant change, it is the shift from analog to digital media – and fashion has embraced this new world. Since the internet became public in the 1990s, the industry has shifted its practices to accommodate the development of new technology. Developing e-commerce and online marketing as powerful tools for image propagation, fashion is also slowly adopting mixed and augmented reality to offer consumers a way to shop virtually by envisioning themselves in clothing. Social media networks have replaced traditional advertising, and celebrity influencers sell goods by example and recommendation. Through their partnerships with the gaming industry, high-end labels are offering skins for avatars that make luxury labels affordable for all socio-economic classes. In an ultimate shift, virtual couture has started making digital-only couture which is meant to be 'worn' and experienced online.

A Cultural History of Western Fashion: From Haute Couture to Virtual Couture provides the reader with socio-cultural context surrounding fashion, highlighting the major designers and styles from the mid-nineteenth century to the present day. Although this volume is not an exhaustive review of the fashion industry's history, it offers a solid foundation for fashion students to analyse and consider the development of the model upon which the contemporary industry is based. Moving forward, the industry at large will continue to undergo necessary changes in order to adapt to the society it serves, developing new materials and ways to integrate garments with lifestyle. Despite some issues created by industry practices, great optimism can be employed to envision a future in which fashion offers solutions to the problems faced by humanity, as it so often has done in the past.

Nazanin Hedayat Munroe

GLOSSARY

Bourgeoisie (Fr.) (n.) a general term designating the middle class; **Bourgeois** (adj.) refers to middle-class tastes, used in the nineteenth century as a derisive term by aristocrats for objects and styles preferred by the middle class. Used during the French Revolution as a counterpoint to Proletariat class values

Bustle pad or frame worn beneath a skirt or gown, to provide fullness in the back of the dress

Cage a steel frame made of concentric rings of steel and connected by tapes (from 1857); worn underneath a full-skirted gown to create a spherical shape on which the dress fabric is overlaid. Also called a hoop skirt

Crinoline stiff fabric made of a horsehair warp and wool weft, used for petticoats to create fullness for skirts from c. 1840 onwards; often combined with the *cage* and referenced as the *cage crinoline*

Conspicuous consumption the display of wealth on one's person, e.g. through expensive clothing and jewellery; a term coined by economist Thorstein Veblen (1899). *Also see: conspicuous leisure*

Conspicuous leisure the indication of wealth displayed through the superfluity and impracticality of ones garments; i.e. the donning of clothes that impeded physical labour; a term coined by economist Thorstein Veblen (1899). *Also see: conspicuous consumption*

Corset a woman's tightly fitting undergarment originally structured with whale bone, extending from the chest to the hips; worn to shape the figure

Couturier (*feminine*, couturière) (Fr.) a French term designating a custom clothing designer using high-end materials and techniques, generally serving an upper class or royal clientele

Couture à façon (Fr.) literally, to sew in a specific way or technique; this denotes a clothing maker who follows an existing style, as opposed to a couturier who is creating original designs

Dandy term used to reference a man who is conspicuously concerned about refined dress and a neat appearance (used after 1815)

Demi-monde (Fr.) literally, 'the half-world'; in nineteenth-century context, it refers to a group whose lifestyles are irrespective of society's expectations of propriety, posing a contrast to the upper class. This term can also refer to women who are supported by wealthy lovers in illegitimate relationships (mistresses, courtesans); possibly coined by the play of the same title, 'Le Demi-Monde' by Alexandre Dumas *fils* (1855)

Digital twin a digital replica of a physical entity, living or non-living; in fashion, usually referencing an avatar on whom clothing can be displayed or fitted

Eco-fashion clothing and other apparel goods made with renewable resources or recycled products that are not harmful to the environment

Fair Trade trade agreements focused on humane treatment, working conditions and fair pay for labourers, often between developed countries and the developing world

Haute Bourgeoisie (Fr.) designating the wealthiest strata of the middle class, who had buying power, i.e. the upper middle class

Haute Couture (Fr.) term used to describe the creation of highly skilled custom-fitted clothing for wealthy clients by a 'house' (Fr., *maison*) owned and operated by a specific designer; includes dress-making and tailoring

Le Bon Monde (Fr.) translated literally from French, 'the good world'; in this context, it refers to the leisure class

Models in haute couture, these are the prototypes for a new design ensemble; in ready-to wear, the job title for people displaying clothing in person or photos

Piece Work in the apparel industry, the practice of paying labourers for finished garments, rather than paying an hourly wage

Sustainability in general terms, processes and action that will not thwart the ability for future generations to continue production at the same rate

Sustainable Fashion clothing that is produced with *fair trade* principles, using eco-friendly materials, with an underlying philosophy of moderate consumption and minimal waste

Toile (Fr.) literally from French, fabric; in fashion, usually indicating the unbleached muslin used to create pattern pieces for garments

Virtual goods objects that only exist in virtual (digital) form

BIBLIOGRAPHY

Albanesi, Melanie. (2020), 'See Rockers in Their Light Up Suits', PBS Antiques Roadshow, 13 April 2020. Available online: https://www.pbs.org/wgbh/roadshow/stories/articles/2020/4/13/see-rockers-their-light-suits (accessed 17 August 2020).

Allen, J. S. (1983), *The Romance of Commerce and Culture*, Chicago: University of Chicago Press.

Anscombe, I. (1984), *A Woman's Touch: Women in Design from 1860 to the Present Day*, London: Virago Press.

Anti-Counterfeiting Group (2005), Available online: www.a-cg.org

Aoki, S. (2001), *FRUiTS*, London: Phaidon Press.

Arnold, R. (2001), *Fashion, Desire, and Angst: Image and Morality in the 20th Century*, London: I. B. Taurus.

Arnold, Rebecca. (2009), *The American Look*, London and New York: I.B. Taurus.

Artley, A. (1976), *The Golden Age of Shop Design: European Shop Interiors 1880–1939*, London: Architectural Press.

Bailey, A. (1988), *Passion for Fashion*, London: Dragon's World.

Baillen, C. (1973), *Chanel Solitaire*, trans. B. Bray, London: Collins.

Banner, L. (1984), *American Beauty*, Chicago: University of Chicago Press.

Barker, E. (1999), *Contemporary Culture of Display*, London: Yale University Press.

Barnard, M. (2002), *Fashion as Communication*, London: Routledge.

Bartlett, D., S Cole and Agnès Rocamora, (ed.). (2013), *Fashion Media: Past and Present*, London: Bloomsbury Publishing.

Barwick, S. (1984), 'Century of Style', in *Harper's Bazaar* (Australia), September, pp. 121–4.

Basye, A. (2010), 'One Day in Fashion: Cinemode', 13 August. Available online: www.onthisdayinfashion.com

Batterberry, M. and Batterberry, A. (1982), *Fashion: The Mirror of History*, London: Columbus Books.

Battersby, M. (1988), *The Decorative Twenties*, Whitney Library of Design, New York: Watson-Guptill.

Baudot, F. (1999), *A Century of Fashion*, London: Thames & Hudson.

Bayer, P. (1988), *Art Deco Source Book: A Visual Reference to a Decorative Style*, Oxford: Phaidon.

Bayley, S. (ed.) (1989), *Commerce and Culture*, Design Museum Books, London: Fourth Estate.

Beard, N. D. (2008), 'The Branding of Ethical Fashion and the Consumer: A Luxury Niche Market or Mass-Market Reality?' *Fashion Theory*, Vol. 12, No. 4, pp. 447–68.

Beaton, C. (1954), *The Glass of Fashion*, London: Weidenfeld & Nicolson.

Bell, Q. (1992 [1947]), *On Human Finery*, London: Allison & Busby.

Bellafante, G. (2004), 'The Frenchwoman, In All Her Moods', *New York Times*, 5 March.

Benaim, L. (1997), *Issey Miyake*, London: Thames & Hudson.

Bender, D. (2002), 'Sweatshop Subjectivity and the Politics of Definition and Exhibition', in *International Labor and Working-Class History*, No. 61, Spring 200), pp. 13–23.

Benjamin, W. (1970 [1936]), 'The Work of Art in the Age of Mechanical Reproduction', in H. Arendt (ed.), *Illustrations*, pp. 219–53, London: Cape.

Berry, J. (2005), 'Re: Collections—Collection Motivations and Methodologies as Imagery, Metaphor and Process in Contemporary Art', unpublished DVA thesis, Griffith University, Brisbane.

Best, K. N. (2010), 'Fashion Journalism', in J. B. Eicher (ed.), *Berg Encyclopedia of World Dress and Fashion*, Vol. 8, London: Berg.

Betts, K. (2004), 'Rei Kawakubo: Comme des Garçons, Avatar of the Avant-Garde', *Time*, 16 February, p. 40.

Betts, K. (2009), 'Will Fashion's Biggest Names Kiss the Runway Goodbye', *Time*, 10 December.

Black, S. (2007), *Eco-Chic: The Fashion Paradox*, London: Black Dog Publishing.

Bliekhorn, S. (2002), *The Mini-Mod 60s Book*, San Francisco: Last Gasp Publications.

Blumenthal, R. (1992) 'When the Mob Delivered the Goods.' *The New York Times Magazine*, (26 July). Available online: https://www.nytimes.com/1992/07/26/magazine/when-the-mob-delivered-the-goods. html (accessed 18 June 2021).

Bolton, A. (2011), 'Alexander McQueen Bumster Skirt Highland Rape' blog for 'Savage Beauty' exhibition at The Metropolitan Museum of Art. https://blog.metmuseum.org/alexandermcqueen/bumster-skirt-highland-rape/ (accessed 18 April 2021).

Boodro, M. (1990), 'Art and Fashion—A Fine Romance', *Art News*, September, pp. 120–7.

Borelli, L. (2002), *Net Mode: Web Fashion Now*, New York: Thames & Hudson.

Bouillon, J-P. (1991), 'The Shop Window', in J. Clair (ed.), *The 1920s: Age of Metropolis*, pp. 162–80, Montreal: Museum of Art Press.

Bouquet, M. (2004), 'Thinking and Doing Otherwise', in B. M. Carbonell (ed.), *Museum Studies: An Anthology of Contexts*, Oxford: Blackwell.

Bourdieu, P. (1984), *Distinction: A Social Critique of the Judgement of Taste*, London: Routledge and Kegan Paul.

Bowman, J. (2008), 'Culture Shock: Comparing Consumer Attitudes to Counterfeiting', in *WIPO 4th Global Conference*, Geneva: WIPO.

Braun, Sandra Lee. (2009), 'The Forgotten First Lady: The Life, Rise, and Success of Dorothy Shaver, President of Lord & Taylor Department Store, and America's "First Lady of Retailing".' Ph.D. Dissertation, University of Alabama, Available online at: http://acumen.lib.ua.edu/u0015/0000001/0000153/u0015_0000001_0000153.pdf (accessed 7 July 2019).

Bray, E. (2009), 'The New Link Between Music and Fashion', *The Independent*, 21 August.

Breward, C. (2003), '21st Century Dandy', exhibition catalogue, in *Art Architecture & Design*, London: British Council.

Breward, C. and Evans, C. (eds) (2005), *Fashion and Modernity*, Oxford: Berg.

Broinowski, A. (1999), 'Japanese Taste: Askew by a Fraction', in B. English (ed.), *Tokyo Vogue: Japanese/Australian Fashion*, exhibition catalogue, Brisbane: Griffith University.

Brown, S. (2010), *Eco Fashion*, London: Laurence King.

Buckberrough, S. A. (1980), *Sonia Delaunay: A Retrospective*, Buffalo: Albright Knox Gallery.

Carbonell, B. M. (ed.) (2004), *Museum Studies: An Anthology of Contexts*, Oxford: Blackwell.

Carnegy, V. (1990), *Fashions of the Decades: The Eighties*, London: Batsford.

Carter, E. (1980), *Magic Names of Fashion*, London: Weidenfeld & Nicolson.

Casadio, M. (1997), *Moschino*, London: Thames & Hudson.

Chadwick, W. (1990), *Women, Art and Society*, London: Thames & Hudson.

Chapman, C., Lloyd, M. and Gott, T. (1993), *Surrealism: Revolution by Night*, exhibition catalogue, Melbourne: National Gallery of Victoria.

Chapman, J. and Gant, N. (eds) (2007), *Designers, Visionaries and Other Stories*, London: Earthscan.

Charles-Roux, E. (1981), *Chanel and Her World*, London: Weidenfeld & Nicolson.

Chenoune, F. (1993), *A History of Men's Fashion*, Paris: Flammarion Press.

Chipp, H. B. (1973), *The Theories of Modern Art*, Los Angeles: University of California Press.

Christodoulides, G. (2009), 'Branding in the Post-Internet Journal', *Marketing Theory*, Vol. 9, pp. 141–4.

Cicolini, A. (2005), *The New English Dandy*, London: Victoria & Albert Press.

Clair, J. (ed.) (1991), *The 1920s: Age of Metropolis*, Montreal: Museum of Art Press.

Cline, Elizabeth L. *Overdressed: The Shockingly High Cost of Fast Fashion*. New York: Penguin, 2012.

Cohen, A. A. (ed.) (1978), *The New Art of Colour: The Writings of Robert and Sonia Delaunay, The Documents of 20th-Century Art*, trans. D. Shapiro and A. Cohen, New York: Viking Press.

Colchester, C. (1991), *The New Textiles: Trends and Traditions*, London: Thames & Hudson.

Copping, N. (2009), 'Style Bloggers Take Centre Stage', *Financial Times*, 13 November.

Craik, J. (1994), *The Face of Fashion*, New York: Routledge.

Crane, D. (2000), *Fashion and Its Social Agenda*, Chicago: University of Chicago Press.

Cumming, C. W. et al. (2017) *The English Dictionary of Fashion, 2nd Edition*. London and New York: Bloomsbury Academic.

Cunningham, B. (2010), *Bill Cunningham New York*, video by Richard Press/Philip Gefter (producer).

Damase, J. (1972), *Sonia Delaunay: Rhythms and Colours*, London: Thames & Hudson.

D'Avenel, G. (1989 [1898]), 'The Bon Marché', in S. Bayley (ed.), *Commerce and Culture*, pp. 57–9, London: Fourth Estate.

Davis, Nancy and Amelia Grabowski (2018), 'Sewing for Joy: Ann Lowe' (12 March), *National Museum of American History Blog,* Smithsonian Institution. Available online: https://americanhistory.si.edu/blog/lowe (accessed 8 June 2020).

De Grazia, V. (1991), 'The American Challenge to the European Arts of Advertising', in J. Clair (ed.), *The 1920s: Age of Metropolis*, pp. 236–47, Montreal: Museum of Art Press.

Delaunay, S. (1978), *Nous Irons Jusqu' au Soleil*, Paris: Editions Laffont.

Deloitte (2017), 2017 Global Mobile Consumer Survey: US Edition, p. 2. Available online: https://www2.deloitte.com/content/dam/Deloitte/us/Documents/technology-media-telecommunications/us-tmt-2017-global-mobile-consumer-survey-executive-summary.pdf (accessed 18 June 2021).

DeLong, M. (2009), 'Innovations and Sustainability at Nike', *Fashion Practice: The Journal of Design, Creative Process & the Fashion Industry*, Vol. 1, No. 1, pp. 109–14.

Di Grappa, C. (ed.) (1980), *Fashion Theory*, New York: Lustrum Press.

Diehl, N. (ed.) (2018), *The Hidden History of American Fashion*, London and New York: Bloomsbury Academic Press.

Dormer, P. (1993), *Design After 1945*, London: Thames & Hudson.

Dowsett, S. and G. Obulutsa (2020), 'Height of Fashion? Clothes Mountains Build Up as Recycling Breaks Down', in *Reuters*, 30 September.

'Electric Girls' *New York Times*, 26 April 1884.

Emery, Joy Spanabel (2014), *History of the Paper Pattern Industry*. New York and London: Bloomsbury.

English, B. (ed.) (1999), *Tokyo Vogue: Japanese/Australian Fashion*, exhibition catalogue, Brisbane: Griffith University.

English, B. (2004), 'Japanese Fashion as a Re-considered Form', in The Space Between: Textiles–Art–Design–Fashion Conference CD, Vol. 2, Perth: Curtin University of Technology.

English, B. (2005), 'Fashion and Art: Postmodernist Japanese Fashion', in L. Mitchell (ed.), *The Cutting Edge: Fashion From Japan*, Sydney: Powerhouse Museum Publications.

English, B. (2011a), Interview with Zang Yingchun, Director of International Fashion and Textile Design Education, Tsinghua University, Beijing, 18 October.

English, B. (2011b), *Japanese Fashion Designers: The Work and Influence of Issey Miyake, Yohji Yamamoto and Rei Kawakubo*, Oxford: Berg.

English, B. and Pomazan, L. (eds) (2010), *Australian Fashion Unstitched: The Last 60 Years*, Melbourne: Cambridge University Press.

Epstein, J. (1982), 'Have You Ever Tried to Sell a Diamond?', *The Atlantic* (February). Available online: https://www.theatlantic.com/magazine/archive/1982/02/have-you-ever-tried-to-sell-a-diamond/304575 (accessed 25 April 2021).

Evans, C. (1998), 'The Golden Dustman: A Critical Evaluation of the Work of Martin Margiela and a Review of Martin Margiela: Exhibition (9/4/1615)', *Fashion Theory*, 2/1: 73–93.

Evans, C. (2003), "Yesterday's Emblems and Tomorrow's Commodities', in S. Bruzzi and P. Church-Gibson (eds), *Fashion Cultures*, London: Routledge.

Evans, C. (2003), *Fashion at the Edge: Spectacle, Modernity and Deathliness*, New Haven: Yale University Press.

Evans, C. and Thornton, M. (1991), 'Fashion, Representation, Femininity', *Feminist Review*, Vol. 38, pp. 56–66.

Ewen, S. (1976), *Captains of Consciousness: Advertising and the Social Roots of the Consumer Culture*, New York: McGraw-Hill.

Ewing, E. (1981), *Dress and Undress: A History of Women's Underwear*, London: Bibliophile.

Ewing, E. (1986), *History of 20th-Century Fashion*, London: Batsford.

Farrar, L. (2011), 'Will Chinese Designers Get Left Behind in China's Fashion Boom?' *CNN*, Available online: www.edition.cnn.com/2011/09-1/living/china-fashion-designers/index.html

Farro, E. (2021), 'Stella McCartney Introduces Her First Garments Made of Mylo, the "Leather" Alternative Grown From Mushrooms', in *Vogue*, 17 March.

Featherstone, M. (1982), 'The Body in Consumer Culture', *Theory, Culture and Society*, Vol. 1, No. 2, pp. 18–33.

Featherstone, M. (1984), 'Lifestyle and Consumer Culture', *Theory, Culture and Society*, Vol. 4, No. 1, pp. 55–70.

Federation de la Haute Couture et de la Mode. Available online: https://fhcm.paris/en/the-federation/history/ (accessed 18 September 2019).

Financial Times (2003), 'The Rise of Asia Gathers Speed', 29 December.

Finkelstein, J. (1996), *After a Fashion*, Melbourne: Melbourne University Press.

Finamore, M. T. (2009), '1: Before 1930', in Finamore, M. T. and Poulson, A., 'Fashion in Film', Oxford Art Online Available online: https://www.oxfordartonline.com

Fletcher, K. (2007), 'Clothes That Connect', in J. Chapman and N. Gant (eds), *Designers, Visionaries and Other Stories*, London: Earthscan.

Foley, Bridget. (2020), "Tom Ford Writes CFDA Members" in *Women's Wear Daily*, May 4. Available online: https://wwd.com/fashion-news/fashion-scoops/fashion-scoops-tom-ford-coronavirus-cfda-letter-from-the-chairman-1203627403/ (accessed 29 July 2020).

Font, L. (2009), 'Christian Dior', Oxford Art Online. Available online: https://www.oxfordartonline.com

Fox, I. (2010), 'British Men Are Too Scruffy, Says Menswear Designer of the Year/Life and Style', *The Guardian* (UK), 10 December.

Frankel, S. (2001), *Visionaries*, London: Victoria and Albert Museum Publications.

Frankel, S. (2006), 'French Fashion Draws a Veil Over Our Faces', *The London Independent*, 9 March.

Freud, S. (1965), *The Interpretation of Dreams*, trans. and ed. J. Strachey, London: George Allen & Unwin.

Friedman, U. (2015), 'How an Ad Campaign Invented the Diamond Engagement Ring,' *The Atlantic* (13 February). Available online: https://www.theatlantic.com/international/archive/2015/02/how-an-ad-campaign-invented-the-diamond-engagement-ring/385376 (accessed 26 April 2021).

Frith, S. (2000), 'Fashion as a Culture Industry', in S. Bruzzi and P. Church-Gibson (eds), *Fashion Cultures*, London: Routledge.

Gale, C. and Kaur, J. (2004), *Fashion & Textiles: An Overview*, Oxford & New York: Berg.

Galante, P. (1973), *Mademoiselle Chanel*, Chicago: Henry Regnery Co.

Galloway, S. and Mullen, M. (2009), 'The Biggest Opportunity for Luxury Brands in a Generation', *The European Business Review*. Available online: www.europeanbusinessreview.com/?p=2391

Garland, M. (1970), *Changing Form of Fashion*, New York: Praeger.

Genova, A. and Moriwaki, K. (2016), *Fashion and Technology: A Guide ot Materials and Applications*, London and New York: Bloomsbury Academic Press.

Gerald, Jonas. (1967), 'Aglow.' *The New Yorker* (28 January). Available online: https://www.newyorker.com/magazine/1967/01/28/aglow-2 (accessed 17 August 2020).

Gill, A. (1998), 'Deconstruction Fashion: The Making of the Unfinished, Decomposing and Re-assembled Clothes', *Fashion Theory*, Vol. 2, No. 1, pp. 25–49.

Gill, A. (2006), 'In Trainers: The World's at Our Feet and the Multiple Investments in High Performance Shoe Technology', conference paper, Cultural Studies Association of Australia's UNAUSTRALIAN conference, University of Canberra, December.

Gilligan, S. (2000), 'Gwyneth Paltrow', in S. Bruzzi and P. Church-Gibson (eds), *Fashion Cultures: Theories, Exploration, and Analysis*, New York: Routledge.

Givhan, R. (2015), *The Battle of Versailles*, New York: Flatiron Books.

Glasscock, J. (2003), 'Bridging the Art/Commerce Divide: Cindy Sherman and Rei Kawakubo of Comme des Garçons'. Available online: www.nyu.edu/greyart/exhibits

Glynn, P. (1978), *In Fashion: Dress in the Twentieth Century*, New York: Oxford University Press.

Golden, A. (1997), *The Memoirs of a Geisha*, New York: Alfred A. Knopf.

Goldberg, R. L. (1979), *Performance Live Art—1909 to the Present*, New York: Abrams.

Goldberg, R. L. (2001), *Performance Art: From Futurism to the Present*, London: Thames & Hudson.

Grail Research (2009), 'Nielsen Global Luxury Brands Study', Fashion Industry Analysis, September. Available online: www.grailresearch.com/pdf/ContenPodsPdf/Global_Fashion_Industry_Growth_in_Emerging_Markets.pdf

Greely, H. (1845), The New York *Tribune*, p. 1 c.3 (June 20); Reprinted in Commons, J. R. (1909), 'Horace Greely and the Working Class Origins of the Republican Party,' *Political Science Quarterly* (Vol. 24, No. 3: Sep. 1909): 472.

Gronemeyer, A. (1999), *Film: A Concise History*, London: Lawrence King.

Grovier, K. (2017), 'When Fashion and Art Collide', *BBC Online* (13 October). Available online: http://www.bbc.com/culture/story/20170929-when-fashion-and-art-collide (accessed 25 May 2020).

Hauffe, T. (1998), *Design: A Concise History*, London: Lawrence King.

Haulman, Kate. (2014), *The Politics of Fashion in Eighteenth-Century America*. Chapel Hill, NC: University of North Carolina Press.

Healy, R. (1996), *Couture to Chaos*, Melbourne: National Gallery of Victoria.

Hebdige, R. (1987), interview in video *Digging for Britain: Postmodern Popular Culture and National ID*, Hobart: Tasmania School of Art.

Hebdige, R. (1997), 'Posing . . . Threats, Striking . . . Poses: Youth Surveillance and Display', in K. Gelder and S. Thornton (eds), *The Subcultures Reader*, pp. 393–405, London: Routledge.

Heinze, A. R. (1990), *Adapting to Abundance*, New York: Columbia University Press.

Heller, N. (1987), *Women Artists*, New York: Abbeville Press.

Herd, J. (1991), 'Death Knell of Haute Couture', reprinted in *Courier-Mail*, Brisbane, 10 August.

Hill, A. (2005), 'People Dress So Badly Nowadays', in C. Breward and C. Evans, *Fashion in Modernity*, Oxford: Berg.

Holborn, M. (1988), 'Image of a Second Skin', *Artforum*, Vol. 27, November, pp. 118–21.

Hollander, A. (1983), 'The Great Emancipator—Chanel', *Connoisseur*, February, pp. 82–91.

Hollander, A. (1984), 'The Little Black Dress', *Connoisseur*, December, pp. 80–9.

Hollander, A. (1988), *Seeing Through Clothes*, Berkeley: University of California Press.

Horyn, C. (2000a), 'On the Road to Fall, Paris at Last', *New York Times*, 1 March.

Horyn, C. (2000b), 'Galliano Plays His Hand Smartly', *New York Times*, 21 May.

Horyn, C. (2004), 'A Store Made for You Right Now: You Shop Until It's Dropped', *New York Times*, 17 February.

Horyn, C. (2006), 'Balenciaga, Weightless and Floating Free', *New York Times*, 4 October.

Howell, G. (2012), *Wartime Fashion: From Haute Couture to Homemade, 1939-1945*, London and New York: Berg Publishing.

The Independent (2010), 'Top Menswear Designers Mix Cheeky with Elegant', 28 June.

International Centre of Photography (1990), *Man Ray: In Fashion*, exhibition catalogue, New York: International Centre of Photography.

Jackson, T. and Shaw, D. (2008), *Mastering Fashion Marketing*, London: Palgrave Macmillan.

Kapferer, J. N. and Bastien, V. (2009), *The Luxury Strategy: Break the Rules of Marketing to Build Luxury Brands*, London: KoganPage.

Kaplinger, M. (2008), 'Combatting Counterfeiting and Piracy: A Global Challenge', in WIPO 4th Global Conference, Geneva: WIPO.

Katz, I. (1996), 'Hollywood's Smash Its', *The Guardian, G2*, 14 August.

Kawamura, Y. (2004), 'The Japanese Revolution in Paris,' *Through the Surface*. Available online: www.throughthesurface.com/synopsium/kawamura

Kaye, L. (2011), 'Textile Recycling Innovation Challenges Clothing Industry', *The Guardian*, 23 June.

Kettley, S. (2016), *Designing with Smart Textiles*, London: Fairchild Books.

Kidd, W. (2002), *Culture and Identity*, New York: Palgrave.

Kidwell, C. B. and Christian, M. C. (1974), *Suiting Everyone: The Democratization of Clothing in America*, Washington, DC: Smithsonian Institute Press.

Kiefer, B. (2017) 'Why Benetton's provocative photographer Toscani thinks advertising is "totally stupid"' (6 December). Available online: https://www.campaignlive.com/article/why-benettons-provocative-photographer-toscani-thinks-advertising-totally-stupid/1452172 (accessed 24 April 2021).

Kinsella, S. (1995), 'Cities in Japan', in L. Skov and B. Moeran (eds), *Women, Media and Consumption in Japan*, Honolulu: University of Hawaii Press.

Knafo, R. (1988), 'The New Japanese Standard: Issey Miyake', *Connoisseur*, March, pp. 100–9.

Lauer, A. 'Under One Sky' and 'From Above, the Cinderella Effect'. Available online: AndreaLauer.com (accessed 23 October 2020).

Laurentiev, A. (ed.) (1988), *Varavara Stepanova: A Constructivist Life*, trans. W. Salmond, London: Thames & Hudson.

Laver, J. (1967), 'Fashion, Art and Beauty', *Metropolitan Museum of Art Bulletin*, Vol. 26, No. 3, pp. 130–9.

Laver, J. (1969), *A Concise History of Costume*, New York: Abrams.

Laver, J. (1995), *Costume and Fashion: A Concise History*, London: Thames & Hudson.

Lehnert, G. (1998), *Fashion: A Concise History*, London: Lawrence King.

Laver, J. and Probert, C. (1982), *Costume and Fashion: A Concise History*, New York: Oxford University Press.

Leitch, L. (2020) 'Creating the Future: How Fashion Designers are Responding to the Crisis', in *Vogue* June/July.

Lemire, B. (1991), *Fashion's Favourite: The Cotton Trade and the Consumer in Britain 1660–1800*, Oxford: Oxford University Press.

Leone, O. (n.d.) #INTERVIEWS, 'Masahiro Nakagawa one of 20471120´s founders'. Available online: https://www.lepetitarchive.com/interviews-masahiro-nakagawa-one-of-20471120s-founders/ (accessed 18 April 2021).

Leong, R. (2003), 'The Zen and the Zany: Contemporary Japanese Fashion', *Visasia*, 23 March. Available online: www.visasia.com.au.

Lewis, John. (1994), 'Attention Shoppers: The Internet is Open', in *New York Times* (August 12, Section D, p. 1). Available online: https://www.nytimes.com/1994/08/12/business/attention-shoppers-internet-is-open.html (accessed 2 August 2020).

Leymarie, J. (1987), *Chanel*, New York: Skira/Rizzoli.

Loho, P. (2019) 'Telling the Forgotten Histories of Bauhaus Women', in *Metropolis Magazine,* 22 August. Available online: https://www.metropolismag.com/design/bauhaus-women-global-perspective/ (accessed 8 September 2019).

Lipke, D. (2008), 'Is Green Fashion an Oxymoron?' *Women's Wear Daily*, 31 March.

Lipovetsky (1994), *The Empire of Fashion: Dress in Modern Democracy*, trans. Catherine Porter, Princeton: Princeton University Press.

Lloyd, M. (1991), 'From Studio to Stage', *Craft Arts*, Vol. 22, pp. 32–5.

Lodder, C. (1983), *Russian Constructivism*, London: Yale University Press.

Loschek, Ingrid (2009), *When Clothes Become Fashion*, Charlotte: Baker & Taylor.

Lowthorpe, R. (2000), 'Watanabe Opens Paris with Technology Lesson', *The London Independent*, 9 October.

Lufkin, Bryan. (2020), 'The Curious Origins of Online Shopping', BBC.com (26 July). Available online: https://www.bbc.com/worklife/article/20200722-the-curious-origins-of-online-shopping (accessed 20 August 2020).

Lynam, R. (ed.) (1972), *Paris Fashion*, London: Michael Joseph.

Lynton, N. (1980), *The Story of Modern Art*, Oxford: Phaidon.

MacDonell, N. (2019) 'Why Safari Style is No Longer Politically Correct,' *Wall Street Journal* (23 January). Available online: https://www.wsj.com/articles/why-safari-style-is-no-longer-politically-correct-11548263049 (accessed 22 April 2021).

Mackerell, A. (1992), *Coco Chanel*, London: Batsford.

Madsen, A. (1989), *Sonia Delaunay: Artist of the Lost Generation*, New York: McGraw-Hill.

Mah, A. (2006), 'Fakes Still Have Their Niche in China', *International Herald Tribune*, 5 March.

Maheshwari, Sapna. (2020), 'Lord & Taylor Files for Bankruptcy as Retail Collapses Pile Up', *New York Times* (2 August). Available online: https://www.nytimes.com/2020/08/02/business/Lord-and-Taylor-Bankruptcy.html (accessed 3 September 2020).

Martin, R. (1998), *Cubism and Fashion*, New York: Metropolitan Museum of Art.

Martin, R. and Koda, H. (1993), *Infra-Apparel*, Metropolitan Museum of Art, New York: Harry Abrams.

Marly, D. de (1980), *The History of Haute Couture 1850–1950*, New York: Holmes & Meier.

Marvin, C. (1990), *When Old Technologies Were New: Thinking About Electric Communication in the Late Nineteenth Century*, Oxford University Press, USA.

Massachusetts Bureau of Statistics (1875), in D. Crane (2000), *Fashion and Its Social Agenda*, p. 75, Chicago: Chicago University Press.

Mayman, Lynette. (2019), 'Loja Saarinen, Lady of Fashion', *Cranbrook Kitchen Sink* (1 March 1). Available online: https://cranbrookkitchensink.wordpress.com/2019/03/01/loja-saarinen-lady-of-fashion/ (accessed 8 November 2019).

McDermott, C. (2000), 'A Wearable Fashion', in *Vivienne Westwood; A London Fashion*, London: Philip Wilson.

McDowell, C. (1987), *McDowell's Directory of Twentieth-Century Fashion*, New York: Prentice-Hall.

McDowell, C. (1997), *The Man of Fashion: Peacock Males and Perfect Gentlemen*, London: Thames & Hudson.

McDowell, C. (2000), 'Fantasy and Role Play', in *Fashion Today*, pp. 460–92, London: Phaidon.

McFadden, D. R. (1989), *L'Art de Vivre: Decorative Arts and Design in France 1789–1989*, Smithsonian Institute, New York: Vendome Press.

McMahon, K. and Morley, J. (2011), 'Innovation, Interaction, and Inclusion: Heritage Luxury Brands in Collusion with the Consumer', in *Fashion and Luxury: Between Heritage and Innovation*, Paris: Institut Francais de la Mode.

McRobbie, A. (2000), 'Fashion as a Cultural Industry', in S. Bruzzi and P. Church-Gibson (eds), *Fashion Cultures*, London: Routledge.

Mendes, V. and de la Haye, A. (1999), *20th Century Fashion*, London: Thames & Hudson.

Menkes, S. (2000), 'Fashion with Bells on It: Haute Couture or Caricature?', *International Herald Tribune*, 13 July.

Menkes, S. (2005), 'Hussein Chalayan: Cultural Dialogues, New Feature', *International Herald Tribune*, 19 April.

Menkes, S. (2006), 'What Is Hidden, Secret and Interior Will Become the New Erotica', *International Herald Tribune*, 2 March.

Menkes, S. (2010), 'Celine's Chic Severity', *New York Times*, 7 March.

Merlo, Elisabetta and Carlo Marco Belfanti. (2019), 'Fashion, Product Innovations, and Consumer Culture in the late 19th century: Alle Città d'Italia department store in Milan', *Journal of Consumer Culture* Vol. 19, Issue 4 (Nov.) (first published online 14 September 2019). Available online: https://journals.sagepub.com/doi/abs/10.1177/1469540519876005 (accessed 19 September 2019).

Metropolitan Museum of Art (1977), *Arts Décoratifs et Industriels Modernes, Paris Exhibition, 1925*, pp. 42–4, New York: Garland.

Metropolitan Museum of Art (2017), *Art of the In-Between,* Exhibition Guide, New York: Metropolitan Museum.

Miller, M.B. (1981), *The Bon Marché: Bourgeois Culture and The Department Store 1869–1920*, Princeton, NJ: Princeton University Press.

Milbank, C. R. (1985), *Couture: The Great Designers*, New York: Stewart, Tabori & Chang.

Mitchell, L. (1999), 'Issey Miyake', in B. English (ed.), *Tokyo Vogue: Japanese/Australian Fashion*, exhibition catalogue, Brisbane: Griffith University.

Mitchell, L. (ed.) (2005), *The Cutting Edge: Fashion from Japan*, Sydney: Powerhouse Museum.

Mitchell, Rebecca N., ed. (2018), *Fashioning the Victorians: A Critical Sourcebook*, London and New York: Bloomsbury Visual Arts,

Miyake, I. (1978), *East Meets West*, Tokyo: Heibon-Sha Ltd.

Moore, B. (2009), 'The Fashion Industry's Old Business Model Is Out of Style', *Los Angeles Times*, 13 September.

Moore, B. (2005), 'Tone in Chic', *Los Angeles Times*, 27 August.

Morgan, A. (2011), 'New Business Degree Makes Sustainability Its Starting Point', *The Guardian*, 14 April. Available online: www.guardian.co.uk/sustainable-business/blog/one-planet-mba-university-exeter

Morris, B. (1978), *The Fashion Makers*, New York: Random House.

Mossoff, Adam. (2011), 'The Rise and Fall of the First American Patent Thicket: The Sewing Machine War of the 1850s', in *Arizona Law Review* (Vol. 53: 2011, 165–211).

Mower, S. (2006), 'Paris Fashion Weekend; Special Report', *The Guardian*, 28 February.

Mulvagh, J. (1992), *Vogue History of 20th Century Fashion*, London: Bloomsbury.

Musée de la Mode et du Costume (1984), *Exposition—Hommage à Elsa Schiaparelli*, Paris: Palais Galleria.

The Nation, (2008), 'DHL Partners with eBay to Enhance Shipping Solutions for eBay Sellers', 9 December. Available online: www.nationmultimedia.com/

Neret, G. (1986), *The Arts of the Twenties*, New York: Rizzoli.

New Policy Institute and Joseph Rowntree Foundation (1993), 'Monotony, Poverty and Social Exclusion'. Available online: www.poverty.org.uk

Newman, A. and Patel, D. (2004), 'The Marketing Directions of Two Fashion Retailers', *European Journal of Marketing*, Vol. 38, No. 7, pp. 770–89.

Niwa, M. (2002), 'The Importance of Clothing Science and Prospects for the Future', *International Journal of Clothing Science and Technology*, Vol. 14, Nos. 3–4, p. 238.

Okonkwo, U. (2010), *Luxury Online*, London: Palgrave Macmillan.

Olds, A. (1992), 'Archives: All Dressed Up in Paper', *ID*, Vol. 39, No. 3, p. 17.

O'Neill, A. (2005), 'Cuttings and Pastings', in C. Breward and C. Evans (eds), *Fashion and Modernity*, Oxford: Berg.

Palmer, A. (2001), *Couture and Commerce: The Transatlantic Fashion Trade in the 1950s*, British Columbia: UBC Press.

Palmer, A., and Clark, H. (eds) (2005), *Old Clothes, New Looks: Second Hand Fashion*, London: Berg.

Palmer, Alex. (2015), 'How Singer Won the Sewing Machine War', in *Smithsonian Magazine* (14 July). Available online: https://www.smithsonianmag.com/smithsonian-institution/how-singer-won-sewing-machine-war-180955919/ (accessed 20 September 2019).

Palmer White, J. (1986), *Elsa Schiaparelli: Empress of Fashion*, London: Aurum Press.

Palmer White, J. (1988), *Haute Couture Embroidery: The Art of Lesage*, New York: Vendome Press.

Palmer White, J. (1991), 'Paper Clothes: Not Just a Fad', in P. Cunningham and S. Voso Lab (eds), *Dress and Popular Culture*, Ohio: Bowling Green State University Popular Press.

Pankhurst, R. (1999), interview with Richard Pankhurst, son of suffragette Emily Pankurst, in *The Suffragettes: 100 Images of the Twentieth Century*, video, New York: CAPA Productions.

Paulicelli, Eugenia. (2009) 'Fashion and Futurism: Performing Dress', *Annali D'Italianistica* 27: 187–207. Available online: http://www.jstor.org/stable/24016255 (accessed 28 August 2020).

Penn, I. (1988), *Issey Miyake: Photographs by Irving Penn*, ed. N. Calloway, A New York Graphic Society Book, Boston: Little, Brown & Co.

PBS.org, 'Edison Outside the Lab' (n.d.). Available online: https://www.pbs.org/wgbh/ americanexperience/features/edison-gallery/ (accessed 30 July 2020).

Peoples Wagner, Lindsay. (2018), 'Everywhere and Nowhere: What It's Really Like to Be Black and Work in Fashion', *New York Magazine*. August 23. Available online: https://www.thecut.com/2018/08/what-its-really-like-to-be-black-and-work-in-fashion.html (accessed 13 November 2020).

Phelps, Nicole. (2020), 'Amazon Launches Luxury Stores on Its Mobile App With Oscar de la Renta as First Brand Partner', *Vogue* (15 September). Available online: https://www.vogue.com/article/amazon-launches-luxury-stores-oscar-de-la-renta (accessed 15 September 2020).

Pinnock, T. (2018), 'Try on, tune in, drop out: the story of Granny Takes A Trip and London's psychedelic tailors', uncut.co.uk. Available online: https://www.uncut.co.uk/features/try-tune-drop-story-granny-takes-trip-londons-psychedelic-tailors-102789/ (accessed 14 June 2021).

Poiret, P. (1915), 'From the Trenches', *Harper's Bazaar*, Vol. 50, No. 2.

Poiret, P. (1931), '*En Habillant L'Époque*', n.p.

Polhemus, T. (1994), *Street Style: From Sidewalk to Catwalk*, London: Thames & Hudson.

Polhemus, T. (1996), *The Customised Body*, London: Serpent's Tail.

Polhemus, T. and Proctor, L. (1978), *Fashion and Anti-Fashion: Anthropology of Clothing and Adornment*, London: Thames & Hudson.

Poulson, A. (2009), '2: After 1930', in Finamore, M. T. and Poulson, A., 'Fashion in Film', Oxford Art Online (https://www.oxfordartonline.com).

Powell, B. (2014), 'Meet the Old Sweatshops: Same as the New', in *The Independent Review* Vol. 19, No. 1 (Summer 2014), pp. 109–22.

Power, D. and Hauge, A. (2006), 'No Man's Brand—Brands, Institutions, Fashion and the Economy', research paper, Centre for Research on Innovation and Industrial Dynamics, Uppsala Universitet, Uppsala, Sweden.

Press, Gil. (2015), 'A Very Short History of the Internet and the Web', in *Forbes Magazine*, 2 Jan. Available online: https://www.forbes.com/sites/ gilpress/2015/01/02/a-very-short-history-of-the-internet-and-the-web-2/#134ba2187a4e (accessed 2 August 2020).

Putman, Tyler Rudd. (2010) 'The Slop Shop And The Almshouse: Ready-Made Menswear In Philadelphia, 1780-1820', Master's Thesis, University of Delaware.

Quantis (2018). Measuring Fashion: Environmental Impact of the Global Apparel and Footwear Industries Study.

Radner, H. (2001), 'Embodying the Single Girl in the 60s', in E. Wilson and J. Entwhistle (eds), *Body Dressing*, pp. 183–97, Oxford: Berg.

Reinach, S. S. (2005), 'China and Italy: Fast Fashion versus Prêt a Porter. Towards a New Culture of Fashion', *Fashion Theory*, Vol. 9, No. 1, pp. 43–56.

Ribeiro, A. (1988), *Fashion in the French Revolution*, London: Batsford.

Richmond, Vivienne. (2013), *Clothing the Poor in Nineteenth-Century England*. Cambridge: Cambridge University Press.

Richter, H. (1965), *Dada—Art and Anti-Art*, New York: Abrams.

Riis, Jacob August. (1890), *How the Other Half Lives*, New York: Charles Scribner's Sons.

Rissanen, T. (2005), 'From 15%–0: Investigating the Creation of Fashion without the Creation of Fabric Waste', presented at the conference Creativity: Designer Meets Technology, Europe 27–29 September, Copenhagen, Denmark, KrIDT and Philadelphia University (US). Available online: www.kridt.dk/ conference/speakers/Timo_Rissanen.pdf

Roberts-Islam, Brooke. (2019), World's First Digital-Only Clothing Sells for $9,500', *Forbes Magazine* (14 May). Available online: https://www.forbes.com/sites/brookerobertsislam/2019/05/14/worlds-first-digital-only-blockchain-clothing-sells-for-9500/#6ff8f0d1179c (accessed 14 August 2020).

Rovine, V. L. (2005), 'Working the Edge: XULY.Bët's Recycled Clothing', in A. Palmer and H. Clark (eds), *Old Clothes, New Looks: Second Hand Fashion*, London: Berg.

Sabin, R. (ed.) (1999), *Punk Rock: So What? The Cultural Legacy of Punk*, New York: Routledge.

Saiki, M. K. (1992), 'Issey Miyake—Photographs by Irving Penn', *Graphis*, July/August, Vol. 48, No. 280.

Saisselin, R. G. (ed.) (1984), *The Bourgeois and the Bibelot*, New York: Rutgers University Press.

Sarabianov, D. and Adaskina, N. (1990), *Liubov Popova*, New York: Abrams.

Scaturro, S. (2008), 'Eco-tech Fashion: Rationalizing Technology in Sustainable Fashion, *Fashion Theory*, Vol. 12, No. 4, pp. 469–89.

Schiaparelli, E. (1984 [1954]), *Shocking Life*, London: J. M. Dent & Sons Ltd.

Schwartz, B. (2009), 'Style-Fashion in Dark Times', *The Atlantic*, June.

Scottish Arts Council (1975), 'Fashion 1900–1939', exhibition catalogue, Edinburgh: Scottish Arts Council.

Seebohm, C. (1982), *The Man Who Was Vogue: The Life and Times of Condé Nast*, New York: Viking.

Settle, Alison. *Clothes Line*, Methuen and Company Limited, London, 1937, p.14.

Shaw, M. (2012), 'Slave Cloth and Clothing: Craftsmanship, Commerce, and Industry', in *Journal of Early Southern Decorative Arts* (Vol. 33). Available online: https://www.mesdajournal.org/2012/slave-cloth-clothing-slaves-craftsmanship-commerce-industry/ (accessed 18 June 2021).

Shonfield, S. (1982), 'The Great Mr Worth', *Journal of the Costume Society*, No. 16, pp. 57–8.

Simms, J. (2008), 'E-male Order: Buying Clothes on the Net Is No Longer Just for Girls', *The Independent*, 28 April.

Simon, J. (1999), '*Miyake Modern*', New York: Little, Brown & Co.

Smith, P. (1968) Body Covering. [Exhibition catalog] Museum of Contemporary Crafts, the American Craft Council, New York

Somerville, K. (2011), 'Rebels & Rulebreakers', in *Manstyle*, Melbourne: NGV.

Sozanni, F. (2011), 'What About Chinese Fashion Designers? And Fashion in China?' Available online: www.vogue.it/en/magazine/editor-s-blog/2011/04/april-1st (accessed 18 June 2021).

Standen, D. (2011), 'John Varvatos style.com', *Runway Review*, 18 June.

Staniszewski, M-A. (1998), *The Power of Display*, Cambridge, MA: MIT Press.

Steele, V. (1988), *Paris Fashion*, Oxford: Oxford University Press.

Steele, V. (1991), *Women of Fashion: Twentieth-Century Designers*, New York: Rizzoli.

Steele, V. (1998), *Paris Fashion: A Cultural History*, Oxford: Berg.

Steele, V. (2000), *Fifty Years of Fashion: New Look to Now*, New Haven, CT: Yale University Press.

Steele, V. (2011), 'Fashion and Art', lecture, November, Queensland University of Technology, Brisbane, Australia.

Stempniak, K. (2019), 'Benetton & Fashioning Controversy', blog for *The Devil's Tale,* Duke University Library (8 April).

Stern, R. (2004), *Against Fashion: Clothing as Art 1850–1930*, Cambridge, MA: MIT Press.

Storey, H. and Ryan, T. (2011), 'Catalytic Clothing', Dezeen Blog Archive, 15 June. Available online: www.dezeen.com/2011/06/15/catalytic-clothing-by-helen-storey-and-tony-ryan/ (accessed 18 June 2021).

Sullivan, J. C. (2013), 'How Diamonds Became Forever', *The New York Times*, 3 May.

Takeda, S. et al. (2015), *Reigning Menswear: Fashion in Menswear 1715-2015,* Los Angeles, CA: Los Angeles County Museum of Art.

The Story of Fashion: The Age of Dissent (1985), video, London: RM Arts Production.

Taylor, L. (1999), 'Wool Cloth and Gender: The Use of Woollen Cloth in Britain 1865–1885', in E. Wilson and A. de la Haye (eds), *Defining Dress: Dress as Object, Meaning and Identity*, Manchester: Manchester University Press.

Taylor, L. (2002), *The Study of Dress History*, Manchester: Manchester University Press.

Thomas, D. (2005), 'If You Buy One of These Fake Bags . . .', *Harper's Bazaar*, April, pp. 75–6.

Thomas, S. (2008), 'From "Green Blur" to Ecofashion: Fashioning an Eco-lexicon', *Fashion Theory*, Vol. 12, No. 4, pp. 525–40.

Tomlinson, A. (ed.) (1990), *Consumption, Identity and Style*, London: Routledge.

Tortora, P. G. and Marcketti, S. B. (2015), Sixth Edition. *Survey of Historic Costume,* London and New York: Fairchild Books.

Townsend, C. (2002), *Rapture: Arts Seduction by Fashion*, London: Thames & Hudson.

Trebay, G. (2001), 'Boys Don't Cry: Fashion Falls for a Tough Look', *New York Times*, 3 April.

Trebay, G. (2004), 'Fashion Diary: Making a Surreal Trip onto a Nightclub Runway', *New York Times*, 4 March.

Trebay, G. (2006), 'Woman Masked, Bagged and, Naturally, Feared', *New York Times*, 1 March.

Troy, N. (2003), *Couture Culture*, Cambridge, MA: MIT Press.

Undressed: Fashion in the Twentieth Century (2001), video, Little Bird/Tatlin Production, London: Beckmann Visual Publications.

Van Godtsenhoven, Arzalluz and Debo (eds) (2016), *Fashion Game Changers: Reinventing the 20th Century Silhouette*, London: Bloomsbury Visual Arts.

Varnedoe, K. and Goprik, A. (1990), *High and Low, Modern Art and Popular Culture*, Museum of Modern Art, New York, New York: Harry Abrams Press.

Veblen, T. (1965 [1899]), *The Theory of the Leisure Class (The Writings of Thornstein Veblen)*, New York: Macmillan.

Von Drehle, D. (2006), 'Uncovering the History of the Triangle Shirtwaist Fire', in *Smithsonian Magazine* (August). Available online: https://www.smithsonianmag.com/history/uncovering-the-history-of-the-triangle-shirtwaist-fire-124701842/ (accessed 2 January 2020).

Von Hahn, K. (2006), 'Noticed Sad Chic', *Globe & Mail*, Toronto, 18 March.

Walsh, M. (1979), 'The Democratization of Fashion', *Journal of American History*, Vol. 66, No. 2, pp. 299–313.

Watson, L. (2003), *Twentieth-Century Fashion*, London: Carlton Books.

Weir, J. (1985), 'Fashion; Closing the Gender Gap,' *New York Times*, 30 June, Section 6, Page 44. (accessed 23 November 2020).

Westwood, Vivienne. Blog, 'The Story So Far', n.d. Available online: https://blog.viviennewestwood.com/the-story-so-far/ (accessed 17 July 2020).

White, C. (1998), 'Celebrating Claire McCardell', *New York Times*, Section B, p. 15 (17 November).

Whitely, N. (1989), 'Interior Design in the 1960s: Arena for Performance', *Art History*, Vol. 10, No. 1, pp. 79–90.

Wicker, A. (2020), 'Fast Fashion is Creating an Environmental Crisis', *Newsweek Magazine* (1 September).

Wilcox, C. and Mendes, V. (eds) (1998), *Modern Fashion in Detail*, London: Victoria and Albert Museum.

Wilson, E. (1985), *Adorned in Dreams*, London: Virago.

Wilson, E. and de la Haye, A. (1999), *Defining Dress: Dress as Object, Meaning and Identity*, Manchester: Manchester University Press.

Winge, T. M. (2008), 'Green Is the New Black: Celebrity Chic and the "Green" Commodity Fetish', *Fashion Theory*, Vol. 12, No. 4, pp. 511–24.

Worth, F. C. (1895), *Some Memories of Paris*, trans. F. Adolphus, New York: Henry Holt.

Wynhausen, E. (2008), 'Following the Thread', *The Weekend Australian*, 6–7 September.

Yamamoto, Y. (2002), *Talking to Myself*, Milan: Carla Sozzani.

Yan, H. (2011), 'Lower Tariffs Might Boost Luxury Buys', *China Daily Business News*, 16 June. Available online: www.chinadaily.com.cn/bizchina/2011-06/16/content_12714105.htm (accessed 18 June 2021).

Yves Saint Laurent Retrospective (1986), exhibition catalogue, Sydney: Art Gallery of New South Wales.

Zola, E. (1989 [1883]), 'Au Bonheur des Dames', in S. Bayley (ed.), *Commerce and Culture*, pp. 53–6, London: Fourth Estate.

INDEX

Note: Italicized numbers indicate a figure